Zora Neale Hurston & American Literary Culture

UNIVERSITY PRESS OF FLORIDA

Florida A&M University, Tallahassee
Florida Atlantic University, Boca Raton
Florida Gulf Coast University, Ft. Myers
Florida International University, Miami
Florida State University, Tallahassee
New College of Florida, Sarasota
University of Central Florida, Orlando
University of Florida, Gainesville
University of North Florida, Jacksonville
University of South Florida, Tampa
University of West Florida, Pensacola

University Press of Florida

Gainesville · Tallahassee · Tampa · Boca Raton
Pensacola · Orlando · Miami · Jacksonville
Ft. Myers · Sarasota

Zora Neale Hurston

& American Literary Culture

M. Genevieve West

Published in the United States of America

First cloth printing, 2005
First paperback printing, 2025

30 29 28 27 26 25 6 5 4 3 2 1

Library of Congress Cataloging-in-Publication Data West, Margaret Genevieve.
Zora Neale Hurston and American literary
culture / M. Genevieve West.
p. cm.
Originally presented as the author's thesis (Ph.D.)—Florida State University, 1997, under title:
Zora Neale Hurston's place in American literary culture.
Includes bibliographical references and index.
ISBN 978-0-8130-2830-9 (cloth) | ISBN 978-0-8130-8108-3 (pbk.)
1. Hurston, Zora Neale—Criticism and interpretation—History. 2. Politics and literature—
United States—History—20th century. 3. Women and literature—United States—History—20th
century. 4. Hurston, Zora Neale—Appreciation—United States. 5. Hurston, Zora Neale—
Political and social views. 6. African Americans in literature.7. Race in literature. I. Title.
PS3515.U789Z94 2005
813'.52—dc22 2005042285

The University Press of Florida is the scholarly publishing agency for the State University System of Florida, comprising Florida A&M University, Florida Atlantic University, Florida Gulf Coast University, Florida International University, Florida State University, New College of Florida, University of Central Florida, University of Florida, University of North Florida, University of South Florida, and University of West Florida.

University Press of Florida
2046 NE Waldo Road
Suite 2100
Gainesville, FL 32609
http://upress.ufl.edu

For Rex Alan West

Contents

Figures

Acknowledgments

I BEGAN THIS PROJECT as my dissertation. Over the years many have offered support. My debts are so numerous I hardly know how to express my appreciation. While writing is a solitary endeavor, envisioning a new project, traveling to peruse unpublished papers, collecting the materials, and revising the manuscript have been collaborative acts. I cannot imagine having completed the project on my own.

The kindnesses of others around the nation have been vital to this project. Only recently has Hurston's correspondence been collected and published. Without the assistance of librarians, I would not have had access to those letters prior to their publication. Librarians also led me to a number of undocumented book reviews in vertical files. I am grateful for access to materials at the Atlanta University Library; American Jewish Archives; American Philosophical Society Library; Amistad Research Center; Beinecke Rare Book and Manuscript Library, Yale University; Chicago Historical Society; John Simon Guggenheim Memorial Foundation Library; Princeton University Library, Schomburg Center for Research in Black Culture, and George A. Smathers Library, University of Florida. Likewise, the Library of America generously shared with me its file of reviews of the 1995 editions of Hurston's writings.

Because I wanted to record others' opinions of Hurston as accurately as possible, quoting from unpublished sources has been central to my work. I am, therefore, deeply appreciative for permission to quote from unpublished papers granted by the Moorland-Spingarn Research Center, Howard University; Harry Ransom Humanities Research Center, University of Texas at Austin; the Institute for Intercultural Studies; Washington University and Brandeis University; Special Collections, Fisk University; Catherine Harris; Department of Archives and Special Collections, Olin Library, Rollins College; Norman F. Boas; and the Carl Van Vechten Trust.

The Zora Neale Hurston Trust granted permission for reproducing the dust jackets, while The Gale Group and TIMEPIX generously gave permission for the reproduction of some of the advertisements included. I am indebted to Karen Blanzy, Media Production, Ferris State University, for digitizing many of those images.

Financial support from a Ferris State University Faculty Research Grant, the University of Southern Mississippi Committee on Service and Resources for Women, and the Aubrey Keith and Ella Ginn Lucas Faculty Excellence Endowment Award at the University of Southern Mississippi helped make the research for this book possible. I am also grateful for the time of Marie McCafferty and Joyce Inman, graduate research assistants at the University of Southern Mississippi. Brett Huddleston's work as my research assistant at Ferris State University was invaluable.

I am deeply indebted to those who have read the manuscript or offered other kinds of assistance. Colleagues Ana Davila-Howard and Steve Symmes kindly translated permission requests into Spanish. David Scott, reference and interlibrary loan librarian, Ferris Library for Information, Technology, and Education, has been a constant help. Dixon Chandler, Anne Wallace, William J. Maxwell, and Meredith Reeves were thoughtful in bringing to my attention recent publications about Hurston. Kimn Carlton-Smith graciously shared her expertise in African American history. Jody Ollenquist has been especially dedicated, searching the entire manuscript for my misplaced modifiers and extra commas.

My two anonymous readers' thoughtful responses challenged me to refine and to clarify my arguments. Juliana Abbenyi, Ruth Mirtz, and Kevin Miller have generously shared their responses to the manuscript at various stages of the drafting process. Reinhold Hill, too, offered thoughtful responses and introduced me to folkloristics. Encouragement from Lisa Langstraat and Julie Lindquist, during a marvelously productive summer, gave me courage to re-imagine the project as the book it has become. Lisa's humor and support have been unflagging. And, without the thoughtful and generous guidance of Joseph R. McElrath Jr., my dissertation advisor, this project would never have begun. Any shortcomings are, of course, entirely my own.

Finally, my greatest debts are to my husband and my parents. Rex, more times than I can count, saved my sanity by fixing my computer glitches and providing endless support. My parents, Leland and Carole Fager, financed research trips while I was still a student. But most important, my husband

and parents have been patient as I have spent weekends, summers, and holidays reading and writing. Their encouragement and patience have made this project possible.

Abbreviations

AJA	American Jewish Archives
AL	Alain Locke
Amistad	Amistad Research Center
APSL	American Philosophical Society Library
Beinecke	James Weldon Johnson Collection, Beinecke Rare Book and Manuscript Library, Yale University
COM	Charlotte Osgood Mason
CSJ	Charles S. Johnson
CVV	Carl Van Vechten
ERE	Edwin R. Embree
FB	Franz Boas
FH	Fannie Hurst
Fisk	Special Collections, Fisk University
Guggenheim	John Simon Guggenheim Memorial Foundation Library
HAM	Henry Allen Moe
HRHC	Harry Ransom Humanities Research Center
JWJ	James Weldon Johnson
MSHU	Moorland-Spingarn Research Center, Howard University
Schomburg	Schomburg Center for Research in Black Culture
Scribner's	Archives of Charles Scribner's Sons, Princeton University Libraries
UF	Zora Neale Hurston Collection, Smathers Library, University of Florida
ZNH	Zora Neale Hurston

Zora Neale Hurston & American Literary Culture

Introduction

Like the dead-seeming, cold rocks,
I have memories within that came out of
the material that went to make me.
Time and place have had their say.

—*Dust Tracks on a Road*

When Zora Neale Hurston opened her autobiography with these words, she alluded to events in her past that had shaped her life and had made her time as a writer possible, but the phrase has proven prophetic, as well, for time and place have continued to have their say in shaping Hurston's personal and literary legacy. The story of Zora Neale Hurston's changed stature in the American and African American literary canons is now legendary: Although she emerged during the Harlem Renaissance or New Negro Movement as an up-and-coming writer, she was by the time of her death in 1960 a literary has-been, a marginalized, out-of-print outsider. Yet today many scholars, critics, and black women writers see Hurston's work as a crucial link in the black female literary tradition. Her fiction and essays appear on reading lists for courses in humor, genre courses on the novel and the short story, and courses devoted to women's, southern, Modern, African American, and American literary traditions. Her folklore collections, likewise, garner respect.

Forty years after her death, Hurston has arrived. The 1995 editions of her work from Library of America placed her in the company of American greats like William Faulkner, Richard Wright, and Edith Wharton. All of her novels and collections of folklore are now in print in multiple editions. *I Love Myself When I Am Laughing*, *The Sanctified Church*, *The Complete Stories of Zora Neale Hurston*, *Mule Bone* (co-authored with Langston Hughes),

Go Gator and Muddy the Water, and *Every Tongue Got to Confess* have made much of her published and previously unpublished work readily available to readers. This increasing accessibility of her fiction and folklore collections will undoubtedly continue to foster growth in Hurston studies as her work becomes more familiar to contemporary readers.

On the foundation laid during the late 1970s by Alice Walker's "In Search of Zora Neale Hurston," Mary Helen Washington's "The Black Woman's Search for Identity," June Jordan's "On Richard Wright and Zora Neale Hurston: Notes Toward a Balancing of Love and Hatred," and Robert Hemenway's *Zora Neale Hurston: A Literary Biography*, a substantial body of serious criticism of Hurston's work has appeared in articles, chapters, and book-length studies. Many of these inquiries focus on her use of language, folklore, and humor; her treatment of race, gender, and politics; as well as her relationship to other black women writers. Increasing recognition of Hurston's contributions to American and African American literature has lent her work—most obviously *Their Eyes Were Watching God*—canonical status. Soon, if this is not the case already, it will be difficult to imagine that Hurston was once a distinctly minor author who died in obscurity.

As Hurston's book-length works appeared in the 1930s and 1940s, critical reception was—in many cases—negative, even though she emerged from the Harlem Renaissance as "one of the best-known black short story writers" (Cromwell, Turner, and Dykes 58). Strong-willed, independent, and unwilling to conform to others' expectations, Hurston increasingly displeased most of the influential African American critics. Reviews from white critics were usually mixed, and often black critics perceived Hurston as a social climber who exploited black culture for her own gain. Too often, white critics inadvertently revealed the ways in which racist readers could manipulate Hurston's work to advance their own ideological agendas. Richard Wright accused Hurston of promoting minstrel stereotypes in *Their Eyes Were Watching God*, and Alain Locke, a former friend and mentor, more than once took her to task for not treating racial conflict more directly. He went so far as to describe her fictional portrait of the biblical figure Moses in *Moses, Man of the Mountain* as caricature ("Dry Fields" 7). Ralph Ellison likewise declared that Hurston had contributed "nothing" to African American literature ("Recent" 24). Her 1942 autobiography prompted a spokesman for the National Association for the Advancement of Colored People, Roy

Wilkins, to describe her as a "handkerchief head" trying to attract readers to her fiction (7). Less than a decade later, Roi Ottley in the *Chicago Defender* echoed Wilkins's indictment of Hurston's character (n. pag.). When she died in 1960, donations paid for her burial in an unmarked grave in a segregated cemetery. At the time of her death, Hurston's literary productions stood only in the margins of American and African American literature: Even her most popular book sold only 5,000 copies (Hemenway, *Zora* 6).

Ironically, the woman who has been reclaimed by the establishment—black and white—died a literary outcast. Given this remarkable change in Hurston's canonical status, we might expect that scholars would have examined this shift thoroughly, but most often critics allude to her changed stature or recount the tale and cite a handful of reviews (including those by Wright, Locke, Ellison, and Sterling Brown) without fully examining them.[1] The generally accepted assumption has been that Hurston's changing fortunes have had something to do with the politics of race and gender. Those who treat her changed stature as more than a footnote typically examine one factor affecting the reception of her work. Cheryl Wall's *Women of the Harlem Renaissance* and Ann duCille's *The Coupling Convention: Sex, Text, and Tradition in Black Women's Fiction* discuss, for example, the ways in which Hurston's gender shaped responses to her work, while John Lowe's *Jump at the Sun: Zora Neale Hurston's Cosmic Comedy* explores the ways in which her gender and her use of humor complicated reception. Similarly, Susan Meisenhelder's *Hitting a Straight Lick with a Crooked Stick: Race and Gender in the Work of Zora Neale Hurston* treats the impact her use of masking had on her audiences.

The introduction to Adele Newson's *Zora Neale Hurston: A Reference Guide* traces Hurston's changed reception. Yet Newson does not provide a contextual framework for understanding the ways in which changes in American culture have shaped readings of Hurston's work. Hemenway in his biography provides brief summaries of critical responses, as does Susan Meisenhelder, but their projects explore other issues, necessarily leaving reception issues less than fully examined. And while *Zora Neale Hurston: Critical Perspectives Past and Present* reprints twenty reviews of her work, the collection neither is comprehensive nor provides contexts for interpretation. In short, no one has yet given the author's changed (and changing) stature in American literary culture the attention it deserves, for Hurston's story is also that of American literary culture and of the almost invisible process of canon formation.

What I hope to provide, then, for academic and nonacademic readers alike, is an understanding of the ways in which "[t]ime and place have had their say," by which I mean to provide a fuller context for understanding how and why Hurston moved from up-and-comer to literary outcast to the subject of substantial critical inquiry and acclaim. The complicated nature of the texts' receptions requires a multifaceted critical approach. My argument is grounded in reviews of Hurston's work and the work of her contemporaries, and other forms of literary commentary, but my interpretations of them are informed by black feminist thought, the work of reception theorist Hans Robert Jauss and formalists Hans-Georg Gadamer and Boris Tomaševskij.

The flow-ebb-flow of Hurston's stature must be studied chronologically, as each text in some way shapes the lens through which reviewers read the following one. Beginning with her apprentice years, I argue that the foundation for negative perceptions of Hurston and her art was laid during the Harlem Renaissance, that *Their Eyes Were Watching God* proved a pivotal text by pushing her to the margins of the literary establishment, and that the works that followed were read through lenses that frequently confirmed preexisting notions of the author and her work. Hurston's literary productions in the late 1940s and 1950s, particularly her opposition to desegregation, made her a literary pariah until the time of her death in 1960. Hurston's recovery began almost immediately following her death, but the converging second-wave black feminist and Black Arts movements, particularly when followed by Robert Hemenway's groundbreaking biography, gave readers new ways of looking at her work and led to her increasing stature and current canonical status.

Zora Neale Hurston and American Literary Culture is to some extent vulnerable to the criticism of "traditional reception study" made by Timothy Morris in his introduction to *Becoming Canonical in American Poetry*: "The traditional reception study is done on a highly canonical author. [. . .] Dismissals of the author seem laughable. [. . .] Teleological history elides the essence of historicity, recasting the contingent outcomes as inevitable by producing causes for them, obliterating the dynamics of past argumentative strategies" (8). My project is admittedly teleological: I cannot, at my own historical moment, help but find Hurston a canonical figure. I can study only that which has already occurred, although I do in the last chapter speculate about ways continuing literary and cultural change might affect Hurston's stature. Her canonization, however, has not been uncontested. Nor can contemporary critics and scholars agree on her value to American literature. Continuing debates about whether *Their Eyes Were Watching God* can be read as a feminist text and whether Hurston possessed a feminist consciousness immediately come to mind, as does Hazel Carby's recent assault on Hurston's canonization in American literature, which I turn to in the final chapter. In no way, then, do I assume that Hurston's stature is secure or permanent. Nor do I find criticisms of her work laughable; more often they make perfect sense within the horizon of expectations that influenced such a reading (an issue I return to shortly). No single reading of a text emerges as correct; rather, each emerges as historically bound by what readers had access to.

Further, following the lead of black feminist critics, I place history at the center of my study. I consider Hurston's works in their historical, social, political, and aesthetic contexts, for it is only in examining the social matrix that we can understand the ways in which the politics of race, gender, class, and art have shaped criticisms of Hurston and her work. Aesthetics are culturally and historically specific, so I address the ways in which the reception of her writing is embedded in changes in American culture and literary studies, specifically the climates of the Harlem Renaissance, the protest tradition, assimilationism, the Black Arts movement, and second-wave black feminism.

In addition, I respond to competing perceptions and readings within the same historical moment. Hazel Carby argues in *Reconstructing Womanhood* that "we must be historically specific and aware of the differently oriented social interests within one and the same sign community" (17). Not all reviewers reached the same conclusions about Hurston's works. This complexity is reflected in the often positive reviews of her books in black periodicals, but those reviewers who liked her work (often female) lacked the credentials and the endurance of Locke, Wright, Brown, and Ellison, making the critical voices of the latter the ones that have shaped lasting perceptions of Hurston.

I treat reviews as texts, rather than documents, that both reflect and promote political, social, and literary ideologies. My approach provides a revealing look at literary history in the making. Writers of reviews dialogically engage the larger public discourses of their time. They write within, from, and to a particular historical moment. The challenge, then, becomes reconstructing that historical moment.

The question of how (and even if) one can reconstruct the past plagues historians and literary historiographers alike. The work of Hans Robert Jauss, however, suggests at least one way to undertake such a process. Jauss, in what is frequently described as his manifesto, "Literary History as a Challenge," argues that it is possible to objectively reconstruct readers' expectations for a given text—in this case for Hurston and her fiction. His theories suggest that it is possible to determine how and why Hurston's work diverged from her contemporaries' popular perceptions and why those interpretations sometimes contrast sharply with more recent evaluations. According to Jauss, a literary work does not exist autonomously, but rather its "life" is created by the "'reciprocal interaction of work and mankind.'" The reception of the text, the interaction between text and reader, constitutes its life and history. Jauss goes still further by asserting that relationships *between* texts further complicate the life of each (15). What Jauss suggests is a dynamic, dialectical relationship between reader and text, and between the text being read and texts already read. Thus, not only are Hurston's texts significant, but her work must in some way be considered in light of that published by contemporaries, black and white, such as Richard Wright, Sterling Brown, Nella Larsen, and Roark Bradford.

To study the life of the text, Jauss argues that it is possible to reconstruct an "objectifiable system of expectations that arise for each work in the historical moment of its appearance"(22). Jauss's notion of objectification is problematic, however, for it follows that such an objectification (a reconstruction), including my own, is bound by the constructor's own horizon of expectations. My own readings, for example, are informed by my identity as a white woman profoundly influenced by black feminist thought and criticism, particularly the black feminist concept of multiple jeopardies, first articulated by Deborah King. King, building on the concept of double jeopardy defined by Frances Beale, suggests that black women experience simultaneously the intersection of various cultural markers. Black women are affected not only by the double jeopardies of race and gender (for they are not black and women, but black women—just as I am a white woman) but also by signs such as class, sexual orientation, and marital status. This intersection of race, class, and gender is a common theme to which I return repeatedly. In addition, black feminist critics Cheryl Wall, Hazel Carby, Barbara Christian, Mary Helen Washington, and Ann duCille have had a tremendous impact on my own horizon of expectations, shaping not only my interpretations of Hurston's texts but also my readings of the other texts, such as reviews and advertisements.[2]

I describe *Zora Neale Hurston and American Literary Culture* as a feminist project, although the term *feminist* is in itself problematic, because critics often use the term, as Ann duCille notes, transhistorically. Certainly *feminist* cannot connote or even denote the same thing early in this century as it did early in the last. Thus, I follow duCille's lead in defining black feminist thought broadly as an exploration and possibly an indirect or direct critique of power relations shaped by cultural attitudes toward race, gender, and patriarchy (*The Coupling Convention* 11).[3] DuCille resists describing the texts she treats, including Hurston's, as "feminist." I follow her lead as well here and describe my interpretations, not the texts, as feminist. Influenced by reader response theory, I believe that the meaning of a text is constituted largely by readers and their historical moments. The letters, words, and sentences on the page are signs that can be—and have been—read differently, depending on the historical moment at which one reads—that is, one's horizon of expectations.

It may be, then, impossible to create as Jauss argues an "objectifiable system of expectations," but Jauss's theory of relationships between texts is, nonetheless, suggestive, for much of the criticism of Hurston's work indicates that her "failure" was departing from accepted norms. For that reason, tension between her writings and other books in the same genre (other novels or other treatments of folklore), others in the same period (the work of her contemporaries), as well as others read over time (how her works relate to existing tradition) help to demonstrate her departure from the expectations of her contemporaries. I use reviews to illustrate reader responses and to trace the evolution of Hurston's reputation chronologically to reveal cumulative effects. I also discuss her writings in the context of writings by her contemporaries. In particular, I focus on writers to whom reviewers repeatedly compare her, including Roark Bradford, Marc Connelly, and Joel Chandler Harris, for such comparisons reveal the unspoken means by which her work is judged.

While I do not privilege some interpretations of Hurston's writings as correct and dismiss others as incorrect, I do, at times, provide alternate, even multiple, interpretations. Having benefit of access to Hurston's entire extant literary output and a significant body of private correspondence, my own horizon differs from that of her contemporaries not only in terms of historicity and feminist values but also in my having the advantage of retrospection and the ability to use transhistorically one text to assist with the analysis of another.

Understanding Hurston's evolving literary reputation, however, necessitates treating more than the life of the text. Drawing from the work of Boris Tomaševskij and Hans-Georg Gadamer, I argue that her persona was (and is) read as a text that informs readers' expectations of her literary work. In the midst of formalist attempts to exclude author biography from literary criticism, Tomaševskij suggested a different approach. While he concurred with formalist prohibitions against biographical criticism, he proposed instead that biography be utilized in studies of the text-reader relationship. Tomaševskij argues, "the biographical legend created by the author" mediates between text and reader. As a result of this mediation, perceptions of Hurston's *persona* become inseparable from readers' horizon(s) of expectations for the *texts* (55).

Tomaševskij's theory is most powerful when considered in light of Gadamer's concept of prejudice. Gadamer builds on Heidegger's claim that interpretation is subject to the pressures of "fore-having, fore-sight, and fore-conception" (qtd. in Gadamer 236). Thus, Gadamer argues, readers never approach a text without existing biases or prejudices, terms I use in the Gadamerian sense (235–52). In contemporary culture, the terms *prejudice* and *bias* carry undesirable connotations that might include biases such as racism. Gadamer, however, uses the term more broadly to include all preexisting ideas or conceptions—positive and negative. Marrying Gadamer's assertions with those of Tomaševskij suggests one of the crucial ways in which Gadamerian prejudice can be created: through biography. In Darwin Turner's words, African American writers are often "condemned or praised for nonaesthetic reasons" (xx). I therefore consider the perception of Hurston's biography, her public persona, as a mediating factor in the critical reception of her work.

A second source of bias I consider is the means used to market Hurston's works, including dust jackets and advertising. In its attempt to sell books, I argue, Lippincott (which published six of her seven books) exploited the author, her race, and negative racial stereotypes. At best the publisher was ignorant of black life and the broad range of concerns held by Hurston's African American contemporaries. At worst, the publisher deliberately manipulated racist stereotypes of black life in order to attract white readers. But regardless of whether Lippincott's marketing decisions were malicious or irresponsible, they had serious consequences. The images and the texts of the ads mediated between readers and the books, proposing interpretations and reflecting on Hurston's literary agenda. I am not suggesting that Lippincott was ultimately responsible for the images her writing generated. Rather, Lippincott's dust jackets and advertising created bias and thereby suggested the way readers should situate her in the literary marketplace, and unfortunately the publisher's decisions often reflected negatively on Hurston.

Additional sources of bias I consider include identifications of Hurston's race and gender, reviewer responses to previous works, and commonly applied literary labels including romance and folklore. With such terms come preestablished expectations that determine, sometimes unconsciously, with what tools a reviewer measures a text.

I also consider the related issues of stereotypes and authenticity. While most scholars rightfully assume readers understand what a stereotype is, more important to *Zora Neale Hurston and American Literary Culture* is understanding how such images function: They, too, mediate between object and viewer, text and reader. Stereotypes are, as Walter Lippmann suggested in 1922, not based in fact. "[W]e define first, then see," putting people, places, images, sounds into categories determined by preexisting biases (55). Because associations are based upon the preexistent, they may be, as Catherine Juanita Starke argues, "more powerful than reality in shaping attitudes" (16). Significantly, stereotypes do not "necessarily [reflect] the world [as] we should like it to be." Rather, stereotypes reflect the "kind of world we expect it to be" (Lippmann 69). In addition, stereotypes serve to defend "our position in society": "In that world people and things have their well-known place, and do certain expected things. We feel at home there" (63).

Thus, stereotypical images serve the needs of those who stereotype by establishing order and confirming one's place in that order. Stereotypes define community membership—who belongs and who does not (Dyer, *Mat-*

ter of Images 14). Richard Dyer argues that the maintenance of "sharp boundary definitions" is "the most important function of the stereotype" (16). As those social boundaries change, however, so do stereotypes. Joseph Boskin's *Sambo: The Rise and Demise of an American Jester* aptly demonstrates the ways in which stereotypes evolve over time. While "neither stereotypes nor their appellations are easily transformed," neither are they static (40).

The psychological complexity goes still deeper. Ralph Ellison explains that while stereotypes "are manipulated" "to control political and economic realities," they also serve other psychological purposes ("Twentieth Century Fiction" 84). For Ellison, "the tenacity of the stereotype springs exactly from the fact that its function is no less personal than political." Black stereotypes are the means "by which the white American seeks to resolve the dilemma arising between his democratic beliefs and certain antidemocratic practices, between his acceptance of the sacred democratic belief that all men are created equal and his treatment of every tenth man as though he were not" (85). Ellison's comments elsewhere are also helpful, for he explains that minstrel figures, a common stereotype, "veil the humanity of Negroes," distill them to a "sign," and permit a white audience to "repress" its "awareness of its moral identification with its own acts" ("Change the Joke" 103). Thus, white Americans find that racial stereotypes not only maintain social and economic boundaries but also emotionally and psychologically legitimize those very boundaries that ironically challenge Americans' notions of self and nation. Individuals cling to stereotypes in an effort to maintain the appearance of psychological and national unity. To disavow stereotypes one must confront the inequities in the practice of American democracy.

Common stereotypical images of African Americans that Starke identifies include the commonly recognized buffoon, mammy, violent youth, happy darky (Boskin's Sambo), rapist or "brute," primitive, and tragic mulatto. To her list I add additional images of black women identified in Barbara Christian's *Black Women Novelists* including the lascivious or "loose" woman; the emasculating Sapphire who is, in general,"[l]oud-mouthed, strong-willed, and practical," and particularly "cold, hard and evil" to black men; and the emasculating black matriarch responsible for "'pathologies' in the black community" (Christian 77–78), particularly that of absent husbands and fathers. Hurston engaged many of these stereotypes, particularly those of black women.

Stereotypical constructions of black identity—male and female—serve to establish, maintain, and justify the subaltern status of blacks in American culture. If Hurston's characters shared any traits with stereotypes, it was likely that racist readers would "define first, then see" (Lippmann 55). Those readers would believe their warped constructions of African American identity had been confirmed by a black author, an insider. Racist readers would, then, continue to accept those images and act accordingly. Thus, stereotypes and the fear of those stereotypes mediated between Hurston's texts and her readers, as did related issues of authenticity.

If stereotypes codify and oversimplify to create false images, then what is the correct or "real" image? An authentic one. But ironically, the label "authentic" can be as limiting as a stereotype. It is a dilemma Gareth Griffiths points out in postcolonial discourse in which writers are frequently hailed as having an "authentic" voice. In Hurston's case, too, reviewers often describe her work as "authentic" or "real," suggesting that as a black woman, she provides insight into that which white writers cannot access or share. Such a remark may seem (and be intended as) a compliment. It suggests that Hurston's characters, plots, and settings mimic reality, but it also poses significant problems by homogenizing African Americans, African American art, and African American culture. Put simply, if her works represent "authentic" "Negro" experiences, then what is it that W.E.B. Du Bois and Jessie Fauset represent in their fictions? Are their middle-class characters less authentic because they are not like Hurston's? For a biased reader, the answer might be "yes." Thus, the issues of who and what are authentic pose significant problems. As black reviewers repeatedly saw white reviewers praise Hurston's treatments of black life as "authentic," as if to suggest that she reveals *the* black experience, powerful black reviewers increasingly countered such assumptions and took Hurston to task for making those assumptions possible.

The first chapter of *Zora Neale Hurston and American Literary Culture* focuses on Hurston's apprentice years from 1919 to 1934. In the context of the Harlem Renaissance, Hurston established herself as a writer and established a well-known, flamboyant persona, thus creating the lenses through which critics would read the novels that followed. This chapter discusses her initial forays into literary life as a poet and her subsequent shift to a fiction writer plumbing the lives and voices of the folk. Her work from this period reveals the evolution of her aesthetics and her emerging interests in women and folklore. Her engagement of negative racist stereotypes of African Americans linked to folk traditions, black dialect, and humor demands that readers look beneath the surface of her work for indirect criticisms of blacks and whites. Hurston's personal rejection of gender norms, her reliance upon patronage, her divided commitments to anthropology and art, and Wallace Thurman's caricature of her in *Infants of the Spring* (1932) contributed to constructions of her Harlem Renaissance identity. When combined with her artistic transgressions, this legend worked to make her following fictional treatments of black Americans suspect.

In Chapter 2 I discuss Hurston's first novel, *Jonah's Gourd Vine* (1934), and her first collection of folklore, *Mules and Men* (1935). In the reviews of *Jonah's Gourd Vine* and *Mules and Men,* the negative perceptions of the author and her work begin to appear. Although many of the reviews are positive, they point to the direction later criticisms take in 1936 and 1937.

The third chapter addresses the reception of what has become Hurston's best-known novel, *Their Eyes Were Watching God* (1937). The initial publication generated very positive reviews, yet it also elicited Richard Wright's resounding condemnation of the author and the novel. In these reviews the divergence between important white and black reviewers becomes clear. I argue that negative perceptions of Hurston became steadfast because of the publication of *Their Eyes*, its reception paving the way among critics for unflattering readings of the books that followed. Although, as Hemenway notes, *Their Eyes* actually contains Hurston's subtle responses to earlier criticisms, the novel firmly established negative perceptions of the woman and her work.

Chapter 4 treats a second closely related pair of texts—*Tell My Horse* (1938) and *Moses, Man of the Mountain* (1939), both of which received mixed reviews. Critical responses to this pair of books illustrate prevailing negative perceptions of Hurston in the late 1930s. Her interpretation of Moses, her use of the black vernacular, and her focus on Voodoo (which was often perceived as pagan and primitive) seem to be of little surprise to reviewers who had already pigeonholed her, particularly Alain Locke, whose discussions of both books are highly critical. Lippincott's description of

Moses, Man of the Mountain as "the majestic chords of the Negro spiritual" drew a clear line between Hurston's work and the protest writings of the time such as Wright's 1938 *Uncle Tom's Children* and his *Native Son*, which followed in 1940.

Chapter 5 addresses Hurston's autobiography, *Dust Tracks on a Road* (1942), which reinforced existing perceptions of her. Hurston—whether by choice or necessity is unclear—avoided discussing her experiences with racism in direct violation of the norms of African American autobiography. Mediating factors exacerbated problems stemming from her omissions. While the volume brought her national recognition and made her a sought-after interpreter of black culture, it also confirmed assumptions among her critics—black and white—that her only goal was self-promotion.

Chapter 6 discusses the remainder of Hurston's career. I discuss her break with Lippincott and the ensuing relationship with Scribner's (which published *Seraph on the Suwanee* in 1948), essays she published in the six years preceding *Seraph*, and selected controversial writings that followed the novel. With politically oriented articles and essays, Hurston attempted to improve her reputation by demonstrating her political consciousness. Her continued use of indirect treatments of racial issues for white readers and direct treatments for black readers, however, probably worked against her by suggesting she would say whatever necessary to see herself in print. Her letter opposing court-ordered desegregation further damaged her reputation, and I argue that by 1955 her reputation was in ruins.

The seventh and final chapter treats the recovery of Hurston's writings and the rapid reevaluation of her place in American and African American literature that followed. I discuss reviews and notices of reprints and collections that began appearing following her death in 1960 through the publication of the Library of America editions of her work in 1995. In particular, I focus on the relationship between Hurston's recovery and the Black Arts Movement and feminism. While the politics of race at work in the Black Arts Movement opened the door to redefining the criteria by which black writers are judged, feminism and black women writers provided a new lens through which to view Hurston's writings and brought her works into American and African American literature classrooms, making her current place in the canon(s) possible.

ONE

Negotiating Ideologies of the Harlem Renaissance

The Politics of Hurston's Art and Identity

[U]ntil we have placed something upon the street corner that is our own, we are right back where we were when they filed our iron collar off.

—"Race Cannot Become Great Until It Recognizes Its Talent"

THE YEAR 1925 was a turning point for Zora Neale Hurston. Working as a manicurist, maid, and waitress, Hurston had been supporting herself while attending Howard University, but her immediate prospects were not bright. Illness had kept her out of school the previous semester, and she was without money to continue her studies. Taking the risk of starting over in a new city without friends or a job, Hurston tells us she packed her bags and headed for the horizon—a move that would place her in Harlem at the height of the Harlem Renaissance.[1] She had been wandering since her mother's death, but this move proved to be the most significant of her life, shaping her aesthetic choices as a writer and establishing her personal persona, what Tomaševskij describes as her "legend." While scholars have devoted little attention to this period of Hurston's creative life, these early years as an apprentice writer before the publication of her first novel in 1934 were formative ones when she searched for an artistic voice in the highly politicized environment of the Harlem Renaissance.

Debates about the Harlem Renaissance are many, but Robert Hemenway's succinct description of the period as "more a spirit than a movement" seems impressively accurate (*Zora* 35).[2] The work produced by Harlem Renaissance artists varies widely in style, form, theme, and ideological orientation. George Hutchinson adeptly argues that attempts to define a distinctly American national identity in large part shaped the historical moment as the most productive black and white writers of the period explored the "cultural wealth of black America" (25). Historian S. P. Fullinwider describes the common tie among artists as "a release from the mode of reform and special pleading" (128). But neither writers nor critics could agree on the nature and function of black art. Assuming art could facilitate social change, should it serve as propaganda designed to offer social amelioration? Or should art be fashioned for its own sake? Was propaganda required of all artistic creations by African Americans? To whom and to what was a black artist accountable?

Such were the issues facing Hurston between 1919 and 1934, years during which she produced a substantial and evolving body of work—more than scholars have given her credit for—including six poems, an unidentified prose piece, two short-shorts, fifteen essays, two plays, and seventeen short stories.[3] I treat the period in two sections. In the first I trace the ways in which Hurston's work engages political, social, and aesthetic debates from the period. Predictably, Hurston's work evolved, and those changes carried political import, making readers more likely to find fault with her writing. In the second section, I turn to biographical issues and the politics of Hurston's identity. I argue here that perceptions of Hurston, as a person, became powerful factors mediating between her writings and her contemporaries' interpretations of them. The convergence of Hurston's early (perceived) artistic transgressions and the politics of her identity laid the foundation for accusations of appropriation and exploitation that followed her throughout her career.

Conservative Experiments with Voice and Genre

While other artists have written at length about the Harlem Renaissance, Hurston mentions it only in passing in her autobiography, *Dust Tracks on a Road*.[4] She credits Charles S. Johnson, founder of *Opportunity Magazine*, with her participation: He had given her hope that she might establish herself as a writer. Following the 1921 appearance of "John Redding Goes to Sea" in Howard University's campus literary magazine, *The Stylus*, Johnson had written Hurston with the "idea of introducing new writers and new material to the public." In response, she sent him "Drenched in Light," which he published in 1924. Johnson also accepted a second story, "Spunk," which appeared the following year. His willingness to publish her work and his encouraging comments in a "kind letter" led her to think of moving to New York and becoming a professional writer (*Dust Tracks* 682). The notion of becoming a writer, however, surely was with Hurston before 1924. While most scholars trace her career from the 1922 publication of "Poem" in Howard's *The Stylus*, from her first short story "John Redding Goes to Sea" (1921), or from the three commonly identified poems appearing in *Negro World* (1922), extant typescripts suggest that she was submitting her work to publishers as early as 1919.[5]

In 1922 Hurston's byline appears nine times in *Negro World*, the weekly publication of Marcus Garvey's Universal Negro Improvement Association. Poems, short-shorts, and an essay present few challenges to readers. They evoke characters familiar to urban readers and rely on traditional forms and subjects. Although Hurston's first story of the Florida folk, "John Redding Goes to Sea," had appeared the previous year, she was publishing more poetry than prose—verse that put her in the company of the era's more conventional and conservative writers.

The titles Hurston selected for her poems reflect traditional romantic themes and rhyme schemes: "Sun Set," "Night," "Journey's End," "Reveries," and "Passion." "Home," like the other poems, explores in elevated diction romanticized universals: "I know a place that is full of light, / That is full of dreams and visions bright" (1–2). "Reveries" poses timeless questions about the nature of life: "Whence come I to this world of strife, / This sphere of love, this vale of sighs?" (lines 1–2). "Passion" casts the joys of a passionate life in natural terms of "the dew of morn" and "the calm of night" (lines 5–6). Hurston's unpublished poem "Twas The Night after Lobster—," a parody of Poe's "The Raven," suggests she experimented with verse that better reflects the wit of her later writings, but nothing indicates that such poems made it into print, which would have confirmed her impulse toward universal, somber poetry.

In her two short-shorts the themes that emerge are similarly universal.

Significantly, however, Hurston for the first time takes Harlem as her subject. Two brief stories under the titles "A Bit of Our Harlem" and "Bits of Our Harlem" recount chance encounters with common Harlem types—a young boy selling candy and a beggar. The stories reveal human connections across class lines and arouse sympathy for the poorest of the community. When a young lady encounters a poor, uneducated child selling candy, she finds in him "the world of sympathy, understanding and fellowship" ("A Bit" 6). The narrator evokes more humor and less pathos in the second piece. She describes herself as a "long-suffering Harlemite" who shudders to see yet another beggar's cup. Nevertheless, the beggar and the unnamed narrator momentarily connect as she looks him full in the face to discover his religious zeal—and his humanity ("Bits" 6).

These early writings from 1922 record an artistic voice most Hurston readers are unfamiliar with, but her report on bibliophile Arthur Schomburg's library bridges the apparent distance between these earliest publications and the fiction that followed. Much of the piece quotes from one of the many volumes "by a Negro or about Negroes" lining Schomburg's shelves. Significantly, Hurston highlights *Journal of a Residence on a Georgian Plantation* by Frances A. Kemble. English by birth, Kemble lived on her husband's Georgia plantation from 1838 to 1839. Both passages Hurston quotes undermine southern stereotypes she must have known well: the chivalrous southerner and poor white trash. That the southerner emerges as a vicious exploiter of black women and the "poor white trash" as "the most degraded race of human beings" make the two quoted selections apropos for Hurston and establish the pattern of criticism through indirection found in the work that follows ("Mr. Schomburg's Library" 6).

Debating the Form and Function of Black Art

By the time Hurston relocated to New York in December of 1925, much had changed, both within the artistic milieu of Harlem and in Hurston's art. The work she produced during 1925 suggests she had by then clearly identified herself as a fiction writer, rather than a poet, and had identified the southern folk as the nexus for her creativity. It was an aesthetic decision with political consequences, for it put her at the center of the most contentious debates of the period.

Hurston's decision to define herself as a fiction writer who explored the black folk experience must have been profoundly influenced by the powerful (predominantly male) figures who advised her and by the larger social and political debates about racial progress and art. Alain Locke and Montgomery Gregory, *The Stylus* faculty advisors, had encouraged Hurston to explore folk life while she was still at Howard (Hemenway, *Zora* 19). While a student at Barnard College, Hurston also studied with anthropologists Franz Boas and Ruth Benedict, both of whom also encouraged her interest in rural folk life. Equally important must have been the precedent established by other writers. W.E.B. Du Bois's *Souls of Black Folks* (1903) and James Weldon Johnson's *Autobiography of an Ex-Colored Man* (1912) and preface to *The Book of American Negro Poetry* (1922) had proclaimed the power and significance of folk influences on American culture. Jean Toomer's *Cane* (1923) had stunned the literary world with its lyric evocation of a passing way of life. White writers, too, were plumbing the experiences of southern blacks, but not necessarily with results black critics appreciated. When Alain Locke included "Spunk," Hurston's fictional treatment of the folk, in *The New Negro*, it further validated her aesthetic choices and placed her among the best-known emerging black writers. Hurston, who in her own words had a "map of Dixie on [her] tongue" (*Dust Tracks* 651), could hardly have resisted the attraction of being part of an emerging movement or the personal affirmation of making art of the Eatonville experience, for to authorize her folk roots was to authorize herself. Her explorations of southern folk, however, challenged readers in an era of active social and artistic debates.

In many ways Alain Locke's signature essay of the period, "The New Negro," set the tone of the Harlem Renaissance: positive, upbeat, expansive. Positive social changes were already occurring, and the work produced by black artists, he believed, would stimulate progress. His essay proclaims the arrival of a "New Negro" "vibrant with a new psychology." Stereotypes of the "Old Negro" that "had long become more of a myth than a man" were passing away in the face of "spiritual emancipation" (3). Black soldiers had fought for democracy abroad and had brought home what Locke describes as a "new vision of opportunity, of social and economic freedom" that was worth fighting for at home. Locke's New Negro was an independent man "trying to hold himself at par" as interactions between blacks and whites increased (8). "[M]utual understanding," he contends, is necessary for continued progress in race relations, and art is the medium of change he touts: "[I]mmediate hope rests in the revaluation by white and black alike of the Negro in terms of his artistic endowments and cultural contributions, past and prospective" (15).

The idea, however, of measuring "the Negro in terms of his artistic endowments" presented issues for critics, general readers and writers. What were a black artist's "endowments"? What kind of work should the black artist produce in order to contribute to the "revaluation" Locke foresaw? The idea that art might facilitate or hamper social change generated two of the central debates of the period that had much to do with the way critics perceived Hurston: what the function of art should be and the ways African Americans should be portrayed.

Classic companion pieces published by Langston Hughes and George Schuyler in 1926 in *The Nation* demonstrate conflicting views of artists creating "racial" art. Hughes's "The Negro Artist and the Racial Mountain" argues for the inherent value of black folk life as a resource for racial art. The "low-down folks, the so-called common element," he contends, "furnish a wealth of colorful, distinctive material for any artist because they still hold their own individuality in the face of American standardizations" (56). If an artist were able to "escape the restrictions the more advanced among his own group would put upon him," Hughes contends he would find "a great field of unused material," and Hurston agreed. But both writers felt the scorn of those Hughes refers to here as "the more advanced," who sided with Schuyler.

In "The Negro Art-Hokum" Schuyler asserts that the folk are a mythical construction of racist whites who used images of folk characters—uneducated, working class or perhaps poor, playful, perhaps religious, unashamed of their slave past—to perpetuate negative stereotypes and oppress.[6] The "racial individuality" Hughes associates with the blues, Schuyler associates with regional and class differences. "Negro art 'made in America,'" Schuyler states, is "nonexistent." Black American artists from his perspective are "just plain American," simply "lampblacked Anglo-Saxon[s]" (51–52). Art that reveals what Hughes calls "racial individuality" promotes "'fundamental, eternal, and inescapable differences' between white and black Americans" that Schuyler maintains were understood by whites to signify inferiority (54).

The issue of difference between blacks and whites was manifest in debates over primitivism, which was often manipulated to serve the needs of the white psyche. Anthropologically, the term *primitive* once implied an evolutionary perspective, a hierarchical privileging of the civilized as more advanced. Franz Boas and other anthropologists challenged such evolutionary assumptions before, during, and after the Harlem Renaissance, but Marianna Torgovnick points out in her discussion of white modernists (including D. H. Lawrence, Freud, and Lévi-Strauss) that the "evolutionary paradigm [. . .] was difficult for ethnography to discard entirely" (8). Nathan Huggins explains primitivism this way: The (white) "civilized man" who "indulged" his "natural passions" risked "neurosis or greater psychic disorders," while the natural (black) man was freer as he remained uninfluenced by the repressive forces of civilization (*The Harlem Renaissance* 87). For some, "Negroes were that essential self one somehow lost on the way to civility, ghosts of one's primal nature whose very nearness could spark electric race-memory of pure sensation untouched by self-consciousness and doubt" (91–92). This hierarchical, evolutionary privileging and new form of stereotyping threatened to keep the "New Negro" bound to images of blacks as less intelligent and more sensual than whites. Although modernist longings for the primitive seemed to pull blacks to the center of public discourse, the evolutionary connotations simultaneously kept blacks on the margins of American culture and continued to cast them in nonthreatening roles similar to older stereotypes.

Primitivism "is not, however, a monolithic discourse," as Tracy McCabe points out (475). It manifests itself in a number of modes other than as the white gaze Huggins describes, including the "romantic and idealizing" (485). Amy Helene Kirschke, in her study of artist Aaron Douglas, suggests that the "romantic primitivism" of Hurston's fellow writers McKay and Cullen "rested on a superficial knowledge of African life" (45), a superficial knowledge that must have been shared by most Americans. The research of Franz Boas helped attract positive attention toward the African past (Hutchinson, *The Harlem Renaissance* 63), and the continent of Africa took on mythic proportions as writers sought connections to a past severed by the Middle Passage. White tourists who went sightseeing in Harlem in the 1920s were still more ignorant of African culture and history than black writers were. According to Kirschke, "[t]o the cabaret visitor, Harlem's blacks seemed to live an honest, free life. Of course, cabaret visitors at three in the morning had a completely different view of Harlem than they would find in the light of day" (49). As Aaron Douglas pointed out, most of Harlem's residents were "church going people" (qtd. in Kirschke 48). White sightseers' ignorance of black life—African, African American or Caribbean—helped make possible their construction of blacks as simpler, more pure, and less inhibited.

Huggins has accused New Negro critics and writers (including Hurston) of capitulating to white demands for primitivistic art, and Hutchinson admits that Langston Hughes and Countee Cullen, to name two, "were capable of 'exotic primitive' tableaus" (*The Harlem Renaissance* 185). Aaron Douglas, too, consciously developed primitivism in his work, as Kirschke indicates. Significantly, however, she describes Douglas's African-rooted primitivism as "a source of inspiration, not an escape," as it was for white tourists sightseeing in Harlem (47). The distinction is worth noting. Hughes's persona in "The Negro Speaks of Rivers" could be lulled to sleep by the Congo, without escaping America's slave past represented by Abraham Lincoln, while Cullen's in "Heritage" could tread the paths of his ancestors without being sure what the romanticized "spicy grove, cinnamon tree" had to do with his own American existence. Their looks toward the African past are rooted in their American present.

McCabe also shows that during the Harlem Renaissance primitivism served as "a vehicle for rebellion and critique" (478). McCabe's examination of McKay's *Home to Harlem* demonstrates that subversive uses of the primitive could simultaneously exploit stereotypical constructions of gender and class, even as artists sought to challenge racist social and artistic norms. Hurston's more primitivistic writings, including "Drenched in Light" (to which I return shortly) and "How It Feels to Be Colored Me," are similar in that they function subversively, but she also works to challenge the gendered constructions McKay relies upon.

The obvious differences in the approaches to African American art outlined above do share one common belief. Implicit in each is the assumption that art not only reflects culture but also shapes it, doing, in Jane Tompkins' words, "cultural work" (ix). Hughes believed art could nurture a distinct African American culture and by implication nurture individual African American identities, while Schuyler suggests that art by black Americans might either advance or impede individuals. Primitivism, too, could be used to promote pride and to critique. Another perspective, advanced by W.E.B. Du Bois, suggested that writers use their art to advance not only individuals but the race as a whole.

W.E.B. Du Bois's 1926 essay "Criteria of Negro Art" argues for what he calls *propaganda*. The term, for many readers, conjures up the worst in literature, yet his argument interestingly aligns him with post-structuralist arguments that language and art are inescapably political. Du Bois believed artists should interpret Beauty and Truth, and ever implicit in that Truth is the repressive structure of American society. Hence, Du Bois argues, "all Art is propaganda and ever must be" (66). Describing the racial stereotypes found in literature created by white writers as oppressive propaganda, Du Bois argues that black artists must fight back with their own form of "positive propaganda" (66).

Locke's 1928 essay "Art or Propaganda" takes up the position of many of the younger artists, notably zeroing in on the problems associated with *propaganda*. Propaganda, Locke argues, "perpetuates the position of group inferiority even in crying out against it" (312). Implicit in the demand for equality made by propagandistic art is acknowledgment and acceptance of the oppressive power structure. Perhaps Hurston and other artists refused to acknowledge and accept the oppressive power structure. Or perhaps they resisted the word *propaganda*, the notion of explicitly political or didactic art, for they could hardly have denied the implicit political import of their own work in challenging classist and racist conceptions of art and of African Americans.

If Hurston believed her writing served a social function, it was the implicit, indirectly pursued function of redeeming the folk—within black and white communities. Inside a few short months of moving to New York, she had the confirmation she needed to continue developing her aesthetics along similar lines when her short story "Spunk" and her play *Color Struck* won second prize in their respective categories in the first literary contest sponsored by *Opportunity*. "Black Death," Hurston's tale of hoodoo revenge, also earned an honorable mention. Each text explores black life in the rural South, a subject Hurston knew in a way that middle-class writers from other regions of the country could not. Folk characters—blue-collar, working-class people—populated much of the fiction and poetry published during the Harlem Renaissance and inspired stylistic choices like the sermonic form and vernacular speech. Hurston, whose mastery of the southern black folk idiom matured over the period, was well on her way.

Hurston's Artistic Transgressions of Race, Gender, and Class

The absence of reviews of short fiction make documenting reader responses to Hurston's stories from the period difficult. There are the positive indicators of her prizes from *Opportunity*'s literary contests. Similarly, *Readings from Negro Authors*, a 1931 anthology, describes Hurston as "one of the best-known black short story writers" (Cromwell, Turner, and Dykes 58). And Andrew Burris's review of *Jonah's Gourd Vine* in 1934, although critical of the novel, describes Hurston's "Spunk" as "one of the best short stories in *The New Negro*" (166).

It is also possible, however, to imagine—given the horizon of expectations—a broader range of responses to Hurston's work. The responses below reflect neither specific readers nor the full range of readings. Nevertheless, the subject matter and the style of her writings, the social and aesthetic debates about the use of dialect and treatment of the folk, and the later responses to Hurston's writings suggest a number of possibilities for interpretation. A closer look at individual stories reveals the complexity of issues related to race, gender, and class that Hurston's readers negotiated.[7]

Hurston's fiction, as many critics have noted, relies on indirection to critique, and this approach is particularly common in her treatment of race, gender, and class. Like Hurston herself, her characters reject conventional gender norms, claim alternate assertive roles, and indirectly critique patriarchy as a source of women's oppression and exploitation. Given her diverse readership, all readers could hardly have had the same responses to her fiction. Some might have seen in Hurston's folk characters the authenticity so often praised in reviews of her novels. Other readers might have seen the folk traditions she recorded as quaint or unusual—an objectification that inevitably belittles by suggesting that folk traditions are rooted in ignorance and provide proof of racial inferiority. Still others may have been disturbed that some of her characters' behaviors overlap with negative stereotypes, particularly those of black men as violent, lazy, and sexually promiscuous. Middle- and upper-class black readers might have found such images of

Hurston's folk regressive. Traditions that reached back to slave culture were, many believed, to be left behind. Some feared writing about such things would only hamper the race. For others the issue may not have been the images Hurston created per se, but potential perceptions of them, for as Walter Lippmann pointed out in 1922, "[w]hatever we recognize as familiar we tend, if we are not very careful, to *visualize with the aid of images already in our minds*" (Lippmann 77; emphasis added). Thus, the more Hurston's characters had in common with stereotypes, the more likely readers were to understand her work as confirmation of those stereotypes—even if she intended otherwise.

Consider the difficulties posed by "John Redding Goes to Sea." The story evokes the sentimentality of her poetry but explores folk culture in a rural Florida setting. Hurston's introduction of folkways, particularly hoodoo, complicates interpretation as the signs of race and class intersect. She recounts a familiar tale of a young man's longing to see the world. John's mother, Matty, remains convinced that his desire to see the world stems from a witch's "travel dust," a notion his father dismisses. For years mother and son remain at an impasse: He vows to see the world, and she uses every means possible to keep him home. To resolve the conflict, Hurston relies on the deus ex machina of an approaching hurricane. John leaves his family to help preserve a nearby bridge as his family rides out the tempest at home listening to a screech owl's "doleful cry" (13). At dawn his family sets out for what remains of the bridge. They find John "prone upon his back" with his "arms outstretched [. . .] . A heavy piece of steel or timber had struck him in falling." Matty laments, "Ah knowed when Ah heard dat owl las' night" (16). The story poignantly ends as John's family allows the current to take him to sea.

The story reveals a sophisticated rhetorical response to her anticipated audience, her fellow students at Howard University. Her nonfiction writings reveal a marked awareness that middle- and upper-class blacks felt themselves divorced from the folk and, in her words, "scorn to do or be anything Negro," that is, anything that would associate them with blacks from lower socioeconomic groups ("Characteristics" 839). However, rather than dismissing Matty's beliefs in hoodoo and omens as mere superstition, as her husband does, Hurston confirms their legitimacy. John's parents serve as character foils: John's father describes hoodoo as "low-life mess" ("John

Redding" 3). The skepticism expressed by John's father mirrors the incredulous or condescending responses Hurston may have anticipated from her educated readership. By story's end even the skeptical husband/father must confront the truth Matty's signs foretold. Hurston's character development pulls readers into Florida folk life and prepares outsiders to believe in that which might seem impossible or ridiculous in another context. Hurston understood her audience's fears of racist, classist stereotyping, but she was unwilling to relinquish or dismiss folk culture.

In "Drenched in Light," race, class, and gender collide in a tale that many read as primitivistic. The story's protagonist, Isis Watts, like John Redding, wants to see what lies beyond her gate. "Perched upon the gate post," looking "yearningly up the gleaming shell road" (17), Isis is forever in trouble with her grandmother, and after a series of confrontations, Isis runs to a nearby benefit picnic. To camouflage her "torn and dirty" dress, Isis grabs a long-stemmed daisy and Grandmother's new tablecloth as a shawl. At the picnic Isis exults in being the center of attention, until Grandmother finds her "dancing before a gaping crowd in her brand new red table-cloth, and reeking of lemon extract" (22). Knowing a whipping will meet her at home, Isis heads to the creek to commit suicide. There a white couple, having lost their way from the picnic, find her. Apprised of her situation, they promise to intervene with Isis's grandmother, if she will consent to helping them find their way. The woman pays Grandmother for the loss of her new tablecloth, and the older woman proudly consents to let Isis accompany the visitor to the hotel to continue her dancing. The visitor explains that she wants "a little of [Isis's] sunshine to soak into" her "soul" (25).

The story brings together for the first time the central theme that links most of Hurston's works: intersections of race, class, and gender in the lives of black women. Central is the tension between Isis and Grandmother, through which Hurston explores constructions of womanhood. Many of their disagreements stem from Isis's refusal to abide by the older woman's ideas of appropriate behavior. Sitting on the gate post is too "[w]omanish," a loaded term. To be "womanish" is to be lower class, bold, even trashy. To abide by middle-class notions of femininity, there are several things "Grandma Potts felt no one of the female persuasion should do—one was sit with the knees separated, 'settin' brazen' she called it; another was whistling, another playing with boys, neither must a lady cross her legs" (941).

Her instructions seem simple enough, but embedded in them are constructions of race, class, and gender. Grandma's notion that Isis must be a lady has clear classist overtones: Being "womanish" is less desirable than being ladylike. Imbued in her repulsion for "settin' brazen" is the historical construction of black women as libidinous and unchaste, an image Hazel Carby explores thoroughly in *Reconstructing Womanhood*.

Implicitly, then, Grandma Potts resists such negative constructions of black womanhood by teaching Isis middle-class white conceptions of womanhood. Isis's refusal to conform suggests a rejection of such prescriptive constructions. Isis has paid for her unconventional behavior before in whippings, yet she refuses to conform and is ultimately rewarded for her individuality. As with most of the stories that follow, Hurston deals with ideology implicitly, questioning both the power of the community to shape the individual and the social strictures that define masculinity and femininity.

Many scholars also read the story biographically, as a reflection of Hurston's own search for an audience. Hemenway describes the story as a "calling card" and "a statement of personal identity" (*Zora* 10). For some readers this story reveals Hurston's use of primitivism—Isis's performance for a white audience mirroring the writer's performance for white readers. Isis does, initially, seem "the stereotypical 'primitive'" (Meisenhelder 5) that Huggins argues was exploited by and for the white gaze. The woman's interest in soaking up a bit of Isis's "joy" would seem to support such a reading. Yet Meisenhelder and I both argue that the story's primitivism is more complex than it appears, in large part because of gender. Hurston puts primitivism to subversive use. Meisenhelder sees Isis's behavior as "acts of racial *and* sexual rebellion against the strangling restraints placed on her as a black female" (7). McCabe's discussion of primitive discourses notes they function differently, sometimes as "a vehicle for rebellion and critique" (478), and in this case Hurston critiques aspiring or already middle-class blacks who sacrifice their values to please whites.

Significantly, Isis's first audience is the racially mixed crowd at the picnic. Isis certainly does not begin her performance or limit her performance for whites. In many ways, as Meisenhelder suggests, Isis emerges as powerful (6–7). She gives the directions, and she has the power to end her encounter with the white couple whenever she wishes. And Isis perpetuates the relationship with her "patrons" for her own reasons: She triumphs over her grandmother and escapes another whipping. Clearly the white couple pursues Isis for different reasons; they do seem to represent a white gaze. Interestingly, however, it is Grandmother (not Isis) who falls victim to racial hierarchies. Isis's behavior does not change for her white audience, but Grandmother's does, for she immediately dismisses Isis's behavior, seizes the five dollars offered, and relinquishes Isis to their care. Isis's "patrons" understand they have gotten her out of trouble, but they cannot possibly understand the long-term power struggle into which they have stumbled. The triad suggests a metaphor for the struggle to control black art. While the couple represents white consumers of black art who understand only one aspect or element of the black experience, Grandmother emerges as the middle-class African American who gives up her own values in order to appease whites. Isis, the subversive artist, remains true to herself and emerges triumphant: She has gotten the best of all three.

The same year, Hurston submitted *Color Struck* to the literary contest sponsored by *Opportunity Magazine*. This powerful one-act play highlights intersections of race and gender, and reveals implicit interracial relations between black women and white men. Set at the turn of the century and in the mid-1920s, the play explores the impact of colorism within the context of southern folk culture. Emma's fear of colorism alienates her lover at a cakewalk, but years later John returns to find Emma with a near-white child and, ironically, a continued obsession with color. Hurston's critique of values within the black community exposes the tragic, warping effect white standards of beauty have when internalized by black women. Society constructs women as objects for the male gaze; to be beautiful is to be desired and loved. Emma has internalized gendered norms, but her race—and particularly her dark skin—make hegemonic standards of beauty unattainable and incredibly destructive. Although Emma always feared her lover was "color struck," her attitude toward her near-white child demonstrates that she, in fact, is the one obsessed with color. Nothing in the story indicates who fathered the child, although Hurston implies he was white. Emma's lost chastity and the absence of a male character in the story to accept half of the responsibility for the child may inadvertently have supported the stereotype of the loose black woman that Hurston's contemporaries complained was all too common. Readers have to discern that Emma does not represent all black women.

"Sweat," one of Hurston's best-known stories, which appeared in *Fire!!* in 1926, also explores intraracial prejudices and male-female relationships. The story foregrounds the politics of race and gender, while the politics of race and class determined the reception of the magazine itself and linked Hurston to the era's most rebellious artists.

"Sweat" is a complex story loaded with biblical and phallic images that chronicles the disintegration of an abusive marriage between Delia, who takes in white folks' laundry to support herself, and her manipulative husband Sykes. With her own sweat Delia has created a bit of paradise, her own Garden of Eden. Sykes, however, wants the home for himself and his girlfriend. To frighten Delia from the house, Sykes installs a box with a large rattlesnake on the front porch, but when he finds that even Delia's terror of snakes will not dislodge her and she threatens to go to the "white folks," his goal changes. Sykes puts the snake in Delia's laundry basket, empties the match safe, and leaves—knowing she will return after dark to a snake-filled basket. In keeping with the notion of poetic justice, however, Sykes gets what he deserves when the snake bites him as Delia listens from outside the house. Delia does not escape unscathed, however. She has learned to hate Sykes and permits him to die alone. He hardly evokes sympathy, but Delia's own Christian values complicate her decision to watch Sykes die without sympathy, compassion, love, or forgiveness.

The porch-sitters know Sykes deserves to be run out of town but fail to do more than talk. Sykes's irredeemable character, when linked with the inaction of the male porch-sitters, suggests a critique of masculinity, but perhaps Sykes, too, has been a victim. A closer examination of the text and the cultural context suggests that Hurston's portrait of black men may not be a monologic one.

The story clearly indicates the violence patriarchy makes permissible against women, but Lillie Howard suggests that Sykes, too, is a victim of oppression. Sykes, to paraphrase Joe Clark, has treated his wife "lak [. . .] a joint of suger-cane," and having ground her until nothing sweet is left, wants to throw her away. When brutality and terror fail to drive Delia away, Sykes attempts murder. The politics of race are clearly evident in Delia's threat that she will go to the "white folks" if Sykes beats her again. Complicating images of Sykes, however, Howard suggests that Sykes's hatred of Delia and her laundry results from his own emasculation as a black man dependent upon his wife's washing of white folks' clothes for support. He has apparently spent most of his adult life un- or underemployed, as perhaps have the other men on the front porch. Delia's tub has "filled [Sykes's] belly" more than his own hands have ("Sweat" 75). From this perspective, then, race and social constructions of masculinity converge to victimize Sykes, who likewise makes his wife a victim. However, less sympathetic interpretations of Sykes may for some readers have come too close to stereotypical conceptions of black men as violent and/or lazy.

Reader responses to the story were also mediated by the venue in which the story appeared, the now legendary *Fire!!* Hurston joined Langston Hughes, Wallace Thurman, Aaron Douglas, John P. Davis, Bruce Nugent, and Gwendolyn Bennett in creating a journal "devoted to the younger Negro artists." Creating a "little magazine" devoted entirely to art, they believed, would provide an important new publishing outlet for emerging black writers. The two national periodicals most receptive to black writers and published for black readers, *The Crisis* and *Opportunity*, were controlled by the National Association for the Advancement of Colored People and the Urban League, both reform organizations. Social missions drove both journals and limited the space devoted to art. *Fire!!* was the younger artists' attempt to open additional pages to art, and the magazine's dedication to aesthetic values allowed for the publication of materials that the two existing magazines would have rejected. In his autobiography, *The Big Sea*, Hughes explains, "the idea [was] that it would burn up a lot of the old, dead conventional Negro-white ideas of the past" (235).

Reader response, however, was largely negative, placing Hurston in the company of the era's most divergent, rebellious voices. Stories by Thurman and Nugent dealing with prostitution and homosexuality were highly controversial. Hughes explains that "[n]one of the older Negro intellectuals would have anything to do" with their little magazine (*The Big Sea* 237). Even Locke, who liked the idea of an independent journal, criticized the direction in which the young artists had taken *Fire!!* ("Fire: A Negro Magazine" 563). Associating herself with such controversial stories would only have furthered images of Hurston as an iconoclast.

In 1933, Hurston's fiction began to explore more explicitly social constructions of female identity and resistance to oppression. "She Rock," a previously undocumented story that appeared in the *Pittsburgh Courier* in

August 1933, demonstrates a more aggressive resistance to male domination and class-specific gender roles in a biblical parody modeled on chapters and verses. The story presents an urban version of the truncated Aunt Caroline section of the commonly documented "The Eatonville Anthology" and the more extended Eatonville version found in *Dust Tracks*. In the rural version, a pair of shoes triggers the central conflict, while in the urban version Hurston substitutes a fur coat.

While in Sanford, Florida, Oscar accepts a job offer in Harlem, hoping to leave Cal'line, "strong of mind and arm," behind. Caroline, however, meets him at the train station. Once in Harlem, Oscar attempts to throw off the ways of Sanford in favor of the ways of Babylon: "[In] August did Oscar put up a coat for her that calleth him daddy that it might be fully paid for when the feast of Thanksgiving drew nigh." But again, Caroline knows more than Oscar thinks. On Thanksgiving day Caroline tracks Oscar to his honey's apartment, drives him out by the fire escape, and claims the fur coat as her own. Oscar, in the end, discovers that "[s]he that toteth the ax in Babylon is narrow of mind, and she that smiteth locks is of little faith." Oscar wonders, "What profiteth a man, if he stand among a multitude of sweet ones if it be forbidden that he possesses even one? For lo, the mind of Cal'line hath not been broadened and her head hath not learned a darned thing. Selah!" ("She Rock" 3).

Oscar's response indicates that Cal'line violates the norm for wives in Harlem. Oscar warns her that "[t]his be great Babylon, not Sanford, moreover thou art no tea for my fever, neither are thou a B.C. for my headache [. . .] . Behold and see thou are still Sanford, while I am Harlem" ("She Rock" 3). Oscar attempts to blame their conflict on geographical differences, privileging the urban woman as more sophisticated and making the rural woman a bumpkin. Yet the story subtly reveals that Harlem's urban, higher-classed norms would relegate Cal'line to the status of a silent wife. Oscar attempts to manipulate his wife by suggesting she is narrow-minded. Broadening her mind would leave Oscar free of guilt or recriminations for violating his marriage vows and leaving Caroline alone in a new urban environment. Caroline, however, claims the folk ethos that empowers her with an ax, a voice, and a mind of her own.

The gender roles in these stories hardly conform to the middle-class attributes Marita Bonner complained women were expected to adopt: silence, gentleness, softness (6–7). In fact, Hurston images Cal'line as "rock hard," an image conventionally more complimentary for a man. Clearly, her "overbearing" behavior is an act of self-preservation in a marriage to an unreliable and unfaithful man. The physical and moral victory belongs to Caroline—because she refuses to bow to social norms, suggesting, as Isis does in "Drenched in Light," the liberation of resisting gender norms.

Negotiating the Politics of Dialect, Folk Traditions, and Humor

If the subjects of Hurston's fiction transgressed gender norms and engaged issues of class and race, so did her stylistic choices. Resisting Du Bois's idea of positive propaganda, Hurston relied heavily on southern black dialect and speech patterns in almost all of her fiction. This use of dialect, or idiom, as she later called it, presented yet another set of issues for readers to negotiate.[8] The long association of dialect with minstrelsy and plantation fiction, its subsequent artistic uses by black writers claiming their folk heritage, and its liberatory functions for white writers would have created substantial difficulties for Hurston's contemporaries. For many readers, use of dialect by black writers during the Harlem Renaissance was "especially dubious" (Gates, *Figures* 182), at least in part because black stage performers had long manipulated the minstrel tradition—ironically imitating white performers purporting to imitate black characters—for personal gain (Huggins, *The Harlem Renaissance* 244–301 passim).

Dialect had also served as a staple of the Plantation Tradition, a southern manifestation of the regionalist writing that flourished following the Civil War. Thomas Nelson Page's collection of stories *In Ole Virginia* (1887) remains a popular example of the tradition through which readers meet loyal former slaves who long for the good old days before emancipation. Page and other local colorists used the frame tale that permits a white narrator to share his encounter with a quaint old "darky." The "standard" English of the frame narrator contrasts sharply with the dialect of his informant, illustrating regional and class differences. It was the form Charles W. Chesnutt borrowed and subverted in *The Conjure Woman* (1899). In 1922 James Weldon Johnson pointed to Paul Laurence Dunbar as the best-known black writer of dialect, but argued that "Negro dialect [. . .] is not capable of giving expression to the varied conditions of Negro life in America" because of "the mold of convention" which lent two stops to dialect: pathos and humor (*The Book* 41–42). While Gavin Jones's *Strange Talk: The Politics of Dialect Literature in Gilded Age America* astutely demonstrates the subversive uses of dialect by writers from the Gilded Age, including Dunbar, prevailing attitudes in Hurston's time made using dialect a complex political and artistic choice.

How could a "New Negro" author use the language of slavery, spirituals, minstrelsy, and plantation fiction to craft the New Negro art that Alain Locke, W.E.B. Du Bois, and Charles S. Johnson believed would bridge differences between the races? Hurston understood that her use of dialect had the potential to alienate middle-class black readers who "scorn to do or be anything Negro." Many of her contemporaries distanced themselves from dialect as a vestige of slavery and an emblem of ignorance and culturally ascribed inferiority. Hurston knew their attitude toward folk life and culture was "[w]e done got away from that now" ("Characteristics" 838–39). Hurston, however, believed she could transform uses of dialect at least in part because the dialect of local color and minstrelsy was as much a myth as the stereotypes that went with it.

The creations that middle-class blacks wanted to distance themselves from existed only in the pages of books. As Alain Locke argued in "The New Negro" that the old Negro was a fictional creation, so too, Hurston believed, was the language ascribed to him. She felt sure that nowhere would readers find the Negro who speaks the argot white writers created. Both the stereotype and his language "exist for only a certain type of writers and performers," she argued. "Without exception" she found such portraits distortions: "I wonder why the black-face comedians *are* black-face; it is a puzzle—good comedians, but darn poor niggers. Gershwin and the other 'Negro' rhapsodists come under this same axe. Just about as Negro as caviar" (Hurston "Characteristics" 844).[9] Hurston's use of dialect reflects a deliberate attempt to write through or transform racist stereotypes into multidimensional, culturally affirmative art.[10]

In her attempt to transform the tools of stereotype and oppression into art and a medium for liberation, however, Hurston had to negotiate biases created by the historical uses of dialect, pathos and humor. Unfortunately, her goals did not align well with that of the "Victorian deans of the Renaissance—Johnson, Locke, Braithwaite, Du Bois," which "was to 'elevate the race' in the eyes of the incredulous white world; *internal function could be only secondary*" (Gates, *Figures* 184; emphasis added); thus the racially internally transformative functions of Hurston's dialect fell victim to culturally external terms of reference—what white readers might think. Hurston's stylistic choice—meant to liberate the nuanced, musical speech of the folk from racist white stereotypes—eventually contributed to images of Hurston, ironically, as an "Uncle Tom."

Minstrelsy and the dialect tradition reflect complex and sometimes competing cultural impulses that evolved as American culture evolved. While earlier scholarship on minstrelsy suggested that it served only to oppress, exploit, and belittle, more recent work, particularly Eric Lott's *Love and Theft: Blackface Minstrelsy and the American Working Class*, suggests that the impulses behind minstrelsy reflect a cultural dialectic marked not only by exploitation and control but also by interest in and attraction to black culture.

At its most basic level, minstrelsy served to reinforce comforting, nonthreatening conceptions of black Americans, particularly black men.[11] The minstrel movement, reaching as far back as the antebellum period, Robert C. Toll's foundational work suggests, met particular needs in the white American psyche: "Although most Northerners did not know what slaves were like, they believed or wanted to believe that black slaves differed greatly from free white Americans" (34). The crudity of the minstrel show manifested the "egalitarian sentiments outraged by the conventional English stage" (North 81). At the same time, however, minstrel shows expressed a desire for superiority: White audience members could "laugh at some of their own difficulties and anxieties while being assured that someone was more ignorant and worse off than they" (Toll 161). Ironically, the stereotypical minstrel characters Jim Dandy and Jim Crow had their origins in white stereotypes, the crude Davy Crockett and Yankee Doodle. They were, Nathan Huggins perceptively points out, "standard American comedy types underneath burnt cork" (*The Harlem Renaissance* 249).[12]

Race acted as a mask behind which white and eventually black performers hid to liberate white audiences. Because African American folk traditions—folktales, songs, dances and dialect—were often perceived as the only creative forms uniquely and indigenously American, adopting black masks provided a means for white entertainers to distance themselves from

British influence and define themselves as American (North 23). It is a process Lott describes as "love and theft," not merely a process of exploitation and control, but also a dialectic marked by expropriation and control of the male body and by sympathetic, albeit condescending, attraction and interest (passim).

The minstrel show had become a stylized staple of American entertainment by the time the local color movement emerged (Huggins, *The Harlem Renaissance* 249). The dialect of local color had its roots in Reconstruction when "the central trope of the movement, the 'disappearing Negro' was serviceable on several levels":

> It functioned as wish fulfillment, revealing the barely submerged hope that the freed slaves would simply die off. It served as a metaphor of the temporal reversal of the post-Reconstruction period, taking readers imaginatively back in time as the South was being taken politically back in time. And it fed nostalgia for a time when racial relationships had been simple and happy, as [sic] least for whites, suggesting that they might be simple and happy again if Southern whites were simply left alone to resolve things themselves. (North 22–23)

For white readers, then, dialect and local color worked also to create a firmly fixed "picture of the freed slave as hapless, childlike, and eager for paternalistic protection" (North 22). While stereotypes of minstrelsy and the plantation tradition differ, they no doubt dialogically informed one another as cultural manifestations that served the psychic needs of whites who constructed both traditions as means of simultaneously securing white authority and disparaging blacks.

Despite these historical uses of dialect, the only way to transform Negro speech was to use it, and use it writers of the 1920s, black and white, did. As North demonstrates, white modernist writers appropriated dialect as a mask to liberate themselves from Anglo-European traditions. So important was dialect to writers of the period that North believes "[l]iterary modernism [. . .] could not have arisen without the example of dialect" (195). However, Hurston's use of dialect was not a mask but an attempt to reclaim and reconstruct the black, rural folk voices that she believed had been too long distorted by and for white readers.

Hurston's attempts to reclaim black folk traditions extended beyond language to include characters and cultural traditions. White writers' expanding "use" of "Negro material" exploited racial stereotypes, Hurston complained, as did Montgomery Gregory and Charles Johnson (North 176). Stereotypes were so common in the late nineteenth and early twentieth centuries that images of "black people as naive, childlike, and just plain stupid" were veritable staples of American culture (Lowe 16). Hurston claimed she had "never seen" a white writer who could make use of Negro material in an "entirely realistic" manner. The elders of the New Negro Movement "wanted to project a positive, even heroic, image of blacks and black life" (Cooper 239). They feared "the well-meant but misguided enthusiasms" of "white critics and admirers of Afro-Americans who, as the movement progressed, seemed bent upon locking blacks into a new version of an old stereotype, that of the primitive" (239), and Hurston's characters often came too close to that stereotype for racist readers to discern the difference.

Hurston's "John Redding Goes to Sea" validated folk traditions, including signs and hoodoo. Hurston also worked to reclaim and reconstruct African American folk traditions from racist, white-imposed frames. Consider again *Color Struck*. Just as readers want to see Emma's color-struck character liberated from white constructs of beauty, Hurston's use of folk life in the play reflects an attempt to situate black folk culture, represented in the play through the cakewalk, within its own cultural context and thereby also remove the play from white-imposed constructions of the minstrel show (North 176–77).

The setting of the cakewalk implies resistance to racist assaults on the black sense of self, but the history of the dance demonstrates the difficulties of trying to reclaim traditions. The dance originally functioned as a source of resistance and release: It originated as a form of parody (Sundquist 278). Slaves, watching through the window of the plantation house, imitated steps from within and then "added to them their own special flair, burlesquing the white folks and then going on to force the steps into a choreography uniquely their own" (Ellison, *Going* 223). It was a "reversal of stereotype," whereby blacks created stereotypes of whites for entertainment. It offered "a significant potential for resistance" (Sundquist 277).

By 1925 when Hurston wrote *Color Struck*, the initially all-black tradition, however, had long been exploited by minstrel adaptations. At the turn of the century the cakewalk was "the most popular element of the minstrel and early black theatrical stage." The dance "could easily be made to correspond to the stereotype of black buffoonery" (Sundquist 277). During the 1890s the dance became the standard conclusion for minstrel shows, so it is difficult to imagine that Hurston could have erased the cakewalk's associations with the tradition, particularly for older or middle-class readers.

Hurston's use of humor also increased the likelihood that educated readers would find her work offensive. John Lowe's perceptive study of her humor, *Jump at the Sun*, notes that "humor played a crucial role in her initial reception by, and later relations with, the other members of the Harlem Renaissance" (51). Humor, Lowe argues, was Hurston's "corrective to any tendency toward sentimental, romantic or egoistic approaches to culture" (2), ironically just what critic and friend Alain Locke accused her of in 1936 and 1938. But how were black readers to know whether Hurston was laughing with them or inviting white readers to laugh at them?

Stereotypes mediated between readers and writer. Critic Nick Aaron Ford complained that "[f]or fifty years the Negro has been the joker in American literature. His idiosyncrasies have been exaggerated and distorted beyond their natural due. [. . .] He has been looked upon as the funmaker of the world rather than a thinker" (97). Ford's critique suggests he sees Hurston's work as an indication that she has "join[ed] hands with [the Negro's] enemies who delight in heaping abuse upon his already bowed head" (98). Perspectives such as Hurston's might "reinforce the already prevalent doctrine of race inferiority." More productive, he believed, was presenting the Negro "in a more favorable light" (99). Hurston, however, refused to be on either the offensive or the defensive. Writing offensively would have smacked of propaganda and special pleading. Writing defensively would have suggested shame. She was neither ashamed of her folk past nor "tragically colored" ("How It Feels" 827).

Consider, for example, the difficulties arising from Hurston's use of humor to treat African American life in "Book of Harlem."[13] Previously thought unpublished, the story appeared in the *Pittsburgh Courier* on February 12, 1927. In this parody Hurston creates humor through the juxtaposition of biblical language and folk characters who have migrated from the South to Harlem. Like "She Rock," the sketch also relies on biblical chapters and verses for structure and records Jazzbo's conflicts with new social mores in Harlem as he searches for a wife.

At home in Waycross, Georgia, Jazzbo hears a traveler praise the women of Harlem, so he asks his father for money to travel to find a wife. Their conversation derives its humor from biblical puns:

6. [B]ut wherefore goeth thou to a far city to seek a wife among Jezebels, when there be Cora, thy neighbor's daughter, a damsel of great piety, who wilt bear thee many sons, and moreover, she is a mighty biscuit-cooker before the Lord.
7. Then did Jazzbo stand before his father and snort with scorn, saying, Wherefore must I wed a cooker of biscuits when I crave not bread? Behold, man was not made to live by bread alone, but upon every thrill that proceedeth from life. (1)

Jazzbo's father consents to the journey, but when the young man reaches Harlem, he quickly discovers that city women will have nothing to do with a man in "mail order britches." Following his roommate's advice, he acquires "much haberdashery," a manicure, and a haircut. He proceeds to a dance hall only to "yearn within his liver and tear his hair" because he does not know the dances he sees being performed. A "maiden with pomegranate lips" rescues Jazzbo, and before long he forgets that "he was a hick, (which being interpreted means dweller-in-the-tall-grass)" (1).

Eventually, thoughts of a virtuous wife return to Jazzbo, who asks his roommate's advice in finding "a maiden, one of exceeding virtue, that I may take her to wife[.]" The response Jazzbo receives is totally unexpected, but fully deserved: "Ha! Ask the maiden herself and she shall tell thee. Thus spake his friend without laughter and Jazzbo was satisfied. For he knew, now, many beautiful maidens who pleased him" (1). Morals in Harlem differ from those Jazzbo knew at home. All of the women he has known in Harlem's dance halls are virtuous.

Because the setting is urban and because southern migrants were so common, readers of the *Pittsburgh Courier* would have been able to relate to Jazzbo. Many of Hurston's readers were probably migrants themselves, who, through Jazzbo, could laughingly recall their own clumsy attempts to adapt to urban life.

But other readers may have been put off by Hurston's irreverent treatment of bread, which serves repeatedly as a metaphor for spirit in the Bible. While her treatment of Matthew 4:4 demonstrates an ironic and powerful manipulation of biblical rhetoric, her use of humor superficially makes light of sin and forces readers to look beneath the surface to find the deeper meaning. The verse states, "Man shall not live by bread alone, but by every word that proceedeth out of the mouth of God." Ironically, Jesus speaks these words after Satan's temptation and after having fasted in the wilderness for forty days and nights. The verse teaches the primacy of spirit over body, even in times of great temptation and physical want—a message lost on Jazzbo. He conveniently omits the last half of the verse. He wanders in his own wilderness of temptation and wallows in physical pleasures. Churchgoing readers would have approved of neither Jazzbo's source of spiritual sustenance nor his use of Harlem dance halls as churches. Only the biblical context of the verse reveals a deeper indirect warning to migrants about the temptations of city life.

Between 1927, when Hurston published "The Book of Harlem," and 1933, when "The Gilded Six-Bits" appeared, the writer's treatment of folkways and humor matured, taking on subtlety and complexity as characters became her central focus against a backdrop of rural folk culture. Her folkloric research had demonstrated the complexity of folkways and beliefs, and her fictional treatments, as a result, became increasingly sophisticated, too, as her use of humor in the last story from the period demonstrates.[14]

"The Gilded Six-Bits" is a tragicomedy that uses characteristic indirection and humor to critique stereotypes of the happy darky. Hurston, as John Lowe notes, establishes an all-black context for most of the story by describing the setting as a "Negro yard around a Negro house in a Negro settlement" (75). As Hurston establishes the relationship between Missie May and Joe Banks, readers see that the couple keeps their marriage "fresh and lively through elaborate games, jokes and rituals" (75). Joe works in the local fertilizer factory and returns home each Saturday to toss money through the door at his wife. Missie May pretends to take offense, a chase ensues, and the ritual ends with Missie fishing in Joe's pockets for the phallically symbolic sweets he brings her each payday.

The arrival of Slemmons, the big-bellied proprietor of an ice cream shop, disrupts their ritual. Joe finds himself initially impressed by Slemmons's round belly—a symbol of prosperity and a life of ease—and the gold pieces pinned to his lapel. Ironically, however, it is Missie May who falls victim to Slemmons. Joe returns home early one day to find Slemmons "fighting with his breeches in his frantic desire to get them on" ("Gilded" 991). Hurston's image of Slemmons "half in and half out of his pants" humorously draws the tragic picture of Joe reaching for the intruder's vest to come away with the "gold pieces" he had used to seduce Missie May—gilded six-bits.

Months pass before Missie May and Joe return to their ritual of tossed coins. Only after Missie gives birth to a baby, "'de spittin' image'" of Joe, does her husband return to the candy store to use the gilded six-bits to purchase Missie's candy kisses ("Gilded" 995). The story's final scene reveals Hurston's indirect critique of the happy darky stereotype. The clerk at the store sees only Joe's happiness at ridding himself of the fake coins: "Whist I could be like these darkies. Laughin' all the time. Nothin' worries 'em" (996).

Hurston's narrative pulls readers, black and white, through a complex relationship and the humorous folk rituals that function internally to keep Joe and Missie's marriage alive. Their relationship reveals the larger functions of humor, ritual, and folk traditions: to preserve and promote a healthy and whole community. From the outside, the clerk models primitivistic assumptions of black folk life as simple, while Missie May and Joe demonstrate its complexity. The irony of the clerk's remark demonstrates how little outsiders know about the lives of folks like Missie May and Joe, and on a larger level, the clerk's mistake cautions readers to look beneath the surface of the humor and laughter associated with the folk. Hurston's use of irony here, with characteristic indirection, borders on satire of simple-minded whites blinded by stereotypes. But her indictment of stereotypes is so subtle that white racist readers might have seen the story's ending as a confirmation of blacks as simple-minded.

Hurston's uses of dialect, humor, and folk traditions might have escaped suspicion had she written protest- or problem-oriented fiction. Langston Hughes and Claude McKay, for example, earned the ire of critics for their portraits of the urban folk, but they also produced work that could make middle-class readers beam with pride. Hughes's *Fine Clothes to the Jew* plumbs common life in Harlem, while his poems "The Negro Speaks of Rivers" and "I, Too" reveal a deep sense of race pride and undoubtedly appealed to those repulsed by his poems about red silk stockings and prostitution. By the mid-1930s, Hughes's fiction and poetry had also taken a more political turn revealed in *The Ways of White Folks* and "Advertisement for the Waldorf-Astoria," the poem that illuminated the distance between Hughes and white patron Charlotte Osgood Mason. Even McKay, whose 1928 novel *Home to Harlem* introduced readers to speakeasy brawls over prostitutes and venereal disease, wrote work that revealed his political conscience, an important factor in the reform-minded decade of the 1930s. While not all black reviewers were critical of the novel, it prompted W.E.B. Du Bois to speculate "how far one could sink in search of money and popularity" (Cooper 244), while Dewey Jones in the *Chicago Defender* complained that "'white people think we are buffoons, thugs and rotters anyway. Why should we waste so much time trying to prove it? That's what Claude McKay has done'" (qtd. in Cooper 245). And yet, that same novel was read through a horizon of expectations that included his best-known verse, including "If We Must Die" and "The White House," both of which record open confrontations with the inequities in American democracy. McKay's and Hughes's most controversial works, then, were mediated by their more politically oriented works. Unlike Hughes and McKay, Hurston and her work continuously resisted propagandistic or overtly political art.

Had Hurston avoided humor and dealt more directly with issues of race—as contemporaries Hughes and McKay did at various points in their careers—it is difficult to imagine readers so persistently questioning her literary agenda. Instead, she relied on humor and indirection to critique. It was this deceptively "neutral" approach that complicated the reception of much of Hurston's work, particularly when readers interpreted her work through the lens of her personal persona.

The Politics of Identity

Hurston's use of indirection, humor, language, and folk traditions challenges readers to work through and move beyond common stereotypes, but her persona presents still other issues to negotiate. Questions about Hurston's identity and motives have been so persistent that for years they dominated Hurston scholarship. As Darwin Turner explained in 1971, "A problem for Afro-American writers is that invariably those who become well-known are condemned or praised for nonaesthetic reasons" (xx). Turner points specifically to the politics of aesthetics and the politics of race as sources for mediating bias, but his mention of expatriates who have "removed themselves from the United States" suggests the ways in which the personal life of a writer also becomes a factor mediating between text and reader (xx). It is an implication that the theories of Hans-Georg Gadamer and Boris Tomaševskij support. Gadamer argues that readers never approach a text without preexisting biases or prejudices. While such biases may be unconsciously held, any reading of a text is mediated by some kind of preexisting knowledge. One source of such bias is, in Tomaševskij's words, "the biographical legend created by the author," which mediates between text and reader (55). Readers cannot, then, read a text without interference from preexisting knowledge of the author. While not all readers had such knowledge, for those of Hurston's contemporaries who did, it proved a powerful source of bias. Hemenway tells us that "'Zora stories' circulated widely" (*Zora* 23). Hurston's unconventional behavior, her relationships with white patrons, and her "schizophrenic" compulsions as a writer and a scientist contributed to a distorted, often unflattering portrait of Hurston as a person.

Breaking the Rules

Hurston's tendency toward unconventional behavior has become nothing short of legendary. Hughes tells the story of Hurston, at a subway stop, taking a nickel from the cup of a blind beggar, saying she needed it more than he did and promising to repay it later (*The Big Sea* 240). May Miller, a playwright who had known Hurston in Washington, recalled her stopping a party after the 1925 *Opportunity* dinner when she "flung" a bright scarf around her, "dramatically calling out 'Calaaaah struuuuk,'" the title of her award-winning play. Similarly, Bruce Nugent recalls Hurston asking if he would walk with her on Seventh Avenue while she smoked a cigarette. They laughed as the passersby stared: It was not appropriate for ladies to smoke in public (Hemenway, *Zora* 60). Both Cheryl Wall and Ralph Story suggest this unladylike behavior proved a source of bias against Hurston (*Women* 1–32 passim; "Gender" 25).

While the Jazz Age is known for "sexual abandon and 'free love'" (McDowell, "Introduction" xiii), Victorian standards for female behavior, like those encouraged by Isis's grandmother, lingered. Hurston violated all of the rules, making her an outsider among other women of the movement. Silence, gentleness, softness were still considered feminine virtues (Bonner

6–7). Young, educated women of color such as Marita Bonner, Jessie Fauset, and Nella Larsen were restricted by social convention. Even a train trip to New York from Washington, D.C., Bonner laments, was impossible; traveling alone was inappropriate for upper-middle-class women.

Black women still felt it necessary to protect themselves from dominant media images of African American women as "a gross collection of desire" (Bonner 5). Elsie Johnson McDougald, in her 1925 essay "The Task of Negro Womanhood," also notes the persistence of "Aunt Jemimas" in advertising and vicious, vulgar stereotypes of the stage (370). "Ladies" from educated families might pursue careers as teachers, nurses, social workers, secretaries, but Eva Bowles, in an article for *Opportunity*, is careful to reaffirm that "a home and the rearing of children" are "first and foremost" the proper concerns for a woman. She further circumscribes the role of women by describing the achievement of "poise" and "charm" which mark "ideal woman leadership" (8–9). Hurston's participation in the renaissance, her work as an anthropologist, and her daily behavior violated all such norms others might have expected a woman from Barnard College to follow.

In contrast, the other two prominent female writers of the period, Jessie Fauset and Nella Larsen, conformed to accepted standards of femininity, thereby making Hurston's departure from the norm more conspicuous. Wall describes Fauset as a woman "bound by cultural dictates" that dominated her childhood in a Methodist parsonage and her education at Cornell University (*Women* 39). Fauset—like Bonner—trained to be a teacher, a role she accepted before and after her tenure as literary editor at *The Crisis* from 1919 to 1926. Although one of the most prolific of renaissance writers, her personal values and her attitude toward fictional portrayals of African Americans were "conservative." Fauset encouraged a number of renaissance writers, including Jean Toomer, Langston Hughes, Arna Bontemps, Countee Cullen, and Larsen, and yet she was "deaf to the poetry of the folk and certain that formal poetry should have rhyme" (65). Not surprisingly, her fiction is peopled with upper-middle-class characters, not unlike those in Nella Larsen's *Quicksand* and *Passing*. Larsen, working as a nurse, librarian, and writer, also led a more conventional, "ladylike" existence than Hurston did. Not only was her working background professional, but her marriage to Elmer Imes, a research physicist who in 1931 became the chair of the physics department at Fisk University, gave her "a proper social pedigree" (93).

Hurston, who was from the poor, rural South, must have been expected to conform to the same standards as her female counterparts. Yet from all accounts she refused.

The Difficulties of Patronage

The most consistent criticism of Hurston, however, stems from her relationships with white patrons. Patronage, in general, presents problems for artists, but the politics of race made such arrangements still more difficult for writers in the Harlem Renaissance. The assumption has often been that if Harlem Renaissance writers "agreed to a patron-artist relationship—especially a financial one—it seemed to obligate them to produce a certain kind of product that would meet the patron(s)' approval" (Story, "Patronage" 289). Such assumptions virtually assured questions about why Hurston's fiction continuously focused on African Americans at the bottom of the socioeconomic ladder.

Among the earliest of Hurston's patrons were Fannie Hurst and Annie Nathan Meyer. When Hurston won her first *Opportunity* award in 1926, she attended the dinner Charles S. Johnson planned to allow winners to mingle with the contest judges, and, Hemenway tells us, she was savvy enough to make the most of the opportunities presented (*Zora* 20). Here she met Hurst and Meyer, who would become her first white patrons. Meyer helped to secure Hurston a scholarship at Barnard College, then the women's division of Columbia University (*Zora* 20–21). Short story judge and novelist Hurst hired Hurston initially as a secretary, but poor typing skills and her lack of attention to detail resulted in her working in a new capacity—that of chauffeur and companion. She stayed in Hurst's home as an employee for more than a year. With the help of Meyer and Hurst, the fledgling writer returned to school in the fall of 1925 without financial worries—quite a feat, considering that she had arrived in New York in January with only $1.50 (*Dust Tracks* 682).

Her professor at Barnard, Franz Boas, was in some ways a patron as well. He helped make possible a $1,400 grant from Carter G. Woodson's Association for the Study of Negro Life and History that permitted Hurston to collect folklore in Florida from February to August 1927. Although the trip was not as successful as she had hoped, it probably enhanced her credibility with

Charlotte Osgood Mason, whom she met shortly after returning (*Dust Tracks* 688). As Hurston's association with Boas had, her relationship with Mason forever changed her life—and altered peers' perceptions of her character.

Mason was an intelligent, wealthy patron of African American art. At the time Hurston met her, Mason was already a patron of Langston Hughes and would make it possible for him to write full-time while completing his first novel, *Not without Laughter* (1930). Alain Locke, editor of *The New Negro* and Hurston's former *Stylus* mentor, was a devoted "confidant" and contact for Mason. It was Locke, Hemenway speculates, who introduced the two women (*Zora* 106), although Arnold Rampersad tells us Hughes "put in a strong word for Zora" (*The Life* 153). Mason provided precious financial security for Hughes through a "generous allowance" and soon did the same for Hurston. After turning her attention to the New Negro, she spent between $50,000 and $75,000 supporting black artists, with nearly $15,000 going to Hurston (Hemenway, *Zora* 104–5).

Hemenway explains that Hurston's relationship with Mason developed quickly (Hemenway, *Zora* 106–7). The two first met in mid-September, and in early December 1927 Hurston signed a contract with Mason that would allow her to collect folklore for all of the coming year. If Hurston did well, Mason suggested she might extend the agreement.

The contract Hurston signed on December 8 proved to be both blessing and curse. The agreement describes Hurston as an "independent agent" hired to "collect all information possible, both written and oral, concerning the music, poetry, folk-lore, literature, hoodoo, conjure, manifestations of art and kindred subjects relating to and existing among the North American negroes." Within the year Hurston was to "lay before" Mason the fruits of her labor. In exchange, the patron was to provide a Ford automobile, a movie camera, and $200 a month. While the financial support allowed Hurston to return south and continue her work collecting folklore, the agreement contained one sharply restrictive clause: she was "not to make known to any other person, except one designated in writing" the material she collected.[15] In short, Mason *owned* the material. She could dictate how and where Hurston might use or publish the material. And Mason did, exerting a powerful influence over Hurston for the next five years.

Mason fully supported Hurston from December 1927 through March 30,

1931, with sporadic financial assistance continuing through September 1932. The original contract with Mason allowed Hurston to spend two years in the field, both in the American South and in the Bahamas. While Hurston was collecting, however, the woman she and other artists called "Godmother" asked her not to publish. Mason and Locke believed that while in the field Hurston should spend all of her time collecting. Time would later be granted for organizing and publishing in a scholarly forum (Hemenway, *Zora* 112–13).[16]

Hurston's perpetuation of her relationship with Mason has been one of the chief complaints leveled by her critics. Louise Thompson, another woman Mason briefly employed, ended her relationship with the patron. She felt the elderly woman was "'indulging her fantasies about Negroes'" (Hemenway, *Zora* 107). Langston Hughes, too, ended his financial relationship with Mason when her limited, primitivistic view of African Americans began to chafe. When he realized he could not fulfill her expectations, he asked her to release him from their financial arrangement, although he wanted to maintain their friendship. Mason agreed to end their financial agreement, but her response also brutally and permanently severed their relationship (*The Big Sea* 324–26). The fact that Hurston did not end her own relationship with Mason has raised questions about her character and her continued fictional focus on the folk.

Nathan Huggins, in *The Harlem Renaissance*, once considered the standard literary study of the period, implies that Hurston exploited herself and popular racial stereotypes in perpetuating her relationship with Mason. Hurston, he says, "seemed to thrive on [. . .] dependency. Her *character*—or perhaps her style—made her into the exuberant pagan that pleased her white friends" (130; emphasis added). Skeptical of Louise Thompson's suggestion that Hurston was "'playing a game'" to manipulate, he points to the discussion of Mason in Hurston's autobiography to suggest that was not really the case (130).

At issue must have been the fact that Hurston's patron was a white woman with a strong interest in the primitive, which is easy to document and was probably common knowledge among Hurston's contemporaries. Hughes explains that she saw American blacks as a "great link with the primitive" but believed that "many had let the white world pollute and contaminate" their innate "mystery and harmony" (*The Big Sea* 316). Thompson saw the woman's primitivism as "self-gratification" (Huggins, *The Harlem Renaissance* 130). The question Huggins implicitly raises in his discussion of Mason's patronage focuses on character: How, in good conscience, could Hurston have perpetuated this relationship? He concludes that "she never did wonder [. . .] about what her 'Godmother' was asking of her" (133). The implication is clear. Hurston, from Huggins's point of view, was uninterested in the larger social ramifications of her behavior. There are, however, other possible motivations for her behavior.

Hurston's newfound commitment to preserving African American folklore may account for her willingness to work under Mason's strictures despite the problems the relationship presented. Much to Hurston's dismay, the treasure of African American folklore was "'disappearing without the world ever realizing that it had ever been'" (qtd. in Hemenway, *Zora* 108). Hemenway suggests that as an unestablished scholar without academic affiliation, Hurston could hardly have expected continued financial support from foundations or scientific societies. Without an advanced degree or a publishing record, she was not taken seriously, as an experience in New Orleans clearly demonstrates. Locke had suggested that she contact Tulane University while collecting. The response—an application for enrollment in social science courses—was not what Hurston anticipated (Hemenway, *Zora* 123). The encounter must have confirmed that Mason was the only source of funding available. Hurston may have believed the ends justified the means. Although differently motivated, she and Mason had the same ultimate goal: the preservation of disappearing African American folklore and revelation of the value of disparaged folk cultures. Hurston could be incredibly persistent, despite serious obstacles, when she pursued something she deeply believed in.

The extent to which Hurston went to bring authentic folk culture to the stage illustrates this commitment. Hurston's *The Great Day*, a one-time stage performance based upon the material she had collected for Mason, was a critical success and a financial failure. Hurston sold her car to put a deposit on the theater and signed a legal contract to borrow $610 from Mason to pay the performers and buy advertising. She had to repay every penny. To put this loan in perspective, the largest royalty Hurston ever received was $943.75. She made an enormous sacrifice to bring "authentic black folk culture to a New York audience" (Hemenway, *Zora* 178). She similarly remained committed to her last manuscript, "Herod the Great," despite rejections from publishers.

Clearly, Hurston's relationship with Mason was motivated—at least in part—by economics. Hughes recalls that Hurston was "always having terrific ups-and-downs about money" (*The Big Sea* 240). More important than financial support, however, was the contract she had signed with Mason in December of 1927.

Mason still *owned* the folklore Hurston had collected. As the break between Mason and Hughes demonstrated, Mason could be brutal. Hughes wanted to sever his financial ties with Mason but retain the woman's friendship. He did not. The message for Hurston was clear: It would be *impossible* to end her financial arrangement with Mason of her own accord and still have access to the material she had collected. Mason, following the performance of *The Great Day*, relinquished control over selected portions of the program, but the remainder of the material that would appear in *Mules and Men* in 1935 was still hers. Hurston had labored to collect, organize, and record the black folklore she loved. It would have been agonizing and foolish to abandon the material and throw away the years she had invested in it.

The question of who manipulated whom and to what degree is at the heart of the issue, and there can be no doubt that the manipulation was not one-sided. Hurston, Ralph D. Story argues, has taken a great deal of criticism for what was at the time common practice. Hughes, Claude McKay, and Aaron Douglas benefited from Mason's support as well. Hurston was, however, the only woman and the only artist whose subject matter was almost exclusively the rural folk. Hughes's description of Hurston in *The Big Sea* as "always getting scholarships and things from wealthy white people" who paid her to be a good Negro omitted the key detail that he, too, had often relied on white patrons (239).

Apparently, Hurston's greatest transgression is that she did not attempt to disguise the game she played. She exposed an unpleasant and uncomfortable aspect of life as a black artist—one most preferred to forget. She revealed the "secret ritual" of courting those who could bestow favors that "most others agreed upon privately and kept off the record" (Story, "Patronage" 289). And while Mason's interests in the primitive were well known, Hurston's contractual obligation to her probably was not. Hughes's fictional treatment of patronage in "The Blues I'm Playing" suggests that a black artist could benefit financially and artistically from a white patron without sacrificing her own artistic impulses. The story was, perhaps, Hughes' attempt to remove suspicions about his poetic focus on Harlem's folk, but his treatment of Hurston in *The Big Sea* implies that she had not maintained her artistic independence. Hughes might have been her ally in the battle of public perception, but their relationship effectively ended in 1932 with their dispute over *Mule Bone*.[17]

Difficult Decisions: Art versus Anthropology

During the same period, Hurston also struggled with her professional identity. Was she a creative artist or an anthropologist? This tension in her life, Hemenway suggests, generated "a kind of vocational schizophrenia," which complicated others' perceptions of her. Langston Hughes and Wallace Thurman, among others, were "exasperated with her denigration of her literary ambitions and with her tendency to dissipate her material in oral presentations" (*Zora* 63–64).

As a student at Barnard College, Hurston encountered two of the most distinguished anthropologists of her time, Franz Boas and Ruth Benedict, both of whom challenged popular conceptions of folk culture as inferior. George Hutchinson describes Boas as an important pioneer of the concept of cultural pluralism who challenged the trend of using science to sanction racism. Where cultural difference had been traditionally attributed to genetically determined racial traits, Boas argued that cultural difference was the result of social and natural environments. He rejected the assumed relationship between race and culture, determining that in fact the two are independent of each other. In addition, his research refuted the idea that racial inequalities evidenced themselves physically, for example, in the size and shape of people's heads. Boas's rejection of a hierarchical concept of culture, in particular, resonated for Hurston. Traditionally "culture" was a monistic term. Groups had been rated on a single scale that placed Northern European culture at the apex. In contrast, Boas argued that cultures developed under specific circumstances and must be understood on their own terms, that groups could not be measured on a single evolutionary scale (Hutchinson 65–66).

Ruth Benedict, trained by Boas and a Columbia University anthropologist, also played an important role in Hurston's career. Benedict, as editor of the prestigious *Journal of American Folklore*, published two of Hurston's scholarly essays on black folklore in 1931. Following Boas's lead, Benedict fiercely resisted "'the absolute singular.'" Her "interpretive anthropological practice" has led to her career being "aptly described as 'one great effort in behalf of the idea of cultural relativity'" (Babcock 40). Hurston must have also later appreciated Benedict's assertion in 1937 that "people's folktales are . . . their autobiography and the clearest mirror of their life" (qtd. in Babcock 50).

Both scholars' willingness to examine each culture within its own context must have appealed to Hurston. Her study at Barnard, then, not only laid the foundation for work as an anthropologist but also must have encouraged her fictional focus on the folk. In keeping with Harlem Renaissance philosophies about the "cultural work" of fiction, Hurston found she could promote folk culture on two fronts. The theories of Boas and Benedict bolstered her faith in the value of the folk and provided a pluralistic, scientific means of examining that culture in context. She had arrived in New York with a strong sense of self and pride in her rural African American heritage. Hurston explains in *Mules and Men* that in Boasian anthropology, she found a "spy glass" through which to see and understand her culture. She found a scientific valuation of her rural background, which was typically devalued by assimilationists who stressed similarities between African Americans and whites rather than differences that might indicate inferiority. Boasian anthropology legitimized her roots.

In addition, Hurston's folk background had scientific, or anthropological, value. Because she was, by virtue of race and experience, something of an insider, the folk opened doors to her that would remain closed to other folklorists. Hurston explains the challenges faced by white collectors: "We smile and tell him or her something that satisfies the white person because, knowing so little about us, he doesn't know what he is missing." The master storyteller adeptly wears masks designed to prevent the "white man" from knowing "everybody else's business" (*Mules and Men* 10). Clearly, Hurston had an advantage in the field, as her first experience with fieldwork illustrated. In 1926 on the streets of Harlem she measured the skulls of passersby as part of Boas's research into physical characteristics. And as Langston Hughes explains, "Almost nobody else could stop the average Harlemite on

Lenox Avenue and measure his head with a strange-looking anthropological device and not get bawled out for the attempt, except Zora" (*The Big Sea* 239).

And yet, Wallace Thurman's 1932 *Infants of the Spring*, a satire of the Harlem Renaissance and its aspiring artists, suggests Hurston's vacillation between artist and anthropologist created an image of her as an opportunist. The novel records a well-known caricature of Hurston in the figure of Sweetie May Carr. Near the end of the roman à clef, Dr. Parks (Alain Locke) encourages Raymond (Thurman) to host a literary salon at "Niggeratti Manor." Sweetie May Carr (Hurston) is the first to arrive, and the narrator gives a detailed description:

> Sweetie May was a short story writer, more noted for her ribald wit and personal effervescence than for any actual literary work. She was a great favorite among those whites who went in for Negro prodigies. Mainly because she lived up to their conception of what a typical Negro should be. It seldom occurred to any of her patrons that she did this with tongue in cheek. [. . .] Her repertoire [. . .] was earthy, vulgar and funny. Her darkies always smiled through their tears, sang spirituals on the slightest provocation, and performed buck dances when they should have been working. [. . .] [B]ut she was too indifferent to literary creation to transfer to paper that which she told so well. [. . .] Sweetie May knew her white folks. (Thurman 229)

Thurman devotes almost two pages to his description of Sweetie May while he describes the other salon attendees briefly. The narrator goes on to relate Sweetie May's justification of her behavior: "'Being a Negro writer these days is a racket and I'm going to make the most of it while it lasts. [. . .] I don't know a tinker's damn about art. I care less about it. [. . .] About twice a year I manage to sell a story. It is acclaimed. I am a genius in the making. Thank God for this Negro literary renaissance! Long may it flourish!'" (Thurman 230). While the description clearly draws much of its venom from Hurston's relationship with white patrons, Hemenway argues that Hurston's "vocational schizophrenia" contributed as well. In the context of Hemenway's discussion of Hurston's struggle to reconcile oral tradition with written literature, Thurman's criticisms lose their bite. Yet whether Thurman's description of Sweetie May resulted from his misunderstanding of Hurston's attempt to resolve her schizophrenia, as Hemenway argues, is largely a moot point: The description has long haunted her. Apparently Thurman's perception of Hurston's literary ambitions was a common one (Hemenway, *Zora* 64), and Hughes's 1940 assertion in *The Big Sea* that Hurston was the "most amusing" of the "nigeratti," and she "was always getting scholarships and things from wealthy white people, some of whom simply paid her just to sit around and represent the Negro race for them, she did it in such racy fashion" (239), only further codified images of Hurston as dilettante and manipulator.[18]

Hurston's Literary and Social Agenda

In a 1934 essay for the *Washington Tribune*, "Race Cannot Become Great until It Recognizes Its Talent," Hurston explained her aesthetic philosophy with characteristic indirection. In the essay she cleverly draws parallels between the oppression of black Americans and the class oppression in England prior to the eleventh century. No one, she notes, thought the English language was suitable for literary expression: "Any thought worth its salt had to be embalmed in French or Latin" (n. pag.). Chaucer changed that attitude. While the English had been physically free, they—like Hurston's African American contemporaries—were "not spiritually free." African Americans are unable to "turn our eyes from the distorted looking glass that goes with the iron collar" of enslavement. The result is "intellectual lynching." Imitation she suggests is fine, but for one crucial fact: "[P]upils never stand on equal footing with the master." Hurston wanted original creations, and the discussion of language with which she begins the essay suggests that she saw the language of the folk and their traditions as crucial to intellectual and spiritual freedom. Without some creation of her own, Hurston argues, the black artist stands where her foremothers did "when they filed [the] iron collar off."

Hurston's nonfiction writings suggest that she set out to reclaim for her contemporaries native folk traditions that had for generations been manipulated and exploited for white benefit. She was not afraid or ashamed of folk traditions. They were the source Hurston wanted to draw from to transform and strengthen the black community from within. But Hurston's repeated use of southern folk characters, even in urban settings, her use of dialect, her use of humor, and her resistance to overtly didactic literature made her the target for criticism from those who wanted to see art publicizing less-well-known aspects of African American life, namely middle-class characters and lifestyles, with whom white readers would have more in common. Finally, and perhaps most important, Hurston's personal persona and aesthetics converged. Neither her relationship with Mason nor the description of Sweetie May Carr would have impacted Hurston's reputation so powerfully if she had been writing about almost any other aspect of black life. Although Hurston had been writing about the folk as early as 1921, six years before she met Mason, her continued fictional focus on folk characters implied that she wrote about them because it pleased white readers, white publishers, and white patrons—like Mason. Thus, the convergence of Hurston's artistic shift from urban, universal subjects to her treatment of rural folk life, her use of dialect, her resistance to propaganda and protest, and her personal reputation combined to lay the foundation for later accusations that she exploited her folk characters for personal and professional gain.

TWO

Making a Way

Fighting "The Line of Least Resistance"

The writer thinks he has been brave in following the groove of Race champions, when the truth is, it is the line of least resistance and least originality . . . .

—"Art and Such"

THE EARLY 1930s brought about profound changes for Zora Neale Hurston, as they did for most Americans. By May 1932, the Great Depression had put an end to "money for research as far as [Hurston] was concerned" (*Dust Tracks* 714). And, while Charlotte Osgood Mason's support for Hurston's field research had provided an invaluable opportunity, it had not enhanced her prospects for working independently. Hurston considered earning a Ph.D. that would give her the additional credentials she needed as a folklorist, but when she broached the subject of returning to school with Mason, the patron was unreceptive.[1] Thus, as Mason's financial support dwindled, so did Hurston's research opportunities.

The Great Depression also changed the literary climate: The bloom of the New Negro Movement was gone. American writers weary of the excesses of the 1920s and strapped by the Depression turned their attention to social issues. It comes as no surprise to students of American literature, as David Minter explains, that "[i]deology played a far more conspicuous role" in the fiction of the 1930s than it had in the 1920s (151). The protest movement climaxed at the end of the decade with Richard Wright's *Native Son* and John Steinbeck's *Grapes of Wrath*, but even as early as 1932, Minter argues, "works of art and even casual remarks were being checked regularly for the range of social concern they reflected" (168). Hurston was caught in a turning tide. The literary mode was no longer celebratory but increasingly protest oriented, a shift that Hurston philosophically and artistically resisted, as did her publisher.

In this context of changing aesthetics Hurston published her first novel and her first collection of folklore. *Jonah's Gourd Vine* brought an overwhelmingly positive critical response and added to her reputation as a fiction writer. In these same reviews, however, the process of dialogic engagement between black and white reviewers begins. With the publication of *Mules and Men* in 1935, Hurston's divergence from emerging protest-oriented norms becomes clear as factors white reviewers praise become sources for black reviewers' criticisms. While my own interpretations of *Jonah's Gourd Vine* and *Mules and Men* suggest that Hurston attempted to transcend, rather than exploit, negative racial stereotypes, the horizon of expectations for her contemporaries permitted racist readers to align her characters with negative stereotypes. The potential for such readings left Hurston and her work increasingly vulnerable to racist interpretations and negative criticisms.

"Wingded Angels" and Missionary Work

When Mason's sporadic financial assistance ended in September 1932, Hurston was living in Eatonville, Florida. In an effort to support herself she contacted nearby Rollins College (Hemenway, *Zora* 184).[2] At Rollins College, Hurston met Robert Wunsch, an English teacher who wanted to interest his students in American folk life. She wrote "The Gilded Six-Bits" and gave it to Wunsch to share with his creative writing class, presumably to demonstrate ways writers make use of folk materials. Wunsch then sent it to *Story*, where editors Martha Foley and Whit Burnett agreed to publish it. Shortly thereafter, four publishers wrote Hurston to inquire if she might be working on a book-length manuscript. One of those publishers was Bertram Lippincott, of J. B. Lippincott. Hurston responded that she was indeed writing a book, although she had not written "the first word" (*Dust Tracks* 715).

As early as March 1927, Hurston expressed an interest in writing a novel, but her folklore collecting, which began soon after, apparently preempted any serious attempt until Lippincott contacted her. In her autobiography,

Hurston explains that the idea for *Jonah's Gourd Vine* had been with her since 1929. She had, however, found the prospect of a book daunting, at least in part because "Negroes were supposed to write about the Race Problem" (*Dust Tracks* 713). Hurston's interest was in "what makes a man or a woman do such-and-so, regardless of his color." Her folkloric training with Franz Boas is evident in her explanation: "It seemed to me that human beings I met reacted pretty much the same to the same stimuli. Different idioms, yes. Circumstances and conditions having the power to influence, yes. Inherent difference, no" (713). Knowing that her philosophies contrasted with what was expected of her, Hurston "was afraid to tell a story the way [she] wanted." There was something, however, in Lippincott's letter that allayed her fears. "Exposing my efforts did not seem so rash to me after reading his letter," she explains (715). Living on fifty cents a week for groceries provided by a cousin, Hurston finished the manuscript in three months. By October 16 she had her first acceptance for a book and the promise of a $200 advance (715–16). Seven months later on May 3, 1934, *Jonah's Gourd Vine* appeared ("Summer Book Index" n. pag.) with an introduction written by former employer Fannie Hurst and a dedication to Robert Wunsch, one of the "long-wingded angels right round the throne."

The Rise and Fall of John Buddy Pearson

Following the rise of John Buddy Pearson, an uneducated, philandering, black folk preacher, the plot of *Jonah's Gourd Vine* hinges on John's refusal (or inability—depending on one's interpretation) to remain faithful to his wives and the problems that ensue. Hurston's portrait of John comes uncomfortably close to (and for some readers is) the stereotypical lascivious primitive. My own feminist reading, however, suggests that Hurston's approach to her protagonist is much more sophisticated and subversive.

John's repeated difficulties as a husband and as a church leader stem from his failures in the domestic or private sphere, an arena typically the focus of fiction about female characters. Hurston's choice of John Buddy as a protagonist signifies on what Ann duCille describes as "the coupling convention." *Jonah's Gourd Vine* can be read as a critique of marriage masked behind a male protagonist.[3] Ann duCille's *The Coupling Convention* points out the "emancipatory" function of marriage and romance in black women's fiction. Extending her argument reveals a transformation of the conventional marriage plot in *Jonah's Gourd Vine*. The central character is not a mulatta female, but a mulatto male, and in keeping with the "emancipatory" project duCille identifies, the series of "romances" or marriages explored in the novel repeatedly critique the notion of marriage as a woman's refuge (3).

John Buddy is, however, the central character. His rise and fall drive the plot of the novel. Finding it easier to run than face his problems, John struggles to understand his own behavior and the consequences it brings. John first runs from his domineering and abusive stepfather. His mother's advice sends John looking for Alfred Pearson, her former master and the man most readers assume is his father. Pearson gives John a job and sends him to school, where he meets Lucy Potts. The two begin to court against her mother's wishes, and they marry. There seems little doubt that John loves Lucy, but he neglects his wife and continues to pursue other women. As Lucy gives birth to their third child, John is in the arms of Delphine, just one in a long line of extramarital affairs.

Eventually, John is driven from town by threat of arrest for assault and an impending visit by the Ku Klux Klan. He starts his life over in the all-black town of Eatonville. After relocating his wife and children, John begins his rise in the community, becoming a preacher, the mayor, and a moderator in the church's state association. In Hurston's own words, he is "a Negro preacher who is neither funny nor an imitation Puritan ram-rod in pants. Just the human being and poet he must be to succeed in a Negro pulpit. I do not speak of those among us who have been tampered with and consequently have gone Presbyterian or Episcopal. I mean the common run of us who love magnificence, beauty, poetry and color so much that there can never be too much of it" (qtd. in Kaplan 298). John's powerful, poetic sermons increase church membership and elevate his status. Nevertheless, as a "natchal man," John still pursues other women. Unhappy with his behavior, the church attempts to remove him, but Lucy guides her husband toward reconciliation, both with her and with the church. For seven weeks John remains faithful. Lucy's most recent rival, however, is unhappy about John's new commitment to his wife. Desperate to end his marriage, Hattie uses conjure to destroy John and Lucy's relationship. As Lucy lies on her deathbed, John slaps her, effectively ending their marriage. Lucy's subsequent passing clears Hattie's path.

Within three months John and Hattie marry. The community, however, grumbles at the pastor's rapid remarriage. As members of the community begin to harass them both, John's support erodes, and he becomes an abusive husband. Unable to understand the situation in which he finds himself, John takes his frustrations out on his wife. Without Lucy's wisdom, John cannot retain his status in the church, and his marriage to Hattie culminates in an ugly, public divorce.

Emotionally devastated to find himself a social pariah, John searches for work as a carpenter in other cities. In Plant City, he discovers the widow Sally Lovelace, who, like Lucy, supports and marries him. John imagines himself a reformed man, but a return trip to his former congregation presents old temptations. John again violates his marriage vows. While he recognizes the seriousness of his error and leaves for Plant City to see Sally, John dies in a collision with a train, an image Susan Meisenhelder suggests phallically reflects the cause of his destruction (46). Ironically, Sally is left with her false illusion that "he wuz true tuh me" (*Jonah's Gourd Vine* 167).

Hurston took the title from the Old Testament book of Jonah. To teach Jonah a lesson in compassion and mercy, God sends a gourd vine to shade the prophet. The next day, however, the vine has withered, bitten by a worm. Jonah finds himself baked by sun and hot wind. God teaches the prophet the pain of loss and the importance of compassion. Many critics have read *Jonah's Gourd Vine* through the biblical text from a patriarchal perspective. Rita Dove, for example, suggests that John, with his rapid rise, is the gourd vine (xi), and this interpretation initially seems to be supported by the novel itself: Deacon Harris twice refers to a "Jonah's gourd vine" that can be cut down (*Jonah's Gourd Vine* 146, 154). John Lowe reads the metaphor differently, describing John's sexuality as the worm and his comfort (including Lucy and his career) as the vine (94).

Yet closer examination of the biblical reference reveals an entirely different possibility, one also advocated by Lillie Howard and Susan Meisenhelder: Lucy as John's gourd vine (Howard 81; Meisenhelder 40). In the biblical text, the vine and the worm are neither of Jonah's making nor within his control. This lack of control suggests that John can be neither the worm nor the vine. Rather, God sends the vine which shades Jonah to protect him from the heat of the desert—from that for which he is unprepared. John Buddy is as unprepared for the heat of public scrutiny as Jonah is for the desert heat.

Lucy serves as John's gourd vine by crafting his prosperity, protecting him, and guiding him. While the biblical vine dies overnight, John's vine—like Lucy—withers slowly, offering him the opportunity to change his behavior.

When Lucy dies, John perishes in the heat and wind of gossip. Hattie offers no respite. Instead she increases the amount of suffering he endures. Sally provides "shelter," perhaps suggesting she, too, might become a gourd vine, but only after betraying her, as well, does John begin to comprehend that he is to blame for the losses he has experienced.

Fallen Preachers and Libidinous Women

As Hurston had in her short fiction, she engages stereotypes—particularly those associated with black men, black preachers, and black women—in *Jonah's Gourd Vine*. While John Buddy is, as Pamela Bordelon indicates, based upon Hurston's father, her treatment of him as a preacher suggests a perceptive awareness of comic stereotypes of black preachers and an attempt to transcend them. Gerald Davis points out in his study of sermons, "'[P]reacher' stories often 'turn on his supposed gluttony, lust, avarice, and ironically, his malapropisms'" (qtd. in Lowe 90). "[E]xcesses or posturing" make a preacher targets for humorous stories and quips (89–90). Hurston's description of John as "neither funny nor an imitation Puritan ram-rod in pants" suggests her awareness of two polar stereotypes. John is neither.

Hurston also had to negotiate images of religion and preachers from Marc Connelly's play *The Green Pastures* (1930), which made humorous, condescending treatments of blacks and religion part of the popular consciousness. The play was, in Nathan Huggins's words, "a phenomenon" (*The Harlem Renaissance* 299). The plot centers on a black Sunday School class's inability to understand the day's lesson. The preacher then transforms his biblical lesson into the language and images of stereotype: black dialect, fishing, barbecue. Its characters are "child-like and credulous," perfect stereotypes that allowed whites experiencing a crisis of religious faith in the post–World War I and Scopes Trial era to "be transported into black innocence" (300).

To distance John Buddy from such images, Hurston situated him between the laughter and the simplicity to reveal the complexity of being simultaneously an imperfect man and an instrument of God. His struggles with women are in many ways rooted in a deeper lack of self-knowledge and an inability to accept responsibility for his own actions, as demonstrated by his repeated flights from confrontation with his stepfather and the law.

Hurston's portrait of John also critiques the primitive stereotypes he superficially approximates. John's sexual promiscuity has none of the positive connotations associated with exotic primitivism's celebration of instinct and sensuality. Admittedly, John's behavior is often unimpeded by the constraints of "civilization" (particularly his marriage vows), and yet the results of his choices—fighting, philandering, abusing, and drinking—are incredibly destructive. There is nothing romantic or desirable in his tale. His tragedy and his ultimate recognition that he bears responsibility for the course his life has taken undermine the stereotype of the carefree primitive. Like the characters in "The Gilded Six-Bits," John is far more complex than the stereotype would allow. John's recurrent encounters with women, however, may for some readers have too closely aligned him with stereotypical images of black men.

Hurston's portraits of black women in *Jonah's Gourd Vine* suggest a similar engagement of gendered stereotypes. Engaging public discourse on black women meant Hurston also had to engage potentially damaging stereotypes of black women as sexually promiscuous. Barbara Christian's *Black Women Novelists: The Development of a Tradition* and Catherine Juanita Starke's *Black Portraiture in American Fiction* treat the stereotype in American fiction.

Hurston's treatment of her female characters in *Jonah's Gourd Vine* suggests a deliberate attempt to counter such images, an attempt similar to those Hazel Carby explores in *Reconstructing Womanhood*. Through her protagonist, Hurston explicitly engages discourse on black female sexuality as John explains to Hambo that the white people in divorce court "wouldn't zarn 'tween uh woman lak Hattie and one lak Lucy, uh yo' wife befo' she died. Dey thinks all colored folks is de same dat way" (*Jonah's Gourd Vine* 140). While the white audience in the divorce court might not discern the differences among black women, Hurston ensures that her readers will not make the same mistake. Not all black women are gin-swilling bundles of libidinous urges. More implicitly, Hurston's creation of three positive female characters counters images of Hattie, who is sexually promiscuous. While Hurston's characterization admits Hatties do exist, she counters, so do

Amys, and Lucys, and Sallys. Such complexities of race and gender, evident from my own horizon of expectations, were lost, however, in Lippincott's marketing of the novel.

Selling *Jonah's Gourd Vine*

The marketing of *Jonah's Gourd Vine* began with the dust jacket, which subtly situates the novel and its protagonist in contemporary culture. Any reader who browses in book stores knows the power a book's cover can have. By hooking readers with the exterior, publishers pull readers into the pages of the book itself, but not without creating some form of bias. Images, word choices, summaries, and quotations from reviewers situate a book in the marketplace. A reader's response to the novel may differ from that suggested by the cover, but subtle differences are easy to miss given the power of stereotypes to encourage people to "define first, then see" (Lippmann 55).

Visible on the exterior of the dust jacket of *Jonah's Gourd Vine* is a black man in a clerical collar surrounded by six other figures, five of whom are female. With arms outstretched, the preacher towers over the others. Immediately, then, the cover orients readers to the black community, the black church, and the largely female adoration of the pastor. To a degree, the image deceives. While John's struggles with the church are important, he does not accept the role of pastor until nearly halfway through the novel. More important to the plot are his marital relationships, but given popular interest generated by *The Green Pastures* and James Weldon Johnson's *God's Trombones*, the church scene may have attracted more readers.

For clues about how to interpret the outside cover, readers need only open it to the inside flap, which provides a plot summary. Although we often think of summarizing as a straightforward process in which opinions are not present, the word choice in such a summary can be incredibly powerful. This summary, for example, identifies John as "a big, lovable Alabama negro." It is an interesting juxtaposition of terms which implies that John's large size might be seen as threatening. To deflect any such implication, the term *lovable* follows. Further down, however, the summary again engages stereotype by suggesting that John is incapable of controlling himself, for he "couldn't seem to help falling for" other women. And while he "preached, prayed, sang and sinned—[. . .] there was *always* another woman." Lippin-

Fig. 1. Dust jacket of *Jonah's Gourd Vine* (1934), on deposit Beinecke. Used with the permission of the Zora Neale Hurston Trust.

cott continued to develop the image in its advertising, an issue I turn to shortly.

The novel's back cover more explicitly situates Hurston in the literary marketplace. It carries praise from three prominent white literary figures: Blanche Colton Williams, Fannie Hurst (who also wrote the introduction), and Carl Van Vechten.

Williams was a well-known English professor, editor, critic, anthologizer, and authority on the short story, who from 1919–32 chaired the

O. Henry Award Committee. In a passage that prefigures much of what reviewers would say, Williams promises readers that "Miss Hurston is a young woman of great promise. Here are the spirit, the dialect and the poetry of the Negro race in a story by one . . . who has the ability to detach herself and see its members objectively. At the same time there is a quality of sympathy which no mere outsider could feel and express." As a scholarly expert on short fiction, Williams's name and her praise were surely included to attract a more literary reader, the kind of reader who might not have found praise from popular writers like Van Vechten and Hurst convincing.

Lippincott's use of praise from Hurst was more problematic. While largely unread today, in the 1920s and 1930s Hurst was an activist and author of twenty-seven books. Her "popular" fiction often focuses on young women's dilemmas with love and employment (Wilentz 21). Hurston had worked as her secretary between 1925 and 1926. Although Hurst's name and endorsement would surely have attracted the white women who read her novels, her *Imitation of Life*, which appeared in 1933 (the year before *Jonah's Gourd Vine*), had prompted debate in the black press (38).[4]

When the film version of the novel appeared in 1935 starring Claudette Colbert, poet and critic Sterling Brown, writing in *Opportunity*, registered his complaints about both the book and the film. He criticized Hurst's stilted dialect and her reliance on stereotypes of black women ("Pancake" 87). The following month's issue contained an angry response from Hurst, but Brown stood his ground ("Miss Fannie Hurst" 121; "Mr. Sterling Brown" 121). The debate continued in yet a third issue when *Opportunity*'s readers weighed in with mixed responses.[5] Donald Bogle explains the controversy this way: African Americans "'hated [Peola] for denying her race; on the other hand, they understood she was fighting for freedom'" (qtd. in Wilentz 38).

When Hurston and Brown both took up residence in Durham, North Carolina, in 1940, his distaste for the novel revealed the powerful impact of the Hurston-Hurst association. In a letter to Hurst, Hurston explains the tenor of her recent encounters with Brown: "He picks on me all the time now. He tells people that he wants to riddle me and otherwise deflate me because he says that *I stand convicted of having furnished you with the material for 'Imitation'*" (qtd. in Wilentz 39). Brown's charge implies that Hurston *gave* Hurst the characters and/or the plot for *Imitation of Life*, or perhaps he suggests as Cary D. Wintz did as recently as 1985 that Hurston served as the model for Delilah (179–80), but all of these possibilities seem unlikely. By the time *Imitation* appeared Hurston had been out of Hurst's employ for more than six years, and Hurston had spent the better part of those years in the South.

Certainly Hurston may have inspired Hurst's interest in black folk characters and dialect, but both folk characters and their speech were very much part of the literary vogue. Brown's own volume of poetry *Southern Road* (1932) mines the speech of the folk as does the work of other contemporaries, including Marc Connelly and Julia Peterkin, white writers who explored black life and drew from southern black oral tradition. Black writers of the period other than Hurston—Claude McKay, Langston Hughes, James Weldon Johnson, and Rudolph Fisher, to name but four—had also drawn inspiration from the vernacular. Hurst's use of dialect, then, was hardly new, but the mediating factors were. Shifting interests in the political intersected with Hurst's portraits of Delilah and Peola to make Hurst and the novel suspect, which reflected negatively on Hurston.

The endorsement from Carl Van Vechten—a well-known music critic for the *New York Times*, novelist, and essayist for popular periodicals like *Vanity Fair* and *Harper's*—presents similar issues. By 1925 many whites considered him an authority on black life. His essays had introduced white readers to Harlem cabaret life, and he confirmed his stature as an expert with what is now his most enduring work, a 1926 novel titled *Nigger Heaven* (Worth 462). To Lippincott he must have seemed the perfect choice for marketing an emerging black novelist to white readers. He had, after all, helped other emerging writers, including Langston Hughes and Countee Cullen.[6] He recommended *Jonah's Gourd Vine* "with unrestrained enthusiasm." Ironically, however, his endorsement may also have made Hurston and her work suspect.

Nigger Heaven—its title, its setting, and its characters—prompted months of debate in black periodicals. White reviewers tended to be more positive about the novel, perhaps because they were "ignorant of fiction written by blacks" about black life (Worth 462). A number of established black critics including Walter White, James Weldon Johnson, and Rudolph Fisher approved as well (White 16; Worth 463). Author and *Crisis* editor W.E.B. Du Bois, however, was an outspoken critic. Describing the novel as "a blow in the face," Du Bois found the novel wanting as a work of art

("Books" 81–82), and most reviewers for the black press concurred. Floyd Calvin, of the *Pittsburgh Courier*, was disgusted by the "immorality" of the novel and accused Van Vechten of "revel[ing] in filth and obscenity on general principles" (qtd. in Worth 464). Six months after publication the novel was still inciting protests ("Two Harlem Bodies" 15). That prolonged debate and the repeated plot summaries in the reviews suggest that even those who had not read *Nigger Heaven* would have been familiar with Van Vechten's name and perhaps even the plot of the novel.

The back inside flap of *Jonah's Gourd Vine* performs its own subtle mediation by establishing the authenticity of the images of black life revealed inside. It includes a small photo of Hurston (which clearly establishes her race) and a biographical description identifying her many memberships in professional organizations, "the American Anthropological Society, the American Ethnological Society, the American Association for the Advancement of Science and the American Folklore Society." It details as well Hurston's educational background at Barnard College and her study with Franz Boas. In sum it stresses her anthropological experience and her current project on "American Negro folklore," which Lippincott had already agreed to publish. Implicitly, the description of Hurston as an educated racial insider stakes the novel's claim to authenticity—providing readers a look at "real" negro life, a claim made more explicitly in the advertising.

The ads for *Jonah's Gourd Vine* appearing in the Sunday book sections of the *New York Times* and the *New York Herald Tribune* are all one column wide and range in length from three to five inches. The small ones contain only text. The larger bear a one-and-a-half-inch image from the book's cover, which the text suggests is a preacher instructing his congregation. Lippincott's descriptions of the novel indicate the firm was depending on the continued currency of primitivism that had marked the peak Harlem Renaissance years. It pitched the novel in language that would be sure to attract readers looking for sensationalism in stories of black life.

For all of its authors, Lippincott's advertising often involved using sensationalized language. Its promotion of *Three Harbors*, "a novel of the American Revolution," for example, describes a "lusty, thrill crammed tale" (35). Claree Longworth de Chambrun's study of "the 2 women in SHAKESPEARE'S LIFE" reportedly reveals "little-known facts, telling of the loves, hates, despairs and triumphs of the greatest genius of all time"

(*Two Loves* 14). The publisher's advertising for Hurston's work, however, is extraordinary. Shocking word choice and exploitative images run through most of the ads Lippincott placed, and the publisher's use of racially charged language made Hurston suspect.

On May 6,1934, the first ad for *Jonah's Gourd Vine* appeared with "He Fought Passion's Fire With Hell's Fire" appearing at the top followed by a description of the novel: " A STARKLY elemental, yet beautiful story of life as it is actually lived down South—told in the life story of a roistering Alabama Negro who became a preacher and a power in his community—but who couldn't still his passions. The author is a brilliant colored woman who knows her race with the insight of a great novelist" (*New York Herald Tribune Books* 18).[7] Beneath in smaller type follows an excerpt from Fannie Hurst's introduction describing the novel as "Negro folk-lore interpreted at its authentic best in fiction form of a high order." The same ad appears on May 13 (*New York Times Book Review* 18).[8] By May 20 the ad in the *New York Herald Tribune* is smaller and has changed slightly. Although it contains the description of the novel quoted above, Lippincott has replaced "He Fought Passion's Fire With Hell's Fire" with the claim that it is "A BOOK NO WHITE PERSON *Could Write*!" An endorsement from Van Vechten follows: "So extraordinary I can only recommend it with unrestrained enthusiasm" (*Books* 14).

By June 3, Lippincott dropped the larger description of the novel in favor of a brief one, "The lusty, revealing story of a big, roisting Alabama Negro, written as only one of his race could write it," and the quotations from both Hurst and Van Vechten have changed as well (*Books* 9). A new passage from Hurst's introduction reads: "It is doubtful if there is any literary precedent for this particular type of accomplishment. It is fiction form of high order." Van Vechten suggests the novel "should serve to place Miss Hurston at once in the very front rank of those (white and colored) who write about the Negro."

In both versions of the advertisements, Lippincott associates John Buddy with the carnal sensualist stereotype Starke identifies. Consider the way the ads describe John. He is an "Alabama Negro," *not a man*, who "couldn't," *not wouldn't*, "still his passions." Even the use of dashes to set off the phrase emphasizes the carnal, while totally eclipsing the identity and personal growth issues central to the novel. The ad implies that John is a character

He Fought Passion's Fire With Hell's Fire

A STARKLY elemental, yet beautiful story of life as it is actually lived down South—told in the life story of a roistering Alabama Negro who became a preacher and a power in his community—but who couldn't still his passions.

The author is a brilliant colored woman who knows her race with the insight of a great novelist. *At all bookstores, $2.00.* (Recommended by The Book-of-the-Month Club.)

'Here in this work of Zora Hurston there springs, with validity and vitality a fresh note which, to this commentator, is unique. Here is Negro folk-lore interpreted at its authentic best in fiction form of a high order"—FANNIE HURST

JONAH'S GOURD VINE by

ZORA NEALE HURSTON

LIPPINCOTT • *Philadelphia*

Fig. 2. Advertisement for *Jonah's Gourd Vine. New York Times Book Review* May 13, 1934: 18.

A BOOK NO WHITE PERSON *Could Write!*

★ The lusty story of a big, roistering Alabama Negro preacher—intimate, earthy, revealing—written by one of the outstanding literary geniuses of the race. It offers you an experience unique in reading—a hitherto unpictured side of real Negro life in the South.

★ CARL VAN VECHTEN SAYS: "So extraordinary I can only recommend it with unrestrained enthusiasm." It is a current recommendation of THE BOOK-OF-THE-MONTH CLUB.

JONAH'S GOURD VINE

LIPPINCOTT *Philadelphia*

Price $2.00

By ZORA NEALE HURSTON

Fig. 3. Advertisement for *Jonah's Gourd Vine. New York Herald Tribune Books* May 20, 1934: 14.

incapable of controlling his primitive urges. Using "lusty" to describe the story of the "*big* roistering Alabama Negro preacher" furthers this impression (emphasis mine). Although Hurston does indeed describe John Buddy as a large man, the description in this context may have conjured up stereotypical images of large black men dominated by uncontrollable sexual urges.[9]

Readers from the 1930s would have been familiar with the stereotypical black man "dominated by violent passions," a stereotype Starke points to in Vachel Lindsay's 1914 *Congo* and DuBose Heyward's 1925 *Porgy* (137). The threat of those "violent passions" is all too clear in Thomas Dixon's 1902 *The Leopard's Spots* and D. W. Griffith's 1915 film *The Birth of a Nation*, which Sterling Brown said "finally fixed the stereotype in the mass mind" (*The Negro* 93). In imaging John Buddy as "a negro who couldn't still his passions," Lippincott tapped into this larger exploitative and demeaning discourse on black male sexuality. Pearson's lack of restraint promised lusty encounters, but because the novel was set in "his own community," white readers could observe safely from a distance.

Why did the J. B. Lippincott Company make decisions that seem highly questionable? One possible answer is that Lippincott wanted a white readership and courted that readership regardless of the implications for the smaller potential black readership. It is also entirely possible, however, that the publisher knew absolutely nothing about the controversy Hurst and Van Vechten generated in the black press. Evidence of Lippincott's ignorance of the black literary world appears in Hurston's correspondence with James Weldon Johnson. On January 22, 1934, Hurston wrote Johnson that Lippincott would be bringing out *Jonah's Gourd Vine* in May. She had seen the list of people to receive advance copies, but there were no African Americans on the list—the publisher did not know to whom it should send them. Hurston added Johnson to the list. On April 20 he responded that he had read the novel, had liked it, and had written the publishers with his praise.[10] And yet the endorsement of an established and well-respected black author whose own book, an autobiography titled *Along This Way*, was garnering "overwhelmingly favorable" responses from black and white reviewers, did not appear in the advertising (Levy 330). Why not? Clearly there would have been time to incorporate his endorsement in the advertisements that ran until mid-June. Regardless of the logic—or illogic—behind the decision, however, Lippincott's use of endorsements from only established white writers may have (erroneously) suggested that only whites with their own preestablished biases would endorse *Jonah's Gourd Vine*.

The advertising also raises complex questions about Hurston's agency. Could Hurston have had any control over the advertising for her work? Her correspondence sometimes reveals which decisions were hers and which were not. Hurston, for example, asked Van Vechten for the advance review of *Jonah's Gourd Vine*, but Lippincott (Hurston says) decided Hurst should write the introduction to the book.[11] Without files from the J. B. Lippincott Company, which have eluded scholars for a number of years, it is impossible to determine with certainty if the publisher consulted Hurston.[12] It seems likely, however, that Hurston's influence was limited. Beyond indicating possible sources for advance reviews and introductions, controlling the content of the ads would almost certainly have been beyond Hurston's province. She would not have had the clout.[13]

Why did Hurston, then, remain with Lippincott through the 1930s? There are a number of possible reasons, although I can only speculate. Perhaps, as her critics have suggested, Hurston wanted only to sell books, regardless of the social and political ramifications. There are, however, other more plausible reasons. In her autobiography, Hurston professed to find something about Bertram Lippincott likable. He had laid to rest her fears about writing a novel (*Dust Tracks* 715). In a life full of professional and economic uncertainty, familiarity may have been a factor. Perhaps during the Great Depression years of the 1930s, she feared her limited success would prevent other publishers from taking her on (an issue I address in more depth in Chapter 3). Or, perhaps, ironically, Lippincott's advertising prompted her to stay.

Lippincott promoted Hurston's work more aggressively in the New York papers than competing publishers marketed work of other black writers. Consider the difference between the ads for *Jonah's Gourd Vine* and those for Langston Hughes's *The Ways of White Folks*, published the same year by Knopf. The weekend following publication of *Jonah's Gourd Vine*, individual ads appeared in both the *New York Times Book Review* and the *New York Herald Tribune Books*. Lippincott continued to promote the novel though June 10. In contrast, there are no ads for Hughes's collection of short stories in the Sunday supplements of either paper. The contrast becomes still sharper. The week after reviewers praised Hughes's collection, Knopf placed a large ad in the *New York Herald Tribune* but failed to promote Hughes's collection. Still more surprising, while Alfred Knopf did describe the volume in his monthly column, "As I See It," in *American Mercury*, I could find no advertisements for the volume in that issue or the ones that follow, even though Knopf published the magazine and advertised in it regularly.

Scanty advertising for black authors in the New York papers seems to have been the norm. Harper, the publisher of Claude McKay's *Banana Bottom* (1933), placed only two ads: one in the *New York Times Book Review* and the other in the *New York Herald Tribune*. Appearing on April 2, the ads promote ten books. A brief description follows a bold title: "In this novel of a brown girl, the author of *Home to Harlem* applies his colorful style and characterizations to life in the West Indies." Only the word *colorful* might evoke the stereotypes Lippincott exploited in advertising Hurston's work. Richard Wright's *Native Son*, which sold 250,000 copies in the first two weeks, is the only novel by a black contemporary for which I could find advertising on three consecutive Sundays in the *New York Times Book Review*.[14] In contrast, Lippincott repeatedly advertised Hurston's work on consecutive Sundays. Such realities might account for Hurston's willingness to defer to the publishing house on the issue of advertising. While the content of the ads is questionable, their size and regularity suggest a commitment to making Hurston's work visible in the white publishing world, a commitment not evident among other publishers.

Reading the Authentic

The weekend after publication *Jonah's Gourd Vine* garnered important positive reviews in the New York weekend papers, most of which heaped hearty praise on Hurston's first novel. Ironically, however, as Hemenway notes, reviewers revealed "their cultural bias, so much so that even their praise becomes suspect" (*Zora* 194). White reviewers saw the novel as a window to the picturesque world of southern blacks. Their effusive praise for an imperfect novel suggests that their standards for black writers were less rigorous than those for white writers. While the overwhelmingly positive tenor of the reviews added to Hurston's stature as a fiction writer, the narrow scope and potentially racist nature of white reviewers' praise raise serious issues about authenticity, race, and class.

Every reviewer—even those who offer substantial criticisms of the novel's development, the development of the characters, or the handling of time—praises Hurston's use of dialect, and most also applaud Hurston's use of folkways. Williams addresses both issues on the back cover of the novel. Hurston's use of idiom, as well as dialect, drew this response from Dewey Jones, reviewer for the *Chicago Defender*: "There is something decidedly new and interesting in the manner in which Miss Hurston's characters talk" (12). It is an assessment echoed again and again. Well-known *Pittsburgh Courier* columnist George Schuyler penned one of the most enthusiastic reviews, promising readers that Hurston's use of "Southern country dialect is superb" (1). Likewise, Margaret Wallace's review for the *New York Times Book Review* notes Hurston's "excellent rendition of Negro dialect" in the first paragraph and returns to it in the last: "not the least charm of the book [. . .] is its language—rich, expressive and lacking in self-conscious artifice" (7). The anonymous reviewer for *The Nation* describes "cotton-country speech [. . .] laden with humor, ancient poetry, and folk wisdom" ("Shorter Notices" 683). Along the same lines, Alain Locke in his annual review of literature for *Opportunity* describes Hurston as having captured a "pure folk quality" ("Eleventh Hour" 10). The "poetry, and sensuous sound, and undaunted mixture of metaphor" led Lewis Gannett to place Hurston in the company of white southerners Julia Peterkin and Erskine Caldwell, although he says he "prefers [Hurston's] work" (n. pag.).[15] Mary White Ovington, who was not particularly impressed by the "plot and character," declares "the material is dressed in magnifificent [sic] phraseology" (4). Even Andrew Burris, who penned one of the most critical reviews for *Crisis*, has to admit that Hurston "has captured the lusciousness and beauty of the Negro dialect as have few others" (167).

A second source of compliments is what critics repeatedly describe as Hurston's "objectivity," and again, Williams's praise on the dust jacket prefigured the larger critical response. Herschel Brickell, in the *New York Post*, describes Hurston as "sufficiently detached" to treat "her people" with the "necessary objectivity" (13). Another reviewer describes Hurston's approach this way: "Hurston writes from the heart of a people of which she is a part with fearless outspoken observation and unflinching gaze"

(R.E.M.J. 4).[16] Martha Gruening asserts that "[c]andor like Miss Hurston's is still sufficiently rare among Negro writers. It is only one of the excellences of this book" (245). Hurston, Josephine Pickney claims, "writes of her people with honesty, with sympathy, without extenuation." Likewise Pickney suggests that Hurston writes with "detachment" in an "objective style" (6). These white critics might well have been describing Hurston's treatment of black characters as "objective" because her portraits did not explicitly challenge existing stereotypes. Interestingly, however, black critic Alain Locke concurs with the assertion that Hurston is objective: "For years we have been saying we wanted to achieve 'objectivity':—here it is" ("Eleventh Hour" 10).

Although none of the reviewers is specific about what merits the verdict of objectivity, the larger contexts of Locke's and Schuyler's reviews provide clear indicators. *Jonah's Gourd Vine* is uniquely situated, particularly in the school of southern fiction. In "The Eleventh Hour of Nordicism" Locke focuses on the degree to which writers endorse existing prejudice or attack it. Hurston's novel falls into neither category. Clearly, *Jonah's Gourd Vine* does not belong to the school of Roark Bradford's apologetic *Let the Band Play Dixie* (1934). Nor does it belong to the school of Clement Wood's race conflict novel *Deep River* (1934). The lack of race conflict in *Jonah's Gourd Vine* also contrasts sharply with the "avowedly propagandistic" nature of Langston Hughes's collection of short stories *The Ways of White Folks* (1934). Schuyler never uses the word *objective*, but his description of the novel certainly echoes the sentiment: "[Hurston] knows her people and loves them, but she is not blind to their faults, their fads or their foibles. She knows their weaknesses and their strength" (1). Unlike most southern fiction from the period, Hurston's novel treats a predominantly black community where whites and their prejudices are peripheral concerns, and she presents both likable and detestable black characters. This unique treatment of African American life defied easy categorizations and merited the label "objective."

Reviewers also praise the absence of white characters, which they perceive as one of the manifestations of Hurston's objectivity. Pickney is the first to point out that white characters play only minor roles in the novel. Significantly, she asserts that Hurston's portrait is without bitterness. Pickney sees Hurston as a writer who will not "be deflected by controversy" toward propagandistic art. Another reviewer suggests that "[i]t is refreshing also in that [the novel] does not deal with the relation of Negroes and white, but merely of men and women—whose skins, incidentally, are black" ("Shorter Notices" 683). Gruening is the only reviewer of *Jonah's Gourd Vine* who recognizes that not all of Hurston's white characters are "bluff and kindly," that "Hurston is aware also of another side" of white people. Describing the divorce scene as "searing" (245), she notes the vivid description of John's discomfort at the "smirking anticipation on the faces of the white spectators," which leaves him feeling like he has "fallen down a foul latrine" (139).

Perhaps the most significant praise, in terms of Hurston's evolving critical reputation, came from reviewers who believed that what they were reading was "real," a notion embedded in Lippincott's advertising. The ads promise that Hurston portrays "life as it is actually lived down South." Thus it is hardly surprising that the reviewer for the *Courier-Journal* describes the novel as "based upon true sources, recorded with accuracy" (W. H. 7). Similarly, Gruening notes that Hurston handles her material "with double authority, a Negro and a student of folklore." She explicitly designates Hurston as "an insider without the insider's usual neuroses" (244). Other important reviewers made similar comments. Brickell asserts that "nothing in the book lacks authenticity" (13). The reviewer for the *Chicago Defender* promises readers that "the dialect is so authentic that one feels himself again in the midst of real people" (Jones 12). Chamberlain in his review for the *New York Times* goes so far as to describe the novel as "excellent anthropology" (17), which suggests Hurston has not created a work of fiction but simply recorded what she observed.

Why were reviewers so certain the book was authentic? The biggest factor seems to be that Hurston writes about "the people of which she is a part" (R.E.M.J. 4). Persistently, every reviewer for the white press distinguishes and circumscribes the novel with Hurston's race. They limit their praise of the novel, as Wallace does, by describing it as "the most vital and original novel about the American Negro that has *yet been written by a member of the race*" (6, emphasis mine). The implication is clear: The novel is a good one for a black writer.

Following the New Negro Movement, it comes as little surprise that reviewers note Hurston's race. These common identifications of race, however, when coupled with reviewers' praise for Hurston's use of dialect and the claim of authenticity, clearly cast Hurston as an interpreter of "Real Negro People" (to borrow the title of Wallace's review) for white readers. At least two of the reviewers who praise the novel's authenticity, Wallace and Brickell, indicate by pronoun reference that their readerships are white. Wallace goes so far as to assert that Hurston's characters "are part and parcel of the tradition of *their* race, which is as different from *ours* as night and day" (6, emphasis mine). She anticipates an entirely white readership in the *New York Times Book Review*. Clearly, then, white reviewers appreciated the novel at least in part because they believed Hurston took them where white writers could not.

In spite of the lavish praise some bestowed on the novel, there were reviewers who offered specific criticisms before recommending it to readers. In many ways Pickney and Sterling Brown best represent this perspective, which endorses the novel with qualifications. Pickney notes the "pungent expressive idiom" but asserts that there is "some uncertainty in the handling of the narrative" (6). Brown, too, states that Hurston is a master "of folk idiom and custom" but "[f]ull characterization and complete plausibility are not achieved" (*The Negro* 12). Chamberlain questions whether the novel is "first-rate," but he endorses the book because it is "both amusing and illuminating" (17). *The Nation* describes problems with the novel as "faults in construction, certain telescoping of years and events" and attributes the difficulties to Hurston's inexperience as a novelist (683). Alain Locke's treatment of the novel in his annual review of literature for *Opportunity* falls into this category as well. Although he notes problems with plot and characterization, he praises both the dialogue and the description (10).

There were other reviewers, however, who had serious complaints about *Jonah's Gourd Vine*, each of them writing for a black audience. Theophilus Lewis, for example, in the *New York Amsterdam News* praises the novel as "interesting folklore." *Jonah's Gourd Vine* is, he says, "a well-executed canvas" in which his black readership might see their own faces or the "the composite features of our daddy and mammy," but he finds a "serious flaw" in that as the novel progresses, "Miss Hurston begins to pay more attention to John's background than to John" (8). Criticisms in *Crisis* and *Opportunity* fell along similar lines but were still more harsh. Andrew Burris, writing for *Crisis*, describes *Jonah's Gourd Vine* as "quite a disappointment and a failure as a novel" (166). Although he ultimately concedes that "there is much about the book that is fine, distinctive and enjoyable," his criticisms are pointed: "She has used her characters and various situations created for them as mere pegs upon which to hang their dialect and their folkways. She has become so absorbed with these phases of her craft that she has almost completely lost sight of the equally essential elements of plot and construction, characterization and motivation" (166). Burris also criticizes the development of John Buddy's character, saying, "In John Buddy she had the possibility of developing a character that might have stamped himself upon American life more indelibly than either John Henry or Black Ulysses" (167). In spite of his attempt to measure the novelist "by the task she has set herself," Burris wants a larger-than-life protagonist, rather than Hurston's very human John Buddy. Likewise Estelle Felton in *Opportunity* writes that "[i]n plot construction and characterization, Miss Hurston is a disappointment." She goes further to assert that Hurston "has not painted people but caricatures of people" (253). Comparing *Jonah's Gourd Vine* to Hughes's *Not without Laughter*, Felton believes, only further illustrates the former's shortcomings.

Critics were not the only ones disappointed, however. Chamberlain's review suggests that Hurston's talents lie in her work as a folklorist, and yet he fails to acknowledge that which came almost directly from the folk. His review claims—much to Hurston's frustration—that John Buddy's sermon "is too good, too brilliantly splashed with poetic imagery, to be the product of any one Negro preacher" (17). Ironically, however, the sermon was nearly word for word one Hurston had transcribed while collecting folklore in the late 1920s (Hemenway, *Zora* 197). In a letter to James Weldon Johnson, Hurston laments, "I suppose that you have seen the criticism of my book in the *New York Times*. [Chamberlain] means well, I guess, but I never saw such a lack of information about us." She complained further that resistance to acknowledging the beauty and power inherent in folk culture was not a white phenomenon: "It just seems that [Chamberlain] is unwilling to believe that a Negro preacher could have so much poetry in him. When You and I (who seem to be the only ones even among Negroes who recognize the barbaric poetry in their sermons) know that there are hundreds of preachers who are equaling that sermon weekly" (qtd. in Kaplan 302). Ironically, refusal to acknowledge the folk, who Hurston had unobjectively planned to champion, clearly disturbed her.

Why were reviews in the black press so much more critical than those in white periodicals? Perhaps, as Hemenway suggests, white reviewers' criteria for black writers were less rigorous. In addition, perhaps embedded in Felton's and Burris's reviews are dialogic responses to white reviewers. Both of their reviews appeared after the laudatory reviews in the New York papers. Burris and Felton may have felt the need to balance or to correct earlier reviews. At the least, they demonstrate a greater awareness of differences within the race. Both point out that Hurston's characters are "backwards Negro people," while Felton notices that John has sexual liaisons with "the prostitutes of his race" (253). Such difference in word choice between these reviews and those in the white press are subtle but significant. Burris and Felton distinguish between classes of African Americans, while white reviewers note only that Hurston writes about "the Negro."

Given white reviewers' reticence to address the shortcomings of *Jonah's Gourd Vine* and their willingness to lavish praise, I wonder if white reviewers believed Hurston's novel so "authentic" because it portrays southern folk characters and does not directly explore racial conflict. And therein lies the rub for Hurston's contemporaries. Were Hurston's working-class characters more authentic than the middle- and upper-class characters populating the fiction of Jessie Fauset, Nella Larsen, or W.E.B. Du Bois? Were white readers inclined to interpret Hurston's characters as "real" because their socioeconomic status more closely aligned with that of stereotype than that of middle-class characters? In addition, whites might have read the all-black world of Eatonville as representative of every southern community. John Buddy has no life-threatening and few pride-threatening encounters with white characters. In an era when the number of lynchings was still in double digits annually, when Jim Crow law ruled the South, Hurston's novel might have been seen as denying the destructive power of racial oppression. And the issue becomes still more complex.

If Hurston, by virtue of her race and her credentials as a folklorist, presents authentic characters and she treats her white characters "without bitterness," what, then, were readers to make of claims by Gruening and Pickney that clearly align Hurston's characters with familiar racist stereotypes? Gruening, for example, sees John as "a magnificent animal following his lusts" (245). She clearly evokes the image of the oversexed black male Lippincott embedded in its advertising. Pickney ends her review in a similar way, tapping into plantation stereotypes by describing Hurston's characters as "childlike, shrewd, violent, and gay" (6). The anonymous reviewer for *Newsweek* goes still further in suggesting that the nature of John's "adventures" mark him as "a man of color" ("Books" 36), as if only black men or black preachers indulge in extramarital affairs. Following the authenticity argument in these reviews to its conclusion suggests that the stereotype, the "magnificent animal" image of John Buddy, is in fact an accurate perception. Thus, it became easy for racist readers and reviewers to believe that the stereotypes they projected on Hurston's fiction reflected the "real." Hurston was, after all, an authority capable of rendering the authentic. Ironically, however, for some reviewers their images of the "real" were intermingled with the constructions of stereotype. From my own horizon, I see *Jonah's Gourd Vine* as a cleverly subversive novel, one that interrogates power, marriage, constructions of gender, and stereotypes, but without access to Hurston's entire body of work, her contemporaries were less certain of her agenda.

Southern Tales of Mules and Men

With the publication of her first book secure, Hurston again turned to her collection of folklore. While she must have been thankful for the acceptance of her much-labored-over manuscript, the publication process presented new challenges. Lippincott hoped the folklore collection would appeal to a popular audience, so Hurston undertook additional revisions to make the material accessible. Exactly what Lippincott required is unclear, but it is easy to imagine that after devoting seven years of her life to collecting and revising the material, Hurston would have gone to great lengths to satisfy her publisher.

In an effort to make the volume appeal to scholars of American folklore, Lippincott in the summer of 1934 asked Hurston's mentor Franz Boas to write an introduction to the collection and sent him a portion of the manuscript. On August 20, Hurston wrote Boas to ask for his consent and to explain the difficult situation in which Lippincott had placed her (Kaplan 308). Lippincott wanted to target a popular audience but still wanted the volume to serve as a reference book. In order to make the collection more readable, as Lippincott demanded, Hurston had inserted narrative between the tales.

Although she knew the approach was decidedly unscientific, she had little choice. No one would publish it otherwise, as her previous search for a publisher had demonstrated.[17] On October 23 she wrote Boas that the publisher had the final version, which included material from her previously published hoodoo article, and suggested that a full manuscript was forthcoming (Kaplan 319). Ultimately, Boas must have been satisfied with the soundness of the collection because he wrote the preface to *Mules and Men*. After Hurston's revisions and nearly a year's delay at the publisher, on October 10, 1935, Hurston's second book, *Mules and Men*, appeared.

The volume contains folktales, stories, sermons, songs, customs, and conjure, but the form of the collection challenged conventional expectations. To make the volume more readable, Hurston framed the folklore within the narrative of her search for material. Thus rather than being the invisible medium through which readers have access to the tales and scholarly interpreter of them, Hurston becomes a central figure, a character, who leads readers from location to location. In the process, she developed a significant innovation. Her narrative provided not only a frame for the lore but also the crucial contexts in which the lore was shared, anticipating current interests in folklore as performance.

Selling *Mules and Men*

To introduce Hurston's collection of folklore, Lippincott chose a plain brown dust jacket. The image on the cover depicts a man playing the guitar and a woman listening, a drawing by Miguel Covarrubias. While the image on the front cover is relatively benign (although perhaps misleading by casting Hurston as a passive listener rather than the active participant she was), the inside of the dust jacket is not. It describes the volume: "One of the most complete collections of American negro folklore that has ever been published forms part I. Authentic descriptions of the weird hoodoo practices carried on by negroes in the South today composes part II." These two brief sentences engage entirely different discourses. The first suggests that the volume represents a scientific achievement, although the claim of completeness virtually invites the critiques from Alain Locke and Sterling Brown that followed. In contrast, the second sentence engages two discourses, claiming both authenticity for the collection, and yet, by implication, simultaneously dismissing it as less-than-serious scholarship. The dust jacket promises the "weird" habits of homogenized "negroes in the South." A more detailed summary follows describing the sermons included as "typical" of "colored preachers." And again in references to hoodoo, Lippincott engages contradictory discourses and reveals racist conceptions of the folk. While Lippincott condescendingly suggests that hoodoo is a practice of "the Southern darky," at once "weird" and "authentic," it erases class and religious differences within the race. The offensive word *darky* would have alienated many a prospective black reader. White readers, it seems, should trust what they find within because Hurston is "herself a member of the richly imaginative race about which she writes." Following *weird* with the word *imaginative* compounds the racial condescension and the linguistic dismissal of hoodoo.

Any reader still unsure of how to situate Hurston and her work in the literary marketplace need only turn to the back of the dust jacket for further indications. The inside rear flap contains Carl Van Vechten's praise of *Jonah's Gourd Vine* as so "extraordinary" that he could "only recommend it with unrestrained enthusiasm." The back cover works to establish the authenticity of what readers will find within. Like the back cover of *Jonah's Gourd Vine*, the back cover of *Mules and Men* establishes Hurston's credentials as a folklorist with biographical information and recounts praise for the dramatic performances she had organized in 1934.

In its advertising for the collection, Lippincott sent similar mixed signals to readers. The initial advertising run was brief but laden with racist stereotypes that challenge the very scientific validity Lippincott claimed. Advertisements for other collections of folklore marketed by Lippincott provide some context for reading the ads for *Mules and Men*. *Hex Marks the Spot* by Ann Hark is an "absorbing" collection containing "200 years [of] stories of witch doctors, quaint old superstitions, strange rituals, such as love feasts, the feet-washing ceremonies, and other legends" (*Books* 21). Only the words *strange* and *quaint* approximate the language used to describe Hurston's books. Likewise, *Body, Boots and Britches* by Harold W. Thompson constitutes "the most complete collection of New York State folklore ever gathered" (*Book Review* 19). Its "river-pirates, Injun-killers, guides, lumbermen, lovers, [and] bandits" are projected as distinctly American folk heroes, however, not the objectified Others found in ads for Hurston's folklore.[18]

On October 13, 1935, the first ad for *Mules and Men* appeared in the *New*

York Times Book Review. The illustration by Miguel Covarrubias from the cover of the book dominates the top half of the ad. Beneath, the publisher describes the collection: "Undoubtedly one of the most remarkable chronicles of Negro life ever published. Part I is filled with folk-tales, Negro songs (with music) and two typical Negro sermons. Part II deals with Miss Hurston's recent amazing experiences as assistant to the foremost Negro Hoodoo doctors" (18). Relying on sensationalism, Lippincott stresses the "remarkable" and "amazing" nature of the collection. Such wording casts the collection as a revelation of oddities rather than a serious anthropological study that would appeal to folklorists. The ads that follow reinforce this image.

A week later, perhaps because the book was selling well and reviews in white publications were positive, Lippincott expanded the ad to two columns wide and lengthened the description (*Book Review* 29). Included is the assertion that the collection "is an astonishing revelation of the inner workings of the Negro mind, and of secret hexes and practices never before fully explained." Such a statement clearly encourages stereotypical perceptions by asserting that there is such a thing as "the" mind of a diverse group.

As the Christmas buying rush approached, Lippincott once again began advertising, and the descriptions become more inflammatory. On December 8 Lippincott placed a large ad in the *New York Times* identifying a number of recent releases (18). *Mules and Men* appears at the top. Quoting a review by Lewis Gannett, the ad touts, "'*I Can't Remember Anything Better Since Uncle Remus*.'" Numerous reviewers made the connection between the two authors, and Lippincott must have hoped that associating Hurston with the well-known Uncle Remus tales by Joel Chandler Harris would boost sales. Clearly, Gannett meant the comment as praise, and as a publisher in the business for profit, using the praise of an established critic must have seemed like a sound marketing decision.

Comparisons of *Mules and Men* and Harris's Uncle Remus tales probably originated with Boas's preface to the volume. Although Boas does not explicitly compare the two, the first line of his preface identifies Harris's tales as the fountainhead for interest in black folklore, inviting the numerous comparisons made by reviewers. While it might have been inevitable for some reviewers to make the connection between Hurston's and Harris's volumes, mentioning Harris and his tales in the preface immediately made them a mediating factor for readers, and any resemblance between the two had serious ramifications.

Arthur Fauset, who collected folklore in Nova Scotia and later studied religion, discusses the problematic nature of Harris's work in his essay "American Negro Folk Literature," which appeared in Locke's *The New Negro*. Fauset concedes that Harris's motives in recording the tales may have been good, but the long-term ramifications of his collections were detrimental. Fauset explains that the character of Uncle Remus represents "a composite picture of the antebellum Negro [. . .] which so many white people would like to think once existed, or even now exists" (240). Sterling Brown agreed (*The Negro* 54; "Negro Character" 184). This "happy darky" stereotype, Fauset suggests, differs greatly from the "folk temperament" reflected in the folklore itself. The danger is twofold. The first lies with readers accepting the material "as an apologia for a social system, or the idealization of the plantation regime" (241).

The second lies in Harris's skewed portrait of African American folklore becoming permanently fixed. Fauset's essay argues that "[m]oralism, sober and almost grim, irony, shrewd and frequently subtle" are the "fundamental tone and mood" often dominating black folklore, while "the quaint and sentimental humor," which dominates the Harris tales, is "an overtone merely." That overtone, however, had come to dominate images of black folklore and to create a false image of black life in the South. Earl F. Bargainnier explains the impact: "The Northern concept of southern life was by 1880 a strange blend of somewhat incongruous elements drawn from Stephen Collins Foster's songs, *Uncle Tom's Cabin*, *In Ole Virginia*, and the Uncle Remus stories. There was little change until the 1930s" (qtd. in Kennan 58). The Uncle Remus tales had worked to establish and promote the illusion of racial harmony in the South (Kennan 58). Because of the popularity of these false images, Fauset believed that black folklore demanded the attention of a "scientific folk-lorist rather than a literary amateur" (243). While Hurston was the scientific folklorist Fauset called for, critics believed that her portrait of black life in the South perpetuated, rather than corrected, the Harris tradition. The historical function of the tales made them highly suspect among Hurston's contemporaries.[19]

In this context, then, Lippincott's repeated attempts to stress the *curiosity*—at least as white readers would see it—of black folk traditions takes on a more sinister tone as it reinforces racist perceptions of the folk. The implication is that the subjects of her book are backward and ignorant, "remarkable" for 1935. But still worse, repeatedly associating Hurston with Harris implied that *Mules and Men* should be read as part of the "quaint and sentimental" local color movement rather than as serious scholarship.

The exploitative tone of the ads must surely have unsettled readers, black and white, who were disturbed by the title of the book itself.[20] Harold Preece, a white critic, suggested that the volume's title revealed Hurston as a "social climber" who exploited "negro art" for her own advancement. There was nothing in the ads to contradict his assertions ("Negro Folk Cult" 364). Rather than stress that *Mules and Men* contains three years of anthropological research, Lippincott suggests a sideshow atmosphere, which could only have created negative bias among race-conscious readers.

Reading *Mules and Men*

Following the cues in Lippincott's advertising, most reviewers read the collection as good entertainment, but critical response was not as swift in coming or as positive as it had been with *Jonah's Gourd Vine*. The *New York Herald Tribune* was the only weekend paper to review the volume promptly, and the *New York Times Book Review* evaluation did not appear until November 10. In contrast, *Jonah's Gourd Vine* had been immediately reviewed and praised. Notably absent are reviews in *Crisis* and *Opportunity*, neither of which ever published another independent review of Hurston's work.

Reviews in white publications were overwhelmingly positive as reviewers encouraged their readers not to be put off by "the label of folklore" (Stoney 7). The *New York Post* review suggests that readers can expect "dozens of good stories" they can read "with the keenest enjoyment" ("A Negro Writer" 13). Samuel Gaillard Stoney, in his review for the *New York Herald Tribune*, describes the collection as "an excellent piece of reporting in such an infectiously interesting style." While Boas's introduction points out the collection's value as "cultural history," Jonathan Daniels in *The Saturday Review* was careful to point out that "[i]t is also valuable to current entertainment" (12). The reviewer for the *Boston Evening Transcript* reached a similar conclusion based on the "picturesque phraseology" of the "southernmost Negro" (H.A.P. 2)

Reviewers of *Mules and Men*, like reviewers of *Jonah's Gourd Vine*, pointed out Hurston's status as an insider as a member of the race. Polly Harris promises her readers a "magnificent chronicle of Negro life" (11), while Brock assures "[a]t the end you have a very fair idea of how the other color enjoys life as well as an amazing roundup of that color's very best stories" (4). It was an insider/outsider dichotomy Hurston herself set up in the early pages of *Mules and Men* as she describes her methodology and the Negro's characteristic "feather-bed" resistance to queries from outsiders (10). Hurston, it seems, willingly took on the role of interpreter of black folk culture, but issues of race, class, and stereotype mediated between her work and her readers.

While reviewers believed Hurston's race lent authenticity to her work, again they were not always able to distinguish between the "real" and stereotype. Consider the following praise from Brock: "The writer has gone back to her native Florida village—a Negro settlement—with her native racial quality entirely unspoiled by her Northern college education" (4). He clearly intends the comment as praise, perhaps to suggest that Hurston has not lost touch with her rural roots, but his word choice also reeks of condescension, as if to suggest that there is such a thing as a "native racial quality" and that education has the potential to "spoil" a good Negro, both of which were common perceptions in the 1930s, particularly in the South.

Other reviewers, all white this time, commented on Hurston's objective approach to "her people." Thomas Caldecot Chubb assures readers that the collection is not "a one-sided portrayal. The gaiety, the poetry, the resourcefulness and the wit are set down, but so also are the impulsiveness, the shiftlessness, the living in the moment only" (181–82). Stoney was the only reviewer to point out that "Florida Turpentine hands and Louisiana Voodoo doctors are only parts of a far-flung and very diverse race," and yet he went on to undercut his own assertion by claiming that in Hurston's lowly characters "may best be seen some of [the race's] essential qualities, and it is only the more encouraging to see these pointed out by one of their own people" (7). So "objective" was Hurston's perspective that Chubb promises, "[H]e who loves the negro, or is amused by him, or burns for his wrongs, or thinks he ought to know his place, will find, each of them, as good a portrayal of the negro's character as he is ever likely to see" (181). C. Leslie Frazier was the one reviewer who saw Hurston's portraits as decidedly unobjective.

In fact, Frazier told his black readership in the *Washington Tribune* that "[o]bviously the book was written and published principally for white perusal."

Of particular interest to white reviewers is the hoodoo section that Hurston had added at Lippincott's request to make the collection longer. Hurston, as a hoodoo initiate and anthropologist, believed the subject of her study a legitimate religion, but most reviewers were not so open-minded. Jonathan Daniels in *Saturday Review* suggests that readers will "halt with skepticism" when reading about hoodoo (12), while the *Boston Evening Transcript* describes this section as "devoted to the weird practices and rituals of voodoo" (H.A.P. 2). Chubb, in his lengthy evaluation for *North American Review*, refuses to "judge" the hoodoo section, but he does suggest it was added for its commercial value, saying, "I have the teasing conviction that [hoodoo] has always been, and always will be overemphasized because of those who like its appeal to the romantically macabre" (182).

In addition to implications of sensationalism, the blending of anthropology and narrative that Lippincott required before publication generated criticisms. Hemenway attributes the "ambivalence" of the text, whether it is about Hurston or about black folklore, to conflicting purposes: "On the one hand, she was trying to represent the artistic content of black folklore; on the other, she was trying to suggest the behavioral significance of folkloric events. Her efforts were intended to show rather than tell, the assumption being that both behavior and art will become self-evident as the tale texts and hoodoo rituals accrete during the reading" (*Zora* 167–68). His explanation, however, fails to take into account the additional mediating factor of Lippincott's influence. Admittedly, Hurston struggled with the contradictory desire to dramatize folk life and the anthropological desire to record accurately, but Lippincott's demand that she write for a popular audience could only have driven her further toward dramatization. Any explicit commentary or interpretation would have pushed the collection beyond a book of marketable stories appealing to a general audience.

Predictably, then, the scholarly journals that reviewed the collection found the blend of folklore and narrative wanting. Although B. C. McNeill in the *Journal of Negro History* describes Hurston's improvisation on the traditional collection of folklore as "unique," he suggests that "[t]he novelist, more than the student of cultural history, seems to have won out toward the end of part I, for her account becomes worth while largely as a record of jookhouse epithets and gambling terms" (225). Joseph J. Williams, reviewer for *Folklore*, was more direct, saying *Mules and Men* "can scarcely be called folk-tales in the usual sense of the word. It is rather an account of the author's quest for folk-tales" (233). Trying to balance the demands of a popular audience with those of scholars was tricky.

Mules and Men received other seemingly contradictory responses from critics. While a number of white critics praised the narrative perspective as objective, other reviewers found they could use the collection to support specific ideologies. Consider the review in the *New York Post*. Reviewed with *Mules and Men* is *God Shakes Creation* by David Cohn. As a transition between his discussion of the two texts, the reviewer explains: "Much of Mr. Cohn's book is about Negroes, naturally, and particularly about their crimes of violence and their reliance upon Hoodoo. Those who suspect that as a white man he exaggerates these matters, may check what he has to say by Zora Neale Hurston's *Mules and Men*" ("A Negro Writer" 7). Clearly, this reviewer uses Hurston's collection to bolster negative stereotypes of African Americans as violent and ignorant. Other reviewers were aware of this same potential. McNeill describes Hurston's contribution as significant, but his final words indirectly critique: "Certainly the writer, if she has not convinced all readers of the powers of Voodooism, has offered new evidence of widespread ignorance and superstition" (225).

The most unfortunate commentary, however, came in the form of repeated comparisons to Harris's Uncle Remus tales. It was a comparison probably sparked by Boas's preface to *Mules and Men*, promoted in Lippincott's advertising for the volume, and repeated in review after review. The comparison, then, became a mediating factor influencing readers' responses, particularly those of race-conscious readers. Hugh Kennan explains that "many blacks came increasingly to disavow such stories until they ceased to tell them even among themselves" (54). While intended by reviewers as a compliment and intended by the publisher to attract a readership, the comparison put Hurston and her work in an unfavorable light, suggesting that readers associate Hurston and the collection with oversimplified stereotypes of African Americans in pastoral southern settings.

Because Alain Locke and Sterling Brown published their reviews in January and February of 1936, respectively, they were well aware of the potential for white readers to use the collection to support "quaint and sentimental" images of American blacks. Both reviewers implicitly respond to praise from white critics that describes the volume as authentic, neutral, or objective by criticizing the "pastoral" nature of the collection. In their reviews is the initiation of the earnest debate about "the nature and value" of Hurston's work (Hemenway, *Zora* 218).

Because the relationship between Hurston and Locke had, by 1935, undergone a number of strains and changes, it bears closer examination. Alain Locke had been Hurston's professor and mentor. He had also mediated between Hurston and patron Charlotte Osgood Mason. Their relationship, however, was contentious. She found him unwilling to take risks by endorsing things others might not approve; she also thought he could be deceptive. In 1929 Hurston wrote to Langston Hughes complaining that Locke "approves anything that has already been approved," a complaint she repeated in 1937 in "The Chick with One Hen" (qtd. in Kaplan 142). Hughes must have shared similar concerns because he advised Hurston to be more selective in what she shared with Locke about her journeys in the South (Rampersad, *The Life* 183).

Hurston did not entirely trust Locke, seemingly with good reason. Hughes's biographer, Arnold Rampersad, describes Locke as "a slippery character, too fond of intrigue and of the pleasures that Mrs. Mason's money assured" (*The Life* 200). He also implies that Locke may have accelerated the split between Hughes and Mason (186–87). In the process, Locke may have avenged himself for Hughes's lack of romantic interest in his mentor (Locke was gay), and Locke may have used the impending split as an opportunity to buttress his position with Mason. Given this history, readers must wonder if Hurston's apparent failure to seek Locke's advice regarding revisions of *Mules and Men* impacted their relationship.[21] It is impossible to know, but certainly his past relationship with Hurston must have mediated his response to her work. But did Locke's biases work for or against Hurston? Perhaps both. His early criticisms are mild but reek of the condescension of an elder for an errant child.

His move toward increasing criticism of Hurston begins in his review of *Mules and Men*. In his annual review for *Opportunity* he praises the "firm grip" Hurston has on her "material," but gone is the optimism that he had expressed ten years earlier in his introduction to *The New Negro*. Locke stops just short of calling for propagandistic literature, but he complains about "the lack of social perspective and philosophy" in *Mules and Men*. Considering the hardships wrought by the Great Depression, Locke felt it his "duty to point out" that "this pleasant Arcady" is "so extinct that our only possible approach to it is the idyllic and retrospective" (Locke, "Deep River" 9). In essence Locke believed that the collection distorted current social realities. His concern is the same one that surfaces not only in Fauset's discussion of Joel Chandler Harris but also in reviews of *Jonah's Gourd Vine*: White readers might read Hurston's work as a confirmation of oppressive racial stereotypes and an assertion that the harsh realities of life under Jim Crow law were overstated.

Sterling Brown's complaint was similar. He, too, had collected folklore in the South, and he argues that Hurston's collection is incomplete (Hemenway, *Zora* 219). Missing for Brown is the "'exploitation, the terrorism, the misery.'" Based on his own experiences, he counters Hurston's assertion that "'the Negro story teller is lacking in bitterness.'" Thus, he rejects her "'socially unconscious characters' whose lives are 'made to appear easy-going and carefree.'" The collection "'should be more bitter,'" he concludes; "'it would be nearer the total truth'" (219).

The title of the collection only compounded concerns about Hurston's goals. Some portion of her black readership found the title offensive, and in critiques of the title, suggestions that Hurston was an opportunist for the first time became clearly stated accusations. Frazier asserts that Hurston's work will prompt "an epidemic" of claims that "'I've got a good nigger story.'" He expects Hurston to "be greatly resentd [sic] by the majority of her colored readers" for using "the words 'niggers' and 'coons,' etc." (n. pag.). The following year, white writer Harold Preece, in a biting essay titled "The Negro Folk Cult," made his accusations still more direct as he noted "the resentment in some Negro circles toward the work of Miss Hurston." He argues that "[w]hen a Negro author describes her race with such servile terms as 'Mules and Men,' critical members of the race must necessarily evaluate the author as a literary climber" (374).

Most studies of the collection published after Hurston's death interpret the title "Mules and Men" in a much more positive way. The title draws from a long folk history of signifyin(g) on the relationship between mules and men. Equated with work animals, slaves adopted the mule (as they did the rabbit) as a symbol for their relationship with the master. Just as a mule worked long hard hours for no reward but food—and paltry helpings of that—slaves did the same. While undoubtedly a beast of burden, a mule is stubborn, wily, and resilient, and often seeks his revenge in a swift, unforeseen kick that gets the best of the master. Slaves, too, were capable of the same kind of subtle, self-preserving rebellion. Thus, the phrase "mules and men" was a mask. The dual meaning subverted the master's attempt to dehumanize and inspired the unpredictable behavior that could get the best of Ole Master. Hemenway explains that the "identification" illustrates the transformation of a negative association into a positive one: The slave was simultaneously a mule and a man (*Zora* 222). And yet, within the context of 1935, demeaning discourses on race, questions about Hurston's literary agenda, and possibly the lack of information about folk traditions made negative responses a logical reaction.

Many of the concerns about Hurston and her agenda for the collection might never have arisen had *Mules and Men* more directly addressed the racial oppression, anger, and exploitation of the folk. The collection appeared the same year of the Scottsboro trial, and by 1935 the Communist Party was enlisting the support of African Americans disillusioned by the broken promises of American democracy. Why would Hurston, a professed advocate of black culture, seemingly erase the social reality against which so many others were protesting? There are other possible explanations besides that proposed by her harshest critics. First, the tenor of the folklore may have something to do with Hurston's having collected it in the years prior to the Great Depression, in years still filled with the promises of change that would be wrought by New Negroes.

Hurston's correspondence also suggests that Lippincott imposed certain "restrictions," although without the Lippincott papers we can only wonder what they were. It seems unlikely, however, that Lippincott would have published a volume openly critical of and hence unlikely to appeal to white readers in the midst of the Great Depression. Recently, Keith Walters has intriguingly suggested that Hurston took a highly subversive approach to mediate the demands of competing discourse communities. She not only revised (and critiqued) current forms of ethnography with *Mules and Men* but also relied on African American oral traditions to create a narrative that signifies to critique her white patrons, including Franz Boas, Charlotte

Osgood Mason, and Annie Nathan Meyer. He suggests that "her very barbed critiques were often couched within the tradition of verbal art of the African American community, recognizable by those who read within the traditions that Hurston [. . .] knew well and described, but often missed or overlooked by those reading within other textual traditions" (n. pag.). In short, Hurston's readers' ignorance of black oral traditions and their expectations that the text would conform to contemporary norms may well have mediated to obscure Hurston's subversive strategies.

Finally, Hurston's own artistic philosophy also demanded that she see black culture and black folks independent of racism. Hurston first wrote about her artistic philosophies in a 1938 essay titled "Art and Such," but that essay remained unpublished until 1990. In it Hurston cautions that an intelligent young man could be convinced that "a tragic accident [. . .] made him a Negro" (907). From her perspective, black life involved much more than being victimized by and responding to racism. Defining the African American experience in terms of bigotry, she believed, circumscribed a wealth of rich cultural traditions into which she wanted to delve. And not only did Hurston want to create affirmative portraits of black life, she argued against propagandistic fiction on aesthetic grounds, saying that the "groove of Race champions [. . .] is the line of least resistance and least originality," that propagandistic art "precluded originality and denied creation in the arts" (908–9).

Hurston's contemporaries, however, had to wait until 1950 when "What White Publishers Won't Print" appeared for any explanation of her refusal to deal explicitly with racial tension in fiction and folklore. Staying the course in turbulent waters, Hurston refused to write propagandistically, a stance that permitted readers to make their own assumptions about Hurston's goals. Typically, white reviewers focused on the quaintness of the world she portrayed and read her work through the lenses of pervasive racial stereotypes. Black critics, knowing that Hurston's work could be used in such ways, felt obligated to dialogically engage and correct racist readings that could be used to oppress.

Hurston was caught in a turning tide. In the early 1930s American writers began to devote their fiction to social causes, and Hurston refused to conform. Resisting the larger trends of the time, Hurston seems to have been unprepared for other writers to question the political implications of folklore that did not explicitly explore the harsh realities of rural, southern black life.

On another front, Hurston faced criticisms from those who believed that portraits of uneducated African Americans—like the folk depicted in her work—fueled bigotry. Nick Aaron Ford voices the conviction felt by many of Hurston's contemporaries: "If the Negro is to rise in the estimation of the world, he must be continuously presented in a more favorable light even in fiction. His ignorance and social backwardness must occupy a smaller place in public representation [. . .]. White writers might balk at such a scheme, but Negro authors owe such loyalty to their people" (99). Ford, in specifically commenting on *Jonah's Gourd Vine*, argues that the novel was "received with small enthusiasm from certain quarters of the Negro race." Hurston had "failed not from lack of skill but from lack of vision" (99). He implies that some black readers objected to not only *who* Hurston portrayed but also *how* she portrayed them.

Likewise, Benjamin Brawley the following year in *The Negro Genius* attributed much of the criticism directed at Hurston to her "broad humor and the lowly nature of her material" (258). Admittedly, Brawley was among the more conservative voices of his generation, but for him and for many other readers, history mediated responses to Hurston's use of humor and folk life.

As had Hurston's short fiction, *Jonah's Gourd Vine* and *Mules and Men* both incorporate humor. While Hurston's portrait of John Buddy Pearson challenges the stereotypical portraits of black preachers, she nevertheless incorporated humor in the novel, as Lowe's careful study establishes (85–155). Much of *Mules and Men* is funny as well. Stories of John getting the best of Old Master, Jack tangling with the devil, tall tales recalling the richest land and biggest mosquitos, and verbal dueling between men and women all are humorous. For Hurston's contemporaries, however, the problems humor presented were the lingering mediation of stereotypes and the traditional uses for black humor by minstrel shows. Joseph Boskin's study of Sambo documents the central nature of humor and comedy to the stereotype. Jessie Fauset, a contemporary of Hurston's, complained that images of black men as "the 'funny man' of America" dominated the American stage. Such manipulation meant the black American's gift for laughter had "been so befogged and misted by popular preconception that the great gift, though divined, is as yet not clearly seen" (161). Boskin argues elsewhere that "[b]y refusing to recognize the complexity and depth of Negro humor, society was able to maintain its caste system and its imbalance" ("Black" 149). While the humor in Hurston's work often functions subversively, a good portion of her readership found their vision "fogged," to use Fauset's term, by historical uses of humor, rural folk characters, and dialect.

Clearly, then, Hurston's choice of subject matter made her suspect. From Ford's vantage point, why would a black writer not present characters "in a more favorable light"? The obvious answer from her contemporaries would have to be personal gain: Hurston appeared to be writing for white publishers and white readers, whom she did not want to discomfit. To most white reviewers she was the black woman who wrote about the quaint folkways of "the Negro." To black reviewers, she was the woman whose literary vision (perhaps inadvertently) promoted social inequality.

Within the cultural and literary context of 1935, Zora Neale Hurston appeared to be exploiting the unusual language and customs of rural, southern African Americans merely to sell books. On the contrary, Hurston believed in the inherent value of the cultural world about which she wrote. Hardly "objective," as the reviewers of *Jonah's Gourd Vine* claimed, Hurston wanted to validate the cultural worth of the folk and wanted to assert the presence of an autonomous black culture. With the pendulum of popular critical opinion about how to portray African American life swinging in the direction of bitter protest, it is easy to imagine that Hurston felt the need to be equally adamant about the existence of an *independent*, affirmative black culture. In the years that followed, however, Hurston's unwillingness to explicitly explore interracial conflict permitted multiple interpretations of her motives. In 1937, with *Their Eyes Were Watching God*, Hurston would attempt to respond to the criticisms generated by *Mules and Men* and yet would be greeted by the most resounding condemnations of her career.

THREE

A Highway through the Wilderness

Ah wanted to preach a great sermon about colored women sittin' on high, but they wasn't no pulpit for me. Freedom found me wid a baby daughter in my arms, so Ah said Ah'd take a broom and a cook pot and throw up a highway through the wilderness.

—*Their Eyes Were Watching God*

After completing work on *Mules and Men*, Hurston set out to make a way out of no way, to support herself as a writer. She took two important steps that should have enhanced her credentials as a serious folklorist and author. First, she applied for and in early 1935 received a $3,000 fellowship from the Julius Rosenwald Fund to pay for two years of graduate study at Columbia University. In 1936 Hurston also received a fellowship from the John Simon Guggenheim Memorial Foundation that allowed her to travel to Haiti, where she wrote *Their Eyes Were Watching God*. Both Hurston's attempt to return to graduate school and the work she produced during her Guggenheim Fellowship should have enhanced her credentials, but they did more damage than good to her evolving reputation. As in the 1920s, the politics of identity and the politics of aesthetics plagued Hurston.

Her encounter with the Rosenwald Fund proved disastrous and confirmed assumptions that she was an unreliable opportunist. When the Rosenwald Fund changed the terms of Hurston's scholarship, she opted to spend the semester writing, rather than return to class as the terms of her scholarship stipulated, essentially turning her semester's academic scholarship into a semester's writing fellowship. Administrators of the fund took a paternalistic attitude toward her, and under those circumstances, I might sympathetically argue that her response to the changed terms of her scholarship is understandable (although perhaps not excusable). The incident, however, could only have damaged Hurston's evolving reputation.

Two years later, *Their Eyes Were Watching God* pushed Hurston to the perimeter of the African American intellectual community. While reviews in the New York papers targeted at white readers were largely positive, reviews in smaller periodicals by prominent black critics, including former mentor and literary critic Alain Locke, *New Challenge* editor Marion Minus, and emerging critic and author Richard Wright, condemned the novel and Hurston for her lack of attention to political and social issues. Lippincott's marketing of the novel encouraged such apolitical readings at a time when the national literary climate was becoming increasingly protest oriented. The movement would climax with Steinbeck's 1939 *Grapes of Wrath* and Wright's 1940 *Native Son*. In the end, *Their Eyes Were Watching God*, which many consider Hurston's masterpiece, appeared to be a romance inappropriate and irrelevant to the crises of Depression-era America. Its reception proved pivotal by pushing Hurston to the margins and paving the way among critics for unflattering readings of the books that followed.

Contradictory Perceptions

Hurston's encounters with the Julius Rosenwald Fund and the Guggenheim Foundation, when combined, create an interesting and contradictory portrait of the writer as an anthropologist, as a fiction writer, and as an individual between 1933 and 1935. In the correspondence of the Rosenwald Fund and the Guggenheim Foundation decidedly different perceptions of Hurston emerge, suggesting that her personality had been and would continue to be a strong mediating factor in perceptions of her work. With Hurston's continuing fictional focus on the folk, her motives were of central interest. Hurston's 1935 encounter with the Rosenwald Fund could only have fueled concerns in the black intellectual community about her character, which was to become a central target of critics in reviews of *Their Eyes*.

In late 1934, Hurston considered earning a degree that would enhance her credentials as a folklorist and make it easier for her to find funding for anthropological work. She completed an application with the Julius Rosenwald Fund in hope of finding financial support.

Robert Hemenway's biography of Hurston provides a detailed account of her experience with the Julius Rosenwald Fund, and the same events can also be tracked through correspondence at Fisk University. Both sources suggest that Edwin Embree, director of the fund, altered the terms of Hurston's fellowship after seeing the course of study she outlined with Franz Boas. Embree had promised Hurston two full years of academic support, in addition to $500 to support fieldwork during the summers. The offer of support explains that the officers believed she would "greatly benefit from two years of study and supervised field work."[1] By January 21, however, the terms of the offer had changed. Hemenway suggests, "The foundation officers decided that her degree plan was unacceptable" (*Zora* 206), even though Franz Boas had approved it. The tone of Embree's correspondence—to Hurston and to others—invites speculation that other forces were at work. Perhaps the officers changed the terms of the fellowship in order to exert additional control over Hurston, or perhaps they began to have second thoughts about Hurston's suitability for graduate study. Whatever the reason, Embree wrote Hurston that the plans she and Boas had outlined "do not indicate a permanent plan on the basis of which we feel justified in awarding a longtime fellowship."[2] The fund would grant her a semester of support, after which she might reapply. Receipt of future awards would be contingent upon the officers' approving her course of study.

We can only imagine Hurston's response. She did write Embree that she was "willing to accept [his] terms and make a later application" after finishing her first semester, but she never did (qtd. in Kaplan 342). In fact, Hurston never began her graduate studies although the fund supported her through June. She wrote Embree that she had tried to make the best of the situation: "You would understand that I would not be able to do anything important toward a doctorate with a single semester of work. [. . .] I wrote the first draft of my next novel which has already been accepted by my publishers. It was six months of most intensive labor, because I considered it *simply must* count constructive (sic)" (qtd. in Kaplan 355). When the Rosenwald Fund changed the rules, Hurston did not hesitate to do the same. It is unclear when she abandoned the idea of pursuing a doctorate. In February she repeatedly wrote Embree about problems with paying her tuition, but out of frustration or anger or lack of motivation, Hurston abandoned the idea of returning to school. In May she wrote Edwin Osgood Grover that she had "lost all [her] zest for a doctorate." Two years of school, she thought, would be a waste "when [she] should be working" (qtd. in Kaplan 351).

The day after Embree wrote Hurston to inform her that she had been granted the $3,000 fellowship, he wrote Charles S. Johnson about her award. Embree's letter is brief but telling. It reveals a strong sense of condescension and prevailing attitudes toward Hurston in important circles. Hurston, he wrote, "has unquestioned ability. On the other hand, she seems to have some rather conspicuous outs. She seems to all of us to need, very badly, further discipline both intellectually and personally. The tempering which comes from hard, even, routine study may turn what in part is still crude iron into fine steel."[3] Hurston and Johnson had been negotiating a teaching position for her at Fisk University, but Embree felt that offering her the position would be a mistake, that two years of graduate study would be better for her. Embree's use of pronouns in the letter suggests that others, perhaps Rosenwald Fund officers, shared his view: "[I]t seems to us that it would be a serious mistake for her to take a post at a college at this time. She would probably cause a great deal of trouble and might simply add to her personal distress and create for herself intellectual confusion." Clearly, Embree sees himself as knowledgeable about what Hurston does and does not need, and his condescension might have been more appropriate had it been directed at a twenty-year-old woman. Hurston, however, was almost forty-five years old, and I imagine that such an attitude would be not only oppressive but also insulting. Nothing suggests Embree was malicious in his dealings with Hurston. His paternalistic attitude may be rooted in gender roles of the period. Embree took seriously his responsibility of distributing the Rosenwald Funds (Harris n. pag.), so clearly something in guaranteeing Hurston two years of funding had appeared risky.

But exactly what happened with the Rosenwald Fund would not have been clear to outsiders. It may not have been clear to Embree himself. He had, after all, suggested that Hurston reapply after completing her first semester of graduate study. In terms of her evolving reputation, however, what happened and why is less important than what appeared to have happened. It may have appeared as if Hurston had spent $700 from the Rosenwald Fund under false pretenses. Her refusal to return to class also confirmed Embree's suspicions that she had "some rather conspicuous outs," making his decision to offer only one semester's support appear to be a wise one. The officers of the fund believed Hurston was completing graduate course work. They had not offered her a semester's writing fellowship, although that is what she took. Hurston's experience with the Julius Rosenwald Fund and its officers, then, could not have enhanced her reputation with those who, before this episode, had thought her in need of "further discipline." Concerns about her suitability for serious study, however, were not confined to advisors for the Rosenwald Fund. The same issues surface in letters Hurston solicited in support of her first application for a Guggenheim Fellowship.

Hurston made her first application to the Guggenheim Foundation in 1933, requesting funding to travel to Africa, where she might study the foundations for American hoodoo. The recommendations she solicited for her application provide an interesting perspective on her, one commensurate with that of Edwin Embree. For letters of support from the anthropological community she turned to Ruth Benedict and Franz Boas, both of whom she had studied with at Barnard College. Neither of them felt Hurston was suited to the work. Boas describes Hurston as a "very good observer" but suggests that her methods are "more journalistic than scientific." His assessment of Hurston as a whole is more direct: "I am not under the impression that she is just the right caliber for the Guggenheim Fellowship."[4] Benedict also criticized: "She has neither the temperament nor the training to present [the material she proposed to collect] in an orderly manner when it is gathered nor to draw valid historical conclusions from it." Both thought Hurston would be able to elicit support for her work from other, in Benedict's words, "more appropriate" sources.[5]

Three other letters endorsed Hurston's application. Fannie Hurst's is surprisingly condescending, given that she supports the application. Hurst describes Hurston as "a talented and peculiarly capable young woman," but she also describes her as an "erratic worker" and "an undisciplined thinker." Such comments may seem straightforward, but they are couched in a larger description of a woman who, Hurst says, has "retained many characteristics of the old-fashioned and humble type. She has a well-trained mind and at the same time has retained strong racial characteristics and preferences which make her a rather unusual combination."[6] One can only speculate as to what Hurst had in mind with this description, but she did, in the end, endorse Hurston's application. Van Vechten, too, supported Hurston's application, but his four-line evaluation must have inspired little confidence in his assertion that "no one" is "so well fitted to do work with folk material."[7]

Only Max Eastman's letter reveals the respect Hurston must have hoped to engender.[8] Henry Allen Moe, director of the foundation, forwarded Eastman four applications. Of the four, Hurston was his second choice. Claude McKay was his first.[9] In his assessment, Eastman declined to address Hurston's anthopological credentials, assuming that others might address that issue more competently. What he did offer by way of assessment, however, notably departed from the norm by commending Hurston for being intelligent and tactful. He also liked her course of study.[10] With such a mixed assessment of Hurston and her work, it is hardly surprising that her first application was unsuccessful. She would have to wait until after the publication of *Mules and Men* for the Guggenheim's support.

Hurston's second application, in late 1935, was successful. This time she proposed "to make an exhaustive study of Obeah (magic) practices" and to look for legends about Moses which she hoped to use as the foundation for a fictional work about the biblical figure (qtd. in Hemenway, *Zora* 227).[11] With Hurston's first novel and *Mules and Men* in print, her credentials were substantially better, as were her choice of topic and her letters of recommendation. All those she asked to evaluate her potential success agreed: She should have the fellowship.

For letters of support, Hurston again turned to Hurst and Van Vechten, and their letters make it clear that the publication of *Jonah's Gourd Vine* and *Mules and Men* had enhanced her credibility. Hurst's second letter of support is remarkably different in tenor from the first. Just two years later, she describes Hurston as "an eloquent and important interpreter of her people." She "warmly" recommends Hurston for the fellowship.[12] Van Vechten's letter, although brief, glows: "Zora Hurston is one of the most important, some might consider her the most important, of the young Negro writers. She has an amazing talent for the collection, selection, and creative application of folk material."[13]

For support from the anthropological community, Hurston turned to a new source. Melville Herskovits of Northwestern University was himself an authority on black folklore—American, Caribbean, and African.

Hurston's ill-fated plan for graduate study at Columbia University had included a semester of work under his supervision. By the time of her second application, the two had known one another for almost twelve years. While at Barnard College, Hurston had done fieldwork in Harlem under Herskovits's supervision (Hemenway, *Zora* 88), and he enthusiastically recommended her for the fellowship. Like Van Vechten, Herskovits believed Hurston was in a unique position to carry out her proposed course of study, describing her as the nation's most knowledgeable scholar of African American folklore. He also offered to assist and consult with her about the project.[14]

The other letters also came from new sources. Two came from those who knew Hurston personally: Harry Lydenberg of the New York Public Library and Edwin Osgood Grover, with whom she had worked to produce her first folk concert at Rollins College.[15] Both letters are enthusiastic. In talking with Hurston, Lydenberg had found her knowledgeable about the published scholarship on her proposed topic. Unlike Boas and Benedict, he believed she had the proper training and would take the necessary objective, scientific approach.[16] Grover, too, had very positive things to say, describing her as the best person he knew to undertake such a project.[17]

The difference in perceptions of Hurston at this point in her career boggles the mind. Boas, Benedict, and Embree believed Hurston to be in need of discipline, unreliable. Hurston needed, Embree thought, "very badly, further discipline both intellectually and personally." Benedict also thought her lacking in "temperament" and "training" while Boas thought her not "the right caliber for a Guggenheim Fellowship." And yet, Herskovits thought her quite suitable. Hurst and Van Vechten, too, by 1935 had come to respect Hurston's work.

Such differences in perspective invite speculation about the influence of mediating factors. The letters from Van Vechten and Hurst indicate that their perceptions of Hurston changed with the publication of her first two books. For them, publication lent credibility. Benedict had not worked with Hurston since she had completed her undergraduate work at Barnard. But Benedict probably had knowledge of Hurston's folklore through Boas, who by 1933 may have seen drafts of a folklore manuscript Hurston had been circulating based on her work for Charlotte Mason.[18] Were Boas's and Benedict's perspectives on Hurston the professional mediated by their experiences with Hurston the student? Were they put off by Hurston's interest in dramatizing folklore? Had Hurston matured over the two years between Boas's and Benedict's letters and the one written by Herskovits? And exactly what had led Embree to suggest that Hurston was unsuitable for teaching at Fisk and in need of discipline remains a mystery.

Whatever prompted Hurston's disastrous encounter with the Julius Rosenwald Fund, the end result would have become an important mediating factor for Boas and Benedict (since Hurston failed to return to class); for black intellectuals, including Embree and Johnson; and for others who worked with the fund. Almost assuredly, others in Hurston's circle picked up bits and pieces of the story. Hurston's character and behavior were already issues, both for those who knew her personally and for those who reviewed *Mules and Men*. Hurston stood poised to confirm or challenge the already divided opinions of herself and her work, and unfortunately, *Their Eyes Were Watching God* did nothing to challenge the worst perceptions of her.

Writing *Their Eyes*

Hurston wrote *Their Eyes Were Watching God* in just seven weeks while in the Caribbean. She explains in her autobiography, "It was dammed up in me, and I wrote it under internal pressure" (*Dust Tracks* 717). That pressure had been building since April when she left behind New York and a troubling romantic relationship.

Hurston devotes most of one chapter of *Dust Tracks on a Road* to P.M.P., the man who inspired *Their Eyes Were Watching God.*[19] The two first met in 1931 and then again in 1935. While they were deeply in love, the relationship was a difficult one: "He begged me to give up my career, marry him, and live outside of New York City. I really wanted to do anything he wanted me to do, but that one thing I could not do" (*Dust Tracks* 747). The desire to write was too strong for Hurston to forsake her work, and for P.M.P., it was an "[a]ll, or nothing," proposition. She turned to her research to "smother [her] feelings. But the thing would not down." Six months after leaving New York, Hurston began writing: "The plot was far from the circumstances, but I tried to embalm all the tenderness of my passion for him in *Their Eyes Were Watching God*" (750).

In Hurston's short fiction—notably "She Rock," "Sweat," and "The

Gilded Six-Bits"—she had begun investigating women's roles in marriage. In *Jonah's Gourd Vine*, she had explored the same theme although the protagonist's wife, Lucy, often remains in the shadows. In *Their Eyes Were Watching God*, Hurston builds on this foundation and zeroes in on the trials and transformations of a thrice-married woman. Black feminist criticism, particularly Ann duCille's subversive reading in *The Coupling Convention*, strongly influences my own reading of the novel. I see Janie as a character struggling to define her own identity and establish her own voice, particularly within marriage. As the following discussion will demonstrate, however, this reading of the text is but one interpretation among many.[20] Initial responses to the novel vary significantly from contemporary critical treatments. Many of Hurston's contemporaries dismissed the novel and labeled her a panderer to stereotypes.

The Search for Self and Love

Hurston begins Janie's story when she is only sixteen. Janie's emerging sexuality prompts her grandmother to arrange a marriage to Logan Killicks, a prosperous local farmer. In Nanny's mind, Logan's age and financial prosperity promise security for her granddaughter, while Janie remains more interested in love. At her grandmother's urging, Janie marries Logan, hoping that love, romance, and passion will be the natural product of marriage. Within the year, however, Janie realizes her mistake. Her marriage holds no warmth, no passion, no playfulness. Once Nanny passes away, so does the bond that holds Janie to Logan. When a handsome passerby invites Janie to join him on his journey to the all-black town of Eatonville, Florida, Janie quite literally walks away from her marriage to Logan.

Once in Eatonville, Jody quickly establishes himself as mayor and Janie as "Mrs. Mayor." Having taken successful white men as his model, Jody wants his beautiful young wife to remain aloof from the average town's folk. Jody isolates and silences his wife, making her a trophy, a symbol of his success. As Jody ages, his verbal thrashings and physical abuse of Janie increase. Nearing forty, Janie decides that she is too old to leave her husband and must simply endure his abuse. One evening, however, Jody's criticisms of Janie become too personal, as if he has "snatched off" her clothing before the community (238). Much to everyone's surprise, Janie responds in kind, implying that Jody is impotent. The exchange devastates Jody but liberates Janie, who has finally found her voice.

A short time later, Jody dies of kidney failure, leaving Janie a wealthy, sought-after widow. Although prosperous black men from across the state pursue Janie, she prefers the company of Tea Cake, a manual laborer and gambler. Much to the dismay of Eatonville's residents, Janie and Tea Cake begin courting. Unlike Logan and Jody, Tea Cake encourages Janie to speak her mind and to participate in the everyday life of the community. Janie finally discovers the passionate relationship she longed for as a girl.

After their marriage, Janie rejects middle-class conceptions of respectability in favor of living on what her husband can provide. She even adopts Tea Cake's migrant lifestyle and journeys into the muck of south Florida in what Mary Helen Washington describes as her descent "deeper and deeper into blackness" ("Foreword" ix). In the Everglades the pair prospers as Janie becomes a full-fledged member of the community, wearing overalls, telling stories, hunting, and working in the fields. Their pastoral life on the muck, however, is cut short by a hurricane.

As the two try to escape the rising floodwaters of Lake Okechobee, a dog threatens Janie, and Tea Cake leaps to her defense. A bite on his cheek seems a small price to pay for saving Janie. Too late to save Tea Cake's life, however, Janie learns that the dog was rabid. In a violent delirium, Tea Cake threatens Janie with a gun, and in what can be read as the ultimate assertion of self, she shoots Tea Cake in self-defense. Although Janie loves Tea Cake, she will not relinquish her own life.

After being tried and acquitted of Tea Cake's murder, Janie returns to Eatonville as a mature woman with considerable insight into life: She has been to the horizon and back. Janie remains unbroken by Tea Cake's death and knows that he is with her in spirit. Reaffirming the positive nature of oral tradition, Janie passes on her story to Pheoby, her best friend, who will in turn share it with the community. Indeed, it is Janie's sharing the story with Pheoby that readers overhear as we become part of that community.

Marketing Hurston's "Romance"

A rendering of the hurricane scene with a Zeus-like god hurling lightning bolts to the flooded Earth beneath greeted those browsing the dust jacket for

Fig. 4. Dust jacket of *Their Eyes Were Watching God* (1937), on deposit Beinecke. Used with the permission of the Zora Neale Hurston Trust.

clues to the contents of *Their Eyes Were Watching God*. While the outer front cover might suggest a story of storms and struggles, the inside flap moves quickly through Hurston's credentials as a two-time Guggenheim Fellow and as an "Honorary Mention in the Book-of-the-Month Club Awards this year."

The plot summary that follows on the front and back flaps establishes the novel as a love story. What distinguishes this summary, however, is its difference from the other dust jackets Lippincott designed to promote Hurston's work. Its word choice and descriptions are much less racially charged. The plot summary is one today's readers would recognize: "Janie's conscious life had begun at Grandma's gate. When Nanny had spied Janie letting Johnny Taylor kiss her over the gatepost she had called Janie to come inside the house. That had been the end of her childhood. Soon after that Janie and Logan Killicks were married in Nanny's parlor." The straightforward summary continues to take readers through Janie's three marriages. Only in the last sentence of the summary do we see any mention of Hurston's race or that of her characters: "This is a story of Miss Hurston's own people, but it is also a story of all people—of man and of woman, and of the mystery that the world holds." The strategy privileges the white audience Lippincott hoped to attract. Lippincott obliquely, almost in code, identifies the race of the author and the characters. Hurston, after all, writes about "her *own* people" (emphasis mine). In the next phrase, however, the publisher suggests that race should not be an issue for readers and that the story transcends race to create a universal appeal.

The final two sentences inside reinforce this universal appeal and praise the novel, but in a way that might have actually worked against Hurston: "In *Their Eyes Were Watching God* Miss Hurston has fulfilled the early promise of her first books. This new novel is one of warmth and humor and rich, transcendent beauty." Read within the horizon of expectations of Hurston's initial audience, it is easy to imagine how such a description intended to bestow praise might also have raised the suspicions of her critics. Consider the context. Both *Mules and Men* and *Jonah's Gourd Vine* had garnered much more positive reviews from white critics than from black critics. White reviewers had also demonstrated the ways in which racist readers could manipulate her work to support stereotypes. If this novel "fulfilled the early promise of her first books," those suspicious of Hurston and her agenda must have wondered about the nature of the "early promise" they would find fulfilled in the pages of *Their Eyes*. That suspicion, then, would have become an increased mediating factor for those readers who were unsure of the agenda promoted in Hurston's first two books.

On the back cover, readers found praise for Hurston's previous book, *Mules and Men*. The text here is also more benign in nature than that found on the previous two covers, in part because Lippincott did not write it. Instead, the publisher quotes five sources of praise for *Mules and Men*. From the *New York Herald Tribune*, the passage reads, "[a]n excellent piece of reporting in an infectiously interesting style." Carl Sandburg's praise for the volume describes *Mules and Men* as a "distinct contribution." Hurston, he says, "brought forth a wealth of bright new material. It is a bold and beautiful book, many a page priceless and unforgettable." The passage from the *Saturday Review of Literature* focuses on Hurston's gifts as a storyteller, promising "[o]nly an ability to write, a rare conjunction of the sense of the ridiculous and the sense of the dramatic, could have produced this remarkable collection of Negro folk tales and folk customs." The passage is obviously intended as high praise, but it also invites speculation about what the reviewer found "ridiculous" in Hurston's volume. Carl Van Vechten calls *Mules and Men* "a grand book, full of the most fascinating lore." The final passage quotes Frederick H. Koch (incorrectly spelled "Hoch" on the jacket), then Kenan Professor of Dramatic Literature, University of North Carolina. While his praise first invokes an anthropological discourse, in the end, he, like Lippincott, invokes stereotypes. *Mules and Men*, he says, "is taking down, at first hand, a hitherto unrecorded body of folk tales and voodoo rituals from her own people in Florida and New Orleans." He goes on to describe the collection as "of incalculable value to the folk-lorists, and a real adventure to anyone interested in the vivid vernacular of the Negro life in the deep South. It is an authentic record, interpreted with imagination and uncanny dramatic feeling." Like many reviewers of *Mules and Men,* Koch appreciates Hurston's uncovering new information, but he also stresses the "authentic" nature of the volume as he simultaneously invites nonscientific readers to "adventure" into southern black life. White readers, from this perspective, become sightseers interested in Hurston's "own people."

While Lippincott clearly hoped to market the novel as a love story that would transcend racial differences, it ironically chose to cover the back dust jacket of the novel in praise from critics that repeatedly identifies Hurston as black and her subject matter as black people, in effect calling attention to the very difference the publisher hoped to transcend. The repeated claims of authenticity and "adventure" also may have reinforced biases against Hurston by implicitly suggesting that readers would find the same kind of racial "adventure" in the pages of *Their Eyes*. The publisher's attempt to sell *Mules and Men* may very well have undercut its attempts to sell *Their Eyes Were Watching God*.

Lippincott began advertising the novel on September 26, 1937, in the

We don't just say—
WE QUOTE:

From The Saturday Review:
GEORGE STEVENS
"The Town of Eatonville (Fla.) is as real in these pages as Jacksonville is in the pages of Rand McNally; and the lives of its people are rich, racy and authentic. There is nothing like it."

From The New Yorker:
CLIFTON FADIMAN
"The book has humor and tenderness, and the Negro dialogue is the realest I've read in years. You might (do well to) look into 'Their Eyes Were Watching God'."

From The Herald Tribune:
EDWARD WEEKS
"Among the books which deserve to be better known and may well reward the explorer, I put this first . . . a colloquial, unimpeachable novel of the South."

From The New York Post:
HERSCHEL BRICKELL
"I hope that readers who say they do not care to read stories about Negroes—why I can't understand—will not let their prejudices cheat them of the pleasure of reading a book so stirring as this."

And Says That Great Novelist:
FANNY HURST
"This is a book shot through with the lightning of an authentic talent. I am anxious to talk to you about it."

• • •

Recommended by the Book-of-the-Month Club. At all bookstores, $2.

THEIR EYES WERE WATCHING GOD

By Zora N. Hurston

Fig. 5. Advertisement for *Their Eyes Were Watching God. New York Times Book Review* October 3, 1937: 20.

Sunday book supplements of the New York papers. The first ad devotes approximately two column inches to Hurston's third novel. Lippincott's ad for *He Did Not Die at Meyerling*, an autobiography by the son of Crown Prince Rudolph of Austria, dominates the top 80 percent of the page. *Their Eyes* is one of four books advertised beneath. The small portion devoted to Hurston follows the pattern set up by the dust jacket of engaging contradictory discourses: "Says Fannie Hurst of this restless rhythmic love story of our own Negro South: 'This is a book shot through with the lightning of an authentic talent.' You will undergo an exciting experience when you read this poignant tale by the winner of a Guggenheim Fellowship in Literature in 1936." Lippincott introduces the novel as a "love story" and targets Hurst's female audience by using her endorsement. And yet, Lippincott also identifies Hurston as a prestigious Guggenheim Fellowship winner. The juxtaposition startles; romance and a Guggenheim Fellowship hardly seem compatible. The ad targets yet a third audience by describing the novel as "an exciting experience" in the "Negro South" to attract those interested in racial or regional sightseeing.

By October 3 *Their Eyes Were Watching God* moved to the top of the page. In addition to the passage above by Fannie Hurst, the ad quotes praise from four reviewers for prestigious periodicals: George Stevens of the *Saturday Review*, Clifton Fadiman of the *New Yorker*, Edward Weeks of the *New York Herald Tribune*, and Herschel Brickell of the *New York Post*. Two of the new endorsements, however, tap into racist discourses. Stevens suggests the characters in the novel are "rich, racy and authentic," while Weeks promises that the novel will "reward the explorer" (*Book Review* 20).

By October 10, the marketing strategy shifted as the space devoted to Hurston again shrank. In the *New York Times Book Review* and the *New York Herald Tribune Books*, Lippincott placed an ad two columns wide running three quarters of the length of the page. *Their Eyes* is one of five books promoted. Lippincott returned to a passage from the *Saturday Review of Literature*, stating, "'No one has ever reported the speech of Negroes with a more accurate ear for its raciness, its rich invention, and its music. There is nothing else quite like it.' A new, epochal novel by the winner of two Guggenheim Awards" (*Books* 20). By this point, Hurston's Guggenheim Fellowship had been renewed for a second year. Lippincott taps into a more anthropological discourse by stressing Hurston's use of language, although even Stevens's word choices (particularly "the speech of Negroes" and "raciness") suggest stereotypes and homogenize African Americans. Also, the words *epochal* and *novel* become possible mediating factors. *Epochal* can suggest that the novel reflects a period in history, which would moderate the homogenizing effects of other word choices, but it can also suggest the book is important. When yoked with *novel* (instead of *romance* or *love story*), *epochal* may represent an attempt on Lippincott's part to suggest that the book is a serious one, one appropriate for the serious times of the Great Depression.

The following week, *Their Eyes* moved to the bottom of a similar advertisement that runs the full length of the page and promotes ten books, including Hurston's. The passage again cites Stevens's endorsement but follows his description with a crucial literary label: "'The town of Eatonville is as real in these pages as Jacksonville is in the pages of Rand McNally; and the lives of its people are rich, racy, authentic.' A memorable love story of our deep South" (*Book Review* 22). Lippincott's advertising again suggests that Hurston introduces white readers to "authentic" or "real" black characters, intimating that black folks unlike her characters are not real or authentic. Notice, too, that *Their Eyes* is no longer an "epochal new novel," but a "love story," a subtle difference that contradicts the earlier advertisements' engagements of anthropological discourses.

The one ad that I have located for Hurston's work in a periodical with a predominantly black readership suggests that Lippincott understood the exploitative nature of its marketing strategy in the *New York Times* and the *New York Herald Tribune*. The ad appeared in the *New York Amsterdam News* on December 11, 1937, and targeted holiday shoppers. One column wide, the ad is topped with a small photo of Hurston and the text reads, "*Give Books by* Zora Neale Hurston" (2). In a much smaller font, the ad goes on to describe Hurston: "America's greatest representative writer of her people, Miss Hurston's inspiring stories of Negro life have become world-known, and her three latest novels are triumphs in literature that should be on every Christmas gift-list." Describing Hurston as the "greatest representative writer of her people" is an interesting strategy, one that might have attracted those who were unfamiliar with Hurston's name and work. It may, however, also have caused those familiar with her work, particularly middle-class readers, to cringe at the implication that her folk characters represent the race.

Below, Lippincott describes Hurston's three books. The language Lippincott uses here is much less inflammatory than the words it used in the *New York Times* or the *Herald Tribune*. The summary of *Their Eyes*, Hurston's most recent publication, stresses the novel as a romance, describing it as a "beautiful, rhythmic story of a daring Negro woman's quest for love in the deep South. . . . 'There is nothing else quite like it.' . . . *Saturday Review of Literature*." In its description of *Mules and Men*, Lippincott again cites a review, "the New York *Herald Tribune* says of this novel: '. . . more than the earth-poetry of Negro speech; it has a fine universality, an understanding of human character.'" In summarizing *Jonah's Gourd Vine*, Lippincott calls the novel "[t]he pulsing, emotional and dramatic story of big John-Buddy of Georgia. . . . 'He wuz uh man and nobody knowed 'im but God.' . . . An extraordinary book of folklore and human interest" (2). The bottom of the ad is a coupon readers might clip to enclose with a money order or C.O.D. request to be mailed to the publisher.

There is nothing in the language of these three descriptions, except *pulsing* in the summary of *Jonah's Gourd Vine*, that approximates the inflammatory or racially charged language used in the other ads Lippincott placed for Hurston's work. There is no mention of dialect, no mention of Uncle Remus, no mention of passion, and certainly no mention of Hurst or Van Vechten. While it is dangerous to draw conclusions based on a single ad, the stark differences between the ads invite speculation that Lippincott's marketing department understood that it was using stereotypes and racially charged language to market Hurston's books to white readers and changed its strategy in an attempt to attract black readers of the *New York Amsterdam News*.

But in terms of Hurston's marginalization, perhaps as important as the racist nature of Lippincott's marketing was its decision to continue marketing *Their Eyes Were Watching God* as a "love story." Promoting the novel as a romance would have created a lens through which her contemporaries, her worst critics among them, read the novel. The designation effectively suggested that Hurston was not a serious writer in a time when the social crises of the Great Depression and rampant racial discrimination demanded serious change. Further, the excerpts Lippincott used in its second round of advertising did nothing to contradict the imaging of the "romance" ads. Her novel is "rich [and] racy" enough to entice white readers to "explore" black life. Her portrait of the South is "warm, rich, mellow" (*Books* 31). Nothing suggests that Hurston deals with issues important in American life. In short, if *Their Eyes* were merely the "racy" love story Lippincott advertised, then it precluded considering her a serious artist and suggested she was not fulfilling her social responsibilities as a black writer.

It is important here to return to the issue of Hurston's agency, particularly as it relates to Lippincott's advertising. As I pointed out in the previous chapter, nothing in Hurston's correspondence suggests that she played any role in the marketing decisions Lippincott made. One might wonder why she stayed with the publisher despite its strategies. By this point Hurston was under contract with Lippincott to deliver three more books; *Their Eyes* was the first of the three that would fill that contract.[21] The sheer volume of advertising I point out in Chapter 2 may also have been a factor, but as the Great Depression deepened and Hurston's books continued to sell poorly, Hurston's reasons for staying with Lippincott may increasingly have depended on the cold, hard economics of Depression-era publishing.

Wayne F. Cooper, in his discussion of Claude McKay's autobiography *A Long Way from Home*, provides some context for interpreting Hurston's decision to stay with Lippincott throughout the 1930s. In contrast to Hurston's books, McKay's 1928 *Home to Harlem* and 1929 *Banjo* had both sold well (237; 258). But in the years after the Crash, "[w]hite patrons and downtown publishers no longer sought out black writers. And the black community itself had precious few resources to share with unemployed writers" (293). The larger economic downturn had important ramifications for black writers like Hurston who had emerged in the 1920s. McKay's 1932 collection of short stories *Gingertown* received "generally favorable" reviews in the black and white press, but "it had poor sales and made no money" (275). *Banana Bottom*, which "American reviewers unanimously agreed" was "McKay's best," also proved to be a "financial failure" (281–82). As a result of such economic realities, Cooper explains, "[P]ublishers were reluctant in 1934 to commit themselves to black authors, especially to someone such as McKay whose last two books had sold very poorly" (298). While McKay's two earlier volumes of fiction had sold well, Hurston's had not—making her position more dire and the likelihood of her finding another publisher slim. While remaining with the publisher may have damaged her reputation, leaving the publisher might well have left her later works unpublished.

Reading *Their Eyes Were Watching God*

Many of today's readers, myself among them, argue that *Their Eyes* is much more than a love story, that the novel is about Janie's developing self, about the ways in which for women "the dream is the truth," and about a woman finding her voice in a male-dominated community.[22] The debates over whether Janie and Hurston can be seen as emerging feminists continue in classrooms and scholarly journals. Secondary and tertiary themes of colorism, spousal abuse, class struggle, cultural pluralism, and racism surface in recent critical commentaries. Many of Hurston's contemporaries, however, read the novel as devoid of any indicators of the author's social consciousness, which is little surprise given the mediation of Lippincott's marketing and the horizon of expectations. Lippincott's ads led readers to expect a love story or romance. Their horizon of expectations also included what they already knew about Hurston as a writer and what they expected of "serious" literature in 1937. Critics could not agree on the success or failure of the novel, and the result is a remarkable array of contradictory critical responses. In these reviews the divergence between important white and black reviewers becomes clear. The very aspects white reviewers praise, most important black critics condemn.

Glowing reviews of *Their Eyes* came from white reviewers Herschel Brickell of the *New York Post* and Sheila Hibben of the *New York Herald Tribune Books*. Both liked the "universal" appeal of the novel. Brickell, who also liked *Jonah's Gourd Vine*, argues that the strength of the novel is a theme "as old as man and as wide as the world" ("Zora" 11). Hibben concurs with the idea that the novel has broad appeal, saying that Tea Cake and Janie have "the perfect relationship of man and woman, whether they be black or white" (2). The description suggests the novel transcends racial boundaries.

There was high praise from others, as well. Lucy Tompkins in the *New York Times Book Review* describes the novel as "beautiful" (29). Still more specifically, she suggests, "[F]rom first to last this is a well-nigh perfect story—a little sententious at the start, but the rest is simple and beautiful and shining with humor" (29). Even M. M., Marion Minus, the reviewer for *New Challenge*, praises the novel as "easily readable." She also appreciates the "framework which utilizes folk knowledge and beliefs in the well-written conversation in dialect" (85). The brief notice for the novel that appeared in *Newsweek* describes it as "charming" ("Other New Books" 41), while native Mississippian Brickell asserts the novel is "a good one" ("Zora" 11). Well-known black novelist and critic George Schuyler went a step further in asserting that "'Their Eyes Were Watching God' is one of the best novels of Negro life ever written" ("Views," *Their Eyes* 12).

A handful of reviewers, their readings perhaps mediated by Lippincott's marketing strategies, describe the novel in the same words used in the ads. Margaret Cheney, in *Scribner's*, describes Janie's story as a "romance" (60). Beck calls it a "book of love, adventure, humor, and tragedy" (18). Brickell, perhaps responding to Hurst's endorsement, describes *Their Eyes Were Watching God* succinctly as a "woman's story" ("Zora" 11).

Only one reviewer responded to Hurston's treatment of classism and colorism in the novel. W. A. Hunton, Howard University professor, argues that "Miss Hurston, it appears, has a healthy scorn for the Negro's endeavor to pattern his life according to white bourgeois standards" (71). He points to Joe Starks and Mrs. Turner as purveyors of the two prejudices. Thus, he argues that "neither isolation or amalgamation, we infer, is the answer to the colored brother's problem" (71), although he is unwilling to endorse the alternative he believes the novel poses, a rejection of middle-class values.

Likewise, only two reviewers even nod at the feminist issues that have dominated Hurston scholarship since the 1970s. Beck's review implies an awareness of feminist issues as he suggests that Janie is a character "who sets out to realize herself, to live fully—not to fulfill the empty and conventional dreams of other people" (18). Schuyler's review more explicitly expresses an awareness of feminist issues as he describes Janie as "the brown feminist who did as she pleased and didn't regret it" ("Views," *Their Eyes* 12).

Hurston's masterful use of language is the most commonly praised aspect of the novel. Her narration of *Their Eyes* mediates between the spoken word of folk traditions and Western literary traditions. Her characters and her narrator not only use dialect but also rely on the idiom of the folk—their word choice, their analogies, their figures of speech, their use of signifying. As with her earlier fiction, Hurston's use of language makes literary art out of the language of working-class, southern blacks, rather than allowing that speech to serve only to mark (and limit) the class membership of those who use it. Her use of this language was the one thing almost all reviewers appreciated.

Sterling Brown, critic, scholar, and poet who had published a volume of poetry inspired by the folk, had high praise for Hurston's rendering of the folk argot. Although one of her critics, he argues that her "forte is the recording and the creation of folk speech" ("Luck" 409). *Their Eyes*, he says, "is chock-full of earthy and touching poetry" (410). Likewise, chair of the National Association for the Advancement of Colored People's national legal committee Arthur Spingarn, in his guide for *Crisis* readers, says the novel reveals "[Hurston's] gift of humor and dialogue" ("Books," *Their Eyes* 47). George Stevens in the *Saturday Review of Literature* argues that "[n]o one has ever reported the speech of Negroes with a more accurate ear for its raciness, its rich invention, and its music" (3). Hunton also agrees that Hurston has a "remarkable ability to translate folk speech into written prose" (72). Reviewers for the *Richmond Times Dispatch* and the *Detroit News* concurred with Schuyler as well, saying "the dialect is perfectly natural" (Leverty 16; Beck 18; Schuyler, "Views," *Their Eyes* 12).

Hurston's use of language, Hibben argues, had improved since the publication of *Jonah's Gourd Vine*. "[T]he sweet speech of black people," she says, "flows more freely, and the roots touch deeper levels of human life" in Hurston's third book. At the same time she praises Hurston, however, she homogenizes African Americans in describing the "unforgettable phrases of colored people" found in the novel (2). Lucy Tompkins recommends *Their Eyes Were Watching God* to her *New York Times* readers who may not appreciate dialect fiction. Hurston's use of dialect, she promises, "is very easy to follow and the images it carries are irresistible" (29). This same use of dialect and idiom, however popular with most reviewers, left her vulnerable to accusations that she was promoting minstrelsy, an issue I turn to shortly.

While most reviewers were impressed by Hurston's use of language, one reviewer objected. Otis Ferguson of *The Republic* liked the plot of *Their Eyes*, but the dialect, he argues, "is really sloppy." He complains that Hurston's transcription of "speech difference" lacks "a different rhythm." His criticisms associate her work with minstrelsy: "To let the really important words stand as in Webster and then consistently misspell all the eternal particles that are no more than an aspiration in any tongue, is to set up a mood of Eddie Cantor in blackface" (276). With blackface makeup a key aspect of the minstrel performance, the implication is clear. Her prose he describes as the "superwordy" and "flabby" work "we are so sick of" (276). Although this criticism of her prose departed from the norm, Ferguson's associating Hurston with minstrelsy suggests the hazards of trying to transform the language of the folk into art.

Readers also disagreed on whether Hurston presented "real" life or pandered to stereotypes in the novel, and linked to this debate are the aspects of black life she chose to depict. Ethel A. Forrest, for instance, praises *Their Eyes* as "a gripping story" depicting "[e]very phase of the life of the Negro in the south, like the self-segregation of the negroes themselves and the race hatred displayed by the southern white man" (107). Brown, again one of Hurston's critics, also conceded that Hurston's portrait of southern life was multifaceted. Although he notes that Hurston "does not dwell upon the 'people ugly from ignorance and broken from being poor,'" Brown points out that "there is bitterness, sometimes oblique, in the enforced folk manner, and sometimes forthright" ("Luck" 410). Schuyler, too, argues that Hurston's "characters are not clothes horses to embellish a tale, but real, living, breathing characters" ("Views," *Their Eyes* 12). Sally Leverty also suggests, albeit condescendingly, to her white readership in the *Richmond Times Dispatch* that Hurston's characters are "so real and alive," that "[t]hey just might be the cook in your kitchen, the washerwoman, the porter boy" (16).

Some reviewers also argue that Hurston's characters are "real" because she avoids the cult of the primitive. Hibben, for instance, points out that Hurston is "not too much occupied with the current fetish of the primitive" (2), while Sterling Brown also quietly claims that her characters "are not naive primitives" ("Luck" 410).

Ironically, however, the very aspects that some reviewers believe make the novel and Hurston's characters authentic smack of stereotype. In this way, Hurston's use of language, character, and plot become linked to stereotypes and exploitation. The anonymous reviewer for *Time* describes the novel as "violent." Hurston's "pictures," he says, are "in glistening blacks and lurid tans." Janie's storytelling he even describes as "mak[ing] her friends' eyes bug out at the tales of what she and life have done together" ("Negropings" 71). W. L. Knickmeyer praises *Their Eyes* and yet unwittingly describes the novel in language that casts Hurston as a panderer to stereotype, for her "tale is, as we say, typical." Although hesitant to generalize (which he does), Knickmeyer states that "the Negro is, because of his simplicity and unselfconsciousness, much closer to the essential quality of living than most white persons can be" (4H). Ralph Thompson, writing for the *New York Times*, does the same as he says the novel includes "childish excitements and endless exuberance," two characteristics of the stereotypical happy, uncivilized "darky" (23). He goes on to argue that the novel has "in abundance" a "racial gayety." It is a literary quality that Thompson connects to both *Mules and Men* and, tellingly, to Joel Chandler Harris. Brickell, although he argues Hurston's characters are not "primitives of the D. H. Lawrence kind," claims that the novel has "a refreshingly pagan undercurrent of the joy of life and an earthy wholesomeness that is both racial and universal" ("Zora" 11). Leverty, too, considers Hurston's characters realistic because of their "gusty living and loving and fighting and gambling," all stereotypical aspects of black life. Each author's discourse evokes the cult of the primitive, suggesting that readers situate Hurston in the literary market as a primitivist. Hurston would explicitly challenge primitivist and essentialist thinking in her autobiography, but by 1942 when it appeared, many readers had already assigned her those very labels.[23]

Inextricably linked to this issue of authenticity is the fact that Hurston was a black southerner and an anthropologist. Lucy Tompkins tells readers of the *New York Times Book Review* that the novel is "about her own people," as does Lockhart, whose title is "Zora Hurston Pens Novel of Own Race." His closing paragraph reinforces this biologically based conception of authenticity, saying that the author of *Their Eyes* "should know the people of whom she writes. She is one of them" (9). These two aspects of Hurston's identity repeatedly surface in reviews and only further support reviewers' beliefs that their perceptions of her characters are accurate, despite the fact that their perceptions are, of course, mediated by their own biases. Their knowledge of Hurston's race and regional affiliation forms the lens through which they respond to the novel as based in reality.

There were some criticisms of Hurston's manipulation of the genre. Stevens describes a "technical" problem as the novel opens: "[It] begins awkwardly with a confusing and unnecessary preview of the end; and the dramatic action, as in the story of the hurricane, is sometimes hurriedly and clumsily handled" (3). Ferguson, who complained about Hurston's use of dialect, also criticizes her technique.

Hurston's ideological perspective, however, generated much stronger objections. Predictably, the harshest criticisms came from reviewers writing for periodicals with explicit agendas: *Current Literature on Negro Education*, *New Challenge*, *Opportunity*, and *New Masses*. Reviewers for these periodicals wanted to see Hurston explicitly tackle social issues in her fiction.[24] Her treatment of black life, they suggest, leaves too much room for white readers, like those cited above, to use her fiction to support stereotypes. These reviews also demonstrate the power of biography as a factor mediating response to Hurston's work.

Hunton, writing for *Current Literature on Negro Education*, bridges the distance between those who praise Hurston's characters as real and those complaining her characters are stereotypes. He argues that her characters are "real" but her narrative treatment of them is not: "one is apt to overlook the fact that her characters remain real only so long as they themselves talk. When the author interprets them, or when we try to see them for their social significance, we find that we are no longer on solid ground, that the characters have their being on a two-dimensional plane" (72). Hunton suggests, then, that Hurston take her work in a new direction. He wants to see her "interpret" the roles of her characters against a larger background, to see her characters become significant on a larger scale, as representative of those struggling with social issues. As it is, Hunton sees a two-dimensional treatment. That limited scope of treatment implies two emotional modes, both of which are typical of minstrelsy—humor and tragedy.

Hunton's review moves on to address very subtly the issue of Hurston's character. He implies that her work has been addressed to a white audience, saying at the end of his review that if she hopes "to make the best use—the honest use—of her universally acknowledged mastery of the idiom and imagery of Negro folk lore, she must likewise change her point of view—and her audience" (72). Such a criticism impugns Hurston's character by implying that she has in *Their Eyes* made dishonest use of her folk materials and that she has been using those materials to advance herself without regard for the social implications of writing for a racist white readership.

The reviewer for *New Challenge*, M[arion] M[inus], has similar complaints: "While Miss Hurston has consistently presented the efforts of her characters to live without showing their relation to the whole of southern life and practices, this sometimes understatement and more often avoidance implies much of what the writer with no aversion to being called 'social conscious' [sic] would make explicit" (*Their Eyes* 86). Like Hunton, Minus wants to see Hurston's characters against a larger backdrop of social ills. She is also obviously aware that Hurston has an "aversion" to using fiction explicitly to advance a social or political perspective. While the "understatement" Minus notes might carry no stigma, "avoidance" certainly did in an era when social issues dominated emerging fiction. Minus goes on: "[O]ne wishes that Miss Hurston had allowed Janie and Tea Cake to be less in love for enough paragraphs to show more fully the depth of [. . .] bitter reaction" to Tea Cake's conscription to help bury the dead (87). And despite her praise for the novel and for Hurston's abilities as a storyteller, she "ask[s] that [Hurston] turn her objectivity to the inclusion of newer interpretations of the Negro's heritage" (88).

As with many of the other reviews, Minus's reveals its sources of mediation. She had been influenced by the rising protest movement in literature, and she believed Hurston should contribute her work to the movement. She also must have known Hurston personally or by reputation, as her knowledge of Hurston's "aversion" demonstrates. The review also reveals Minus's knowledge of existing criticisms of Hurston's work. Those earlier criticisms, then, mediate between Minus and the novel, which she implies supports those criticisms of Hurston's work: "Out of the South herself, she has an understanding and knowledge of Negroes which make her able to enter one particular segment of life at the point where she can best probe its reality. There are times, however, when she does this with a lightness which has resulted in the criticism that she uses her story-telling and showmanship ability to exaggerate for a white audience intent upon sensational details regarding the lives of Negroes" (86). Minus's accusation that Hurston deliberately moderates her fiction for a white audience and Minus's use of *exaggerate* and *sensational* engage the discourse of minstrelsy, suggesting that which Wright's review of the novel makes explicit.

Paula Snelling, writing for the *North Georgia Review*, has a complaint that comes close to Richard Wright's. Although she praises Hurston's use of dialect, she also suggests that "the author seems content again to write a book which scarcely rises above local color and tall tale" (8). Snelling intimates that Hurston has little "to say."

Even Hurston's former Howard University mentor and advisor Alain Locke criticized her approach. For Locke, "setting and surprising flashes of contemporary folklore are the main point." He describes her characters as "pseudo-primitives" in language that also implies Hurston's novel amounts to minstrelsy. The "reading public," he says, "loves to laugh with, weep over and envy" the kinds of characters in the novel.

Locke, like Hunton and Minus, wants to see Hurston delve deeper, and even as he compliments, he criticizes: "Her gift for poetic phrase, for rare dialect and folk humor keep her flashing on the surface of her community and her characters and from diving down deep either into the inner psychology of characterization or to the sharp analysis of the social background" ("Jingo" 10). He wants her to "come to grips with motive fiction and social document fiction." In a final blow he writes, "Having gotten rid of condescension, let us now get over over-simplification" (10).

The best-known and most negative review of *Their Eyes Were Watching God* came from Richard Wright, and it is the most open assault on Hurston's character. In an attack more direct than those of Sterling Brown, Alain Locke, or Marion Minus, Wright argues that Hurston promotes "minstrel technique that makes the 'white folks' laugh. Her characters eat and laugh and cry and work and kill; they swing like a pendulum eternally in that safe and narrow orbit in which America likes to see the Negro live: between laughter and tears" ("Between Laughter" 25). Like Locke, Wright's horizon of expectations and mediating factors eclipse some elements of the novel while highlighting others. He misses the treatments of racism that Brown and Forrest point out and the treatment of class that Hunton discusses. In his closing comments Wright turns to Hurston's character, indirectly suggesting that the problems with her novel are not "those of an honest [wo]man trying desperately to say something." Instead, he tells readers that "[t]he sensory sweep of her novel carries no theme, no message, no thought. In the main her novel is not addressed to the Negro, but to the white audience whose chauvinistic tastes she knows how to satisfy" (25). From Wright's perspective, Hurston "exploits that phase of Negro life which is 'quaint,' the phase which evokes a piteous smile on the lips of the 'superior' race" (25). Wright's pointed and brutal assessment left nothing to the imagination.

There are critics who disagreed with his execration of Hurston's novel. Sterling Brown's review, while mixed, argues that Hurston's characters "are not naive primitives." George Schuyler agrees. Sheila Hibben makes a similar claim (2). Even Jack Lockhart, reviewer for the *Memphis Commercial Appeal*, contends that Hurston's characters are uniquely human: "The characters are not the painted dancers on mechanical boxes that Octavus Roy Cohen presents, nor the sullen persecution-crazed hulks that Faulkner drives to nothingness. Strangely—to the South—the Negroes here are human beings" (9). Wright's review, however, was the most resounding, its lingering power evident in the now pro forma references to it in contemporary (particularly feminist) scholarship on the novel. While many have suggested that Wright's assessment of the novel was incorrect, his condemnation of Hurston seems logical from within his horizon of expectations.

Part of that horizon would have been an essay published in 1936. Harold Preece's stinging 1936 essay titled "The Negro Folk Cult" for the first time explicitly condemned Hurston as an exploiter of black folk traditions. While Sterling Brown's and Alain Locke's reviews of *Mules and Men* had implied that Hurston's motives were questionable, Preece's *Crisis* essay (appearing between the publication of *Mules and Men* and *Their Eyes*) attacked directly. The essay initiated explicit, published questions about Hurston's character. Preceding the release of *Their Eyes*, the essay would have become a mediating factor for a number of black readers, including Hunton, Minus, Locke, and Wright.

In his essay Preece yokes Hurston with what he describes as exploitative writers, such as Carl Van Vechten (whose praise for *Jonah's Gourd Vine* Lippincott had used to market the novel in 1934). Charging that "[t]he professional collector of Negro folklore simply capitalizes upon the artificial peculiarities of a group kept in systematic impoverishment and ignorance," Preece assaults Hurston and her livelihood (364). He goes one step further by associating black folklore, and thereby Hurston, with minstrelsy, the very word Richard Wright used a year later to demeaningly describe *Their Eyes Were Watching God*.

Preece's response to Hurston and her work was itself subject to mediating factors, including earlier commentaries on her work. He complains, "'Uncle Remus' is a familiar symbol to every American school boy, but Nat Turner remains a vague figure on the edge of history" (364). It can hardly be coincidence that white critics the year before had repeatedly compared

Hurston's *Mules and Men* to Harris's Uncle Remus tales and that Lippincott had used those comparisons to market the novel. By again associating Hurston with Harris, Preece insinuates that Hurston deliberately promotes the minstrel-like "happy darky" stereotype that white readers found appealing, while rejecting the revolutionary Nat Turner and similar icons that, to his mind, would more positively portray realities of black life. He believed that Hurston had deliberately perpetuated the tradition begun by Harris. Preece's criticisms become pointed when he claims that the title of *Mules and Men* reveals her to be a "literary climber" (374).

The second set of mediating texts for the vocal critics of *Their Eyes Were Watching God* ironically includes the positive reviews in other publications—including their use of the novel to support stereotypes. Hunton, Minus, Wright, and Locke would have had time to read the first reviews of *Their Eyes Were Watching God* before penning their own. The anonymous review in *Time*, which describes the novel as "violent" and Hurston's "pictures" as "glistening blacks and lurid tans," appeared September 26 ("Negropings"). Brickell, although he argues Hurston's characters are not "pseudo-primitives of the D. H. Lawrence kind," claims that the novel has "a refreshingly pagan undercurrent of the joy of life and an earthy wholesomeness that is both racial and universal" ("Zora" 11). His review appeared September 14. Stevens's September 18 review says Hurston's characters are "rich, racy, and authentic," while Tompkins on September 26 suggests that to enjoy the novel one must not be "so civilized" as to have "lost the capacity of glory." All of these praises for the novel evoke racist stereotypes of African Americans as violent, uncivilized, primitive. Such inflammatory language in the reviews of Hurston's novel by white reviewers in "white" publications suggests that her harshest critics were reading the novel through these early reviews. While Hurston did not intend for racist readers to use the novel to support stereotypes, these early reviews indicate that is precisely what happened. Hurston's critics, most African American, must have been aware of such racist interpretations of the novel.[25] Their reviews dialogically engage the racist discourse in many of the earlier reviews. Hurston's critics may have felt the need to challenge those racist assertions, which would have influenced their own readings of the novel.

Social and cultural concerns also became mediating factors for Hurston's initial readers. Today's readers approach the novel with a more broadly conceived understanding of political consciousness informed by a more diverse educational system than that available in the 1930s, by second-wave feminisms, and by the articulation of culturally specific aesthetics. In contrast, Hurston's original readers' horizons included the economic crisis of the Great Depression, legal social inequalities based on race, the Communist Party's attempts to restructure American life, and the looming danger of fascism in Europe. With these changes taking place, "[i]t was probably inevitable" for writers to attempt "to create a new form of art and a new conception of the intellectual's place in American life" (Pells 151).

There were diverse perspectives on art in 1930s. Entire book-length historical studies grapple with the competing philosophies of the decade. Proletarian perspectives demanding social commitment competed with the philosophies of the Agrarians, while conservative voices argued for the artist's need to remain outside political and social debates. It was also a period when American artists turned to documentary forms as a means of recording life. Works Progress Administration (WPA) projects produced local guidebooks, murals, and collections of folklore and slave narratives. While competing philosophies of life and art found voice throughout the period, Marxist thought had the greatest impact on Hurston's critics. The discussion that follows, then, focuses on those influences.

Daniel Aaron's classic study *Writers on the Left: Episodes in American Literary Communism* argues that the movement to the Left was not "a new fad"; it had been slowly happening through the 1920s (150). For many intellectuals, the execution of Sacco and Vanzetti in 1927 proved pivotal by drawing attention to class tensions in American life (172). And with homeless and unemployed Americans sleeping in doorways, standing in bread lines, or roaming the country, the relative prosperity and advancement in the U.S.S.R. made Communism seem a hopeful alternative to American's capitalism (152). According to Aaron, "it was the times, not the party, that made [artists and intellectuals] radicals. The party attracted them because it alone seemed to have a correct diagnosis of America's social sickness and a remedy for it" (160). Aaron lists Theodore Dreiser, Sherwood Anderson, Waldo Frank, Malcolm Cowley, Clifton Fadiman, and Lionel Trilling among those whites making "literary radicalism" a "'mainstream affair'" (190). Black writers, too, were making the same move.

Robin D. G. Kelly's *Race Rebels* argues that the Party appealed to blacks for a number of the same reasons it appealed to whites. Langston Hughes and Richard Wright, along with black intellectuals Arthur P. Davis, E. Franklin Frazier, and Ralph Bunche, focused on class more than on race (Young passim 35–63). Influenced by "the intellectual currents of the time," the younger thinkers viewed the needs of black Americans, indeed all Americans, through "an economic frame of reference" (62). Most important was the Party's involvement in issues important in black communities: the economy, social justice, and the end of racism (Kelly 110).

Unlike their stance in the previous decade, writers sought group solutions to group problems. For those on the Left, including Hurston critics Wright and Minus, "[i]ndividual moral gestures suddenly appeared out of place when men desperately needed collective solutions" (Pells 154). To help inspire authors to produce reform-oriented work, the Communist Party had created the John Reed Clubs in 1929, which helped draw Wright into the communist fold. Periodicals, including *Modern Quarterly* and *New Masses*, campaigned for proletarian literature. *New Masses* literary editor Granville Hicks believed the artist needed to provide "the moral guidance America so desperately needed" (Pells 173). Michael Gold, perhaps the foremost Marxist literary critic of the period, made specific aesthetic demands. He wanted writers to focus on the actions of characters more than on their thoughts. He argued that "'individual tremors, lyricisms, emotions, [and] eccentricities'" required "some 'large objective pattern'" (qtd. in Pells 177). Wright delineated his own expectations for authors in "Blueprint for Negro Writing" in 1937 (the same year *Their Eyes* appeared).

Young intellectuals' move toward the Left, however, was not uncontested. James O. Young's *Black Writers of the Thirties* documents the debates over race and class among black intellectuals. Elders—W.E.B. Du Bois, James Weldon Johnson, and Kelly Miller—remained more focused on issues of race than on issues of class.[26] The younger generation, more focused on class, accused the men of "black chauvinism" (passim 3–34). Black historians, too, emphasized race in their effort to improve black America. Their approach used "Negro history as a source of race pride and as a force in race advancement" (Young 107). They wanted to instill a sense of pride in black American history and the accomplishments of black Americans. Historians as varied as Lawrence D. Reddick, Joel Augustus Rogers, and Carter G. Woodson attempted to make history a "'lever of racial progress'" (Reddick qtd. in Young 106).

There were, of course, many writers and intellectuals (black and white) who were on neither the Left nor the Right. Most existed somewhere between the two poles. What seems central, however, was the need for "writers to redefine more precisely their relationship to the larger society" (Pells 152). Whether writers believed in remaining outside observers of society, committing to social issues, or joining the Communist Party and adhering to its artistic directives, the issue of commitment resurfaces. Pells explains, "two of the gravest crimes the 1930s could conceive" were to create literature "'indifferent to action and unconcerned with the group'" (155).

Even in the latter half of the decade as concerns about Hitler's rise in Europe prompted an increased emphasis on "the mores and customs of the common man" (Pells 313), Hurston's critics demanded a more group-oriented focus. As the decade progressed, political purges in the U.S.S.R. and the rising threat of fascism in Europe prompted a renewed interest in things distinctly American, which might have made Hurston's portraits of black southern life appealing but did not. Hurston's focus on one woman's journey lacked the class-oriented or race-oriented group struggle that might have appealed to those focused on race and class issues.

Amid debates over race, class, and (increasingly) fascism, feminist thought virtually disappeared from hegemonic discourse. This shift, too, made Hurston's social commitment difficult to discern. Because working women were often perceived as the cause of male unemployment, feminist organizations in the 1930s struggled to preserve earlier advancements (Strom passim). Women on the Left often responded to "women's issues," and yet, Sharon Hartman Strom points out, most "refused to associate themselves with the legacy of the movement for women's rights" (270). Communists did not address "women's issues"; they believed that "women's problems would automatically be corrected with the arrival of true communism" at some date in the future. As a result, feminist concerns were "superseded by the overall struggle of the working class" (270). Thus, as economic crisis, recovery, and Marxist thought dominated the horizon of expectations in the 1930s, for most readers, feminist issues receded beyond view.

Within the context of the 1930s, surviving the struggle against class-based and race-based oppression seemed much more critical than addressing gender inequities within the race. Battles against racial and economic oppression could unite black and working-class communities, while gender issues could only have divided already embattled populations. In many ways,

Hurston was writing about issues with which Americans were psychologically unable to contend. In contrast, the changed American political and social climates (from the 1970s to the 1990s) have made gender issues more crucial to current interpretations of the novel. For many of Hurston's initial readers, however, the 1930s' social and political horizon combined with the mediating importance of protest literature made her novel seem socially unconscious, even socially irrelevant. Although I disagree with their assessment, to her contemporaries, *Their Eyes Were Watching God* appeared to tap into neither of the dominant discourses.

Hurston's Response

Hurston was well aware of the accusations of exploitation being leveled at her. Locke's review is the one to which we have her written response. She penned a passionate response entitled "The Chick with One Hen" and sent it to *Opportunity* insisting they publish it. Her reply takes issue with two specific points in Locke's January 1938 review of *Their Eyes*. First, Hurston disagreed with his contention that recording "contemporary folklore" is the point of the novel. But still more infuriating to Hurston was Locke's suggestion that she condescends to the folk by creating "pseudo-primitives." In response she charges that Locke knows nothing about the daily lives of most African Americans, that he is too far removed from the folk to speak knowledgeably about them.

Hurston believed Locke's negative review was motivated by something other than an honest opinion. Ironically, just as she herself was accused of exploiting others for personal gain, she charges that his mendacity is driven by his desire to be a leader. Because he lacks original ideas, Locke, she says, promotes only safe ideas that are already being accepted. She argues that his dissatisfaction with her work stems from two sources. First, she did not confer with him about the novel, and second, she did not write like Sterling Brown. Arguing for artistic freedom, Hurston explains that both she and Brown are entitled to write as they please, but Locke's perspective denies her creative independence. Brown, she says, is the one chick who consults the hen-like Locke, and thus Locke uses Brown's work to set the artistic criteria by which he judges the work of other artists. Inverting the metaphor of the hen with one chick, Hurston charges that since Brown is the source of ideas, he is the chick with one hen, Locke.[27]

Their Eyes Were Watching God also suggests that Hurston had been reading criticisms of herself and her work. The novel reveals a rhetorical strategy subtly, perhaps too subtly, designed to resituate herself and her work in the literary marketplace. My own reading and that advanced by Hemenway suggest that *Their Eyes* responds to the criticisms directed at her earlier works (*Zora* 240). Shifts in Hurston's work suggest she tried—to a small degree—to align herself with two contemporary literary trends: the move away from primitivism and the move toward social protest fiction. With *Their Eyes*, Hurston began focusing more on the internal aspects of identity than on external behavior, a necessary change considering that Margaret Mitchell's *Gone with the Wind,* complete with its cast of stereotypical characters, was a best seller that year. In addition, Hurston also acquiesced to the demand that fiction deal with social issues: Both Nanny and Tea Cake battle racism (Nanny as a slave and former slave, and Tea Cake as a conscript to bury the dead), and after the hurricane, readers see the manner in which black victims are placed coffinless in a mass grave while whites are buried individually in coffins.

Hurston's clearest response, however, is to those who believed the title of *Mules and Men* was an insult. In the opening paragraphs of *Their Eyes* Hurston explains that members of the community "had been tongueless, earless, eyeless conveniences all day long. Mules and other brutes had occupied their skins. But now, the sun and bossman were gone, so the skins felt powerful and human" (175). Here Hurston performs two important tasks. First, she furnishes an explanation and a defense of the title of her collection of folklore, and second, she announces to the reader that the novel takes place at a time when the mask of servility has been removed (Hemenway, *Zora* 242). In removing oppressive outside influences, Hurston sets up an affirmative tone for the novel.

Hurston, however, was not content to let the matter of mules rest there. Instead, mules function as one of the central symbols in *Their Eyes* as Hurston's rhetorical strategy teaches readers about the importance of mules in black folk traditions and working-class communities. Nanny's now often-quoted description of the black woman as "the mule of the world" (186) is more than a feminist observation. It is also a literary declaration of independence and an affirmation of a historic image some saw as negative. In addition, the subplot of the novel involving Matt Bonner's mule, taken from

Mule Bone (which Hurston and Hughes to some degree co-authored in the late 1920s) signifies on the role of the mule in working-class communities. The mule is the center of much of the verbal play that takes place on the store's front porch, and when the mule can no longer work, Jody purchases and frees it to enhance his own stature. In the process, he also purchases the respect of the community members, in spite of having worked them as Matt Bonner did his mule. When the community drags the dead mule out of town and holds a mock funeral, Jody literally climbs on the mule and uses it as a platform for his speech—in much the same way he has used the community to launch his rise to power. The mule is repeatedly a source of humor and a symbol of power relations in the community. Hurston, despite misunderstandings, stood her ground and refused to abandon folkloric icons in her work.

There is no indication that Hurston's contemporaries noted her literary response to Preece's charges that she must be a "literary climber." The damage was done, as his essay paved the way for additional personal criticisms in response to *Their Eyes Were Watching God*. In refusing to write explicitly about social issues, Hurston was fighting the surging emphasis on protest fiction. Wright's "Blueprint for Negro Writing" provides a means for measuring the degree to which Hurston diverged from popular trends.

Hemenway has attributed Locke's criticism of *Their Eyes* to a conception of the folk different from Hurston's. The same can be said of Wright. Hurston "wrote of black life after the warrior stances preserving self-dignity in a hostile environment have been set aside for community fellowship" (*Zora* 242). In their reviews of *Their Eyes* neither Locke nor Wright acknowledges the affirmative nature of the all-black community and its oral traditions. In essence, Locke's review "denies the validity" of Hurston's fictional world (242). Likewise, Wright's description of African American folklore as "moulded out of rigorous and inhuman conditions of life" ("Blueprint" 55) suggests that he, too, saw it as largely a response to white oppression, a concept Hurston implicitly refuted in her fiction and folkloric collections.

Wright and Hurston also held differing views about the role of African American art. Wright argues that social realism should be the goal for black writers, whose task is to "create values by which his race is to struggle, live and die" ("Blueprint" 59). And while Hurston adamantly opposed using fiction for political purposes, Wright asserts, "[A] simple literary realism which seeks to depict the lives of these people [Negro workers and the Negro middle class] devoid of wider social connections, devoid of the revolutionary significance [. . .] must of necessity do a rank injustice to the Negro people and alienate their possible allies in the struggle for freedom" (59). Unlike Du Bois, Wright explains that he does not advocate propaganda, but a particular "perspective," or "that fixed point in intellectual space where a writer stands to view the struggles, hopes and sufferings of his people" (61). In contrast, Hurston argues for the necessity of artistic freedom. Explicitly promoting a political perspective, in Hurston's words, "preclude[s] originality and den[ies] creation in the arts" ("Art and Such" 909).

Wright and Hurston also held very different perspectives of southern life. Wright's experiences with racism, detailed in "The Ethics of Living Jim Crow" and his autobiography, were horrific. *Black Boy* records no positive images of the South or southern life. He recalls poverty, exploitation, intimidation, and violence. His fiction records similar images of southern life. In contrast, Hurston's autobiography, although less than reliable, records few such encounters. Jacksonville, Florida, taught her what it meant to be black in the South, but race and white folks remained on the periphery of life in Eatonville, Florida. Unlike Wright, Hurston returned to the South and lived most of her adult life there after completing her education. Her fiction, too, reveals an affirmative folk experience and psychology foreign in Wright's Mississippi. Obviously, their vastly different experiences form the foundation for vastly different fictions of southern life.

Despite their differences, Wright and Hurston were united on one artistic front. Both contended that the folk were appropriate subjects for literary creations although their perspectives were influenced by different factors. William Maxwell argues convincingly that critics weighing in on the "Wright-Hurston debate have blinded themselves to more-than-trivial points of contact between the two writers" (157). Both, Maxwell points out, journeyed out of the rural South to find scientific lenses through which to view black folk culture. For Hurston the "spy glass of Anthropology" offered distance and perspective, and for Wright Communism offered the same. According to Maxwell, "[b]oth [. . .] allowed a constructive sort of African-American double consciousness: an untorturous twoness allowing one to see birth cultures as both subject and object, thus ensuring that black difference could not be interpreted as black deficiency" (164). Maxwell even argues that Wright's short story "Fire and Cloud," which appeared in *Uncle Tom's Children*, intentionally signifies on Hurston's early short story "The Fire and the Cloud" (173).

Maxwell distills Wright's complaints about Hurston to this: "To [Wright's] mind, Hurston's welcome challenge to pathologizing accounts of rural black communities thus needed to challenge the facts of rural white ownership, facts that at best hindered the flowering of black folk culture into black self-determination and at worst threatened the folk's very existence by demanding removal north" (173). Wright and Hurston were both engaged in kinds of cultural work that, ironically, complement one another. Hurston set out to nurture a positive sense of self within the race, while Wright set out to inspire action against oppression. Although Wright and Hurston opposed one another and critics have since followed their cue, typically accepting the polarity, as June Jordan points out, a healthy community needs both nurturing and inspiring to resist oppression (4–8).

Hurston's literary perspective, to borrow Wright's term, put her in an awkward position in 1937 America. On the one hand, Nick Aaron Ford in 1936 in *The Contemporary Negro Novel* and others argued that portraying common African American characters, like those populating Hurston's work, inhibited social progress. Marion Minus in her essay "Present Trends in Negro Literature" also addresses the concern that the realist explores "depths best left unplumbed" (11). On the other hand were those artists, including Wright, who argued that not only were the folk an appropriate subject but that African American writers had the responsibility "to depict Negro life in all of its manifold and intricate relationships" ("Blueprint" 59). Both schools of thought rejected Hurston's work. Writing about the folk excluded Hurston from the first group while her treatments of black life failed to meet the demands outlined by Wright and Locke.

Although notable for the strength of its condemnation of Hurston, Wright's review should not have come as a surprise. The perception that Hurston was manipulating black stereotypes had been growing for twelve years. When Lippincott published *Their Eyes Were Watching God*, questions about her character seemed to be answered. Wright pointedly accused her of exploitation for personal gain. Much more than a single review, Wright's evaluation is the dialogic culmination of preceding biased reviews written by white critics, of Lippincott's racist marketing strategies, of Wallace

Thurman's description of Sweetie May Carr in *Infants of the Spring*, and of Hurston's reliance upon white patrons, all of which resonate in Wright's assertion that Hurston "exploits the phase of Negro life which is 'quaint,' the phase which evokes a piteous smile upon the lips of the 'superior' race" (25). By his standards, Hurston had sold out to a white readership that would buy only books confirming nonthreatening stereotypes of African Americans.

Hurston took the negative reviews of *Their Eyes* personally—and made her rebuttals personal—for good reason. By January 1938, when Locke's review appeared, Hurston was on the defensive. Critics of her fiction had begun to refer more frequently to her character in their discussions of her work. Hurston's response to Locke's review has been described by Hemenway as "unfair" (*Zora* 241), but her frustration is understandable. After all, most turn-of-the-century readers and a handful of Hurston's contemporaries argue that *Their Eyes* documents social reality for women in a broad way, exploring the roles of women in a misogynistic community, exploring class conflict, and probing colorism within the black community.

Locke, Wright, and Brown, however, apparently wanted Hurston to document racial conflict or class-based conflict rather than be socially conscious in a more broad-minded way. Their dismissal of the issues that today's scholars discuss, however, was not unique. The three readers who did comment on what today's readers see as the more substantive themes in the novel were alone in their observations. In *Their Eyes,* Nanny sets out to "throw up a highway through the wilderness" for her daughter (187), and Hurston was doing the same for her literary descendants. In creating a path of her own, Hurston rejected the one prescribed for her by a predominantly male literary establishment, reinvigorating matrilineal literary traditions for the black women writers who would follow.

Ironically, *Their Eyes Were Watching God*, today considered Hurston's best novel and accorded canonical status, had a devastating impact upon her evolving critical reputation. It pushed her to the periphery of the African American literary community. Accused of opportunism, Hurston would have encountered less resistance had she conformed to the existing trend of explicitly treating social issues, and she might have also sold more books if she had done so. But Hurston effectively dug in her heels and refused to capitulate to those who would limit or direct her artistic endeavors, as her next two books would demonstrate.

FOUR

Voodoo

Fact and Fiction

> But there are other concepts of Moses abroad in the world. Asia and all the Near East are sown with legends of this character. They are so numerous and so varied that some students have come to doubt if the Moses of the Christian concept is real.
>
> —*Moses, Man of the Mountain*

Zora Neale Hurston's fourth book, *Tell My Horse*, appeared in 1938. Less than a year later, her fifth, *Moses, Man of the Mountain*, followed. *Tell My Horse* is based on the folkloric research Hurston did in 1936 and 1937 on her Guggenheim Fellowships in Jamaica and Haiti, while *Moses* follows the biblical figure from birth to his apparent death outside the Promised Land. Both Haitian Voodoo, which dominates *Tell My Horse*, and Moses were topics that had recently been treated by other authors with success, and clearly Hurston's publishers hoped that her books would be successful as well.[1]

Ironically, however, neither sold well, and neither enhanced Hurston's reputation. The reception of *Tell My Horse* was subject to several important mediating factors. First was her existing reputation as an exploiter of black culture for white readers, which immediately made her work suspect. Second, the subject of Voodoo lent itself to sensationalism, and the controversial nature of Voodoo and zombies was only compounded by the form the volume took and by poor editing at the publisher. Lippincott's sensationalized marketing of the volume as a travel narrative made matters still worse. Its advertising created negative bias by suggesting the volume was not serious anthropology but rather an exploitative adventure for sightseers. While there were vague praises for *Tell My Horse* from white critics, most reviewers found fault with the volume. Once again her worst critic was Alain Locke. In the end, the publication of *Tell My Horse* confirmed the worst speculations among Hurston's critics.

A year later, *Moses, Man of the Mountain*—had it been read as a contribution to the protest movement or a serious exploration of slave psychology—might have redeemed Hurston. The novel, however, was subject to similar mediating factors that created bias against her. Likewise, Lippincott's marketing *Moses* as "the majestic strains of the Negro spiritual" proved prejudicial by placing Hurston outside the dominant, serious literary movement of the period, the protest tradition. The increasing move toward protest fiction made it inevitable that some readers would judge Hurston's work by similar standards. While several reviewers noted the political undertones, most who had published reviews of Hurston's prior books, including Locke, failed to see the novel as a serious one.

Hurston's Search for Truth

Hurston's interest in hoodoo can be traced to the *naissance* of her literary career. Her first published short story "John Redding Goes to Sea" deals with the power of witch Judy Davis's "travel dust" to make John leave home. Conjure was present in the central Florida of Hurston's childhood, and financial support from Charlotte Osgood Mason made it possible for Hurston to turn the "spyglass of anthropology" toward the subject.[2] The second half of *Mules and Men* dramatizes Hurston's New Orleans apprenticeship to Luke Turner, nephew of famed Voodoo priestess Marie Laveau. At one time Hurston attempted to publish what biographer Robert Hemenway describes as a "conjure manuscript" (*Zora* 160), one presumably devoted to the subject and perhaps the material that became the second half of *Mules and Men* or perhaps a version of "Hoodoo in America," which appeared in the October–December 1931 issue of the *Journal of American Folklore*.

Hurston's first request to the Guggenheim Foundation to study in Africa had been denied, so it seems logical that when she reapplied for a fellowship, she turned her attention to a geographical area closer to home and to a topic more closely linked to her already published work. The Guggenheim Foundation granted Hurston's request for support in March 1936, and she resigned her position with the Federal Theater Project to embark on an arduous physical and spiritual journey.

Hurston spent the first half of the fellowship living in Jamaica. She studied Maroons—descendants of Africans who had escaped slavery. In the Maroon community at Accompong, Hurston discovered a medicine man who could make "millions of frogs in the trees" on a nearby mountain peak stop "chirping as suddenly as a lightning flash" (*Tell My Horse* 300–301). This same medicine man taught Hurston the "terrors and benefits" of plants such as Cow-itch, Madame Fate, and Marjo Bitters (298). She witnessed the ceremony known as "The Nine Night." Descended from West African tradition, the rite appeases the dead so they will not harass the living (309–25).

Hurston also turned her emerging feminist's eye toward Jamaican culture. More directly than she had when exploring women's roles in rural African American communities in *Mules and Men* and *Their Eyes Were Watching God*, Hurston frankly points out misogynistic traditions in Jamaican culture. "[A]ll women are inferior to men by God and law," she explains. A man has "no obligation to a girl outside of his class, and she has no rights which he is bound to respect" (*Tell My Horse* 328). Any man who tires of his bride can "discard" her by claiming that he "was not the first" (330). Regardless of her innocence, the woman can offer no proof and "has no redress." The man destroys her honor and preserves his own.

After six months of study in Jamaica, Hurston traveled to Haiti in September 1936. She collected folklore during the day and wrote *Their Eyes Were Watching God* at night. The wealth of material she collected convinced her that she needed more time to devote to her subject. On January 6, 1937, she applied for a renewal of her fellowship. She hoped to write a thorough book on Voodoo and explained in a letter to Henry Allen Moe, director of the Guggenheim Foundation, that "the task is huge, so huge and complicated that it flings out into space more fragments than would form the whole of any other area except Africa. It is more than the sympathetic magic that is practised by the hoodoo doctors in the United States. [. . .] It is like explaining the planetary theory on a postage stamp" (qtd. in Kaplan 390–91).

The foundation granted Hurston's request for renewal in March 1937.

She was by then back in the United States, but by May 23 Hurston was again on Haitian soil. Her research initially went very well. That great influx of information, however, came with what she termed "repercussions." On July 6 Hurston wrote Moe that she had become violently ill, so ill that she had feared for her life: "It seems that some of my destinations and some of my accessions have been whispered into ears that heard. In consequence, just as mysteriously as the information travelled, I HAVE HAD A VIOLENT GASTRIC DISTURBANCE" (qtd. in Kaplan 403). She had spent two weeks in bed recovering and hoped to do her "polishing on American soil." Hemenway reports that Hurston remained convinced that "her illness and her voodoo studies were related" (*Zora* 248). Disturbed by what had happened, she had sought assistance from the U.S. Consul (247). Was Hurston being overly dramatic? A bit paranoid? Why would someone want to poison her? The answer may lie in the pages of *Tell My Horse*.

In November 1936 Hurston had encountered Felicia Felix-Mentor, a zombie, in a hospital in Gonaives. Believed dead and buried twenty-nine years earlier, the woman had been found wandering near her family's home. Both her brother and husband had made positive identifications. Doctors speculated that documented zombies were produced by a vegetable poison that induced deathlike symptoms and destroyed particular areas of the brain (*Tell My Horse* 468–70). A mere shell of a human being—body intact but mind decimated—could be removed from the grave and exploited as a slave.[3]

Tell My Horse records both Hurston's earnestness in learning the secret of Bocors (those who use evil means to achieve goals) and the Haitian doctors' caution that she "would curse the day" she began such a search (470). Handed down through secret societies that often take refuge under the name Voodoo, a list of ingredients that would produce zombies could not be bought or discovered through any means. Hurston also relates the process of "give man," where a supplicant who desires wealth or power sacrifices someone close to him each year in return for the Petro Loa, or Petro god's work.[4] Hurston's discussion of secret societies, zombies, and "give man" in *Tell My Horse* suggests that her research might have represented a threat to the secrecy necessary for making zombies and for the operation of secret societies such as the Sect Rouge. If she were indeed poisoned, fear of disclosure seems a likely motive. Where Hurston was headed at the time of her illness or what she had acceded to is unclear, but her rapid reevaluation of her goals is unmistakable. She backed away from her quest to learn all there was to know about Voodoo, secret societies, and zombies. In *Tell My Horse*, she explains only that "[w]hat is involved in the 'give man' and making of Zombies is a question that cannot be answered anywhere with legal proof" (464).

Hurston returned to New York in late September 1937. She promoted *Their Eyes Were Watching God* and talked of her next book. Her name and movements appear regularly in the pages of the *New York Amsterdam News*. By December, Bertram Lippincott was asking for Hurston's Voodoo manuscript (Hemenway, *Zora* 248). Hemenway explains that because preceding books about Haiti had been popular, both Lippincott and Hurston expected the book to sell well (248).[5] And yet, it did not.

As Hurston had divided her research time between Jamaica and Haiti, she divided *Tell My Horse* into two sections in which she records her studies in both countries. The first tells of her experiences among the Jamaican Maroons, dealing especially with their folk beliefs and their treatment of women. The second, longer segment explores Haitian history and politics, and the intricacies of Haitian Voodoo. A combination of travelogue, political commentary, anthropology, and history, the volume is sometimes narrative, sometimes analytical, sometimes based on fact, other times based on speculation.

The title, *Tell My Horse*, indicates Hurston's desire that readers accept the volume's veracity. Taken from Haitian Voodoo, it suggests that Hurston reveals hidden truths. Guedé is a spirit or Loa who mounts believers. A believer mounted by Guedé may fling insults at his boss or reveal a compromising event in someone's history with impunity, for it is not the individual who speaks, but Guedé. The speaker is merely the channel Guedé chooses. Each revelation or insult is begun with the phrase "Parlay Cheval Ou," tell my horse (495–97). In titling the collection *Tell My Horse*, Hurston hoped to convince readers that she was merely the channel by which the truth about Voodoo traveled, but American readers were not quite sure what to make of her treatment of Haitian life and culture.

Sometimes disorganized and incomplete, the text can baffle readers unfamiliar with Haitian history and Voodoo. Consider, for example, Hurston's passing mention of Trujillo in a discussion of Haiti and Santo Domingo. Readers must continue for two pages before Hurston provides the necessary information, explaining that Trujillo is president of Santo Domingo. Likewise, her rapid chapter summaries of Haitian history lack a clear organizing principle, and as the volume progresses, lengthy descriptions of Loas (gods), though initially captivating, can become repetitive for the unscientific reader Hurston hoped to target. Similar inconsistencies arise as Hurston translates some Creole for readers and leaves other passages untranslated.

The problems stem from a number of sources. First, Lippincott was pressing Hurston to deliver the manuscript, which means she did not have the time she would have liked to have to write. Second, it seems that she and perhaps Lippincott were unsure of their audience, or perhaps trying to appeal to audiences with very different needs. Hurston's application for her Guggenheim Fellowship suggests that she wanted to write for both scientific and popular audiences. *Tell My Horse*, in trying to target each of these audiences, missed both. She considered "writing two books, one for the anthropologist and 'one for the way I want to write it'" (qtd. in Hemenway, *Zora* 248). In the end, however, she apparently tried to combine the two with results that are less satisfactory than in *Mules and Men*.

Even before Hurston had finished the volume, her topic and her approach to black folk life generated hostility. On December 11 the *New York Amsterdam News*, a black weekly newspaper, ran a story reporting that her "uncomplimentary remarks" about "Haiti and its religious beliefs" had generated indignation and anger that "threaten[ed] to engulf her" ("Raps" 4). Hurston's treatments of "folk tradition among the race's illiterate," it reports, "aren't a bit cool." In the comments that follow, class distinctions and the dangers of homogenizing blacks become clear. One *New York Amsterdam News* reader, Mrs. Julia E. R. Clark, had written from Haiti after hearing of Hurston's comments, made apparently at a lecture in New York. Hurston's "unfavorable comments on Haiti" were not appreciated, and neither were comments she had made about American blacks while lecturing in Haiti: "'I was amazed to hear of the many voodoo practitioners, who are called doctors, who amass great fortunes and are held in great respect among us!'"(4).

The letter quotes two published responses to lectures on African Americans that Hurston gave during her time in Haiti. Hurston, it seems, had dwelled too heavily on the "faults" of African Americans for the reporter who hoped that "some day she [would] tell us of the progress the American Negroes have made in their march towards civilization" ("Raps" 4), a statement that reveals its own class bias. Hurston's second lecture had received an even harsher response, intimating, as had her American critics, that she had dealt too long with the folk: "[I]n association with these people [the folk] she has to a degree forgotten that there are others" (4). Clark, the author of the letter, suggests that the subject of Voodoo had been studied at length by Haitians, "whose writings are the result of years of diligent research and investigation into African origin." In contrast, she charged that Hurston's "observations on the subject after a few months of superficial 'study'" represented a form of "impertinence" (4). Precisely what Hurston said in her lectures is unclear, but the responses to her subject matter indicate the complex race and class issues involved in her treatment of black folk life and traditions. Lippincott's marketing of the volume only exacerbated such concerns.

Selling Stereotypes

As it had with Hurston's earlier books, Lippincott's marketing of *Tell My Horse* relied on racist marketing strategies. Divided, contradictory discourses tried to attract both scientific readers and those interested in the bizarre or unusual. Readers unsure of how to interpret the volume's full title, *Tell My Horse: Voodoo and Life in Haiti and Jamaica*, needed only open the dust jacket for direction. Lippincott's rhetorical strategy used Hurston's credentials to hook readers, then played on stereotypes to pull them into the book.

The opening paragraph inside the cover stresses Hurston's scientific credentials. Hurston, it says, was unable to find an "adequate account" of Voodoo "as practiced in Haiti and Jamaica." In her search for answers "[s]he presented her idea to the Guggenheim Foundation, and they awarded her a Fellowship, and a year later an extension of that Fellowship, to go down to the Islands, get the facts and write the story. *Tell My Horse* is the result." Immediately, then, Lippincott stresses Hurston's status as a Guggenheim Fellowship winner and the accuracy of the volume. Hurston, after all, went after "facts." In the paragraphs that follow, however, Lippincott's discourse no longer engages issues of her credibility. Instead, Lippincott exploits stereotypes to attract nonscientific readers.

In the second paragraph, Lippincott's description of the volume again fashions Hurston as a black insider sharing the unusual with white readers, and as it does so, the language becomes inflammatory. Lippincott first stresses the authenticity of the volume, for Hurston is "*an initiate*, of voodoo in Haiti and Jamaica." The events she took part in "are celebrated with all the wild, savage abandon of the native blacks." Lippincott promises readers that "[t]his is folklore as only Zora Hurston can write it—the story of esoteric superstitions, savage voodoo ceremonies, strange customs of the little known Negroes of Jamaica and Haiti. All the mystery, weirdness, horror and comedy of the transplanted African Negro run through the book and color [pun intended?] its pages." Obviously, the word choice is intended to grab the reader's attention, but in describing Hurston's observations as "strange," weird, horrible, and funny, Lippincott engages the discourse of minstrelsy. Only the publisher's claim that Hurston went after "the facts" suggests it is a scientifically based volume. Readers encountering Voodoo for the first time would have found nothing on the cover to suggest that it is a complex, legitimate religion. Instead, readers were encouraged to look at the subject of her book, Haitian and Jamaican blacks, as themselves weird, "savage," and "wild." And Lippincott's promise to readers that the volume is one "only Zora Hurston [could] write" may have been intended as a compliment, but given questions about Hurston's political agenda and her treatments of black life, that very phrase must have raised the suspicions of some readers, particularly given the larger context of the dust jacket.

Readers not put off by the inside front flap of the dust jacket found on the inside back flap and on the back cover descriptions of *Mules and Men*, Hurston's first collection of folklore. The inside cover encourages readers who liked *Tell My Horse* to purchase the preceding volume, while the outside rear cover, which cites positive reviews of *Mules and Men*, suggests this new volume will be well received. The language on the back portions of the dust jacket is less inflammatory but still appeals to stereotypes.

The inside rear flap says that *Mules and Men* is probably "the greatest and most sympathetically recorded collection of Negro folklore in the world." The volume includes "folk-tales, typical sermons by colored preachers and a number of Negro songs with complete musical accompaniment." The claim that Hurston's subjects are "typical" is obviously problematic. By homogenizing, it created questions about her literary agenda. As the description moves on to the second section of the volume, the publisher more blatantly invokes the language of stereotype:

> In the second section the author's equally exhaustive first-hand study of hoodoo practices of the Southern darky is clearly evident. She explains the weird practices and rituals of the famous Marie Leveau of New Orleans, her successor and many other hoodoo doctors. No more vivid atmosphere could be created as a background for this authentic material, no more intimate facts could be told, than those which Miss Hurston brings to us here—herself a member of the richly imaginative race which she writes about.

While Lippincott again closes the passage with claims about the authenticity of Hurston's work, more troubling is the word *darky*. Nothing in Hurston's text suggests the condescension embedded in the term.[6] The word, however, becomes a source of bias for those who might read *Mules and Men* after reading this passage, and it becomes a mediating factor for those who move beyond the dust jacket of *Tell My Horse*. The word invites readers to adopt a racist prejudice against the subjects she explores and her folkloric sources. The wording, too, invites readers to adopt a particular view of Hurston: She becomes an exploiter of black cultural traditions that white readers find titillating.

The back cover is more benign in nature, in part because Lippincott did not write the text. Instead, the publisher quotes the same five sources of praise for *Mules and Men* that appear on the back cover of *Their Eyes Were Watching God*. From the *New York Herald Tribune* the passage reads, "[a]n excellent piece of reporting in an infectiously interesting style." Passages from Carl Sandburg, the *Saturday Review of Literature*, and Carl Van Vechten promote Hurston's folklore from the American South. The final and most notable passage quotes Frederick H. Koch, then Kenan Professor of Dramatic Literature, University of North Carolina. While the first passage of his praise invokes an anthropological discourse, in the end, he, like Lippincott, invokes stereotypes. *Mules and Men*, he says, "is taking down, at first hand, a hitherto unrecorded body of folk tales and voodoo rituals from her own people in Florida and New Orleans." Koch appreciates Hurston's uncovering new information, but he also stresses the "authentic" nature of the volume as he simultaneously invites nonscientific readers to "adventure" into southern black life. White readers, from this perspective, become sightseers interested in Hurston's "own people." The implication for *Tell My Horse*, the book packaged within the dust jacket, is that it offers a similar kind of adventure. Lippincott would make matters worse, however.

Lippincott's advertising for *Tell My Horse* in the New York newspapers took the use of inflammatory language to its height. As had been the case with Hurston's previous books, Lippincott's advertising for the volume en-

Fig. 6. Dust jacket of *Tell My Horse* (1938), author's copy. Used with the permission of the Zora Neale Hurston Trust.

couraged the belief that she was exploiting black stereotypes for personal gain. In the established pattern, Lippincott exploits Hurston's race and creates a sensationalized lens through which readers can approach the volume.

Consider the first ad in the New York papers on October 16, 1938. Lippincott placed an ad on the bottom third of a page of the *Herald Tribune*, the left column of which promotes *Tell My Horse*. The column is topped by a wallet-sized photo of a black man. Beneath it in italics reads, "*No white person ever saw these things*!" In smaller type, the advertisement stresses that Hurston is an "*initiate* of Voodooism" and a racial insider: "She witnesses ceremonies no white person has ever seen," and "her exceptional ability to express the thoughts and emotions of her own race makes this book" (*Books* 21).

The ad's engagement of differing discourses suggests the "fractured audience" Lippincott and Hurston hoped to attract (Meisenhelder 5). The text promises, "Whether you read it for sheer entertainment, or strictly from an educational viewpoint, you will find every page a fascinating adventure." The text goes on to point out that Hurston was a Guggenheim fellow, establishing her credentials as a folklorist and thereby establishing the scientific value of the volume. At the same time, however, the exploitative language undercuts the credibility of the volume. Even when mentioning the "educational" value of *Tell My Horse*, the publisher retreats to the language of exploitation by describing it as "a fascinating adventure" (*Books* 21).

The following week Lippincott placed a much larger ad for the volume in the *New York Times Book Review* (23), and within the intervening week, Lippincott it seems decided to focus its advertising strategy on a nonscientific readership. The ad drops mention of Hurston's fellowship and focuses on attracting readers interested in the bizarre and the unusual. In short, its strategy shifted to appeal to those interested in racial and cultural sightseeing. Lippincott moved *Tell My Horse* to the very top of the page, where it would be sure to attract attention. Dominating the top one-third of the page in one-inch type is the phrase "VOODOO *as no* WHITE PERSON *ever saw it!*" The left side of the ad depicts the same wide-eyed black man, and the caption beneath him reads, "Actual Photo of a Voodoo Priest." The smaller text beneath the headline provides a brief summary: "THE amazing experiences of an *actual initiate* of Voodooism, whose race enabled her to witness secret ceremonies seemingly incredible in these modern times" (23).

Endorsements from William Seabrook, whose own book on Haitian

THE NEW YORK TIMES BOOK REVIEW, *October 23, 1938.* 23

VOODOO *as no* WHITE PERSON *ever saw it!*

THE amazing experiences of an *actual initiate* of Voodooism, whose race enabled her to witness secret ceremonies seemingly incredible in these modern times. Writes William Seabrook: "I must tell you how terrifically excited I am by this new book of Zora Hurston's. Papa Legba opened wide the gate for her — and Zora has come through as no white ever could." Says George Stevens in his Book-of-the-Month Club Recommendation: "For general color, life and readability, *Tell My Horse* is hard to beat. She tells some hair-raising stories." 24 remarkable photographs. $3.00

TELL MY HORSE

VOODOO LIFE IN HAITI AND JAMAICA

by Zora Neale Hurston

Fig. 7. Advertisement for *Tell My Horse*. *New York Times Book Review* October 23, 1938: 23. Photo by Rex Hardy, Jr. Used with the permission of the Zora Neale Hurston Trust and TIMEPIX.

Voodoo had sold well, and George Stevens, critic for the *Saturday Review of Literature*, follow.[7] Seabrook exclaims, "'I must tell you how terrifically excited I am by this new book of Zora Hurston's. Papa Legba opened wide the gate for her—and Zora has come through as no white ever could.'" Stevens's comments follow: "For general color, life and readability, *Tell My Horse* is hard to beat. She tells some hair-raising stories." While Seabrook focuses on Hurston's status as racial insider, Stevens's comments undercut the volume as a serious folkloric work. His use of the term *color*, for instance, invites connections to pejorative, limited, and limiting uses of black folk culture by local-color writers. Likewise, his mention of "hair-raising stories" situates the volume as a titillating thrill-ride, rather than a volume of folklore collected by a serious anthropologist.

The advertising space Lippincott devoted to *Tell My Horse* dramatically decreased after October 23, although brief mention of the volume continues to appear in full-page Lippincott ads promoting several volumes. Interestingly, the approach Lippincott uses to promote the book changes, perhaps in a dialogical response to the reviews appearing in periodicals across the nation. Consider the one column-inch devoted to *Tell My Horse* in the *New York Times Book Review* on November 6.[8] The sensational language is still present but less inflammatory, and the publisher uses a review to situate the volume as a memoir or travel narrative: "Awarded a Fellowship by the Guggenheim Foundation, this talented negro author traveled to Jamaica and Haiti and became an actual *initiate* of Voodooism. These are her memoirs of that incredible trip, during which she took part in ceremonies bordering on the unbelievable. Says George Stevens in his Book-of-the-month Club Recommendation: '*Hard to beat among current books of travel*'" (23). The organization and structure of the volume clearly left it wanting in the eyes of folklorists, a subject I turn to shortly, so in response, Lippincott tried to find another niche for the volume—memoir or travel narrative—neither of which demands scientific objectivity. It was an interesting strategy that suggests the difficulty Lippincott's marketing department had in imagining an audience for Hurston's work.

Folklore or Fiction?

When *Tell My Horse* appeared October 13, 1938, it generated fewer reviews and more anonymous reviews than previous books, and critics again disagreed on the value of the work. Harold Courlander's review for the *Saturday Review of Literature* summed up the critical response: "*Tell My Horse* is a curious mixture of remembrances, travelogue, sensationalism, and anthropology. The remembrances are vivid, the travelogue tedious, the sensationalism reminiscent of Seabrook, and the anthropology a melange of misinterpretation and exceedingly good folk-lore" (6). Despite *Tell My Horse*'s claim to veracity, most reviewers were unsure of what to believe and what to dismiss. While some reviewers praised Hurston's work and/or the volume, no one recommended it to readers, and several of those who did praise the volume may have been biased in Hurston's favor.

The most direct praise for the volume came from brief reviews. Burton Rascoe's mention of *Tell My Horse* in *Newsweek* promises readers that Hurston's book is one of only two scholarly books on Voodoo (of the eighty-three he claimed to have read) that is "worth reading" (4). The reviewer for *Modern Quarterly* went one step further, arguing that *Tell My Horse* is "by far the best book on voodoo that has to date been written" (S. M. 96). Neither reviewer comments specifically on the volume, so it is impossible to know what they liked or respected about the work.

Carl Carmer's praise, while more effusive, is also strangely vague about the volume's merits. Carmer, a white novelist and folklorist from New York, reviewed the volume for the *New York Herald Tribune*.[9] He introduces Hurston to his readers as "a trained scholar" and "one of the most delightfully alive personalities of our day," comments that clearly indicate a personal bias in her favor. Her work, he says, is "the best that [he] know[s] in the field of contemporary folklore" (2). His review of *Tell My Horse* was also probably mediated by the fact that Hurston had written a positive review of his *The Hurricane's Children: Tales from Your Neck o' the Woods* for the *New York Herald Tribune* the previous December.[10]

Carter G. Woodson's review for the *Journal of Negro History* is similar to Carmer's in that the review is positive, but most of it treats Hurston's credentials and past publications rather than *Tell My Horse*.[11] Woodson stresses that Hurston collected the information herself and "described [it] in [the] highly literary, even poetic, language of which she is capable" (117). The "superstition," "primitive rites" and "strange customs," he says, "are presented as mystery, weirdness, comedy and tragedy which give convincing evidence of the transplantation of African culture to America." While he suggests that the book "is an important chapter in the conflict and fusion of culture" (117), his description of the volume as containing "mystery, weirdness, comedy and tragedy" is difficult to interpret. Whether the word choice reflects his subtle dismissal of *Tell My Horse* as unscholarly or simply reflects Woodson's own biases against Haitian culture is impossible to discern. In his final assessment, however, Woodson tells readers that "[t]he work is entertaining and at the same time one of value which scholars must take into consideration" (118). It is unclear precisely what Woodson thought of the volume, but his discussion of factors besides the collection itself suggests that his previous contact with Hurston and knowledge of her work were mediating factors to her advantage, probably in part because her first grant for folkloric work had been funded by Woodson's Association for the Study of Negro Life and History.

Those who indicated specifically what they liked about the volume focused on Hurston's ability to transport them in time and space, her ability to make them present at the ceremonies she describes. One reviewer suggests that Hurston "captures the ineluctable spirit of voodoo [. . .] without distorting or sensationalizing it" (S. M. 95–9). The anonymous reviewer for the *New York Times Book Review* also praises Hurston. This reviewer treats the volume in more detail, describing it as "the result of [. . .] long and intimate research." The reviewer promises, Hurston "writes [. . .] with sympathy and levelheaded balance, with no sensationalism, in a style which is vivid, sometimes lyrical, occasionally strikingly dramatic, yet simple and unstrained" ("Lore of Haiti" 12). Gertrude Martin, writing for the *Chicago Defender* also, finally, appreciated *Tell My Horse* "for its treatment of the voodoo." She believed it was "definitely good reading" (19). Not all reviewers were so capable of avoiding sensationalism.

Carmer's comments, for example, praise but also invoke stereotypes: "Miss Hurston's book is so filled with the spirit of her subject that the whole feeling of its spine-chilling supernatural grotesquerie encompasses the reader" ("In Haiti" 2). Much of *Tell My Horse* is given to detailed descriptions of ceremonies, but it is also full of history and culture, which would be hard to interpret as "spine-chilling." It seems likely that stereotypes of Voodoo and zombies created bias for Carmer and thus became the elements of the volume he remembered most vividly.

Other reviewers more explicitly invoked stereotypes, some of them connected to Hurston's racial identity. With her previous books, her racial identity as she (sometimes) and Lippincott (always) constructed it made her an insider able to access that which whites could not, and reviewers frequently responded to that construction. As one writer put it, "that what she says *about* the Negro comes *from* the Negro has an obvious significance" (Alsterlund 586). With *Tell My Horse*, Hurston's status as a black woman generated yet another response, one reductive, essentializing, and dismissive. Consider Courlander's claim: "The Voodoo resolves out of her anthropological training. But it is in her blood, and would be inevitable under any circumstances. As one observer said, 'She'd find Voodoo in anybody's kitchen'" (7). Such a comment indicates that in this case, Hurston's racial identity makes the veracity of what she reports suspect. If she would "find Voodoo in anybody's kitchen," then one must wonder about the truth, accuracy and perspective of her treatment of the subject, for clearly Voodoo, as a complex set of religious beliefs and cultural values, is not to be found in "anybody's kitchen." His comments also dismiss Hurston's training as a folklorist. For Hurston to find Voodoo was "inevitable"—because she was black. Carmer, who was also known as an authority on African American folklore, makes a similar claim that Hurston's race and "natural reactions" permitted her "to report the Haitian Negro's observance of folk customs" (Carmer, "In Haiti" 2). While he clearly believed that Hurston's race had given her access to ceremonies that might not have been accessible to whites, his references to her "natural reactions" smack of stereotyping and essentializing. What, exactly, in *Tell My Horse* did he imagine demonstrates Hurston's "natural reactions" rather than her training? Perhaps responding as a competitor, Courlander felt compelled to assign reasons for her success to race, which minimized and dismissed her achievement.

The anonymous reviewer for the *New York Times* made a similarly racist remark: "As a Negro author, Zora Hurston could not only go among the simple and secret people of the island hills and valleys but she could understand them. She could talk with them almost casually, listen to old legends [. . .] be received among the initiates at voodoo ceremonies, even photograph a real zombie" ("Lore of Haiti" 12). Probably without realizing it, this reviewer attributes Hurston's knowledge of Haitian French Creole and Haitian society to her racial heritage, rather than to her study of language and culture. The reviewer also reveals his or her cultural bias when describing the information Hurston assembled as "strange," as did Carmer.

Other comments, however, were more blatantly racist. The anonymous review in the *New Yorker* called *Tell My Horse* a "witches' brew bubbling in the stewpot of a transplanted African culture (71).[12] *New Republic*'s brief mention of *Tell My Horse* calls it "mumbojumbo translated for Americans, but still accompanied by the beat of the tom-toms" (155). Both comments call up primitivistic stereotypes that reveal the biases of the reviewers. In spite of having read Hurston's volume, obviously neither is willing to accept Voodoo as a legitimate religion. "Witches brew" dismisses, while "mumbojumbo" suggests the volume is a fabrication.

Still other readers were unsure of what they could accept as truth in the volume. Carmer's praise has an edge as he points out that the reader "has a hard time convincing himself that he is reading the authentic work of an honest, painstaking scholar" ("In Haiti" 2). We might take Carmer's comment at face value to mean that the atmosphere Hurston creates is horrifying, but it might also imply that she had pushed the limits of scholarly treatment. The anonymous reviewer for *New Republic* suggests his or her own skepticism by saying that Hurston's "sympathy" for Voodoo "comes close to belief" (155). The comment clearly indicates that the reviewer did not accept as fact the information Hurston recorded and felt a bit put off by her apparent acceptance of Voodoo and zombies as fact rather than myth.

Some reviewers for popular periodicals were more direct with their criticisms. Courlander complained about the lack of a glossary for translating the Creole and suggested that the volume was "not properly edited before publication." The material, he suggests to his readers, "was not completely digested" (7). The *New Yorker* called the volume "disorganized" (71). Courlander also criticized the photographs in the volume. They are "exceptionally good," he concedes, but he believes that many of the scenes depicted "were enacted in Port-au-Prince and accessible to the average run of tourists" (6). Gertrude Martin "would have liked for Miss Hurston to have given a few more facts to tie together [her] impressions." She also wondered if Hurston had failed to realize that black American women often fall victim to the same privileging of white features she notes among Jamaicans (19).

Reviewers who took a more scientific approach to *Tell My Horse* were also divided in their assessments. Henry Nash Smith, counselor in American history, Harvard University, and reviewer for the *Boston Evening Transcript*, generally praises the work. He suggests that Hurston's credentials and close observations lend a "vantage" that "dispels some of the spurious aura cast about voodoo by earlier writers." As a result, "the rites gain interest under Miss Hurston's careful study" (2). Edgar Thompson, writing for *Rural Sociology*, however, is far less positive. He compares *Tell My Horse* to the work of Melville Herskovits, who was to have advised Hurston, and finds Hurston's work lacking: "Dr. Herskovits, as evidenced in his *Life in a Haitian Valley*, was able to discover as much or more, to report what he discovered more systematically, and to interpret it more significantly" (261). The bulk of his review treats Voodoo and Herskovits's work, rather than *Tell My Horse*, the book under review.

The most caustic review, however, again came from a black, male reviewer. Alain Locke's brief treatment of the volume for his annual review of literature for *Opportunity* is dismissive, condescending, and critical: "Unless it be characterized as the breezy biography of a cult, Zora Neale Hurston's story of voodoo life in Haiti and Jamaica is more folklore and *belles lettres* than true human or social documentation." He assures readers that "[s]cientific folklore, [*Tell My Horse*] surely is not" ("The Negro" 38). He found it too full of "personal reactions and the piquant thrills of travelogue." More specifically, Locke indicts Hurston for her approach to the material: "Too much of *Tell My Horse* is anthropological gossip in spite of its many unforgettable word pictures" ("The Negro" 38). His criticisms are reminiscent of those he had for *Their Eyes*. Hurston, he thought, had used her gift for language for the wrong ends. Rather than documenting, he thought, she was gossiping. He found nothing of scientific or cultural value in *Tell My Horse*. Although Locke concedes that the photographs are "worth the price of the book" and that the "social and political criticism [. . .] is thought provoking," he is obviously skeptical of Hurston and her goals. Perhaps he intended to insult Hurston, whose credentials as a folklorist are repeatedly lauded in the earlier reviews of the volume. What is clear, however, is that Locke wanted to remove the protective and justifying label of anthropological research from her work. If it did not have scientific value, then it must be intended to entertain—and by implication—exploit, unfortunately a perception supported by Lippincott's marketing of the volume.

As a whole, reviewers sensed Hurston's struggle to balance her desire to dramatize with the need to report objectively what she had observed. Courlander pointed to "a constant conflict between anthropological truth and tale telling, between the obligation she feels to give the facts honestly and the attraction to (as one of her characters says in 'Mules and Men') the 'big old lies we tell when we're jus' sittin' around here on the store porch doin' nothing'" (6). Reviewers also were responding to Hurston's resisting the genre norms for folkloric work and her targeting two readerships with decidedly different needs. The unresolved tensions, coupled with Lippincott's exploitative advertising and existing concerns about Hurston's motives, undercut her legitimacy as a folklorist or anthropologist doing serious scholarly work.

The decreasing number of reviews and the increasing number of anonymous reviews suggest that critically Hurston had reached her zenith. *Tell My Horse* had offered her the opportunity to reassert herself as a serious scientist. Her extended essay on hoodoo in the *Journal of American Folklore* illustrates that she was capable of conforming to scholarly norms, but she resisted. She yoked her dramatizing narrative with anthropological detail. This lack of conformity to the conventions of scientific writing supported existing assumptions about Hurston's character and her motives: Uninterested in the larger social or cultural ramifications of her work, Hurston seemed interested only in selling books.

Writing *Moses, Man of the Mountain*

The fountainhead of *Moses* can be traced to Hurston's 1934 short story "The Fire and the Cloud." The story draws from Deuteronomy 31–34. As the Israelites prepare to cross the River Jordan without Moses, the 120-year-old leader selects Joshua as his successor. Retiring to the mountain of Nebo, Moses, according to the Bible, dies and is buried in a valley in the land of Moab.

Hurston's rendering relies largely on dialogue between Moses and a talking lizard. In Moses' conversation with the lizard, he reveals his isolation as leader and the people's lack of appreciation for his sacrifices. As the journey of God's chosen people ends, Moses is once again being called on to restrain their willful nature. To keep his impatient followers from crossing the River Jordan for another thirty days, Moses builds his own tomb and leaves his staff waiting for Joshua, his successor. Moses, in his final sacrifice, buries his role as leader. In his tomb, Moses inters "the voice of Sinai, the stretched-out arm of Moses, the lawgiver, and nationmaker" ("The Fire and the Cloud" 120). Out of respect for his apparent death, the people must remain where they are to mourn his passing. Moses, still living, crafts himself a new staff and walks away from his tomb. The Children of Israel need and have a new leader to take them into the Promised Land, and they must wait the prescribed thirty days to complete their journey. While Hurston's focus is more secular than religious in its exploration of the foibles of human nature and the struggle for freedom, she carefully draws from the Bible her description of the chosen ones as "stiff-necked people," a biblical adjective she uses verbatim.

Inspirations

Hemenway speculates that Hurston began expanding her study of Moses soon after completing the short story. She was working on a novel during the spring of 1935 (*Zora* 256). Over the following years, her research in Haiti apparently renewed her interest in the subject. At the least, her time abroad presented new perspectives on Mosaic lore. In *Tell My Horse* Hurston notes,

> All over Haiti it is well established that Damballah [head of the Rada gods] is identified with Moses, whose symbol was the serpent. This worship of Moses recalls the hard-to-explain fact that wherever the Negro is found, there are traditional tales of Moses and his supernatural powers that are not in the Bible, nor can they be found in any written life of Moses. [. . .] All over the Southern United States, the British West Indies and Haiti there are reverent tales of Moses and his magic. (378)

Lippincott had great hopes for the novel, and Carl Van Vechten told Hurston that *Moses* was "the best thing that [she had] done" (Hurston qtd. in Kaplan 422). Hurston, however, did not share their sense of enthusiasm when the book appeared the second week of November 1939.

Drawing from the tradition of comparing the bondage of African Americans to the slavery of God's chosen people and from a literary tradition replete with explorations of the Exodus, Hurston crafted a commentary on human nature and the struggle for emancipation. Earlier treatments by African American authors include Frances E. W. Harper's *Moses: A Story of the Nile* and Paul Laurence Dunbar's "Antebellum Sermon."[13]

Hurston's white contemporaries were also also using the Bible for creative inspiration. In addition to the numerous biblical films (more than forty) that appeared between 1908 and 1939 (Lowe 217), Hurston also saw white contemporary Roark Bradford's short stories stereotype southern blacks and their Christianity. Those stories inspired *The Green Pastures*, a widely successful play which Hurston despised. In addition, in 1928 Louis Untermeyer had published a novel based on Moses' life.[14] John Lowe speculates that Untermeyer's humorous treatment of Moses may have inspired Hurston's own approach to the biblical figure (213).

I would argue, however, that the most important influences on *Moses* come from Hurston's knowledge of and use of folklore. Her preface alludes to her knowledge of unwritten Mosaic lore she had collected in the American South and in Haiti. She understood the way legends grow. As an anthropologist and recorder of black cultural traditions, she wanted to inscribe the unwritten, culturally specific legends surrounding Moses as a powerful Voodoo master. Although Hurston clearly draws from African American culture, she makes an effort in the introduction to prevent readers from seeing the novel as *the* black American conception of the biblical leader. As she points out, "Asia and all the Near East are sown with legends of this character. They are so numerous that some students have come to doubt if the Moses of the Christian concept is real" (337). In short, Hurston crosses cultural traditions and treats the Pentateuch as *folklore* rather than as a sacred, static text.

Moses blends myths reflecting alternate perceptions of Moses and recasts them in black oral tradition. Hurston's rendering of the Pentateuch returns the tale to its oral foundations. As a written story enshrined in the King James Bible, the tale became static or "desiccated," to borrow Lowe's term (212). Hurston brings it back to life. At work in the novel are what folklorist Barre Toelken calls the twin laws of the folklore process (34–35). Folklore by nature evolves as new people tell the tale, as contexts for transmission change, and as a culture evolves. If folklore does not evolve to meet the needs of successive audiences, it loses its relevance and may cease to be transmitted. Not all elements of folklore evolve simultaneously, however. Select elements, "dynamic" ones, evolve to keep a story alive and maintain its relevance to contemporary life. As these elements change, other elements, "conservative" elements, remain the same. Conservatism is evident, for example, in Hurston's use of the plagues, the parting of the Red Sea, the burning bush. The dynamism is manifest in her use of hoodoo, dialect, contemporary social references, and personal relationships not detailed in written sources. The dynamism of tellers shaping tales for specific audiences produces what folklorists describe as variants and versions of tales, which are common. Novelist and raconteur Julius Lester, who notes Hurston as a profound influence on his work, explains it this way. Transmitting folklore is much like pouring water from one container to the other. The water, the essence of the story, remains basically the same, but the container, the taleteller, shapes the tale as she tells it, shaping it to her own time and audience (*Black Folktales* ix).[15]

As a folkloric taleteller, Hurston shares the tale in the language of her own time, complete with contemporary cultural references to make the tale newly relevant to African Americans' continuing struggle for equality in post-emancipation America. Although Hurston has frequently been accused of being politically and socially unconscious, her use of black vernacular—

both in dialogue and narration—helps establish parallels between the plights of the Hebrews living under Ramses, black Americans living under a discriminatory United States government, and European Jews living under Hitler. These parallels are also evident in the plot. When Moses as leader of the Egyptian military suggests integrating Hebrews into the military and extending voting rights, Pharaoh's negative response echoes those of white Americans who objected to extending suffrage and military service to black Americans. Likewise, when Moses attempts to focus on internal Egyptian problems rather than conquests abroad, his grandfather tells him, "'Egypt has no home problems that I can see,'" again mirroring American preferences for colonizing abroad rather than addressing problems at home (395).

Hurston's rendering challenges readers by transcending traditional Western binaries of secular and religious. Both exist simultaneously in *Moses* just as the serious themes of the story coincide with the humor it evokes. Readers, particularly Christians, must see beyond their own horizons and imagine a more culturally and genre-diverse aesthetic for what scholars term a novel. Like Hurston's irreverent treatment of bread in "The Book of Harlem," her rendering of Moses' story posed (and continues to pose) challenges for readers who may resist its dynamic elements or find troubling her use of humor in a classic biblical tale.

Historically, *Moses, Man of the Mountain* has been dismissed or neglected. More recently, critics have described *Moses* as a major novel, a masterpiece. Lowe, Plant, and Meisenhelder all successfully argue that Hurston's rhetorical strategies highlight elements of race, class, and gender. By blending allegory, parody, satire, and humor, Hurston takes aim at her characters, various groups and a wide range of issues. Aaron, Zipporah (Moses' wife), Jethro, Miriam, race leaders, patriarchy, greed, ambition, irresponsibility, the Hebrew people, the Egyptian leadership and America's governmentally sanctioned social inequality are all satirized at various times. While Plant argues that Hurston saw Moses as "the ideal to which other men should aspire" (127), I disagree. Moses, too, comes under scrutiny, much like the preacher does in *Jonah's Gourd Vine*. Moses, like John Buddy, is a man—human in his condescension toward women and his manipulation of people's desires for their own good.

A final factor influencing Hurston's treatment of Moses came from the looming threat of war in Europe. Richard Pells points out that in the late

1930s "many writers on the Left" began looking backward "for habits and precedents that had sustained the country through previous crises" (314). *New Masses* urged writers to reinterpret history and sought to illuminate "similarities between past and present." Hurston, staunchly anti-communist, ironically undertook this very process in *Moses*, but her contribution to reinterpretations of history went unrecognized. She could not afford to address inequities in American culture more directly. Situated between World War I and World War II, Hurston's developing text would have been restricted by a "repressive climate" (McDowell, "Lines of Descent" xvi). With World War II on the horizon and World War I within memory, McDowell speculates that Hurston recalled attempts on the part of the U.S. government during World War I to "stifle any publications that did not lend their full support to the war effort," a pattern that continued during World War II and was still perceptible two decades after the treaty of Versailles was signed (xvii). Had Hurston's criticism of the United States been more direct, she might have faced Lippincott's censorship, as she did with her autobiography.

Hurston's Rendering of the Exodus

Moses, Man of the Mountain generally follows the Pentateuch. As part of Hurston's exploration of racial issues, however, her account of Moses' birth diverges from the biblical account. She suggests that the Old Testament leader may well have been Egyptian, and the legend that he was a Hebrew child raised in the palace might well have originated in the Hebrew Miriam's excuse for her negligence in tending her little brother. Sent to watch her infant brother on the Nile, Miriam falls asleep and awakes to discover "[t]he child and his basket were gone, that was all" (363). Seeing the princess bathing nearby and removing a floating basket from the river, Miriam creates a story to stave off punishment from her mother—that the infant Hebrew child was in the basket the princess took from the river: "Others conceived and added details at their pleasure and the legends grew like grass" (371). As those in the palace question Moses' racial purity, the concept of pursuing purity is satirized. Who can prove his purity and to what end?

Similarly, Hurston fictionalizes Moses' childhood in the Egyptian palace, which the Bible does not detail. As an inquisitive child, Moses is guided by

Mentu, a storytelling stableman, who teaches Moses the ways of nature, equestrian skills, and strategies for warfare. From this mentor, Moses learns of the Book of Thoth, sunken in the river of Koptos and guarded by a deathless snake. Distracted by other responsibilities and unable to pursue the wisdom promised by the book, Moses becomes leader of the Egyptian military and triumphs against other nations. With Moses' conquests, his stature increases, and his jealous uncle plots to destroy him by spreading rumors that Moses is a Hebrew. Moses' interest in the plight of the Hebrew people and his murder of an Egyptian foreman further fuel speculation about where his loyalties lie. The Hebrew slaves he saved by murdering the Egyptian foreman repay their debt by telling Moses' secret: "The will to humble a man more powerful than themselves was stronger than the emotion of gratitude" (403). Warned by an attendant that Pharaoh plans to imprison him, Moses flees Egypt.

In the land of Midian, Moses takes Zipporah as a wife. For twenty years Moses worships the god of Jethro, his father-in-law, and studies magic, learning to turn water to blood and create a plague of frogs on command. Only after Pharaoh's death does Moses travel to Egypt to search for the Book of Thoth. Upon his return, he is able to "command the heavens and the earth, the abyss and the mountain, and the sea. He knew the language of the birds of the air, the creatures that people the deep and what the beasts of the wilds all said" (448). Having seen Moses fulfill his greatest desire, Jethro asks if his son-in-law might grant his own wish: to spread the word of God by converting the godless Hebrew people. Although resistant to Jethro's request, Moses consents when the burning bush asks the same of him.

Proving himself a man of service unconcerned with his own glory or the prospect of becoming a ruler, Moses uses his power as the world's greatest Voodoo practitioner to release the plagues on Egypt. Passover breaks Pharaoh's resolve, and he consents to the slaves' freedom. The Hebrew people, however, remain unprepared for what lies ahead. Hoping to fish and relax, the people see no need to leave Egypt immediately, but Moses insists and leads them to the edge of the Red Sea where he parts the waters so they can cross. In keeping with biblical tradition, Pharaoh reverses his decision and pursues the Hebrews through the sea only to drown when the walls of water descend.

Although crossing the Red Sea means the Hebrews are free of Pharaoh, they are far from free in spirit, and Hurston begins to explore the psychology of freedom through her cast of biblical characters. With each new obstacle on their journey to the Promised Land, the people turn to Moses, expecting him to provide for all of their needs. They are unwilling to take responsibility for their own well-being and even long for the security of slavery. They question Moses' motives, and when Zipporah, Moses' wife, joins the travelers, Miriam's jealousy at her loss of power intensifies. Moses' rise to power displaces Miriam as a prophet, and Zipporah's beauty and jewels attract the envy of all the Hebrew women, who no longer look to Miriam as leader or model.

When Moses ascends Mount Sinai for forty days to receive God's commandments, the people are quick to doubt their leader and their newly found God. As in the Bible, Hurston's Hebrews cast a golden calf to worship under the leadership of Miriam and Aaron. In the power struggle that follows, Miriam and Aaron claim they, like Moses, have been called by God and deserve status equal to that of Moses. They also use Zipporah's dark skin as a means of attacking Moses, saying, "the ladyfolks don't want her ruling over them, dark as she is" (556). To resolve the issue, Moses leads them to the tabernacle where Miriam receives her punishment for self-serving ambition: seven days of leprosy. Ironically, Hurston points out, Aaron, her coconspirator and maker of the golden cow, remains unpunished.

In the years that follow, Moses rejects the people's desire to name him king. He would, he says, rather lead than rule. Zipporah, who had her own ambitions, returns to Midian with her hopes of becoming a queen unfulfilled. Despite their increasing power, however, the people still complain: "We want fresh meat and vegetables and fish and fruit and if we don't get it, we can get another leader that can take us back to Egypt" (562). On the edge of Canaan, the people fight their first battle without Moses or the Ark of the Covenant and lose. Moses, in order to "grow men and women in the place of slaves," leads the people of Israel into the wilderness for forty years in hope that "'the third generation [under his leadership] will feel free and noble'" (570).

Following their years of wandering, the Hebrews rest on the shores of the River Jordan, and Moses, near the end of his service, ascends Mount Nebo. As Hurston had done in "The Fire and the Cloud," she recreates Moses' last moments. Pleased with the sounds of life in the valley below,

Moses reflects on his failure "to make a perfect people, free and just" (590). He recognizes that "no man may make another free. Freedom was something internal [. . .] the man himself must make his own emancipation" (590). Moses' reflections are crucial to interpretations of the novel as an interrogation of freedom and emancipation. Here is the marrow: Hurston's belief that true freedom can neither be taught nor purchased nor given. It must come from within the individual. Self-serving Miriam and Aaron represent the moral corruption and impotence of self-proclaimed "race leaders." While Meisenhelder argues that Moses relinquishes the more egalitarian religion of his youth in favor of a patriarchal one, he does emerge as the best of the three, sacrificing to serve the people (128–29). The complexity of Moses' character indicates Hurston's appreciation for the flaws in all leaders, even those divinely sanctioned.

From my own horizon, Hurston's message is innately political, timely, and important. Race leaders who assume power to better themselves cannot improve the race as whole. Leadership requires self-sacrifice, and freedom requires an individual, sometimes arduous journey—not a proclamation. The self constructed in order to survive oppression must be transformed to partake of spiritual, emotional, and psychological freedom. Such a reading of the novel clearly would cast it as "political," for what could be more political in America in 1939 than the struggle for freedom? Black Americans were still fighting for equality in a nation founded on democratic principles, while Hitler loomed on the European horizon. Most reviewers, however, discussed other issues.

Marketing Mired in the Past

This book, more than any other of Hurston's, reflects the power of Lippincott's marketing tactics to situate her in the literary marketplace and to create bias. The dust jacket and advertisements Lippincott created for the novel confirmed the worst assumptions about Hurston's agenda and her character. While Lippincott's use of racially charged language is less noticeable on this book cover than on the cover for *Tell My Horse*, the publisher's attempt to connect Hurston to a previous hit, *The Green Pastures*, was an incredibly powerful and damning decision.

The front cover of the novel depicts a bearded Moses holding the tablet

Fig. 8. Dust jacket of *Moses, Man of the Mountain* (1939), author's copy. Used with the permission of the Zora Neale Hurston Trust.

on which God inscribed the Ten Commandments. The top of the inside flap says, "Moses, from the point of view of the American Negro, as the great 'Voodoo Man' of the Bible." What follows is a summary that probably created more confusion than clarity for Hurston's readers, for Lippincott's description creates questions about the volume's genre. Lippincott's clues to readers suggest the volume is both a biography and folklore, each genre of course having very different conventions from those of the novel, a work of fiction. Admittedly, *Moses* fails to fall neatly into any genre, but rather than marketing the volume as a blending, an experimental exploration, or an innovation, Lippincott vacillated between established, inadequate genre labels.

The first paragraph of text introduces the volume: "This life of Moses, the greatest and most fascinating character in the Old Testament, is more than a biography." Immediately readers face the question of whether the volume is a biography. Readers of biography, perhaps naively, expect to learn facts, while readers of folklore expect a rendition of an often-told tale. Each genre has its own conventions, and experienced readers bring to texts knowledge of those conventions. Implicitly, a reader measures one text by others in the same genre. Thus the contradictory literary labels of "biography" and "folklore" establish bias and invite confusion about what readers should expect of the volume.

In the remainder of the first paragraph, Lippincott emphasizes Hurston, as author, rather than the contents of the volume. Hurston, "in her inimitable way," it says, "treats the great leader from the point of the American Negro—as the great 'Voodoo Man' of the Bible." Twice in fifteen lines of text Lippincott identifies the perspective of the author as "Negro" and associates Moses with Voodoo, the controversial subject of Hurston's previous book. Hurston "brings to Moses's life all the characteristic brilliance she showed in her previous books." As with *Tell My Horse*, the descriptions of the volume as "characteristic" of Hurston's work and her "inimitable way" would have attracted fans of her earlier works and from one perspective suggest praise. At the same time, however, another horizon of expectations exists for those skeptical of or offended by Hurston's earlier works. The phrases must have raised the suspicions of readers who already had questions about Hurston's literary agenda and those who had already assigned her the label of sellout.

Also of importance is that when Lippincott listed Hurston's other works, the publisher chose to identify by name her two collections of folklore, suggesting that perhaps it hoped the volume would have folkloric appeal. Descriptions of *Tell My Horse* and *Mules and Men* also appear on the back cover. Consider, too, that the dust jacket twice identifies the story as "from the point of view of the American Negro," suggesting it has a foundation in folklore. So, again, readers of the dust jacket confront the question of genre. Nothing on the dust jacket suggests that *Moses* is a novel although recent scholarship treats it as one.

As readers turn to the back flap, the publisher makes an unexpected (given past marketing tactics), vague, and largely ignored attempt to make the novel socially relevant: "The retelling of the story of Hebrew persecution and bondage in Egypt has special significance today because the modern Hebrew is undergoing a similar fate in some parts of the world at this time." The passage of course alludes to Hitler's attempt to exterminate European Jews. The parallels between Hurston's volume and current events was not lost on all of her initial readers. Annie Nathan Meyer, one of Hurston's early patrons and herself Jewish, wrote J. Bertram Lippincott about those similarities, and at least one reviewer picked up on the same issue.[16] Most of Hurston's reviewers, however, were sidetracked by the closing paragraph on the inside of the dust jacket.

In the final paragraph devoted to *Moses*, Lippincott, as it had in marketing *Mules and Men*, tried using a celebrity text to position the volume in the literary market. Lippincott promises readers, "The majesty of the old Bible story is here, but in addition there is the special feeling the Negro has always had for Moses as the great magician—the greatest voodoo man of all. The play *The Green Pastures* had this same feeling in its portrayal of the Negro conception of God. Now, Zora Hurston, with her singular genius for interpreting her race, writes a book that is unique and unforgettable." *The Green Pastures*, by Marc Connelly, had been phenomenally popular in 1930, and Lippincott must have hoped that associating Hurston's work with the play would attract readers, and it might have. The same connection, however, would have made other readers dismiss *Moses* and conclude that Hurston was exploiting black culture.

Inspired by Roark Bradford's short stories, the play portrays African Americans as stereotypically simple and childlike. The plot centers on the transformation of biblical stories for a black Sunday school class (that cannot understand its lesson) into black vernacular and stereotypically black cultural contexts. Readers who had found Bradford's or Connelly's treatments of black life simplistic, reductive, or condescending would have assumed that Hurston approached her characters and subjects in the same way.

As it had with Hurston's other books, Lippincott invites sightseeing, and connecting Hurston to *The Green Pastures* would have done nothing to allay fears about the *way* Hurston was portraying black life. A 1939 reader of *Moses, Man of the Mountain* might have been attracted to Hurston's work for its anthropological value or because of an interest in the Bible or biblical history. Yet within the horizon of expectations, much more critical responses to the dust jacket were also possible. Readers of the dust jacket came to its text with already established biases that might have included knowledge of Hurston's other works, knowledge of concerns about her literary agenda, and knowledge of *The Green Pastures*. All of these elements helped form the biases of readers, particularly reviewers.

Lippincott's use of the play to promote Hurston's work suggests, as I have elsewhere, that she played no role in determining how to market her work. Hurston detested this play. In "Girl Stalks Negro Lore," an interview from 1934–35, Hurston argued that Connelly's hit was a "good spectacle, but damned poor Negro" (J. Mitchell n. pag.). In 1937, just the year before *Moses* appeared, Hurston expressed similar sentiments in "The Chick with One Hen," her response to Alain Locke's review of *Their Eyes*. She recalled his appreciation for *The Green Pastures*, which she considered "'anything you want to call it but the truth'" (qtd. in Lowe 251 n. 11). Hurston intended to correct Connelly's racist interpretation. We can only imagine Hurston's response to Lippincott's marketing. She must have been frustrated and angered at seeing her attempt to correct racist depictions of folk religion described in the very terms she sought to challenge.

On November 5 the first advertisement appeared in the *New York Times Book Review*. While the top of the full-page Lippincott ad is dominated by Christopher Morley's *Kitty Foyle*, the bottom right one third promotes Hurston's forthcoming novel. It is the only advance advertisement for her work, suggesting the high hopes Lippincott had for sales. The content of the ad, taken out of context, might appear benign, but in the context of Hurston's evolving reputation, the consequences of Lippincott's imaging of the novel are clear. The top of the ad describes *Moses* as offering "[t]he stark simplicity of 'THE GREEN PASTURES'" and "the majestic chords of a Negro Spiritual" (*Book Review* 23). While Lippincott hoped the association would attract readers (and it may have attracted some white ones), it almost certainly also drove away some. The implication was that Hurston, like Connelly, drew on and exploited negative stereotypes that white readers would find comforting or acceptable. In addition, the play's financial success, coupled with concerns about Hurston's agenda, led some reviewers to speculate that money had been the driving force behind her depiction of Moses.

The ad, like the dust jacket, asserts that Hurston represents Moses as "seen through the eyes of the American Negro" (*Book Review* 23), a statement that directly contradicts her introduction to the novel. She explains that the conception of Moses as a magician "is not confined to Negroes. In America there are countless people of other races depending upon mystic symbols and seals and syllables said to have been used by Moses to work his

Fig. 9. Advertisement for *Moses, Man of the Mountain* (1939). *New York Times Book Review* November 5, 1939: 23.

wonders" (337–38). Lippincott, however, was in the business of selling books, and its strategy again relied on implications that black Americans have quaint, unusual ways that white readers can access through Hurston's work.

By November 26 the advertisement is topped by "'A truly extraordinary quality.'" A description building on the first ad reads, "Here in the simple, sensitive spirit of 'The Green Pastures,' is the Book of Exodus as it would be written by the American Negro tradition. Moses has always been the Negro's favorite Biblical character—the powerful, wonder-working Voodoo 'let my people go'" (19). How the advertising department at Lippincott reached the conclusion that *Moses, Man of the Mountain* is "simple" or "sensitive" is a puzzle. What follows, however, compounds the effects of linking *Moses* to *The Green Pastures* by again suggesting that Connelly's interpretations—and by implication Bradford's short story interpretations of black life which had inspired Connelly—were accurate: "Miss Hurston, as one of the foremost interpreters of her race, here presents Moses in a fresh, vivid, human role" (*Book Review* 19). By describing Hurston as "one of the foremost interpreters of her race," Lippincott attempts to establish her credentials and the authenticity of her novel. The statement also creates an insider/outsider dichotomy implying that Lippincott anticipated a white readership. It is after all *her* race Hurston writes about, not *our* race.

The horizon of expectations for these ads is broad, given Hurston's status and concerns about her literary agenda. Those unfamiliar with her work might have been attracted by Lippincott's attempt to establish her as "[t]he world's outstanding Negro author" (*Book Review* 19). Those who had liked Hurston's earlier works might also have been attracted. But middle-class blacks or black readers who had never even considered the possibility of Moses as a Voodoo master would have been bewildered, angry, or disturbed by the implication that her comedic treatment represented their conception of Moses. And finally, those readers who had been troubled by Hurston's earlier works would have found in comparisons of *Moses* and *The Green Pastures* confirmation that she was indeed exploiting stereotypes for financial gain. Any and all of these responses would have become mediating factors creating bias for readers who ventured beyond the image into the pages of *Moses, Man of the Mountain*.

A brief look at the advertising for Richard Wright's books that appeared both before and after *Moses* provides a sharp contrast. Lippincott's and Harper and Brothers' strategies for marketing the two authors are substantially different. While Harper and Brothers did little advertising for *Uncle Tom's Children* in the New York Sunday papers, *Native Son* is the only book from the period by a black writer that garnered larger and more frequent advertisements than Hurston's works.

Uncle Tom's Children earns only three lines in a full-page Harper and Brothers ad. The quote from reviewer Lewis Gannett claims, "Terror grips you as you read these swift-moving tales of black life. This man can write" (17). This brief description labels the subject matter as "black life," but the ad neither labels the author as African American nor invokes stereotypes. The passage "this man can write" indicates the writing is powerful, but nothing entices white readers to venture into black life.

With the publication of *Native Son*, Harper and Brothers' strategy included promoting Wright as a "Spokesman" for "an entire Race" (*Book Review* 21), claiming authority for Wright's work but not the authenticity that Lippincott claimed for Hurston's. *Native Son* is the "amazing drama of American life which received an unprecedented critical ovation" that has "immediately established its author as one of America's most distinguished novelists, compared by critics to Steinbeck, Dreiser, and Dostoevski" (21).

Grapes of Wrath, which had appeared the previous year and critiqued the plight of America's migrant workers, is repeatedly the celebrity text Harper and Brothers uses to promote *Native Son*. Everything in Harper and Brothers' advertising suggests the novel is important and current. Nothing links either book to stereotypes, although some readers have felt the violence and lack of humanity of Bigger Thomas, Wright's *Native Son* protagonist, evoke stereotypes of the violent, depraved black male.[17] Instead, the ads stress that Wright presents something new and powerful. The publisher indicates that Wright's subject is African American life and that he is African American (often with a photo), but the ads fail to create the titillating insider/outsider dichotomy Lippincott exploits. Readers are compelled to purchase *Uncle Tom's Children* and *Native Son*—not enticed.

The difference is subtle but real. There is nothing in the ads for *Uncle Tom's Children* or *Native Son* that mirrors the racially charged, stereotype-laden language Lippincott used to market Hurston's work. Admittedly, her *Moses, Man of the Mountain* is substantially different from the books Wright published, but the approach Harper and Brothers used to market Wright invites speculation that Hurston's reputation might have fared better had she worked with a different publisher.

Reading *Moses, Man of the Mountain*

In general, readers of Hurston's fifth book were intrigued but not overwhelmed by her portrait of Moses. Connecting her novel to *The Green Pastures* drew a wide array of responses, and most were not what the publisher was hoping for. Only a handful of reviewers considered the political implications of the novel. Three of those reviewers were writing for predominantly black audiences, and they appreciated what they felt was Hurston's treatment of race issues. Ironically, however, once again, black men were Hurston's harshest critics, reminding us—as Hazel Carby points out—that "we must be historically specific and aware of the differently oriented social interests within one and the same sign community" (*Reconstructing* 17).

General praise came from *College English* where the anonymous reviewer promises that "[o]f all the fall books none is more fascinating than this retelling of the story of Hebrew persecution" ("In Brief" 465). The *New Yorker*'s "Briefly Noted Fiction" section calls it "[t]he real thing, warm, humorous, poetic" (75). Carl Carmer, a fan of *Tell My Horse*, also appreciated *Moses*, calling it "a fine Negro novel" that reveals Hurston's "uncommon gifts as a novelist."[18] He also appreciated her "use of Negro speech rhythms to tell the story" (5). Percy Hutchinson, too, praises the novel as "an exceptionally fine piece of work far off the beaten tracks" (Review 21). Hazel Griggs, writing for the Associated Negro Press, describes the style of the book as "distinctly Hurston": "poetic weaving shot through with sparkling Negro witticisms and the strong fabric of the Negro's philosophy" ("Moses" 20). She says, "he really lives for the reader" (20). *Booklist* told its readers that the volume has "a Negro folklore quality that is warm and human" (150). Beatrice Murphy's response to the novel surprised her. She admits to readers that "Miss Hurston rather gets under my skin because, while conceding the fact that she knows her own race, I can never quite forgive her for the subtle and patronizing ways in which she pokes fun at its members" (n. pag.). Despite the mediation of her past responses to Hurston's work, she found the book compelling, telling readers, "I couldn't put it down." In the end she promises readers "that you can't afford to miss 'Moses.' You will enjoy it" (n. pag.).

Those who liked the book offered more substantive assessments than most reviewers had of *Tell My Horse*. Griggs suggests that "[t]he race question is the underlying theme of the book, having been the dominant issue of the time, and the problems Moses encounters trying to help his oppressed people are strikingly similar to current situations faced by today's leaders" (20). Richard Greenleaf made a similar connection, and in the process rejected Lippincott's attempts to situate the novel in the marketplace. "[T]he jacket of the book" indicates the novel is

> Zora Hurston's presentation of Moses as 'the great Voodoo man.' Much will be said (the publishers start the ball rolling here too, by a neat trick of misdirection) about the plight of the Hebrews in the days of Pharaoh and their plight now in the day of Hitler. This last point is of course important, but I cannot accept either of these as the principal aspect of the book. Zora Hurston, I think, has taken this way of telling the story of the forging of her own people. (n. pag.)

He then quotes from the novel about the ongoing difficulties of creating and maintaining freedom, suggesting in the end that he read the novel as an examination of emancipation that "bear[s] study by black and white, Jew and Gentile" (n. pag.). Griggs, too, made the connection between Hitler's treatment of the Jews and Hurston's novel (20).

Philip Slomovitz made a similar connection between the novel and American history and praises Hurston's "biography" of Moses as "invaluable": "Her distinctive contribution is her brilliant study of the problem of emancipation, done as perhaps only a Negro could do it" (1504). He describes *Moses* as "a splendid study of slave emancipation." These reviewers approach the novel as a serious contribution to American discourses on race relations, and yet other reviewers found the novel entirely devoid of social value.

Most criticisms of the novel deal with Hurston's execution. May Cameron told her readers that although "[t]he experiment is bold," Hurston "was not so successful with her venture as she manifestly thinks she was" (16). She points to "all its frequent faults—such as impossibly clumsy dialogue" and "horrifying words such as 'teenincy,'" but she ultimately recommends it as "a book for anyone's money" (16). Slomovitz's one criticism is that the novel "is weak in its interpretation of the ethical contributions of the prophet and in its treatment of the code of laws handed down by him" (1504). Louis Untermeyer was more generally disappointed: "[T]he whole is less successful than the parts, and the total effect is that of unfilled expectation" ("Review" 11).

The harshest critic of such formal issues or of Hurston's execution is George Schuyler, who had liked her earlier books, but was particularly critical in his assessment of this one. While Schuyler concedes that the book is "readable" and contains "much of the homely wit and corner-store philosophy which is the author's stock in trade," he also warns readers that "[t]aken as a whole 'Moses' is pedestrian, insincere, and alive with annoying incongruities. It is, to be brief, painfully disappointing, and there are times when one wonders why it was published at all" ("Looks" 7). The concept, he points out, had great potential to capture the Moses of "the country Negro preacher lecturing to his flock" or the opportunity to "tell the story of the Exodus from [a] proletarian class angle" (7). Instead, however, he argues that the novel is an "inadequate re-hash": "What could have been a masterpiece becomes little better than burlesque, interspread with cotton-patch dialect" (7). He also complains about inconsistencies in that dialect.

In addition to revealing their likes and dislikes, reviewers also revealed the mediating power of Lippincott's marketing. Lippincott's claim that *Moses* is "the Negro version" of Moses' life is repeatedly echoed. Greenleaf, Untermeyer, the anonymous reviewer for *College English*, Slomovitz, Carmer, and Hutchinson all made the mistake Lippincott's marketing department made in designing the dust jacket and in advertising the novel. Hurston's introduction to the novel works to undo this perception, but most readers missed her attempt to guide them. Lippincott's marketing created a powerful bias, as would have readers' own stereotypical perceptions of Hurston and African Americans in general.

That some reviewers read *Moses* through such stereotypical lenses is clear in their commentary. Hutchinson's review states outright what the others only imply by their references to *Moses* as "the Negro" conception: "All primitive peoples have an inordinate love of magic or what appears to be magic and the African most of all." Here Hutchinson reveals his bias, which is a condescending attitude toward "primitive peoples." For him this group includes people of African descent. He suggests that Hurston's endowment of Moses with powers that other conceptions of Moses attribute to God "is undoubtedly due to the fact that it was easier for a primitive mind to endow a human being with mystical power than to grasp a purely rational concept of deity" (21). Hutchinson never even entertains the possibility that his own conception of Moses (or God for that matter) is one of many of equal value.

While many reviewers suggest that Hurston's portrait presents *the* "Negro" perception of Moses, three readers were more discerning, and it should come as no surprise that all three were writing for a primarily black audience. Arthur Spingarn in his mention of *Moses* in his annual review of literature for *Crisis* carefully describes the volume as "[t]he story of the life and death of Moses as seen through the eyes of *a* Negro" ("Books" 46; emphasis mine). Griggs's review for the Associated Negro Press explains to readers that "the story of the people of Goshen is told from the point of view of *a member* of another oppressed people" (20; emphasis mine). Murphy describes the novel as "told from the point of view of an American" (n. pag.).[19] Again the difference in word choice is subtle but significant.

Another powerful source of mediation was the publisher's proposed connection between *Moses* and *The Green Pastures*, which a number of reviewers discuss. Percy Hutchinson reaches back to Roark Bradford, whose fiction inspired *The Green Pastures*, for comparison. Again, any resemblance had serious ramifications. *The Green Pastures* and Bradford's fiction, for many readers, suggest condescension and stereotype, both of which became mediating factors not only for reviewers but also for those reading their reviews.

Carmer, like Hutchinson, also mentions Bradford but attempts to transcend the mediation of stereotypes by promising that "Miss Hurston's characters are less naive." Hurston's have "much the same humor, the same directness, but they are more sophisticated and more wise—as befits a serious novel" ("Biblical" 11). Greenleaf, too, argues that the condescension of *The Green Pastures* and other similar works, "good and bad," "is made impossible by Zora Hurston's book" (n. pag.).

Untermeyer also made the connection only to reject it outright, but for other reasons. He did not see *The Green Pastures* as condescending, but he believed the comparison was unfair to the play, doing *it* a disservice: "The publishers imply that Miss Hurston's fifth book has the same feeling as 'The

Green Pastures' in its portrayal of the Negro conception of 'our' Christian God. But this is unfair to both volumes. If Miss Hurston's fantasy lacks the combination of humor and poignancy which characterized the Roark Bradford-Marc Connelly collaboration, it has a genre quality of its own" ("Review" 11). Untermeyer does not associate the play with stereotypes but finds Hurston's novel too different from the play for comparison. In fact, his comments suggest he preferred *The Green Pastures* for the "humor and poignancy" others found offensive.

Unlike Untermeyer, Hurston's by-now frequent critic Alain Locke thought the comparison a fair one, but his evaluation of the play and Hurston were very much to her disadvantage. His criticisms echo his assessments of *Their Eyes Were Watching God*, but in this review, he is more direct and more accusative. He condemns the novel as a "cleverly adapted *Green Pastures* in conception, point of view, and execution," suggesting that Hurston's treatment of her characters and subject matter exploits and condescends. But still more surprising is that Locke finds *The Green Pastures* superior to Hurston's *Moses*: "[L]acking the vital dramatization that superb acting gave to *Green Pastures*, it sinks back to the level of the original Roark Bradford." Believing the novel "caricature instead of portraiture," he asks readers, "What if the stereotyping is benign instead of sinister, warmly intimate instead of cynical or condescending?" ("Dry Fields" 7).

Locke takes issue with Hurston's conception and her ideological "perspective," to borrow Richard Wright's term. The larger context of his "Annual Review of Literature" suggests why he found the novel so offensive. Again, almost as if the essay were written with Hurston in mind, he opens with a delineation of "two traditions in the portrayal of Negro life and characters: the realistic and the romantic" ("Dry Fields" 4). In the next paragraph, Locke connects *The Green Pastures* to the romantic tradition which focuses on the "poetically picturesque," "the naive, the zestful and the exuberantly imaginative," all of which he sees as "baneful social misrepresentat[ions]." Demonstrating his interest in protest literature and social criticism, he hopes that "the recent vogue of *Grapes of Wrath*" will interest more readers in realistic fiction ("Dry Fields" 4). It hardly seems a coincidence that his paragraph-long assessment of *Moses, Man of the Mountain* mentions *The Green Pastures* as well.

Why is it Locke failed to see the political import other critics recognized?

The lens through which he read *Moses* was shaped by specific factors not present for other reviewers. Locke and Hurston had a long history together. He had reviewed all of her books and increasingly found them lacking. While he had initially supported her use of folk life, his review of *Their Eyes Were Watching God* had promoted Hurston's virulent response, creating (or perhaps exacerbating) a personal bias against her. In addition, Hurston's previous apolitical stance had violated Locke's artistic and social agenda. His review, then, was shaped in part by the fact that he did not *expect* Hurston to address political concerns. Other readers of *Moses, Man of the Mountain* came to the text without those preexisting biases.

Locke also had a literary agenda, which the novel violated. The larger context of his annual retrospective of literature clearly reveals the measuring stick by which he assessed the novel. Locke's frustration stemmed from his feeling that "picturesque" treatments of black life were giving most readers, black and white, what they wanted, rather than what they needed. He was frustrated by the reality that "folk life, as poetically picturesque, enjoys a more than ten-to-one advantage over folk life as prosaically pictorial. A small section of reformists, a disillusioned intelligentsia, will accept sociological realism [. . .] but on the whole and in the long run, romantic versions of life, especially minority life, are bound to have a greater currency and popularity." If, as Locke claims, Hurston was indulging in the romantic and stereotypical, then she was not providing readers with the kind of fiction he felt they *needed* to be reading. He asserts, "We need more informative and less escapist literature and art" ("Dry Fields" 4). As a well-educated woman, Hurston should have been a member of Locke's "intelligentsia" and should have been willing to meet her social responsibilities.

Locke's implication is that Hurston had sold out for financial reasons, and Schuyler reaches the same conclusion. He opens his review with the suggestion that "the pecuniary success of 'The Green Pastures'" motivated Hurston's *Moses, Man of the Mountain* ("Looks" 7). Ralph Ellison reached a similar conclusion two years later. He tells readers of *New Masses* that "the blight of calculated burlesque" has "marred most of her writing" ("Recent" 24). Hurston's treatment of Moses he describes as "a fictional biography" that "sets out to do for Moses what *The Green Pastures* did for Jehovah; for Negro fiction it did nothing" (24). Notice that he describes the burlesque as *calculated*, suggesting that Hurston had deliberately distorted black life. His reference to *The Green Pastures* indicates the enduring power of Lippincott's comparison.

The Big Picture

When *Their Eyes Were Watching God* appeared in 1937, most black critics believed they had already seen enough of Hurston's work to conclude that she exploited stereotypes for white readers. *Tell My Horse* offered her the opportunity to redeem herself in the eyes of her critics. Although the subject of Voodoo is controversial and is easily sensationalized, Hurston might have approached the subject as an anthropologist, rather than as a novelist reporting anthropological data. Her early work in the *Journal of American Folklore* proves she was capable. Had she uncovered the secret of zombies and had she felt safe continuing her research in Haiti, she might have been more inclined to write the definitive—and by implication scientific—study of Voodoo, which was her original goal. Her sudden illness, her personal inclinations, and pressure from her publisher undoubtedly combined, however, to push Hurston toward creating a book that the average reader might find appealing. And for Lippincott, attracting such a readership meant that the more sensational the volume was, the better. That reality alone, however, would not have generated all of the reviewers' criticisms of *Tell My Horse*. The relatively haphazard manner in which the material appears and the poor editing suggest that Lippincott rushed the volume to press. The consequences included criticisms directed not only at Hurston's approach to her subject but also at the form. Although her volume is now considered an important resource for those interested in Haitian Voodoo, the impact of the text on her critical reputation in 1939 was negative. Readers who were suspicious but unconvinced that Hurston was guilty of exploitation would almost surely have found the volume to be a confirmation, and those already convinced of her guilt would have found their views unchallenged.

Moses, Man of the Mountain only compounded the effect. Obviously, Lippincott connected the novel to *The Green Pastures* in hopes that the play's popularity would translate into book sales. Instead, the connection suggested that readers see in Hurston's work the same stereotypes that nine years earlier had made the play a success. Lippincott's decision was an ironic and powerful one that delivered two blows to Hurston's reputation. Not only did she appear guilty of creating stereotypical images of African Americans, but she was also writing outside the dominant literary trends of the period, which stressed social and group commitments.

When *Moses* appeared, protest fiction was at or near its peak. Wright's 1938 collection of short stories *Uncle Tom's Children* had sold well, in addition to being a critical success.[20] Confrontations between blacks and racist southern whites link the stories. Steinbeck's study of exploited, starving farm workers, *The Grapes of Wrath*, appeared the same year *Moses* did. When *Native Son* followed in 1940, it sold 250,000 copies the first year (Rampersad, "Introduction" xxvi). In contrast, none of Hurston's books "sold more than 5,000 copies before going out of print" (Hemenway, *Zora* 6). Her exploration of slavery and emancipation has clear political implications, and the novel might have been marketed as an innovative contribution to the protest tradition—a move that would likely have bolstered sales and Hurston's sagging reputation. Lippincott, however, drew from the popular stereotypes of the 1920s to situate the novel in the marketplace.

Reading *Moses, Man of the Mountain* as "the majestic strains of the Negro spiritual" excludes Hurston from being a serious artist; nevertheless, during this period she was thinking seriously about her own work and the role of the black artist. In January 1938, after finishing *Tell My Horse*, she directly revealed for the first time one of her aesthetic principles: resist convention. Hurston wrote "Art and Such" to be included anonymously in the projected WPA volume *The Florida Negro*. Here she confronts the attitude that "a tragic" accident makes a person "Negro" ("Art and Such" 907). This conception, popular among what Hurston terms "Race Leader[s]," had influenced Florida arts. The pressure on black artists to explore the "sorrows" of their race stifled their individuality. The creative result, Hurston argues, is that "the same old theme, the same old phrases get done again to the detriment of art" (908). The writer who believes he has been brave in championing his race, she argues, has in fact taken "the line of least resistance and least originality—certain to be approved" (908). Conforming to this pressure "precluded originality and denied creation in the arts" (909).

She continues in the essay by discussing her own work in the third person. Hurston, she explains, had introduced "two new things in Negro fiction." The first returns to the reviews of her first novel, *Jonah's Gourd Vine*. Reviewers of the novel had repeatedly praised her "objective point of view" that portrayed American blacks "without bias." The second element she had introduced was telling a story "in the idiom—not the dialect—of the Negro." Hurston had begun to write with the rhythm, idiom, and humor of black folk culture rather than simply altering spelling to reflect a changed pronunciation. The approach lent "verisimilitude to the narrative by stewing the subject in its own juice" ("Art and Such" 910).

The essay reveals Hurston's tenacious drive to create without being pressured by either bigots or race leaders. It remained unpublished until 1990, however, so her contemporaries could only speculate about what motivated her to continue producing work that could be used to bolster negative stereotypes. Money was the obvious answer.

Hurston's 1938 essay reveals little about the feelings engendered by negative reviews of her work, but it portends her continued approach to her art. Rather than conform to "the line of least resistance," she stayed her course. In addition, the issue of Lippincott's influence looms large and raises questions about the kind of work Hurston might have produced had her publisher been more supportive of folklore with a better defined audience and more willing to confront racial issues. The criticisms of *Tell My Horse* and *Moses, Man of the Mountain*, however, did not deter Hurston from seeking her own way. When her autobiography appeared three years later, she had again written a text that challenged convention.

FIVE

"The Tragedies of Life"

> I regret all of my books. It is one of the tragedies of life that one cannot have all the wisdom one is ever to possess in the beginning. Perhaps it is just as well to be rash and foolish for a while. If writers were too wise, perhaps no books would be written at all.
>
> [P]eople are prone to build a statue of the kind of person it pleases them to be.
>
> —*Dust Tracks on a Road*

When Zora Neale Hurston wrote in *Dust Tracks on a Road* that she regretted all of her books, she surely meant to include her autobiography. Hurston was trying to "build a statue of the kind of person" she wanted to be with her life story, and yet the statue built in the pages of *Dust Tracks*, as it appeared in 1942, hardly represents the person she was. The drafting and revision processes for the book were difficult. The version Lippincott printed, for years the only one available to readers, is 10 percent shorter than the final version Hurston submitted to the publisher (Wall, "Note" 983). Only in 1995 did the Library of America editions of Hurston's work restore the passages Lippincott excised from the last draft and simultaneously make available four chapters eliminated during the revision process.[1] In part due to her revisions and Lippincott's editing, the effects of *Dust Tracks on a Road* on Hurston's literary reputation were among the tragedies of her life.

Initially, it might have seemed that *Dust Tracks* would be a success. It won the 1943 Anisfield Award for "creative literature" that deals with "racial problems" ("1943 Anisfield Awards" 11). And yet, important critics—black and white—were highly critical of Hurston's treatment of race. Hurston resisted discussing her own experiences with racism, fighting the genre expectations of African American autobiography. Her resistance of these norms and her sometimes effusive thanks to white patrons made the volume suspect for her contemporaries and continues to discomfit readers today.[2] When it appeared, the autobiography made Hurston a sought-after celebrity who interpreted black America for white readers and confirmed critics' perceptions that she was an opportunist. She appeared to be exploiting herself and oversimplifying the realities of black life in America in order to avoid offending white readers. An ill-timed newspaper interview reinforced this perception.

My own reading of *Dust Tracks* is more positive. Hurston's final intention for the autobiography reveals her standard use of subversive tactics to address issues that critics have claimed she ignored. In addition, the manuscripts on deposit at the Beinecke Rare Book and Manuscript Library offer glimpses of the autobiography that might have been, although extant chapters neither reveal Hurston's original intention nor make clear what revisions Lippincott required. Her earlier drafts almost certainly would not have won a race relations award but might have provided a more complete look at her beliefs and earned her more respect.

Writing *Dust Tracks on a Road*

Hurston began writing her autobiography, somewhat unwillingly, in the spring of 1941. Having plumbed the Eatonville community, biblical lore, and folklore with less success than she and her publisher had hoped for, she needed a new project. Bertram Lippincott suggested she try autobiography. Although Hurston initially resisted on the grounds that "her career was hardly over," she relented (Hemenway, *Zora* 275). Katherine Mershon, a wealthy friend, offered Hurston a place in California where she could write, and by mid-July 1941 she had finished the first draft. Uncharacteristically, however, the required revisions were time-consuming. The revelatory nature of autobiography and the United States' entrance into World War II presented new challenges. It took nearly a year for Hurston to deliver the final draft to Lippincott.

Hurston later explained to a friend that she "did not want to write" *Dust Tracks* because it was "too hard to reveal one's inner self" (qtd. in Kaplan 478). Her difficulty, however, extended beyond trying to reveal her inner self. Her quandary stemmed in part from attempts to conceal an inner self that she could not or did not want to share with the reading public (Raynaud, "Autobiography" 112). Could she trust herself to revisit formative and perhaps painful experiences? Could she trust readers to share those experiences? How much could she say and not violate her own artistic and life philosophies? How much could she say and avoid the publisher's and censor's scissors? The pressures must have been tremendous.

It is also important to remember that autobiography is an art form subject to shaping and shaving. No autobiography can present every life event. Each autobiographer chooses which events are important enough for inclusion and which should be omitted, which secrets will be told and which kept, which aspects of a life to emphasize and which to diminish. It is, as Hurston's reference to building a statue indicates, a means of self-construction for public viewing. Scholar Claudine Raynaud goes so far as to call *Dust Tracks* a "Lying Session" that subverts the "autobiographical mode" ("Autobiography" 131). While the process of telling one's life story may seem straightforward, autobiography may be among the most difficult narratives to construct. Fiction is subject to the author's imagination, but the expectation of truth telling and concerns about whose truth will be told make the autobiographical process a complex one under the best of circumstances. Hurston had not only her own impulses to satisfy but also those of her publisher, imposed at a particularly difficult historical moment.

It should come as no surprise, then, that the version of *Dust Tracks* Lippincott published in 1942 is elusive and—at times—deliberately deceptive. Hurston, for example, claims to have been born in the all-black town of Eatonville, Florida. Yet Cheryl Wall's research with census records reveals that she was actually born in Notasulga, Alabama (*Women* 143). Likewise, Hurston never reveals her birth date in the autobiography, perhaps because she had misstated her age for most of her adult life, often citing 1901 as the year of her birth instead of the 1891 date recorded in census records. As an autobiographer, Hurston was apparently unwilling to disclose too much of herself, and this pattern of resisting self-revelation continues, helping to make her and the volume suspect.

The first eight chapters of *Dust Tracks on a Road* chronologically explore Hurston's childhood. Within the chapters themselves, however, she often leaps from one memory or story to another from a different time period. She relates her parents' courtship, her family's settling in Eatonville, her childhood dreams, and the books she read. She also records her father's infidelities, the death of her mother, her father's remarriage, and her violent loathing of her stepmother.

The chapters that follow are what Joanne M. Braxton describes as portraiture (145). In these later chapters the chronological narrative gives way to thematically linked summaries of significant experiences and opinions, creating a multifaceted but often superficial portrait. Static description of carefully selected moments creates a summary of who Hurston is. The narrative with which she begins the volume disappears. One group of summaries deals with an assortment of subjects: research, love, religion, and friendship. Hurston's treatment of white patrons in this group helped to make her and her work suspect, but the second, more problematic group focuses on her thoughts on race and politics. Notably absent from both are discussions of her encounters with racism, her participation in the Harlem Renaissance, her relationships with other black writers, and her travels as a folklorist to the American South, the Bahamas, Jamaica, and Haiti.

Because African American autobiography is a genre with specific conventions, readers brought with them clear ideas about what *Dust Tracks on a Road* would be, and these expectations mediated between readers and the text. Traditionally, slave narratives and the autobiographies that have followed are more than personal accounts. Individual struggles often represent the larger efforts of the community. Autobiographers also inspire or give hope to others trying to improve their lives. Given the racist nature of American cultural, social, and political institutions, Frances Smith Foster explains, "the quest for an ideal freedom and justice" traditionally has been an important aspect of African American autobiography (272). The history of slavery and continued racial oppression complicate the black individual's attempt to achieve. Thus, the individual's confrontation with or an examination of her experiences with racism has become a requisite part of the search for freedom and justice. But as Hurston had done so many times before, she rejected the established norm.

Within the autobiography, Hurston had opportunities to conform and to explore her experiences with racism, and yet she declined—whether at her own discretion or at the demands of the publisher is unclear. Instead, negative experiences enter the text subversively, dialogically, as narratives divert attention from potentially inflammatory themes. Several examples illustrate a prevalent pattern. Each episode invites Hurston to expound on race relations in the South, but each time she instead deals indirectly with memories of racism. She might have chosen to deal with these episodes indirectly under the best of circumstances, but she may also have believed that more direct confrontations with the issues would be cut by Lippincott.

Hurston, for example, recalls being chastised by her grandmother and father for sitting on gateposts, "looking dem white folks right in the face! They's gowin to lynch you, yet" (*Dust Tracks* 589). Hurston attributes her grandmother's fear to the woman having known slavery. Hurston might have related being chastised without mentioning her grandmother's fear of lynching, but as an adult narrator, she feels that the memory (which also records her fearlessness) should be included in the autobiography. Ascribing her grandmother's fear of lynching to the past, Hurston softens an element of protest but does not silence it. She also records her father's prediction that "white folks were not going to stand for" her behavior, that she would "be hung before [she] got grown" (573). She attributes her father's concern to her refusal to follow her sister's "meek and mild" example (573). In both cases, Hurston subtly indicates that fears of racial violence still lingered in the Florida of her childhood, despite the friendly race relations she describes in the first chapter of *Dust Tracks*. The history of race relations in the South enters the text dialogically.

In "My People! My People!" Hurston explores a related memory of a man's beating. She recalls hearing a man's "terrible cries" that stirred "[old] fears and memories" (726–27). Afraid the cries came from a fellow African American, the black men of Eatonville gathered to "go git him" only to discover that the white residents of Maitland were beating a poor white man for courting out of his class. What was so important about this memory that it warranted inclusion in her autobiography? Hurston had a lifetime of memories to draw from as she crafted her autobiography. The inclusion of this event, like the gatepost story, suggests that she was playing the trickster. Later in the autobiography, Hurston suggests that blacks and whites should all "be kissing-friends" (762). And yet here she subtly records the not-so-recent past (and in some regions then-present) of race relations in the South. Hurston also fractures any image of a unified white South by revealing class prejudices. What she does not address directly appears more subtly embedded in stories where editors and censors would be unlikely to identify it as criticism of America.

Hurston made similar decisions when exploring her educational experiences. After her mother's death, Hurston's father sent her to school in Jacksonville, Florida, where she apparently encountered racism for the first time: "Jacksonville made me know that I was a little colored girl. Things were all about the town to point this out to me. Street cars and stores and then I heard talk around the school" (621). She alludes to painful moments, but she neither reveals the details nor explores her reactions to the experiences. In the same way, when relating her experiences at Barnard College, Hurston claims, "I have no lurid tales to tell of race discrimination at Barnard" (683). And yet, Hemenway has pointed out that her letters to Annie Nathan Meyer, her benefactress, reveal that the woman ordered Hurston not to attend the Barnard Prom. Perhaps Hurston attributed the decision to the woman, rather than the school, and hedged with her word choice. She did write in 1959 that she could "see no tragedy in being too dark to be invited to a white school social affair" ("Court Order" 958). Perhaps Hurston dismissed the apparent racism of a woman who otherwise had helped her in so many ways. She did dedicate *Mules and Men* to Meyer. Or, perhaps, Hurston simply did not want to open such moments in her life to public scrutiny.

Years later, Hurston would relent and explicitly explore an encounter with racism in "My Most Humiliating Jim Crow Experience." The essay relates Hurston's visit to a white New York physician's office, where the nurse escorted her to a closet in which they stored soiled linen, rather than to an examination room. After a few questions, the racist physician demanded his twenty dollar fee, which Hurston declined to pay. Why did she neglect to include this experience in *Dust Tracks*?

Attributing the contents of the autobiography to any one factor, I believe, would oversimplify. My own understanding of the absences in *Dust Tracks* is informed by four factors. First, Hurston's artistic philosophy suggests that she wanted to define her work and her life in positive rather than in negative terms. Elizabeth Fox-Genovese argues that Hurston's unwillingness to explore the impact of racism illustrates denial of "the relevance of previous oppression to her sense of herself" (174). But an important difference exists between what she understood privately and what she acknowledged publicly. Autobiography is an act of self-construction for public consumption. It would have been strangely ironic for Hurston, a staunch individualist, to devote pages of her autobiography to those who had belittled her. She repeatedly eschews the idea of blaming others for her problems, saying "bitterness is the under-arm odor of wishful weakness. It is the graceless knowledge of defeat" (*Dust Tracks* 765). In this context, her refusal to treat racism explicitly is not necessarily a denial of it, but it may be a choice to write as an individual resisting being bound by a literary and political convention. Explicitly discussing racism would have meant allowing convention to dictate her art, which would have been a departure. In her 1938 essay "Art and Such," Hurston denounces those who conform to the norm by treating the "Race Problem," rather than creating art.

Second, June Jordan has suggested that Hurston's fiction reflects her childhood in the "supportive, nourishing" all-black town of Eatonville, Florida (6). We can extend Jordan's assertion to address Hurston's autobiography as well. In her work preceding the autobiography, white people are incidental. Hurston's characters operate in largely black worlds that need and have no justification. This environment is crucial to her construction of black psyches thriving in black communities in spite of white racism. In addition, the core of Hurston's identity was formed before leaving the Eatonville community and before confronting blatant racism. Consequently, her later encounters with racism would have been less defining and less significant than they might have been for other autobiographers, including Richard Wright.

Hurston's drafting of and the reception of her autobiography were further complicated by a third factor: editorial concerns about white readers.[3] Her comments in "Seeing the World as It Is" would almost certainly have infuriated white readers. In her discussion of domestic policy, Hurston points out that "President Roosevelt could extend his four freedoms"—freedom of speech and expression, freedom of worship, and freedom from fear—"to some people right here in America" (*Dust Tracks* 792). The country she saw was one she was willing to "fight for" but not to "lie for" (792). In directly turning her attention to white Americans, Hurston is equally caustic. She wanted the "Anglo-Saxon to get the idea out of his head that everybody else owes him something just for being blonde. I am forced to the conclusion that two-thirds of them do hold that view" (793).

When Hurston moves on to address the Communist Party, her ideas are potentially explosive: "If the leaders on the left feel that only violence can right things, I see no need to fingernail warfare. Why not take a stronger position? [. . .] Kill dead and go to jail. I am not bloodthirsty and have no yearning for strife, but if what they say is true, that there must be this upset, why not make it cosmic?" (*Dust Tracks* 794). Hurston's dig may have been at the verity of what the Communist Party advocated without being willing to "[k]ill dead and go to jail," but it is hard to imagine readers, particularly those unaffiliated with the Left, interpreting the remarks as anything other than antagonistic.

In contrast, the final chapter Lippincott published is conciliatory. None of Hurston's criticisms of white Americans, American policy, or foreign affairs appears. Instead, her conclusion proposes putting the legacy of slavery behind America, which would have been widely accepted by white readers. The published version suggested that Hurston was uninterested in the ongoing battle against racial inequality, which is far from the truth, as is evident in the earlier version of the conclusion.[4]

The fourth mediating factor was America's entrance into World War II. Chapters not included in the final draft suggest that Hurston's original version included harsh criticisms of whites and of American democracy. The Japanese attack on Pearl Harbor, however, forced her to eliminate those criticisms. Three chapters omitted from the final draft reveal a tone far less conciliatory than the one in the version Lippincott published in 1942.

"Seeing the World as It Is," once the final chapter, demonstrates the changes Hurston made after the United States entered World War II. After dismissing the concepts of "Race Pride" and "Race Unity," which would have offended a number of black readers, Hurston takes on a subject that might have made those same readers cheer: the failures of American democracy, at home and abroad. Attacking the double standards of American foreign policy, she points out, "All around me bitter tears are being shed over the fate of Holland, Belgium, France, and England. I must confess to being a little dry around the eyes. I hear people shaking shudders at the thought of Germany collecting taxes in Holland. I have not yet heard a word against

Holland collecting one twelfth of the poor people's wages in Asia. Hitler's crime is that he is actually doing a thing like that to his own kind" (*Dust Tracks* 792). Her point is clear. Colonizing the darker peoples of Asia (and Africa) was considered more acceptable than Hitler's colonization of Caucasian Europe. She originally intended this chapter on race and world politics to close the autobiography. It is difficult to imagine that Hurston went from the version above to "let's all be kissing-friends" in the published version without some significant prodding (769). She may not have had a choice, however, if she wanted to see the book in print. Deborah McDowell points out that the U.S. government had established during World War I a precedent of stifling media critical of America or American policies ("Lines of Descent" xvi-xvii). It seems logical that Hurston would have been expected to quash her negative perceptions of America as her contribution to the war effort. Unity on the home front, or at least the appearance thereof, would have been vital to the war effort.

Clearly the excised and revised manuscript chapters might have prevented Hurston from receiving the Anisfield Race Relations Award, but they also might have improved black critics' reception of the volume. The earlier versions reveal an aspect of Hurston's persona concealed by the published version, showing her to be a politically aware woman willing to speak her mind. In some ways, the portions Lippincott refused to publish more accurately reflect the audacious, outspoken Harlem Renaissance legend than the woman portrayed in the autobiography.

There can be little doubt that the pressures to conform to Lippincott's expectations were enormous. One of the manuscript pages reflects an editor's perspective as he "'[s]uggest[s] eliminating international opinions as irrelevant to autobiography'" (qtd. in Hemenway, *Zora* 288). By the end, however, Hurston must have felt that she could compromise no more. When she donated the final typescript to the James Weldon Johnson Collection of Negro Arts and Letters, she wrote, "'Parts of the manuscript were not used for publisher's reasons.'" With typical indirection, Hurston's one sentence only hints at the negotiations that must have taken place in getting the manuscript accepted. The version Lippincott published represented neither her original intentions nor her final intentions for her life story. Although Hurston must have consented to the changes, she could not have been satisfied.

Selling Hurston to White Readers

The front of the dust jacket Lippincott designed for *Dust Tracks on a Road* depicts Hurston's journey from rural Florida to New York, while the back cover places her autobiography squarely within the World War II era with its advertisement for War Bonds and Stamps. Between the two, readers found Lippincott's attempts to make Hurston a worthy subject for readers. By using quotes from white reviewers, Lippincott hoped to attract readers who, if not interested in her fiction, might at least be interested in an important black female author. The dust jacket also works to promote three of Hurston's previous publications, *Tell My Horse*, *Their Eyes Were Watching God*, and *Mules and Men*. Interestingly, the jacket contains no mention of her most recent work, *Moses, Man of the Mountain*.

The front cover interprets Hurston's journey. The upper left corner, on the distant horizon, depicts a small log cabin with two women on the front porch. A wide road passes from the cabin beneath the title of the autobiography to an urban skyline in the lower right-hand corner. The cabin is framed in a half circle, perhaps even a setting sun casting shadows, but in a rounded, softer frame. In contrast, clean, hard lines frame the urban skyline, suggesting a kind of pastoral image of Hurston's past in opposition to the more cosmopolitan environment of the woman who had written the autobiography.

For clues about how to interpret the cover, readers found on the inside flap a quote from May Cameron of the *New York Post*: "Among those Negroes who have left an imprint on our letters, few I think, are more significant than Zora Neale Hurston." Immediately, then, Lippincott tells prospective readers that the autobiography chronicles an important black author. Lippincott follows the title with "author of *Their Eyes Were Watching God*, *Tell My Horse*, etc." Lippincott again turns to a critic to establish the value of the autobiography: "Of Zora Hurston, Lewis Gannett once wrote, 'She has the gift of storytelling.' Now, in *Dust Tracks on a Road* she uses that gift to tell the exuberant story of her own life, the story of a young Negro girl who was to become one of the most respected anthropologists of her race, of a girl who grew into a novelist praised by the leading critics." Twice Lippincott tells potential readers that Hurston is an important black author who has attracted the praise of white critics. The publisher emphasizes her racial identity, which it will later exploit, and makes her identity important to potential white readers.

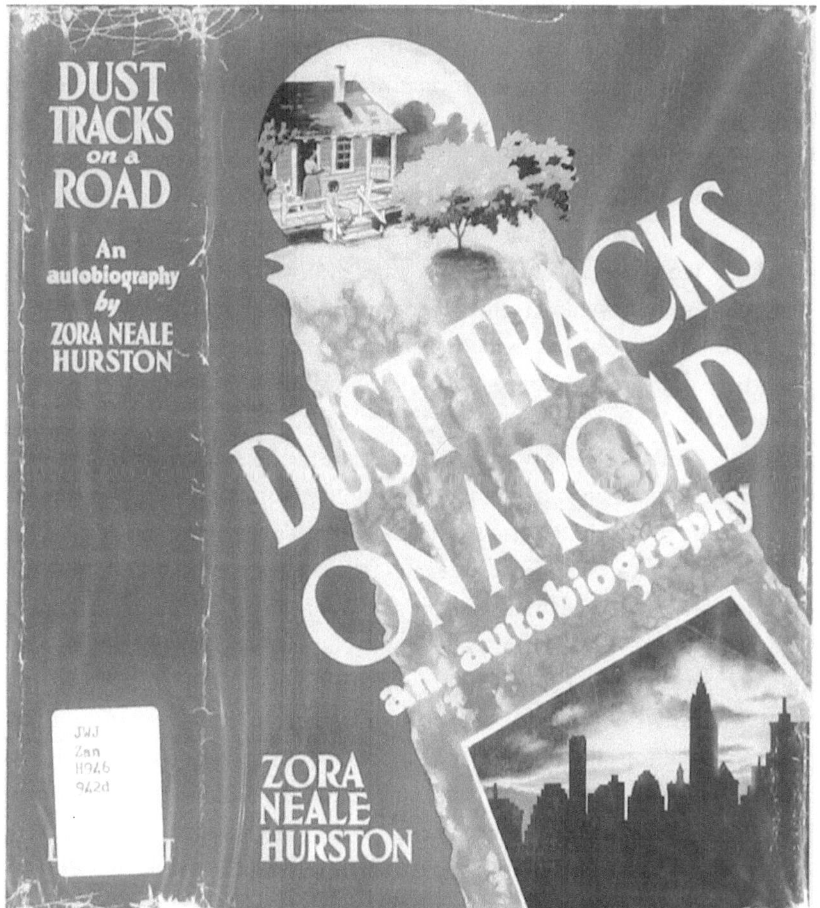

Fig. 10. Dust jacket of *Dust Tracks on a Road* (1942), on deposit Beinecke. Used with the permission of the Zora Neale Hurston Trust.

The next passage provides a summary of Hurston's life and zeroes in on Eatonville's claim to fame as "the first incorporated Negro town in America," perhaps in an attempt to distinguish her background as unusual and to attract readers interested in American history. What follows, however, comes dangerously close to exploiting the cult of the primitive. The cover tells readers that "[o]ut of her childhood memories she creates a picture, full of humor, gusto, and vitality, of the life of a colored family. The road that began there was a long one. It took her, after many turns and byways, to Barnard and Columbia where her ability and ambition won her scholarships and fellowships." The trio of "humor, gusto, and vitality" subtly invokes the cult of the primitive, the stereotypical notion that African Americans were somehow more in touch with the earth, lived freer of civilization's burdens, and were to be admired for their simplicity. And in the passage that follows the link becomes more clear as Lippincott tells readers that Hurston lived in "primitive simplicity" in Haiti, a black nation.

The dust jacket then takes readers where the autobiography does not. Consider what the jacket promises that the book does not deliver: "A Guggenheim fellowship given in recognition of her work in anthropology took her to Haiti. She has lived in primitive simplicity in remote communities where folklore is a part of daily life; she has lived in the inner circles of literary New York, has known the glamour of Hollywood. All this comes to life in her story." The very things Lippincott mentions here are among the most notable omissions of the autobiography. Hurston doesn't even mention *Tell My Horse*, much less record her experiences living in Haiti, as the dust jacket implies. Nor does she discuss fellow black artists or her time as an artist in New York. She briefly mentions moving to New York, appreciating Charles S. Johnson's assistance and Annie Nathan Meyer's work on her behalf, and working for Fannie Hurst (which all take place in New York), but she avoids any discussion of the Harlem Renaissance and its artists. Likewise, she mentions life in California in passing but makes no note of Hollywood. Were all of these elements once present in a draft of the autobiography? Did the marketing department create the dust jacket based on a preliminary version of the autobiography? Or did the marketing department craft the dust jacket from knowledge of Hurston's life rather than from the autobiography itself?

The dust jacket continues with its summary of the contents, although more accurately: "Reflections on Negro religion and culture, philosophy and humor, pungent with wit and startling in revelation, make this book rich fare." Once again, Lippincott crafts Hurston as an insider willing to reveal the hidden or surprising to white readers, and still worse, those revelations make "rich" reading. In closing its description of the autobiography, Lippincott moves to make it part of the war effort, saying, "It breathes a spirit which should give every reader courage for the future of America," an idea that at least one reviewer would develop more fully.

The inside back cover of *Dust Tracks* promotes *Mules and Men* with condensed passages from its dust jacket, while the back outer cover contains a request from Hurston that readers buy war bonds: "Freedom is a cemetery-flower—rooted in struggle and nourished in blood. Now our young men are in the field offering and giving that last and final possession—life—that we may be secure in possessions and peace, liberty and life. Can we do less than give freely of perhaps the least of all things which they are guaranteeing to us with their all? Buy War Bonds! Buy Savings Stamps!" Hurston's name follows the passage. The strategy makes her a good American as a means of creating bias in her favor. Readers' perceptions of Hurston as a patriot would, then, mediate their interpretations of the book. And for one reviewer, that feeling led to an ironic quote Lippincott would use to market the volume in newspapers.

Lippincott advertised *Dust Tracks on a Road* far less often in the New York papers than it had advertised her other books. I can locate few ads. Most play up the link Lippincott made on the dust jacket between the autobiography and American democracy. In a full page ad promoting fourteen books, Lippincott advertises *Dust Tracks* with a single quotation from John Chamberlain, reviewer for the *New York Times*: "If you want to feel warm inside about the whole of American democracy this is a book among many for you to read." A second ad, appearing December 6 in the *New York Times Book Review*, makes the exact same claim (39). Such feel-good reactions must have been exactly what Lippincott was hoping for when it put Hurston's encouragement to buy war bonds on the back cover of *Dust Tracks.*

It was an incredibly ironic choice given that Hurston's earlier drafting had included harsh criticisms of a nation she was willing to "fight for" but "not lie for" (*Dust Tracks* 792). She loved her country and remained a staunch defender of democracy throughout her life, but she also understood the irony of America's push for democracy abroad when much remained undone at home. Hurston had, at some point, intended to highlight the failings of American democratic ideals. Instead—because of the nation's entrance into World War II—Lippincott used *Dust Tracks* to glorify the imperfect.

Reading *Dust Tracks on a Road*

As with Hurston's other books, the initial reception of *Dust Tracks* was generally favorable, and Hemenway indicates that it "was commercially successful. It did not offend whites, it sold well, most critics liked it" (*Zora* 288). And yet, there were still fewer reviews than there had been of her previous books. Those who liked the autobiography liked the story, and ironically, several liked the apparent honesty of the autobiography. Hurston, however, drew serious fire from old acquaintances, Arna Bontemps, a fellow Harlem Renaissance writer, and Harold Preece, the white critic who had first openly accused her of exploitation in 1936. Alain Locke, the black critic and former mentor who had so regularly condemned her work in annual reviews of literature for *Opportunity*, did not publicly weigh in. He did not publish his annual review that year.

General praise came from several quarters. In his annual article for *Crisis* noting "Books by Negro Authors," white bibliophile Arthur Spingarn praises the autobiography as a "vivid and gusty account" that makes "swell reading" ("Books" 45). Beatrice Sherman, reviewer for the *New York Times Book Review*, also liked the book. She promises her readers a "thumping good story" (44). Phil Stong, the reviewer for the *Saturday Review of Literature*, seems particularly fond of what he calls Hurston's "charming practicality," a quality he associates with her description of her father as a man who "would have fetched a high price for stud stock" in the days of slavery (6). Although he describes the book as "more a summary than the autobiography it advertises itself as being," he thought it "delightful," "wise," and "full of humor" (6). The anonymous reviewer for the *New Yorker* reaches a similar conclusion in describing the autobiography as "[w]arm, witty, imaginative, and down-to-earth" (79). Even the *Pittsburgh Courier* reviewer, Ruth Elaine Caston, recommended *Dust Tracks* as "the grandest of [Hurston's] career." She found it "very attractive, simply written" (7). Ernestine Rose thought it "absorbing reading" (950), and a fellow Floridian told readers that "you must buy and read this book if you want a real treat, in the humorous, salty, but kindly, philosophy of life of this rare product of Florida. All Floridians have a lot to be proud of in Zora Hurston" ("Florida Local Color"). Hazel Griggs, writing again for the Associated Negro Press, argues that the autobiography is a "brilliant and analytical portrait" and a "rewarding experience" ("Zora" n. pag).

The most notable praise, however, came from John Chamberlain, reviewer for *The New York Times*. After providing a summary of Hurston's biography and calling it "as beautiful as Cape jasmine—and as vulgar as a well-liquored fish fry," he made the fateful promise to his readers that Lippincott borrowed in its advertising: "If you want to feel warm on the inside about a concrete individual at one end of the scale, and the whole of American democracy at the other, 'Dust Tracks on a Road' is a book among a hundred for you to read" (13).[5] Clearly, Lippincott's dust jacket mediated here. For Chamberlain, and other reviewers, Hurston's treatment of race relations, her insistence on leaving behind the legacy of slavery and making her own way, and her willingness to criticize her fellow African Americans made Chamberlain feel that despite its past, American democracy—that which men were dying for in Europe—was in fact a success. It never occurred to him she might also have criticisms of American whites as well.

Embedded in similar praise were other comments that must also have rankled Hurston's critics, to whom I turn momentarily. Fans of the autobiography praise her treatment of race and unquestioningly accept the veracity of her autobiography, as Chamberlain does, despite its obvious omissions. Sherman summarizes Hurston's feelings on race in a manner that suggests approval: "The author regards the Negro race much as she regards any other race—as made up of some good, some bad and a lot of medium" (44). Stong goes further and calls "My People" "the most sensible passage on the subject" of race. Griggs portrays Hurston as "wholly unrace-conscious in its devitalizing sense" ("Zora" n. pag.).

Hurston's treatment of race, they believed, made the autobiography appeal to all readers, regardless of race. Sherman suggests that "[a]ny race might well be proud to have more members of the caliber and stamina of Zora Neale Hurston" (44), although not all readers felt the same. Griggs told her readers that her book treats "with candor and humor the story of her people and herself" (n. pag.).[6] Stong was more specific and in the process revealed his own bias against more confrontational treatments of race: "The race consciousness that spoils so much Negro literature is completely absent here" (7). For that reason, he thought it would appeal "to anyone, white, black or tan." Rose went so far as to suggest that *Dust Tracks* offers "a good documentary film of the growth of a Negro intellectual in this modern day" (950), which almost certainly infuriated Alain Locke given his past criticisms of Hurston's artistic and political choices.

Three other reviews deserve specific treatment as they reflect markedly different approaches to *Dust Tracks* and to Hurston, one a thoughtful consideration of the merits and flaws of the autobiography, one a very craftily constructed and ambiguous criticism, and the third a brutal attack on the autobiography and on Hurston.

W. Edward Farrison, Howard University professor, penned the review that appeared in the *Journal of Negro History*. His is the most thoughtful treatment of *Dust Tracks* to appear in 1942. Although he does not recommend it as "a great autobiography," he argues, "it is a worthwhile book" (352). Unlike the reviewers cited above, he recognizes the complex nature of autobiography. He asserts that there is "much" of both "fact" and "fancy" in it. He recommends it as "interestingly presented."

Farrison also, however, had a number of criticisms. He points out that Hurston's "twelve visions of destiny [. . .] remain not only indistinct but elusive" (352).[7] He notes, too, what he describes as "hash warming": "She has re-presented much of the folk material she had previously used in *Jonah's Gourd Vine* (1934) and *Mules and Men* (1935)" (354). He fails to recognize that her parents' marriage, detailed in *Dust Tracks*, provided the inspiration for *Jonah's Gourd Vine*. Farrison's discussion of *Dust Tracks* as a Cinderella story veils his criticism of Hurston: "[A]lmost always, it seems, when she gravely needed sympathy and assistance, she found herself in contact with those willing as well as able to help her" (353). Farrison does not consider the possibility that her "fancy" includes omissions of difficult times when she remained unaided.

Arna Bontemps wrote the most difficult to decipher review for the *New York Herald Tribune Books*. Bontemps was an old acquaintance: He, too, was living and writing in Harlem in the 1920s. In the 1930s he had published *God Sends Sunday* (1931), *Black Thunder* (1936) and *Drums at Dusk* (1939), but his work failed to attract the attention Hurston's did. Perhaps equally important to his review, Bontemps and Langston Hughes had remained close friends over the decades. Bontemps's review of the autobiography, then, was mediated by his competition with Hurston as a fellow author, his personal knowledge of her, his friendship with Hughes, and his knowledge of Hughes's autobiography, *The Big Sea* (1940). Bontemps's criticisms of Hurston are subtle but clear. After a lengthy introduction to her life story, Bontemps makes the first remark that signifies. It delivers two totally different meanings based on one's horizon of expectations: "In a number of ways

[*Dust Tracks*] is a book that many people have been waiting for Miss Hurston to write. Visions and all, it is fascinating work" (3). Those unaware of the ongoing interrogation of Hurston's literary agenda might read the comment as praise. However, for those skeptical or critical of her, Bontemps implies that the autobiography clarifies and supports assumptions that she has been (and continues to be) guilty of exploitation. "Visions and all, it is fascinating work" has a similar bite.

Eventually, Bontemps turns to the "line of substantial friends who saw in the exuberant unspoiled colored girl the kind of Negro they wanted to encourage" (3). This comment, too, signifies. African American readers would have understood Bontemps's comments as criticism, suggesting that Hurston had manipulated white patrons by being who they thought she should be rather than being true to her own values. At the same time, however, naive or racist white reviewers might have found the comment proof that, as Chamberlain touted, American democracy works.

Bontemps also differs from the other reviewers in his response to Hurston's treatment of race. He closes his review with terse commentary on Hurston that leaves much unsaid for readers to ferret out for themselves: "Miss Hurston deals very simply with the more serious aspects of Negro life in America—she ignores them. She has done right well by herself in the kind of world she found" (3). Readers might have seen in this statement confirmation that black Americans can rise, but the comment also implies that Hurston had built her career by taking the world as she found it. Other African Americans not so fortunate be damned. "The more serious aspects of Negro life" she avoids because they might complicate her ability to do "right well" (3). The image of Hurston that emerges hardly flatters.

The final review worthy of mention comes from an old Hurston nemesis, Harold Preece. Preece's 1936 essay "The Negro Folk Cult" had for the first time openly accused Hurston of exploitation for personal gain. In his review of *Dust Tracks* he makes explicit what Bontemps implies: "Six weeks before this book appeared, two Negro children were lynched in Mississippi. And while this book is having its brief hey-day, armed mobs in the South are terrorizing Negro communities" (58). His assessment of Hurston's character is brutal: "*Dust Tracks on a Road* is tragedy and only technically autobiography. It is the tragedy of a gifted, sensitive mind eaten up by an egocentricism fed on the patronizing admiration of the dominant white world" (58–59). A more appropriate title, he suggests, would be "Dust in My Eyes" (59).

The one concession Preece makes is to suggest that Hurston's collections of folklore have made a "contribution," but he takes issue with "her whole interpretation of folklore" (59). While some writers, he suggests, "see in folklore the profound creative capacities of the people," others—including Hurston—"turn them into so much vaudeville material for bored sophisticates" (59). Again Preece accuses Hurston of passing off minstrelsy as art. The works of John Steinbeck and Margaret Walker, a then-emerging black Mississippi poet, were mediating factors for Preece. He believed they, in contrast to Hurston, made art of the folk experience. Predictably, Richard Wright's work also mediated Preece's response to *Dust Tracks*: "Books like Miss Hurston's seem hollow and puerile after Richard Wright's *Native Son*. The awakening world expects more of its artists than self-haunted dreams" (59). Wright's open confrontation with racism had altered expectations in the literary world.

Obviously, past knowledge of Hurston and her work proved a powerful mediating factor for Bontemps and Preece, who were also probably reading *Dust Tracks* through bias intensified by Langston Hughes's autobiography, which had appeared just two years earlier. In *The Big Sea*, Hughes (unlike Hurston) details his time in Harlem in the 1920s and discusses his fellow artists, Hurston among them. His portrait of her, like his treatment of the *Mule Bone* affair, is discreet, but not without its bite. Hughes subtly capitalizes on the assumption made by many of the Harlem Renaissance artists that Hurston was guilty of manipulation and exploitation. The perception was not new, but Hughes resurrected it just two years before *Dust Tracks* appeared. Although he admits that Hurston was a "fine folk-lore collector," the description that follows is not flattering: "In her youth she was always getting scholarships and things from wealthy white people, some of whom simply paid her just to sit around and represent the Negro race for them, she did it in such a racy fashion. [. . .] To many of her white friends, no doubt, she was a perfect 'darkie,' in the nice meaning they give the term—that is naive, childlike, sweet, humorous, and highly colored Negro" (*The Big Sea* 239). Admittedly, Hughes's description of Hurston is the same one Wallace Thurman developed in his 1932 novel *Infants of the Spring*. Hughes's relationship with Hurston, however, must be considered a mediating factor that makes his portrait of her suspect. Their friendship had died years earlier in their dispute over *Mule Bone*.

Hughes's treatment of Hurston's reliance on patronage also makes the passage doubtable. The "wealthy white people" might allude to Charlotte Osgood Mason, who was, Hughes neglects to mention, his own patron. Or it might allude to Fannie Hurst. Either way, his rhetorical strategy distances his criticism of Hurston's reliance on patronage from discussion of his own patron, which appears in another portion of *The Big Sea*. Hughes had other white patrons throughout his life as well. For initial readers of Hughes's and Hurston's biographies, however, *The Big Sea* confirmed the worst about Hurston's character, and there was nothing in Lippincott's advertising or *Dust Tracks* itself to challenge such perceptions.

Evidence of *The Big Sea*'s mediation appears in Bontemps's review of *Dust Tracks*. It can hardly be a coincidence that Bontemps's review returns to Hughes's stories of Harlem in the 1920s. Bontemps specifically mentions Hurston taking friends to "a certain little Sanctified Church" and "borrowing car fare from a blind man," both of which are stories related by Hughes in *The Big Sea* (Bontemps 3; Hughes 240).

Aftereffects

The Anisfield Award made Hurston a sought-after personality, and she must have initially enjoyed the attention. Yet she learned that popularity could quickly become notoriety. A February 1943 interview with the *New York World Telegram*'s Douglas Gilbert further damaged her reputation. While Hurston claimed that Gilbert had misquoted her, the damage was done. As Hemenway explains, Hurston's interview, as reported by Gilbert, echoes the "'raceless'" stance of her published autobiography, explaining that she did not "'see life through the eyes of a Negro, but those of a person'" (n. pag.). While this statement reiterates her earlier ones, she reportedly went further and claimed that "'the lot of the Negro is much better in the South than in the North,'" a statement that might have anticipated her controversial opposition to desegregation—had she actually made it. Combined with her repeatedly affirmative portraits of black southern life, the statement must have confirmed for many a black reader that Hurston had been so influenced by white patrons that she could deny the brutality of southern racial oppression. Still worse, however, was Gilbert's report that she claimed the "'Jim Crow' system works" (n. pag.).

When the interview appeared, it must have rankled a number of black readers. Roy Wilkins wrote a response for the National Association for the Advancement of Colored People that appeared in the *New York Amsterdam News*, while J. A. Rogers, columnist for the *Pittsburgh Courier*, also took Hurston to task. Wilkins's response is among the most direct condemnations of Hurston's character ever published. He chastises her as one "who knows better" and makes it clear that he believes she would say or do anything to sell her books: "Now is not the time for Negro writers like Zora Hurston to come out with publicity wisecracks about the South being better for the Negro than the North" (7). Citing racial inequities in her home state of Florida, Wilkins argues, "Under Miss Hurston's anthropological nose" the "race is fighting a battle that may determine its status for fifty years. Those who are not for us, are against us" (7). Hurston, Wilkins implies, is against "us." Rogers reaches a similar conclusion. He intimates that a segregated North, like the South Hurston reportedly praises, would have kept her from studying at Barnard with Franz Boas. He ultimately concludes that "Prof. Boas must certainly have turned over in his grave" to find a former student endorsing "racial inequality" (n. pag.). His final insult is to tell readers that "Miss Hurston is the author of six or seven books on the Negro which have a large sale among white people" (n. pag.).

Hemenway accepts the Gilbert interview as accurate, but Hurston claimed it was not (Hemenway, *Zora* 289). She wrote Gilbert to correct his description of her views and complained bitterly to friend Claude Barnett, founder of the Associated Negro Press, a black wire service (Kaplan 474–78). In a more public attempt to minimize the damage, she defended herself in an interview with the *Atlanta Daily World*. She argues that Gilbert misquoted her. Her comments in the Atlanta interview, intended to be corrective, more closely resemble her published and unpublished writings on the wholeness of the black community and on socially mixing with whites—suggesting that Hurston was, indeed, misquoted. In the corrective interview, a "bitter" and "disappointed" Hurston stops just short of calling Gilbert, the *New York World Telegram* reporter, a liar. Instead, she staunchly maintains that her words were "twisted": "I deny categorically that I ever said that

Negroes are better off in the south. Neither did approve [sic] of segregation in the south or anywhere" ("Zora Hurston Denies" 3). She tries, then, to clarify her position. She states that prejudice is not "sectional." The difference is that "the south by opportunity of long practice has worked out a system, while the north, caught between its declarations of no prejudice and its actual feelings [. . .] was groping around for the same thing, but with fine phrases." Hurston uses Harlem, a segregated neighborhood, as an example of the ways in which prejudices in the North mirror those in the South. In the statement that follows, it becomes clear how Gilbert might have deduced that she believed life in the South better. While condemning "northern abstractions about justice," Hurston claims to have said that "in some instances the south is kinder than the north [. . .]. [T]he north adds the insult of insincerity to its coldness" (3). The point that she apparently was trying to make is that African Americans living in the South know the racism they face; oppression is openly practiced. The false promise of equality in the North, she suggests, can be still more devastating for those who find a more subtle—but equally powerful—brand of racism.

On the matter of Jim Crow, Hurston says she was also misrepresented. Rather than asserting that the "Jim Crow system works," she explains that "Negroes were happy in their own social gatherings and had no more desire to associate with whites than the whites had to associate with them." She points out that southern blacks "have their own theaters and places of amusement." Her implication is that blacks do not necessarily want to mix socially with whites. She uses this idea of separate, whole communities to refute the idea that "Negroes are eager to marry into white families" ("Zora Hurston Denies" 3). Long used to deny "equal opportunity," this argument concocted by racists is, in Hurston's words, "a red herring."

The *Atlanta Daily World* interview intimates that Hurston's goal in the original interview was to dismantle existing conceptions of the "race problem." In keeping with her belief in the existence and value of whole black communities, she suggests that there is nothing inherently attractive about being white or socializing with whites. For those who believed that black men represented a threat to the perceived purity of white women, Hurston says, in essence, look again: Black men (and black women by implication) do not *need* whites to lead happy, fulfilling lives. She also wanted to associate the hypocrisy of northern whites with the behavior of southern bigots.

It seems unlikely that Hurston's response to Gilbert's interview was widely reprinted. Corrections seldom generate the furor that mistakes do. Coming on the heels of her unconventional autobiography, the article could only have further damaged her battered reputation.

Hurston's goals as a writer had long been suspect. Her "raceless" approach to American life, particularly given her criticisms of fellow African Americans and her apparent failure to criticize whites in *Dust Tracks*, confirmed those suspicions. The perception, advanced by Wilkins, was that she would say anything in order to sell books. Her thoughts on race, however, were neither new nor crafted for the readers of her autobiography. Hurston had explained her philosophy to Nick Aaron Ford years earlier. In *The Contemporary Negro Novel* (1936), Ford records an encounter with her in Florida where she explained, "I have ceased to think in terms of race; I think only in terms of individuals. I am interested in you now, not as a *Negro* man but as a *man*. I am not interested in the *race* problem, but I am interested in the problems of *individuals*, white ones and black ones" (96). Clearly, then, Hurston's 1942 position on race was not fabricated to appease whites, but the selectivity enforced by Lippincott proved the failure of the autobiography. Her criticisms of whites and of American democracy in the discarded chapters would have provided an entirely different perspective on her.

Just as *Their Eyes Were Watching God* marked a significant turn in Hurston's career, *Tell My Horse* and *Moses, Man of the Mountain* had offered her the opportunity to redeem herself in the eyes of her critics as a socially responsible black artist and as an anthropologist. When *Dust Tracks* appeared, it offered her the opportunity to correct existing misconceptions of her character. Hemenway, too, sees it as "a pivotal book in the Hurston canon" (*Zora* 288). When the publisher's concerns collided with the historical context and Hurston's staunch individualism, another door closed. If she regretted her previous books, surely she regretted this one as well. *Dust Tracks* was to have been the life story of a woman who "made it," but in the end it must also have been a painful reminder of her lack of agency as a black female writer.

Ironically, earlier drafts of *Dust Tracks on a Road*, complete with attacks on racism, American democracy, and international colonialism, might have generated a reevaluation of Hurston's character. Even had she avoided her experiences with racism, a more candid approach to life in America could and probably would have earned her the respect of more discerning readers. A more direct approach, however, would have required Lippincott's support.

Instead, the version of *Dust Tracks on a Road* that Lippincott published gave Hurston's critics exactly what they anticipated. She violated the genre norms for her autobiography, and she painted a picture of an America where anyone with enough gumption could rise to the top, regardless of race. Thousands of black Americans knew that was not necessarily true. A letter written in 1943 from Arna Bontemps to Langston Hughes describes Hurston as "the muse of black-face comedy" (qtd. in Nichols 128), which implies that her writings on race had been detrimental to the struggle for racial equality. In spite of this perception by Hurston's black contemporaries, the autobiography and the Anisfield Race Relations Award that came with it made her a much sought-after celebrity who would interpret black America for white periodical readers in the years that followed.

SIX

Talking Back

Taking a Stand on Race and Politics

My knees have dragged the basement of Hell and I have been in Sorrow's kitchen, and it has seemed to me that I have licked out all the pots.

—*Dust Tracks on a Road*

WHEN ZORA NEALE HURSTON told readers of her autobiography that her "knees had dragged the basement of Hell," she had no idea that there were more extraordinarily difficult times still to come (782). The eighteen years of her life after *Dust Tracks on a Road* were full of trials, in spite of the publicity brought by the Anisfield Race Relations Award. Hurston underwent a number of changes, artistically and personally. In the years between *Dust Tracks on a Road* and *Seraph on the Suwanee* in 1948, she abandoned her overtly apolitical stance as a writer. Popular periodicals provided a forum for Hurston to express her views. Her politics were controversial, and her personal life was no less difficult. She battled poverty and poor health, worked as a maid in Miami, and fought allegations she had molested a child. They were tumultuous years.

For many white readers, Hurston's receipt of the Anisfield Award confirmed the authority (and perhaps nonthreatening nature) of her depictions of African American life. That recognition made her a sought-after spokesperson for and interpreter of black culture for white readers. Rather than apolitically discussing the folklore that had so often been her subject,

Hurston's writings from the period—particularly her nonfiction—focus on issues related to politics and social change in America.

It seems likely that two events motivated Hurston's change. First, having been restricted and directed—even in telling her own story in *Dust Tracks*—must have heightened Hurston's awareness of her circumscribed agency as a black woman writer. The autobiography that Lippincott consented to publish represented only those aspects of her life and opinions that would be unlikely to offend white readers. Her frustration increased in 1948 when Lippincott rejected a book-length manuscript about middle-class black life, a manuscript she believed defied popular stereotypes.

It also appears that years of attacks on Hurston's subject matter had finally registered. Whether she simply wanted to refute those attacks, wanted to demonstrate that she had more artistic breadth than she was credited with, or changed her mind about trusting readers' racial sensibilities is unclear. Perhaps all three in some part account for Hurston's published acknowledgments that American art and politics are tightly interwoven. She had been accused of depicting African Americans who could be used to confirm negative stereotypes, and she had defended herself based on aesthetics, not politics. By 1944, however, Hurston had seen her fiction, her folklore and her autobiography manipulated by racist readers to support their own assumptions about black life. No longer was she remaining silent about life in the nation she would "fight for" but not "lie for" (*Dust Tracks* 792).

In 1944 Hurston gave an interview to Constance Curtis of the *New York Amsterdam News*. For the first time she spoke about the realities of being a black author in a white publishing world. Her comments suggest that she had come to understand or finally accepted (which is unclear) that she and her work had been manipulated by white publishers. Hurston explains that as a black author writing about black characters her "material is controlled by publishers [. . .] who think of the Negro as picturesque" (n. pag.), ironically a word critic Alain Locke had used more than once to describe Hurston's work.

As she discusses publishers' restrictions, it becomes clear that she often felt she had little choice in dealing with the J. B. Lippincott Company. Hurston explains, "[I]t is not sensible to buck the will of the people who have final authority" over the decision to publish: "Rather than get across all the things you want to say you must compromise and work within the limitations set you." It was better to say something, rather than nothing. Hurston hoped to buck the trend of "oversimplification" which depicted "the Negro" as "happy picking his banjo" or "miserable and crying" (n. pag.). She wanted to capture the "inbetween and above and below." Interestingly, Hurston's description of what she wanted to avoid engages the discourse of minstrelsy—the poles of humor and pathos. Was she dialogically engaging criticisms of her past books and working to distance herself from them? Was she engaged in a bit of public relations work on her own behalf? Perhaps both. If Hurston indeed regretted "all of [her] books" as she claimed in *Dust Tracks* (717), she probably understood that the portraits of black life Lippincott had published could be considered complicit, even though she had not intended to support stereotypes. Hurston understood what people had come to think of her, and she wanted to change their minds.

Hurston wanted to reveal who she was and what her values were. Although she told Curtis she did not believe that artists should be "pamphleteers," she felt compelled to point out, "Don't forget [. . .] that although I'm not a politician, I consider it important that the Negro fight for complete repeal of all Jim Crow laws" (n. pag.). In speaking about artistic oppression and the repeal of Jim Crow laws, she hoped to counter skepticism about her life and art.

By this point in her career, however, Hurston's efforts proved too little too late. Instead of altering opinions of herself, between 1942 and 1955 she created a new series of occasions for readers to ascribe her motives to opportunism. Although Hurston's new regard for the politics of art answered a criticism that had long been leveled against her, the essays she wrote for national periodicals between 1942 and 1945 too often attacked problems within the black community in forums conducted principally for white readers. Hurston did write a number of items unconcerned with American politics (most of them book reviews and reportage on the murder trial of black Floridian Ruby McCollum), but I focus on pieces that would have complicated existing perceptions of her in the years after *Dust Tracks*. Hurston was already on the margins of the black intellectual community, and her status as interpreter for white readers coupled with her failure to strenuously and directly criticize white racism further eroded her reputation. Was Hurston "tomming"? No. Readers, however, came to her work from the period with preexisting biases against her and her previous work. By the time *Seraph on the Suwanee* appeared in 1948 with a cast of mostly white characters, Hurston was very much a literary outsider perceived by many as an opportunistic exploiter of African Americans and African American culture. Being accused of child molestation the same year encouraged Hurston to isolate herself and may have made reviewing the novel virtually impossible for black periodicals. The work Hurston published after 1948, when read through the lens of existing bias against her, reinforced perceptions of Hurston as an opportunist. When her letter opposing court-ordered desegregation appeared in 1955, it proved the death knell for her reputation with her contemporaries.

Periodicals and the Politics of Race

Between 1943 and 1945, Hurston's byline appears seven times in popular periodicals, but only two of those essays are in black periodicals. The two sets of essays are remarkably different, revealing very different rhetorical strategies for different audiences. Hurston's *American Mercury* essays often attempt to inform white readers about black Americans and implicitly promote an integrated America. In contrast, her *Negro Digest* essays explicitly tackle racial discrimination. As this series of essays appeared, America was still a nation at war, and Robert Hemenway, Hurston's biographer, speculates that in writing for *American Mercury*, "[w]hat Zora apparently hoped for, like many other black public figures during the war, was a mood of racial cooperation and a recognition of black people's patriotism" (*Zora* 292). Hurston's stature as an interpreter of black culture and her choice of subject matter for a predominantly white audience again put her in the position of an insider relating little-known facts to whites. While the information she revealed was more politically oriented, her audience, her criticisms of black Americans, her lack of direct criticism of white Americans, her alternating between rhetorical strategies, and her existing reputation compounded the perception that she was pandering.

In May 1943, just two months after she received the Anisfield Race Relations Award, Hurston's essay "The 'Pet Negro' System" appeared in *American Mercury*. She explores the complexities of race relations in the South. Beginning and ending in mock sermonic form and tone, the essay suggests that northern liberals and race champions had oversimplified race relations in the South. Any mode of thought or action that sought to identify a "solid black" or "solid white" South "[would] run into a hornet's nest," if it failed to account for personal relationships (918). Hurston offers as an example a hypothetical "Colonel" who will do all he can to advance his black "pet" because he "*likes*" him (916, Hurston's emphasis). It is a system, she points out, that "a lot of black folk, I'm afraid, find mighty cozy" (915). While both the Colonel and the pet will generally assert that they dislike people of the other race, they are, she suggests, genuinely friends. Offering examples of friendship across the color line from well-known figures including W.E.B. Du Bois and Joel Spingarn, she explains, "The thing doesn't make sense. It just makes beauty" (921).

The "pet" system, she explains, "tends to stabilize relations" and "prevent hasty explosions" (919). There are problems, of course, in the system. Some "pets" profit personally from that which is meant to benefit the community, while white officials often believe a kind of "pet" tokenism in political appointments should satisfy the black community. And there are those "pets" who are unqualified or dishonest yet find themselves appointed to office. For those who profit from the system, it is "somehow useful" and deeply rooted (919).

The essay reveals an idea that had long been crucial to Hurston's thinking on race relations: Taking into account environmental differences, all people are basically the same. Although she does not explicitly state her view on race, her theories on the lack of inherent racial differences between blacks and whites underlie her assertion that people of different races can indeed be friends. Was Hurston naive enough to believe that a Colonel was not motivated by paternalism? No. She was writing for a predominantly white readership, however, and she had consistently resisted judging groups in favor of judging individuals. Hurston's rhetorical strategy called for avoiding that aspect of the patron/pet relationship. Had she taken on the issue of paternalism, she might well have offended and lost the trust of the very readers she wanted to reach with two more important and recurring ideas: first, that race relations in the South are more complex than northerners have acknowledged and, second, that blacks and whites are basically the same.

It is easy to imagine a range of responses to the essay. Northerners might have appreciated learning something new about race relations in the South.

At the same time, the title, which Hemenway describes as "unfortunate," probably enraged many a reader, black and white (*Zora* 291). The title of the essay, "The 'Pet Negro' System" is loaded with paternalistic and animalistic connotations suggesting ownership. Given the history of slavery in America, Hurston must have known she would offend with her word choice, if not with her ideas, but she tells readers that "[w]hether they like [her view] or not, is no concern" (921).

Clearly, then, Hurston knew her essay would generate hostility from some quarters. Hemenway points out that "most black professionals in the South earned their status in spite of, rather than because of, white paternalism" (292). Was Hurston hoping to anger blacks and whites benefiting from the "pet" system and thereby make it a less comfortable relationship? Did she want white patrons to understand the irony of their befriending the individual and dismissing the group? Did she want blacks who benefited from "petting" to understand they might be complicit in slowing progress for others? Or did she simply hope that a greater level of awareness of the complexities of race relations in the South would help facilitate change? Hurston likely wanted to do all of the above.

With an outdated patronage system still dominating southern life, African Americans could prosper only if they abided by the status quo. If, as Hurston said, she wanted to see Jim Crow eliminated, blacks and whites alike needed to confront the system that kept aging and restrictive powers at work in a changing world. Such a reading, however, is informed by my own horizon of expectations, by Hurston's other writings and interviews. These sources create bias in her favor, a bias not available to her contemporaries.

The essay reached a secondary audience Hurston could hardly have initially anticipated, that of *Negro Digest*. A condensed and revised version of the essay, "The South's Other Side," is followed by a description that distorts the meaning of the original essay: "Famous author claims all is not dark for Negroes in deepest South" (37). The mock sermon that opens and closes the original essay is gone. The condensed version also omits Hurston's paragraph-length description of the "pet system." The changes in text combined with the new title result in a less inflammatory tone. But her exploration of southern power structures may still have unsettled black readers. She may have appeared to attack the few southern "friends" of blacks rather than the system that privileged a few and oppressed the majority.

There were so many inequities in southern culture, some readers must have wondered why Hurston opted to criticize behavior that, at least superficially, helped black southerners prosper. But again, America was still at war. A black woman's criticism of white America would have appeared divisive to white editors and readers. As a black woman, however, Hurston could criticize within her own community without rupturing a "united" nation.

In October of the same year, *American Mercury* enlisted Hurston's support of the war effort. Hurston frames the lore of High John de Conquer with the idea that he might serve as a national "hope-bringer." She instructs readers, "[I]f the news from overseas reads bad, [. . .] listen hard, and you will hear John de Conquer," who helps his believers "overcome things, they feel they could not beat otherwise" and "brings the laugh of the day" ("High John" 931). Her use of John the Conquer relies on signifyin(g). The frame for the folklore was, in part, a concession to the editor. She wrote Alain Locke, "What I did for the Mercury has no scholarship of necessity. Besides the editor had to have it sugared up to flatter the war effort. That certainly was not my idea, but sometimes you have to give something to get something" (qtd. in Kaplan 490).

Hurston uses John the Conquer to transcend racial divisions and to suggest that African Americans and their culture have important contributions to make to the wider American culture, both of which were important ideas for her. She opens the essay by telling readers that "nationally and culturally, we [African Americans] are as white as the next one. We have put our labor into common causes for a long time" (922). However, the essay also signifies by offering a masked warning to white Americans that most probably missed. Couched in the essay are subtle hints that John may also pose a threat to white Americans who continue to fail to meet their democratic obligations at home. She warns, "[N]o matter how bad things look now, it will be worse for those who seek to oppress us" (931). In her final paragraph she advises that readers "be sure our cause is just." If it is just, John will offer strength. Both of these passages signify. John may offer black and white Americans endurance during difficult times, but he also sides with the oppressed against the unjust. He is, as Hurston promises, in the "'Be' class. *Be* here when the ruthless man comes, and *be* here when he is gone" (924). Who falls into the category of "us" depends on one's horizon of expectations.

Hurston subtly advises black Americans struggling against an oppression more immediate than Hitler to be patient, for "it will be worse" for whites whose domestic cause is unjust. Simultaneously, she cautions white oppressors that American blacks will endure and eventually prevail.

Hurston's rhetorical strategy in this essay is crafty. She signifies to address two different audiences to send two very different messages. Hurston's reputation, however, would not have inspired the trust of black readers. It is difficult to know how many of Hurston's black readers decoded her secondary message. She played the trickster, but she did not necessarily come out on top.

The following month, a third essay, "Negroes without Self-Pity," appeared. It, too, tells white readers that black Americans are ready and able to participate equally in American life. Hurston points to a meeting of the Florida Statewide Negro Defense Committee as evidence of "something in the offing" (934). Hurston quotes from one speaker: "'I know that citizenship implies duties as well as privileges. It is time that we Negroes learn that you can't get something for nothing. [. . .] If we expect to be treated as citizens, and considered in community affairs, we must come forward as citizens and shoulder our part of the load'" (932). Hurston records a second speech that encourages proactive behavior to influence community events. She admits that there may be nothing "world shaking" in what she records, but she believes the meeting represents a "profound" change. What preceded this meeting, she believed, was "self-pity without a sense of belonging to America" (933). In its place, Hurston finds "a new and strange kind of Negro meeting—without tears of self-pity" (934).

Again, the essay signifies. To white readers, the essay argues that black Americans are no longer looking to the past of slavery or reconstruction. Instead, she introduces them to two well-spoken black businessmen clearly able to participate in American political life. For those readers with limited racist and classist perceptions of African Americans, such well-spoken professionals might have been a surprise. At the same time, however, Hurston holds these two men up as examples for African Americans to follow. Her message here is similar to that in *Moses, Man of the Mountain*: Individuals must take responsibility for their own freedom.

In March 1945, Hurston's last essay for *American Mercury* appeared. "The Rise of Begging Joints" focuses on small black southern colleges, which she saw as little more than "Begging Joints" (937). She contends that the unaccredited colleges often provide a standard of education more appropriate for 1880. Wealthy white donors and uneducated black parents unknowingly support the founder's need for expensive automobiles and prestige rather than quality education. Hurston lays this foundation to argue for eliminating the double standard in American educational practice: "The raising of the Negro educational standard is an obvious necessity, since the inefficient are a drag on all" (942). She promises readers that she is not soliciting funds, but she wants readers who believe themselves a "friend of the Negro" to know that they can best help by contributing to established programs such as those at Fisk, Howard, and Atlanta universities.

Hurston was again apparently unworried about offending, but she probably did. While uninformed white readers might have been thankful for the advice, black readers' responses may not have been so positive. The range of responses might have included frustration at her airing "private" problems and increasing the scrutiny to which black colleges were subject. Faculty working for these unaccredited programs, however, would have been more troubled by her attack on their livelihoods. Hurston's generalization about black colleges may have made it more difficult to find funding for those institutions, regardless of the quality of academic training they offered.

During the same period, she also published two essays targeted at a black readership. These essays tackle subjects readers might have expected her to treat in her autobiography: experiences with racism and her thoughts on American democracy. They reveal a side of Hurston carefully masked in books and periodicals targeting white readers. In writing these two essays for black readers, she removed the mask, but again, her decision to deal openly with racism and the failings of American democracy was not sufficient to repair her reputation, particularly since during the same period she was also relying on rhetorical indirection and subtlety when addressing white audiences in *American Mercury*. Despite the difference in strategy, however, a common theme emerges among all her essays from this period. Hurston reminds Americans that race relations are far more complex than most acknowledge.

The first essay Hurston drafted specifically for black readers appeared in June 1944 in *Negro Digest*, which had printed a revised version of her "The 'Pet Negro' System." "My Most Humiliating Jim Crow Experience" records an encounter with racism in a New York physician's office. Hurston chose the episode carefully. It not only records her experiences but also demonstrates an idea that repeatedly surfaces in her other writings: Racism still flourishes in the North, not just in Dixie. In the first sentence, Hurston points out the irony of having her "most humiliating Jim Crow experience [. . .] in New York, instead of in the South as one would have expected" (935). While still supported by patron Charlotte Osgood Mason, Hurston had returned from the Bahamas with stomach problems. At the behest of Mason's attorney, a New York specialist consented to see her. When Hurston arrived at the physician's office, however, she was hastily shown to a closet filled with soiled linen—rather than to an examination room. Instead of leaving, she waited "to see just what would happen, and further to torture [the physician] more" (936). After a cursory examination and extracting bile from her gall bladder, the man asked for his twenty dollar fee. Hurston explains, "I got up, set my hat at a reckless angle and walked out, telling him that I would send him a check, which I never did. I went away feeling the pathos of Anglo-Saxon civilization." She knew "that anything with such a false foundation cannot last" (936).

Hurston maintains a strong sense of self and refuses to feel victimized, an attitude in keeping with her revulsion for self-pity. Instead of anger or pain in the face of discrimination, she expresses pity. The strategy places her on the moral high ground, as if she were above such insipid behavior. It also offers encouragement and advice to others who might have had similar experiences. Hurston walks away from her Jim Crow experience unchanged and so might her readers. At the same time, however, the strategy fails to illustrate the potentially devastating consequences of racism. She simply walks away from the physician's office without reflecting on the emotional or physical consequences of the encounter. Many of her contemporaries had experienced far worse treatment, and it seems likely that at some point in her life she did, too. But the essay, for Hurston, was not necessarily about self-disclosure. She made rhetorical choices to convey a particular political point: Racism is not only a southern problem. Hurston's choice signifies on an established African American literary trope that reaches back to slave narratives. Autobiographers who migrate North typically demonstrate the continued reality of white racism despite their changed geography. Her essay taps into this tradition.

Hurston's second essay written specifically for the readers of *Negro Digest* appeared after the end of World War II, and the difference between this essay and the other four is remarkable. In "Crazy for This Democracy" Hurston finally aired the opinions she had expressed in the discarded drafts of *Dust Tracks on a Road*. "Since 1937 nobody has talked about anything else" but democracy, she tells us. Her rhetorical strategy pulls in readers with a folksy persona that she will gradually abandon: "All this talk and praise-giving has got me in the notion to try some of the stuff [democracy]. All I want to do is get hold of a sample of the thing, and I declare, I sure will try it. I don't know for myself, but I have been told that it is really wonderful" (945). The meaning takes a moment to sink in. Hurston—although American—has never experienced democracy.

She continues by suggesting that perhaps she "mistook" the late President Franklin D. Roosevelt's description of America as the "arsenal of democracy." Perhaps, she should "go out and buy [herself] a dictionary" or a "spelling book" (945). Given events around the world, however, she decides instead that Roosevelt must have described America as "arse-and-all of democracy" (946). The phrase "arsenal of democracy" comes from the 1941 Atlantic Charter Roosevelt had outlined with British Prime Minister Winston Churchill. The charter outlines four basic freedoms essential to human rights: freedom of speech, freedom of expression, freedom of worship, and freedom from fear. But those freedoms, Hurston points out, need extending elsewhere. She sardonically notes that the Atlantic Ocean "does not touch anywhere but North America and Europe" (945). America was unwilling to fight for the same freedoms elsewhere. America's hypocritical and selective support of democracy made it "the arse-and-all" of democracy.

Hurston points out that the American "arse-and-all" had sent "millions" of soldiers to "carry the English, French, and Dutch [. . .] back on the millions of unwilling Asiatics" (946) to reestablish colonial rule. Imagine a Javanese man "[w]anting the Dutch to go back to Holland and go to work for themselves! The very idea!" (946–47). She points out, too, that "not one word has been uttered about the freedom of Africans" (946). She dwells on the uncomfortable reality that the nation's interest in protecting democracy extended only to Europeans.

With tongue in cheek, Hurston then draws a parallel between her own experience and that of the Javanese, bringing her criticisms home: "The only thing that keeps me from pitching headlong into [democracy] is the presence of numerous Jim Crow laws on the statute books [. . . .] I am crazy about the idea of this Democracy. I want to see how it feels. Therefore I am all for the repeal of every Jim Crow law in the nation here and now" (947).

This voice is the one readers of *Dust Tracks on a Road* lost in the revision process. With World War II ended, Hurston could freely criticize American democracy. She had been stifling her criticism of Roosevelt and American democratic hypocrisy since 1941, and it must have been vindicating to see her ideas finally in print. She also had to have been responding to existing opinions of her, including the idea that she endorsed Jim Crow that appeared in the Douglas Gilbert interview in 1942. Hurston could finally say what she thought and work to rehabilitate her reputation. And yet, nothing indicates that her essays in *Negro Digest* generated a reevaluation of her character. Existing perceptions of her as an opportunist were too deeply entrenched. Her next and final book, which focuses on white characters, could, then, only have confirmed that her singular interest was attracting a white readership.

A New Beginning

Seraph on the Suwanee is the last book Hurston published but not the only one she wrote in the years after 1942. As she wrote her series of essays for *American Mercury* and *Negro Digest*, she drafted two very different novels. The first fits the description of the book she told Constance Curtis about in 1944, the book that would not oversimplify (n. pag.). This manuscript, like the essays, represented a significant departure for Hurston. Rather than write about the folk, she drafted a serious book about "the upper strata of Negro life." She had titled the novel *Mrs. Doctor* and was "2/3rds done, when I think Lippincott (timid soul) decided that the American public was not ready for it yet" (qtd. in Kaplan 529). When that idea died, she told Carl Van Vechten she turned to a more familiar subject: "I have done a book on my native village, starting with the material of Mule Bone and weaving a story about a village youth expelled from town by village politics going places, including Heaven and Hell and having adventures, and returning after seven years to achieve his childhood ambition of being a fireman on the railroad, and the town hero" (qtd. in Kaplan 529). According to Hemenway, the J. B. Lippincott Company "did not like the manuscript." After Lippincott turned down the second manuscript, Hurston passed a difficult period through the winter of 1946 (303–4).

The spring of 1947, however, brought new possibilities. Fellow Floridian Marjorie Kinnan Rawlings put Hurston in touch with her own publisher, Charles Scribner's Sons. In April, the well-known editor Maxwell Perkins became Hurston's editor at Scribner's, and the publisher purchased an option on Hurston's next novel.[1] With an advance in hand, Hurston journeyed to Honduras to write. Perkins, however, died in June, preventing the two from working together. Burroughs Mitchell became her new editor (Hemenway, *Zora* 304–5).

In September 1947 she mailed a draft of her new book to New York. The subject grew from personal experience. She wrote Mitchell that she wanted to create a female character similar to an insecure man she had known: "You go along thinking well of them and doing what you can to make them happy and suddenly you are brought up short with an accusation of looking down on them." Such insecurity had destroyed her relationship. It was, she believed, "a very common ailment" that formed the foundation of the novel (qtd. in Kaplan 558). Hurston's novel about the marriage of Florida crackers appeared on October 11, 1948 (Hemenway, *Zora* 307).

Many readers unfamiliar with *Seraph* are startled to find that it treats white characters. From one perspective, Hurston's decision to focus on white characters would seem to make her disregard for black characters and black people complete. Considering Hurston's own horizon of expectations, however, offers another rationale. Each time she had written about folklore or the folk, racist readers had manipulated her work to support racist assumptions. When she attempted to interest Lippincott in a story about middle-class black life, the publisher had rejected it. An emerging movement among fellow black writers offered an appealing alternative. Writing about white characters would not only free her of criticisms that she exploited lower-class black life for white readers but would also establish her prowess as a writer.

Bernard W. Bell, in his standard study of the African American novel, argues that the 1940s "increase in the number of writers who published novels in which the protagonists and the majority of characters were white" was one of the most "momentous changes" of the period (186–87). Willard

Motley's *Knock on Any Door* and Ann Petry's *Country Place* both appeared in 1947, the year before *Seraph on the Suwanee*, and both deal only incidentally with black characters. These authors are but two of the black writers who took white characters as their subject matter in the late 1940s. Richard Wright followed the trend in 1954 with *Savage Holiday*.

Critic Robert Bone, in *The Negro Novel in America*, suggests the trend developed for two reasons. He sees the novel by black authors about white characters as a response to the limitations of the protest novel. And he suggests that writing about white characters reflected "an understandable but unsophisticated desire for an 'integrated' art" (168). That the protest novel held limited artistic possibilities is confirmed by Bell, and certainly, following World War II and the move toward the abolition of "separate but equal" social practice, black writers were arguing for integration. Hurston's essays from the early 1940s repeatedly argue that African Americans and Anglo-Americans are very much the same.

Bone takes a troubling turn, however, when he attempts to psychoanalyze those he terms "assimilationist." From his perspective, "Assimilation is in this sense a means of escape, a form of flight from 'The Problem.' It involves a denial of one's racial identity, which may be disguised by such sentiments as 'I am not a Negro but a human being'—as if the two were mutually exclusive" (4). He claims that the minority writer's identification is "so strong that it results in an indiscriminate appropriation of the dominant culture, including even its antiminority prejudices" (5). Bone's study appeared just ten years after *Seraph on the Suwanee*, and it is easy to see how the study might have mediated for later readers of *Seraph*. Hurston had repeatedly argued that she thought in terms of individuals, human beings, not in terms of race. Bone's quip that being a Negro and human being were not "mutually exclusive" ignores the fact that too often "Negro" and "human" *were* mutually exclusive. A darker skin indicated intellectual and social inferiority to many whites.

Hemenway's discussion of Hurston's choice of white characters provides yet another influence to consider. While contemporary explorations of race treat whiteness as a race, during the 1940s the term *race* implied minority.[2] As Hemenway argued in 1978, "the critics assume that the ultimate transcendence is to not write about black people at all, believing for some reason that white people carry no racial identity" (*Zora* 307). Writing about white characters, then, created "raceless" art. Philip Butcher in 1948 wrote an essay titled "Our Raceless Writers" in which he traces the tradition of black authors writing about white characters to Paul Laurence Dunbar. He argues that "there is no reason why Negro writers should be restricted in their material to the problems of the segregated minority" (115). For Butcher "colored novelists [. . .] taking as their canvas all the aspects of American life which are within the range of their varied personal experience" constituted "a step forward" (115). Hurston wrote Carl Van Vechten that she hoped to "'break'" the "'old silly rule about Negroes not writing about white people'" (qtd. in Hemenway, *Zora* 308). Such "rules" constituted a form of artistic and intellectual segregation.

Hurston had long advocated artistic freedom, so the move, within her own horizon of expectations, seems logical. J. Saunders Redding in a 1949 essay, "American Negro Literature," argues that black writers are no longer forced to make a decision about the race of their audience. Instead he saw the "gulf" between black and white "closing" (116). Black writers, therefore, were "finding it easier to appeal to the two audiences without being either false to one or subservient to the other" (116). The ability of the black author to "concern himself almost entirely with white characters" constituted a new form of artistic freedom, one which Hurston claimed for herself.

Hurston, however, did not undertake *Seraph* alone. She was working with literary agent Jean Parker and Scribner's editor Burroughs Mitchell. What readers see in the pages of *Seraph* represents neither Hurston's original intention for the novel nor her final intention. The version we read today was very much a collaborative project. Correspondence between Parker and Mitchell indicates there were three versions of the novel (or large sections of the novel) that would become known as *Seraph on the Suwannee*. Hurston, who had been writing in Honduras since May 1947, completed work on the novel in late November. She waited through December and into January 1948 for acceptance of the manuscript. Mitchell wrote her that he, like Parker, thought some sections of the second version better than the third. He had blended the best of each and passed along *his* revision to another editor for a fresh reading. When Scribner's finally agreed they could publish the composite version, Hurston returned to make additional revisions that would marry sections of the second and third versions.[3]

Hurston's *Seraph*

At its most basic level, the novel follows the courtship and married life of female character Arvay Henson Meserve, a self-proclaimed Florida cracker. The novel opens with the twenty-one-year-old "spinster" in love with the new preacher, whom her sister has married. In the past, Arvay has kept suitors at bay with fits, but Jim "cures" her fits by dropping turpentine into her eye. Arvay, however, is not convinced Jim really wants her. He, after all, comes from an old aristocratic southern family while she is only a cracker. Jim tells Arvay before they marry, "Love and marry me and sleep with me. That is all I need you for. Your brains are not sufficient to help me with my work: you can't think with me. Let's get this thing straight in the beginning" (630). Jim rapes Arvay under the tree she played house in as a child, thus foreshadowing a difficult marriage. Arvay imagines Jim has ruined her only to have him marry her.

The two move to central Florida, where Jim builds a citrus grove, and Arvay raises three children. Their first child is mentally and physically disabled, but as a young adult he is strong enough to attack a local girl. The event leads to the death of their first-born, but the other two children grow to lead happy and prosperous lives. For Arvay and Jim, however, life is not happy. Arvay lives in perpetual fear that Jim will desert her. The two communicate poorly. Arvay never knows when Jim is joking with her, and he lacks sensitivity. Jim tries to earn his wife's admiration, and Arvay feels Jim looks down on her.

In a misguided attempt to win Arvay's admiration, Jim picks up a large rattlesnake only to have it coil around his chest. When Arvay finds him, the snake is constricting, and Arvay, deathly afraid of snakes, stands frozen. The snake slowly killing Jim represents the extent to which he has adopted constructions of masculinity which are strangling his marriage, the very thing he is trying to save. Arvay's horror at Jim's overwhelming, suffocating masculinity is to stand transfixed. Only the arrival of Joe, Jim's hired man, saves him. Arvay's inaction proves the last straw for Jim, who "is sick and tired of hauling and dragging [her] along" (840). He leaves Arvay, hoping that she will change. He gives her exactly one year to become the woman he "married her for" (841).

When Arvay's mother becomes ill, the trip home becomes a catalyst for change. She finds her sister and brother-in-law living in filth and perched like vultures waiting for her mother's death. When her mother dies, Arvay, thanks to Jim's hard work, can bury her mother in style. After the funeral, Arvay finds her sister and brother-in-law have stripped the homestead of all value and disappeared. In an attempt to cleanse, Arvay burns the old home and breaks the bonds of her class consciousness. She tells a neighbor, "I can't see that I belong here no more" (880).

Arvay's next move is to find her husband. She first wins over Joe, her husband's hired man, and then begins work on Jim, who has taken up shrimping off the east coast. She flatters Jim, notes his prosperity, and takes an interest in his fleet of three shrimping boats. Repeating and revising the incident with the snake, Arvay finds her husband with a frightened mate grasping him. The mate fears Jim will break up the ship, but Arvay hits the man in the face until he retreats. Rather than fearing the mate's masculinity, she takes control of it. The pair make up, and the end of the novel finds Arvay "snuggled down again beside her husband" at the sunrise of a new day (920).

If *Moses, Man of the Mountain* was Hurston's most ambitious novel, *Seraph* is her most complex. Neither of her white protagonists emerges as entirely likable: Jim is insensitive, and Arvay is whiny and insecure. Hurston was drawing from personal experiences as she crafted the novel, but she reversed the gender roles of her characters, perhaps to better mirror social norms. Jim's frustration with Arvay mirrored Hurston's frustration with "this man that [she] cared for" (qtd. in Kaplan 558). She wrote Mitchell, "Have you ever been tied in close contact with a person who had a strong sense of inferiority? I have, and it is hell" (558). Jim doesn't emerge as a hero, however. Jim's faults reveal Hurston's ambivalences about white masculinity. The development of her two central characters must also have been complicated by merging versions of the novel. Perhaps this factor accounts for some inconsistencies in character development and for Arvay's rapid transformation at the end of the novel. While a number of Hurston's white contemporaries liked the novel, for today's readers, feminist thought and race relations prove powerful mediating factors.

The absence of three-dimensional black characters surprises many. Today's readers come to *Seraph* often after having read *Their Eyes Were Watching God* and/or Hurston's short fiction. After experiencing these texts' rich portraits of black life, readers are often troubled by *Seraph*'s flat, minor black characters who are the loyal friends of Jim Meserve. The relationship between Joe and Jim is friendly, for the two men seek each other's advice and support, but Joe calls his friend "Mister Jim," which suggests a boss-employee relationship rather than friendship. In addition, their lack of economic parity and Joe's dependence on Jim for advancement illustrate the "pet" relationship Hurston had explored in "The 'Pet Negro' System." It seems unlikely, however, that she was endorsing in fiction what she condemns in her essay.

Hurston wanted to mirror realistically racial relationships in the early years of the twentieth century. Mitchell queried her, for instance, about Arvay's use of the term "nigger." Hurston agreed the term was offensive, but she staunchly argued that a woman of Arvay's class and time would have used the word (Kaplan 555). Hurston wanted "to give a true picture of the South" (qtd. in Kaplan 561). This attempt to provide a realistic view of the South and its people may account for the marginalization of her black characters. Arvay and Jim are the central characters, and we see life through their eyes. The flat images of Joe and Dessie, then, may be Jim and Arvay's—not Hurston's. However in choosing aesthetic values over political ones, Hurston opened herself again to the accusation that she was exploiting stereotypes. In this case, Joe appears to be the nonthreatening, loyal retainer white readers would have been familiar with.

Arvay and her relationship with Jim prompt similar problems for today's readers. Many approach *Their Eyes Were Watching God* from a feminist perspective. They believe Janie finds herself and her voice. And yet, in Arvay, Hurston presents a character who at the end of the novel is committed "to serve" (920) a man who believes he must think for her. Scholar Janet St. Clair has suggested that in crafting the Meserves' reconciliation, Hurston was responding to her own time. She argues that the novel's ending "reflects the oppressive traditionalism of the so-called reconversion period when the capable and independent figure of the wartime woman worker is 'transformed into the naive, dependent, childlike, self-abnegating model of femininity in the late forties'" (39). Hurston's portrait of marriage, however, is more complex.

Hurston was masterful at indirectly critiquing. First, she critiques both Arvay and Jim to portray the complexity of marriage, a complexity she knew personally, having married and divorced three times. Meisenhelder has pointed out that in *Seraph*, Hurston also targets oppressive white masculinity, the exploitation of women and people of color, vapid white culture, and the desire to dominate nature (95–96). Jim is a sometimes foolish man's man who measures his value by what he can provide his family and by what he can control. Arvay's missing sense of humor is yet another of Hurston's targets. Lowe's reading of the novel as Hurston's "'comic masterpiece,'" complements Meisenhelder's. The novel, he argues, "explores contemporary problems of race, class, and gender while providing a Freudian case study of the consequences of rejection. Humor's diagnostic and therapeutic role in dealing with all these issues proves considerable" (260–61). If Arvay and Jim had learned to laugh together, their marriage might have been a much happier one.

Ann duCille's subversive feminist reading of the novel, more in line with my own, unveils more complexity. Arvay's apparent transformation can be read as a form of role-playing. DuCille argues that Arvay understands Jim's need for a serving wife and permits him to believe she will play that role but in doing so takes control of the relationship (*Coupling Convention* 138–39). Hurston understood this aspect of conventional male/female relationships. She wrote Mitchell that "a woman is most powerful when she is weak." A man "fights like a tiger to protect some alluring, weakly thing" (qtd. in Kaplan 562). Arvay's "transformation," then, becomes a calculated choice to embrace Jim's strength and prowess, to enable his success (by fighting off the terrified mate), and thereby ensure her own prosperity. It is hardly an endorsement of feminist independence, but Hurston wanted to create a realistic portrait of southern life, where manipulation and passive-aggressive behavior have been the conventional means for middle- and upper-class women to attain power in their relationships.

Such interpretations, however, are mediated by elements outside the horizon of expectations for the first readers of *Seraph*. Within Hurston's own time, critics largely read the novel as a Freudian exploration of Arvay's character, which Charles Scribner's Sons' advertising may have prompted.

Selling *Seraph on the Suwanee*

The dust jacket Charles Scribner's Sons created for *Seraph on the Suwanee* is quite different from the ones the J. B. Lippincott Company created. Gone are repeated references to Hurston's past works and to her race. Gone is the inflammatory, racially charged language. Instead, Charles Scribner's Sons lets the novel and Hurston speak for themselves. Rather than trying to connect the author to literary tradition, the publisher works to establish the novel as something new. In terms of Hurston's evolving reputation, the ads did no damage and even worked to create new perceptions of her.

The front cover of *Seraph on the Suwanee* is simple. Wide, vertical bands of sea green on the outside edges surround a deep blue center. The title *Seraph on the Suwanee* dominates the top half. Beneath it lies a small image of a palm tree on the water with birds flying overhead. The deep blue, sea green, and palm trees suggest the lushness of the novel's Florida setting. "A NOVEL BY Zora Neale Hurston" appears at the bottom.

Readers looking for clues about how to interpret the title found on the inside front flap a description of the novel and a summary. Very little here links it to the advertising Lippincott did for Hurston's other novels. The publisher describes the novel as "unique in its warmth, in its irrepressible zest for life, in its rough, sometimes bawdy humor which has a way of merging into honest tenderness most disconcertingly." The summary that follows is a fairly straightforward recounting of the plot. When Jim and Arvay moved south, because of Jim's "gumption," they "prospered and their world expanded—a world which Miss Hurston creates with flowing authenticity." Only the publisher's claim to authenticity ties it to Lippincott's advertising. That claim to authenticity, however, has nothing to do with race but rather with the region Hurston writes about. The source for her authenticity is identified on the back cover, to which I turn shortly.

The back inside flap identifies the "heart of the novel" as "Arvay's long, stumbling progress toward self-discovery and fulfillment. She could not believe that people counted her as high as they did or that she deserved to hold her head up in the good life Jim was fixing for her. It made suffering for her—and for her family as well—before she was able to find out where she belonged." The description of Arvay's search for "self discovery and fulfillment" subtly engages the discourse of feminism and may have been intended to target female readers. Notice the description of the novel focuses on Arvay's internal development, not rape, her love for her brother-in-law, or even her self-proclaimed status as a cracker. Each might have been exploited to attract readers interested in salaciousness.

The closing paragraph of the back flap focuses on the language Hurston uses in the novel: "Miss Hurston has heightened the idiom of her characters with her own inimitable style and achieved something quite different from the 'dialect' novel." Unlike Lippincott, which repeatedly tried to connect Hurston to past traditions, Charles Scribner's Sons tries to distance her from past traditions to suggest that her work is new and inventive.

The back cover of the dust jacket is a biographical sketch written by Hurston about herself in the third person. In recounting the location of her birth as Eatonville, Florida, she indirectly identifies herself as African American, which makes the back cover the only aspect of Charles Scribner's Sons' promotional materials for *Seraph* that identifies Hurston's race. Much of the cover describes her early interests in books and her father's abhorrence for her reading novels and writing poetry.

As the narrative progresses, however, it suggests Hurston's move to Scribner's was more than a change of publishers; it was an attempt to reinvent herself as a writer. She states on the cover, for instance, that she wrote her first story "after college and it was read by Robert Wunsch," who she says forwarded it to *Story Magazine*. When that story led to the acceptance of Hurston's first novel, she tells readers, "Zora was being evicted from her house for $18 rent." Hurston describes here the publication of "The Gilded Six-Bits" and the acceptance of *Jonah's Gourd Vine*, which appeared in 1933 and 1934, respectively. She makes no specific mention of her other books, perhaps at the request of Charles Scribner's Sons or perhaps to distance herself from her literary past.

Hurston had been writing and publishing for almost a decade before "The Gilded Six-Bits" appeared, so why does she imply that her career as a writer began in 1933? Did she hope to leave behind the accusations of exploitation? Did she consider "The Gilded Six-Bits" her first serious story, and thus her first story? Or does her erasure of those years simply illustrate her willingness to shave fact for effect? The image, or statue, she creates of herself takes on new drama as her discovery seems more sudden and the acceptance of her novel a well-timed rescue.

In terms of the bias created by Charles Scribner's Sons, the dust jacket demonstrates a remarkably different approach to selling the work of Zora Neale Hurston. Nothing suggests the publisher was interested in exploiting Hurston or her racial identity. The word choice on the dust jacket is generally unremarkable, unsalacious.

The advertisements Charles Scriber's Sons placed for *Seraph on the Suwanee* reflect the same attitude. The ads are simple but large. They appear frequently in October—despite accusations that Hurston had molested a child, which surfaced in mid-October. The publisher continued to promote the novel in the New York papers, a testament to its faith in Hurston and in the novel.

On October 10 the first large ad appears in the *New York Herald Tribune*. It describes the novel as "*warm and zestful*" "*with a* really different *flavor*." A brief summary is followed by the claim that "[n]o brief synopsis can possibly suggest the hearty man-woman relationship" between Arvay and Jim. References to key humorous scenes, including "the seduction scene which becomes hilarious rather than salacious," are used to entice readers before asserting "[a] lot of people are going to enjoy the honest relish for living that shines through *Seraph on the Suwanee*, its extraordinarily colorful idiom, and above all, the satisfaction of a story well told" (11).[4]

By October 14, the initial reviews of *Seraph* were good enough to prompt five more advertisements in the *New York Times* and the *New York Herald Tribune* during the last two weeks of the month.[5] On October 24, Charles Scribner's Sons advertised five books in a large ad. Here it describes *Seraph* as "A Surprise Hit." Brief quotations from reviewers follow. "It is by turns tender and tough, clean and lusty: it makes you laugh and cry" from the Associated Press appears first. Brief praise from Carl Van Vechten describes it as "[a] superb creation," while the passage from the *New York Herald Tribune* describes Hurston's as "an astonishing, bewildering talent" (15). It was an

Fig. 11. Advertisement for *Seraph on the Suwanee* (1948) published by Charles Scribner's Sons. *New York Times Book Review* October 24, 1948: 15. Reprinted by permission of The Gale Group.

interesting choice given that the accusations against Hurston had made the front page of black weeklies less than two weeks before. The ads simply ignore her legal battle. The publisher's use of praise describing the novel as both "lusty" and "clean" strikes an interesting balance. Recall the previous ad had described the "seduction scene" as "hilarious rather than salacious." The image that emerges is of a well-rounded novel intended for adult readers with a sense of humor.

On the last day of the month, Charles Scribner's Sons ran another large ad, two columns wide and three fourths the length of the page. The strategy is consistent with that on the dust jacket: Hurston's novel offers something unusual. In type of various sizes and fonts the ad reads, "Unique is the word for *Seraph on the Suwanee* the new novel by Zora Neale Hurston." What follows again are five quotations from critics. Including longer versions of the endorsements from the previous week's promotion, the new ad also quotes reviews from the *New York World Telegram* and *Book of the Month Club News*. The first calls *Seraph* "[a] grand show of vitality," while the second promises that "[t]he racey, pungent speech, the expressions so vivid and so unexpected, the unforgettable flavor of local customs and superstitions give this book an altogether unique quality and color" (14).

The advertisements Charles Scribner's Sons created to situate Hurston's work in the marketplace are subtle. Scribner's attempts to attract readers by offering something unique, unusual. Hurston's use of language, her Florida setting, and her often humorous treatment of Arvay's life all attract readers. The publisher's focus on Arvay's evolution and her marriage target women readers looking for love stories. But nothing in the advertising places the novel in a narrow category or suggests it would strongly appeal to a particular kind of reader. While Lippincott's attempt to attract readers with various backgrounds often resulted in contradictory discourses and contradictory images of Hurston's work, attempts by Scribner's to attract a broad readership suggest that the novel transcends traditional labels—the very labels Lippincott had relied on.

If the ads by Charles Scribner's Sons created bias, for a number of readers it was a positive one, creating interest in and curiosity about Hurston's "unique" novel. Those familiar with her work, however, probably read the cues well enough to understand that a story about Florida crackers was about white folks. What form of bias her choice of subject matter created among her critics is impossible to discern. There are no contemporary reviews of *Seraph* in the black press.

Reading *Seraph on the Suwanee*

The critical response to Hurston's last published novel is neither overwhelmingly negative nor positive. Nevertheless, *Seraph* sold better than any of her previous books, and Scribner's ordered a second printing (Hemenway, *Zora* 323). In general, reviewers liked Jim Meserve, the prototypical American man caring for his family and prospering through hard work. Hurston, however, had her doubts. She wrote Marjorie Kinnan Rawlings that she was unhappy with the final version: "I am not so sure that I have done my best, but I tried. I need not tell you that my goal still eludes me. I am in despair because it keeps ever ahead of me" (qtd. in Hemenway, *Zora* 315). Reviewers were inclined to agree. While the responses were generally positive, many believed the novel failed to fulfill its potential.

As the quotes Charles Scribner's Sons used to promote *Seraph* might suggest, the language Hurston used attracted a good deal of praise from the white press. In fact, her use of language is one of only two consistent sources of praise. The anonymous reviewer for the *Christian Science Monitor* counts Hurston's use of language as the second most impressive element of the book, the first being "the background" (11). Harnett T. Kane reports that Hurston has "caught so magnificently the speech, the movement, the nuances of thought among the lesser whites" (58). Herschel Brickell, too, appreciates "Miss Hurston's wonderful ear for the vernacular, for the picturesque phrase and the poetical turn of words" ("A Woman" 19). He suggests that anyone who "grew up in the South will find himself encountering on every page the familiar expression of his childhood, half forgotten and invoking nostalgia" (19).

Hurston's development of the Florida setting also elicited consistent praise. One anonymous reviewer describes the novel "as earthy as a vegetable garden planted in rich soil and as wholesome" (11). Frank Slaughter, writing for the *New York Times Book Review*, concludes that Hurston "knows her people, the Florida cracker of the swamps and turpentine camps intimately, and she knows the locale" (24). The background, he says, is "excellent." Kane seems to appreciate the fact that Hurston is no local colorist or travel writer. In fact, he suggests "her scenes have bite and stink and, as often as not, a lusty, chucklesome laughter" (58). Brickell praises the novel as "simple, colorfully written, and moving" ("A Woman" 19).

The endorsements, however, were not overwhelming. An anonymous reviewer for *Kirkus* calls it "[a] fair enough novel" (415). Kane's review suggests the novel is "concerned more with the charting of strong emotion than with literary technique. Sometimes, in fact, she is guilty of bad writing, overstraining and overtelling" (58). Brickell also thought the narrative "inclined to be stiff and somewhat graceless" (19). Hedden, writing for the *New York Herald Tribune Book Review*, explains that he wishes Hurston had "used the scissors and smoothed the seams" (2).

Reviewers were more harsh about Hurston's development of her characters. Hedden suggests that her treatment of Arvay's "domestic routine" is "less than successful" (2). Although Hamilton likes Hurston's use of language, he tells his readers that the novel's quality declines, in part because Hurston "neglects motivations and assigns uncharacteristic actions to her" characters. The point of view, he complains, "shifts" in this last third as well (355). He mistakenly believes *Seraph* is Hurston's first novel and as such, he believes it "shows promise if ever a book did" (355). Only Carl Milton Hughes (writing five years later) disagreed, saying, Hurston's "[c]haracterization[s] of Arvay and Jim are competent portraits by an author who develops animated characters that live throughout the novel" (*The Negro Novelist* 175).

Three reviewers read Arvay's character through a Freudian lens. Hughes was the most positive of the three in his suggestion that Hurston "gives a study of the hysterical woman," rather than returning to the Freudian vogue of the 1920s and 1930s, which focused on "uninhibited sex" (172). He describes Hurston as "more or less" of "the avant-garde in Freudian literature among Negro authors" (175). Hedden suggests that she "knows every intimate detail of Arvay's physical self and reveals it to the point of absurdity, but she has to construct a visible Freudian network to give us understanding" (2). Slaughter singled in on parallels between Arvay and Freud's hysterical neurotic. He finds Arvay a "textbook picture." He suggests that Hurston "took a textbook on Freudian psychology and adapted it to her needs perhaps with her tongue in cheek while so doing" (24). In the end, however, he concludes that the novel is "a curious mixture of excellent background drawing against which move a group of half-human puppets" (24).

Only Hughes's commentary on the novel ties it to Hurston's essays from the period. He notes the many scenes in the novel where black and white characters interact. He indicates, "The scene at the railroad station is typical. The little white and Negro children, playing with affection and enjoyment, together" (175). He sees the scene as Hurston's "subtle comment on the paradox entailed in the adult world." Hurston's characters, he points out, "accept racial equality [. . .] as a matter of course" (175).

The most interesting link between reviews for *Seraph* lies in what they do not say. Reviewers of Hurston's earlier books repeatedly refer to her as a "Negro novelist" and her books as "Negro novels." Both descriptions circumscribe by limiting her abilities and the appeal of the works. Most often, however, reviewers of *Seraph* identify Hurston as a southerner or Floridian, for it is from her longtime residence in Florida that the novel derives the authenticity Charles Scribner's Sons describes on the dust jacket. Brickell and Slaughter even refer to Hurston's white characters as "her people."

While reviewers avoided such limiting descriptions of Hurston, three did reveal bias in their surprise at her ability to record white speech. Hamilton's reference, the least offensive, surfaces in his description of *Dust Tracks*, which he liked, as relating "how, as a Negro, she came up the hard way" (355). Kane, on the other hand, seems impressed that Hurston, as a black woman, had been able to capture "so magnificently the speech" of her "lesser whites" (58). Hedden, too, thought it "incredible" that she could be the "biographer" of Florida crackers. Such comments reveal condescension. And yet, the reviewers do not limit Hurston with the label Negro novelist, suggesting that if she intended to establish her artistic prowess by crossing racial lines, she, at least in part, succeeded. Although her use of language and her choice of setting had not changed, the race of her characters prompted a changed response from white reviewers as they failed to link the quality of the work with the author's race. Why did black critics fail to review the novel? Events in Hurston's personal life may be to blame.

Hurston's "Basement of Hell"

Despite the good sales of *Seraph on the Suwanee* and a handful of positive reviews, the success Hurston dreamed of was not to be. On September 13, 1948, less than a month before *Seraph* appeared, New York police arrested Hurston for child molestation. Because court proceedings regarding children are closed to the public, it took time for the story to leak to the media. In a letter to Carl Van Vechten, Hurston tells us that "a Negro who works down in the courts secured the matter and went around peddling it to papers" (qtd. in Kaplan 571).

When the *New York Age* and another black weekly, the *Baltimore Afro-American*, went public with the story, Hurston made the front pages with bold, salacious headlines. On October 16, just four days after the release of *Seraph*, the headline from the *Age* in the lower right-hand corner of the front page reported: "Morals Charge Hurled at Zora Neale Hurston." According to the paper, the Society for the Prevention of Cruelty to Children had signed the complaint charging Hurston with "committing an immoral act with a 10-year-old boy" ("Morals Charge" 1). The information at this point was accurate, if not supposed to be public knowledge. A week later, however, the facts became grossly distorted.

On Saturday, October 23, both the *New York Age* and the *Baltimore Afro-American* ran large front-page stories with headlines above the fold line about the accusations. The *Age* headline reads, "NOTED NOVELIST DENIES SHE 'ABUSED' 10-YEAR-OLD BOY." While other headlines on the page follow the standard pattern of capitalizing first letters of words, this headline capitalizes them all, in the same way it was capitalizing on Hurston's misfortune. Bill Chase reported that Hurston, near hysterics, had "vehemently denied the accusation," but the number of victims had increased from one to "three under-teen age boys" (1). Hurston, he said, produced her passport as proof that she was not in the country on the dates the alleged abuse had occurred—between April 1947 and April 1948. She had been in Honduras. On another date specified by the boy's mother, Hurston pointed out that she "had proof that she was in Rhinebeck N. Y." with Constance and William Seabrook. Those facts, however, did not keep Chase from describing the charges against Hurston as "the most sordid and perverse ever revealed" (1). The charges, according to Chase, were based solely upon the word of a child undergoing psychiatric treatments and his mother, whom Hurston described as jealous.

While the New York paper had misstated the number of victims, the Baltimore paper went still further in exploiting the situation: *Seraph* and reviews of it were used as a weapon against Hurston. The headline in two-inch letters states, "Boys, 10, Accuse Zora." The headline beneath it reads,

"Novelist Arrested on Morals Charge" and beneath that "Reviewer of Author's Latest Book Notes Character Is 'Hungry for Love'" (1). In the novel, Jim tells Arvay that he "is hungry as a dog for a knowing and doing kind of love" from his wife. The newspaper implies that this phrase means something perverse, that it somehow reflects on the charges against Hurston. The article quotes from an unnamed reviewer (Worth Tuttle Hedden) a passage that attempts to psychoanalyze Hurston through the novel and in the process suggests there is something unnatural about her character: "'Incompatible strains in the novel mirror the complexity of the author. Miss Hurston shuttles between the sexes, the professions and the races as if she were a man and woman, scientist and creative writer, white and colored'" (1). Clearly, Hurston's refusal to conform to expectations for a black woman are used against her here. She "shuttles" between the narrowly defined roles the reviewer obviously found comforting and necessary. To make matters worse, the article on Hurston's "Morals Charge" sits among a sordid collection of headlines: "7 Men Held in Sex Orgy Cases Probe," "Jealous Woman, 58, Slays Pastor, 68, for Scorning Her," and "Nude Woman's Body Found: Sex Killer Sought in Attack, Murder" (1). The *Baltimore Afro-American*'s version of the story was picked up by one of the wire services and probably made papers across the nation.[6]

To clear Hurston's name, her attorney, Louis Waldman, appealed to the Manhattan District Attorney. The District Attorney, after hearing the limited evidence against Hurston and seeing her passport as proof she had not even been in the country when the alleged events took place, initiated an investigation that ultimately cleared her. The case was not dismissed, however, until March 1949.

Hemenway suggests that because the "morals charge went unreported in the major white newspapers," "it did little damage to the promising initial sales of *Seraph on the Suwanee*" (323). The ordeal did, however, have other wide-ranging consequences, financial and emotional. The episode was devastating for Hurston. She would not "subject herself to public scrutiny" to promote the book (Hemenway, *Zora* 323). As she told Bill Chase, "if 'such injustice can happen to one who has prestige and contacts, then there can be absolutely no justice for the little people of this community'" (1).

Her letters to Carl Van Vechten and Fannie Hurst about the affair reveal the depth of the financial and psychological damage. Although Scribner's issued Hurston a monthly advance on her next book that would help her get through the winter (Hemenway, *Zora* 323), by February 1949 Hurston was asking for financial assistance from Fannie Hurst, who had hired Hurston as a secretary in the twenties and written the introduction to *Jonah's Gourd Vine*. Hurston explains that she had paid her attorney $1,000, which depleted her cash, pawned her typewriter, and still needed $76 immediately.[7] Hurst apparently made the loan, and Hurston's letter of thanks reveals her frustration: "[B]oth my race and my nation have seen fit to befoul me with no excuse whatsoever." And as she had pointed out in her published essays of the period, she noted that "this foul thing did not happen to me in the Deep South, but in enlightened New York City" (qtd. in Kaplan 574).

The struggle of dealing with her legal problems had taken not only a financial toll but a psychological one as well. She told Hurst, "[M]y soul is dead, and I care about nothing anymore." She made a similar statement to author Carl Van Vechten and wife Fania, who had written to inquire about her well-being in the midst of the ordeal. In reply she wrote, "A dozen times since this horror struck me, I have crept to the phone to talk about it with you, but the horror and the loathing of the filth that had been spewed upon me was so great and so unbelievable, that I could not bring myself to take it in my mouth" (qtd. in Kaplan 570).

She wrote the Van Vechtens, "I care nothing for anything anymore. My country has failed me utterly. My race has seen fit to destroy me without reason, and with the vilest tools conceived of by man so far" (qtd. in Kaplan 571–72). When she had spoken to the representative from the Society for the Prevention of Cruelty to Children, which had made the complaint, she had successfully countered each of his accusations. She decided, however, that the man "was not seeking the truth, but to make his charges stick. Horror and disbelief took me. I could not believe that a thing like that could be happening in the United States and least of all to me" (571). She felt "hurled down a filthy privy hole" (574). Dismissal of the charges must have been a relief for Hurston, but in Hemenway's words, "the damage had been done" (*Zora* 320).

Not only was the damage personal (for not only Hurston's New York friends knew about the charges, but word spread to Marjorie Kinnan Rawlings and one can only imagine how far beyond), but there were also professional consequences.[8] While the accusations of child molestation had not been picked up by the white press and *Seraph on the Suwanee* had sold well, there were only a handful of reviews in white periodicals and no reviews in black periodicals. Were reviewers—black and white—hesitant to review the novel of an accused child molester? Did black critics not review *Seraph* because its central characters are white? Did they simply not think the volume worthy of note? It is difficult to be certain, but Ann Petry's treatment of white characters in *Country Place* did get reviewed in the black press, suggesting that other factors, either Hurston's declining literary reputation or her status as an accused child molester, kept *Seraph* out of the black press.[9]

Hurston's Progression Toward the Fall

There is also the matter of "The Conscience of the Court" as an indirect effect of the accusations leveled at Hurston. The story has been read as evidence that she utterly and completely bought into the myth of white superiority. She published "The Conscience of the Court" in the *Saturday Evening Post* in March 1950. Read in the context of her other works, it continues the pattern of Hurston's periodical publications between *Dust Tracks on a Road* and *Seraph on the Suwanee*: writing very different pieces for different audiences.

Critics have read "The Conscience of the Court" as a biographical treatment of the American judicial system, and such readings have damaged Hurston's reputation by suggesting that she was an "Uncle Tom." "The Conscience of the Court" follows the trials of Laura, a black housekeeper wrongfully accused of assaulting a white loan shark. Laura and her husband had followed Celestine from Savannah to Jacksonville. When Laura's husband passed away unexpectedly, Celestine had assumed the cost of his memorial service and had taken out a loan to pay for his burial. The loan shark tells the court he was trying to collect on that debt when Laura barred him from the house and tossed him over the fence. After the white judge coaxes a resigned Laura into telling her version of the story, he requests the contract that the plaintiff says gave him permission to collect the furnishings. Once that contract is produced, Laura is exonerated. The loan shark had tried to collect his debt months prior to the date specified in the contract. He had tried to steal the furnishings, and Laura, the loyal housekeeper, had protected them. In a contrived twist readers learn that Celestine, who might have cleared up the entire matter, did not know the trial was taking place. The conniving loan shark had intercepted Laura's request for assistance.

Hurston may again have been trying to demonstrate that friendship crosses the color line, but most have read the story biographically as her panegyric to the benevolent, white legal system that exonerates Laura and had cleared Hurston of the morals charges made public by a traitorous black court employee. Only recently has Susan Meisenhelder suggested an alternate reading of "The Conscience of the Court," one that turns previous readings inside out. She convincingly argues that Laura "is saved not by American judicial ideals or the benevolence of the white judge but by her own wits." She sees the story as Hurston's "final trickster tale" where the author crafts a tale with "a servile, even racist overt theme" only to send "a message with much more subversive implications" (185). Meisenhelder's interpretation is an insightful one that demonstrates the extent to which Hurston's biography has proven a mediating factor for scholars. Most have failed to look beneath the surface of the story to explore the ways in which "The Conscience of the Court" might continue, rather than depart from, traditions Hurston relied on in her other works.

Further complicating the matter, "the story was heavily edited by the *Post*'s staff" (Hemenway, *Zora* 327). It is difficult, then, if not impossible, to know what Hurston originally intended. Within her own horizon, however, the tale, like her other writings during this period, appears to have invited two very different perspectives. For white readers, the story would have confirmed, as did *Dust Tracks*, that American democracy works. The judge deals fairly with Laura, and the real criminal is discovered. At the same time, however, Hurston's critics would have found in the story confirmation of her willingness to promote oversimplified images of American democracy in order to publish her work.

The following month, Hurston's essay "What White Publishers Won't Print" made public in *Negro Digest* her most open criticism of the white publishing world. She takes white publishers and their white readers to task for showing so little interest in "the complicated emotions of minorities" (951). American whites, she says, have two conceptions of black Americans—both of which she links to minstrel characters and their poles of laughter and tears—they are unwilling to relinquish. The first, obviously the "happy darky," is "seated on a stump picking away on his banjo and singing and laughing." The other character Hurston roots in the minstrel tradition but modifies slightly. He is the "most amoral character before a share-cropper's shack mumbling about injustice. Doing this makes him out to be a Negro 'intellectual'" (952). While Hurston has extended this stereotype to include the "race man," he represents a modern version of the minstrel stereotype she had been accused of exploiting. White readers are only interested, she says, in stories with racial tensions.

Hurston's central point is that white publishers refuse to publish works that challenge stereotypes for fear that white readers will refuse to purchase them. Because publishers refused to accept and publish such works, white readers continued in their mistaken conceptions of African Americans. And the problem, for Hurston, extended beyond the publishing world: "[F]or the national welfare, it is urgent to realize that the minorities do think, and think about something other than the race problem. That they are very human and internally, according to natural endowment, just like everybody else" (952). Hurston, too, suggests that the "'exceptional' as well as the Ol' Man Rivers has been exploited" (954). The solution, she tells readers, lies in "[t]he realistic story around a Negro insurance official, dentist, general practitioner, [or] undertaker" (954).

Hurston may have been preaching to the choir, however. The essay appeared in *Negro Digest*, where she was likely to find a sympathetic audience. In the pages of *Negro Digest*, her criticism of whites probably did little to reinvigorate her reputation.

Later the same year, Hurston's November 1950 essay on vote-buying in Miami, "I Saw Negro Votes Peddled," generated another round of controversy. The essay initially appeared in *American Legion Magazine*, but *Negro Digest* condensed and reprinted it in September 1951. Hurston's account of the Senate primary race between Claude Pepper and George Smathers may have suggested that African Americans would sell their votes and therefore should not be allowed to vote. There was during the primary, Hurston tells readers, a substantial amount of "one-shotting," the process by which a voter is told how to vote on a single race and to leave the booth after casting that one ballot. To compensate voters for their "support," she alleges, an organization paid African Americans one dollar each to register to vote, and after actually casting their ballot, some were paid an additional two dollars, supposedly to compensate for having taken time off from work. Other voters, she says, were provided or promised household linens, groceries and even automobiles. Hurston points out that poor whites have long been guilty also of selling their votes, but she admonishes that African Americans have a special responsibility to honestly discharge their duties as citizens, as the right to vote had only recently been restored: "[N]o fairly intelligent Negro has any right to be deceived by any political 'friend' who offers to buy his vote. The fact that he offers to buy it tells you what he thinks about your character, and the petty amount gives you his estimate of your intelligence. Lumped together, you are two dollars worth of integrity and brains" ("I Saw" 59). Hemenway suggests Hurston may have been bitter about her candidate's large losses in Miami's black neighborhoods (328). But whatever her motive, the essay generated harsh responses from across the nation.

Less Granger argued in the *California Eagle* that Hurston made black voters look "'childishly gullible'" (qtd. in Hemenway, *Zora* 329). An Alabama reader wrote *American Legion Magazine* and called Hurston's article "contemptible." In his letter, the mediating power of her existing reputation becomes clear. He states that Hurston's claims of vote-buying were untrue, based on her "record of lambasting the race." What he knew of Hurston and her work made the essay on vote-buying unreliable. He dismisses her as "relatively unimportant" but questions how "any member of a group struggling as hard for acceptance as the Negro is forced to do, could sink so low as to write such despicable lies" ("Letter" 8). He doesn't even consider the possibility that her account might be accurate, as another letter to the editor claimed. An Oklahoman thought he saw in Hurston's story parallels between vote-buying in Miami and the practice of buying votes from "farmers, or any other group" (Athey 8). The Oklahoman interpreted the story from his own horizon of expectations. He gives no indication that he knows Hurston's work or reputation, and he implies that he has seen similar practices in the Midwest. Two very different interpretations emerge based on the biases of the readers, but the perception that Hurston might have fabricated the charges of vote-buying to sell a story stands as a powerful testament to the condition of Hurston's reputation in 1950.

The following year, Hurston's last politically oriented essay appeared in *American Legion Magazine* in June 1951. Her longest journalistic piece of the period, "Why the Negro Won't Buy Communism," outlines her early suspicions about communism and details what she saw as the Communist Party's strategic mistakes in trying to recruit African American members.

The plan, Hurston explains, had failed for a number of wide-ranging reasons. First, the Communist Party had "lauded to the skies" the idea of peasantry, while it "glorified skilled labor in words" (56). The mistake, she suggests, was in forgetting "that the Negro is the most class-conscious individual in the United States" (56). The American dream of upward mobility and of being the boss were too deeply rooted for American blacks to abandon in favor of collectivism. The party had also tried to link the fate of Asians and African Americans, but Hurston suggests that "[t]here never has been any bond between us and the Chinese" (57). The attempt to convince black Americans that they could not succeed in a capitalistic and racist America was, she suggests, countered by "Negroes in numerous fields" who had succeeded (58). The party's disregard for the average black American's religious grounding had presented another problem. She wonders how the party expected black Americans "to turn godless in a lump" (59). Other failures of the party include "under-rating our intelligence and self-esteem," promoting an "anti-white campaign," and forgetting "that nationality is stronger than race" (58–59).

The theme of the essay is similar to that of the essays Hurston wrote for *American Mercury* between 1942 and 1945. The essay repeatedly asserts that African Americans are primarily Americans. She points out that black men are dying fighting communism in Korea. She tells white readers that most American blacks are good, patriotic Americans who cannot be misled by the false promises of communism. This goal is very much in keeping with her arguments that black Americans were ready for the repeal of Jim Crow laws. The essay, however, serves another purpose for black readers who find themselves included in Hurston's essay as "we" and "our." Implicitly, the essay outlines the reasons black Americans should not be misled by communist organizers. She reminds both black and white readers that "[w]e"—African Americans—"are Americans."

Hurston's ethos, however, probably continued to work against her. The ethos she constructs fails to inspire trust that her criticisms are thorough, well-researched, or unbiased. The broad scope of the essay, her rapid movement from idea to idea, and the lack of organization all fail to inspire trust in a skeptical reader. In fact, in these late essays her attempt to establish her personal political values in a public arena probably worked against her by making her appear biased or reactionary rather than stimulating reevaluations of her character.

During the years between 1948 and 1954 Hurston also published a handful of book reviews and a series of essays on the trial of a Florida woman named Ruby McCollum, who was accused and convicted of killing her lover, a white physician. But by far the most memorable and most damaging of her other published writings was her letter opposing court-ordered desegregation following the *Brown v. Board of Education* decision in 1954. This letter delivered the final blow to Hurston's reputation. With her repeated attempts to persuade white magazine readers that black Americans were ready and capable of assuming the full responsibilities of citizenship, her opposition to desegregation in 1954 may appear puzzling, but read within her horizon, her opinions make sense.

On August 1, 1955, Hurston wrote a letter to the editor of the *Orlando Sentinel* explaining her opposition to desegregation. How could the woman who more than once called for an end to Jim Crow law oppose desegregation? Her response was complex. She explains, "The whole matter revolves around the self-respect of my people. How much satisfaction can I get from a court order for somebody to associate with me who does not wish me to be near them?" ("Court Order" 956). She understood that her response to the court order would prompt many to believe that she wanted to "deny the Negro children of the South their rights" and to label her "one of those 'handkerchief-head niggers' who bow low before the white man" (956). She believed that looking at her view logically, however, would prove such charges untrue. Hurston contends that there is nothing inherently better about attending school in "the presence of white people." She argues that Negro schools in Florida are "in good shape and on the improve." To her mind, the Supreme Court might have better used its power to enforce compulsory education for black children (958). In the desegregation order she saw a "spurning [of] Negro teachers and self-association" that was antithetical to "race pride."

In many ways, Hurston was right. The presence of white students would not inherently improve the quality of education for black students. Undoubtedly, there were well-qualified black teachers, and of course, enforcing compulsory school attendance among black students would have boosted the numbers of students attending. On the matter of desegregation, Hurston's other writings suggest that she would have preferred individual schools or school districts voluntarily undertaking desegregation. Unfortunately, such an ideal might never have realized itself. Her pride in black teachers, black communities, and black schools obscured the reality that separate but equal had long been a sham designed to reinforce class and race hierarchies.

Hurston's criticism of court-ordered desegregation was reprinted and read in newspapers across the nation, from Dallas, Texas, to Greenville, South Carolina.[10] The response was not what she must have hoped for. Unfortunately, segregationists used the letter to bolster their own positions. The Raleigh, North Carolina, Advisory Committee on Education wanted to reprint her letter in the form of a pamphlet to distribute as a rebuttal to African Americans demanding integration.[11] A rabid white supremacist expressed her support for Hurston's stance by sending her a postcard that claimed NAACP stood for "Negroes Are Advocating Communist Peace."[12]

Black activists responded as well. Roi Ottley in the pages of the *Chicago Defender* called Hurston a "handkerchief head" and a "flannelmouth" (n. pag.). He "wonders under what rock she has been sleeping for the last decade to be so out of step with contemporary events." But perhaps most telling is the following statement: "The fact is, I do not believe Zora actually believes what she says—it is her way of attracting attention. After all, we haven't heard from her in nearly a decade. But we are sorry she had to choose this moment to open her trap." The statement indicates a common perception of Hurston—that she would say anything to publish.

In December, Hurston wrote a friend that she was amazed at the controversy her letter had generated (Kaplan 743). Her thoughts expressed here inform my readings of her letter to the *Orlando Sentinel*. She was not opposed to desegregation, but opposed to *court-ordered* desegregation. The distinction may seem minute, but for Hurston it was vital. She explains in her letter that she does not find any value in forced associations. The physical presence of a white person meant nothing to her if the mind was not also in agreement. What her letter to the editor did not say was that years of associating with "liberal" whites had taught her to recognize hypocrisy when she saw it. Hurston had discovered that a white person's willingness to associate with African Americans was often driven by a self-sacrificing sense of nobility—not respect. In other words, when a white person stooped to share his presence with her, the action was often an egotistical one, making the white person feel high-minded and kind. The subtext of Hurston's letter is that legally changing human relations would change very little. She wanted meaningful internal, not meaningless external, change. Hurston, however, had not revealed herself fully in her letter, and sadly, this imperfect expression of her ideas was her last piece of writing to win a national readership. Her time in the national spotlight ended on a ruinous note.

By 1943, it seems Hurston recognized the need to change existing perceptions of her character. She also wanted to continue supporting herself as a writer and begin promoting political change. Unfortunately, her essays for *American Mercury* placed her in the position of criticizing black culture—rather than oppressive white culture. More than her criticisms of black life, however, her failure to criticize white oppression in the 1940s suggested that she had aligned herself politically and socially with white readers who would buy her books. *Seraph on the Suwanee* did nothing to challenge those assumptions. For years the novel was read as Hurston's contribution to assimilationist aesthetics and evidence of her lack of regard for black life and culture. She *appeared* to have abandoned exploitative black folk characters for white crackers and their black, nonthreatening "pets." Likewise, "The Conscience of the Court" appeared to honor the white justice system, which often dispensed racially segregated brands of justice to her contemporaries. In 1950 when she criticized blacks for selling votes, she was accused of fabricating the story in order to publish. When Hurston did criticize whites, such as in "What White Publishers Won't Print" and "Crazy for This Democracy," it did little to enhance her reputation and may have furthered images of her as one who would say anything in order to sell her work. She had relied on masking for so long that readers were unable to discern between the mask and the "real" Hurston. Her 1955 letter to the *Orlando Sentinel* opposing court-ordered desegregation was the final insult for black (and probably white) intellectuals. By inadvertently bolstering segregationist arguments by suggesting that blacks were also opposed to desegregation, Hurston had made herself a literary pariah. By 1955 her reputation was in ruins.

SEVEN

The Making of an Icon

Nothing that God ever made is the same thing to more than one person. That is natural. There is no single face in nature, because every eye that looks upon it sees it from its own angle. So every man's spice-box seasons his own food.

—*Dust Tracks on a Road*

IN THE YEARS between Zora Neale Hurston's 1955 letter to the *Orlando Sentinel* and her death in 1960, she published very little. Aside from articles and a series of columns titled "Hoodoo and Black Magic" in the *Fort Pierce Chronicle*, her only other published work appeared in 1956. Hurston's chapter-length account of the trial of Ruby McCollum, a black woman who was tried and convicted of murdering a white physician in 1953, appears in William Bradford Huie's *Ruby McCollum: Woman in the Suwanee Jail.*

In late 1957 Hurston moved to Fort Pierce, Florida, where she could supplement her small income by writing for the local paper. Biographer Robert Hemenway tells us her health was poor: She was overweight and struggling with high blood pressure, an ulcer, and gall bladder attacks. In 1959 she suffered a stroke and was forced to enter a nursing home (Hemenway, *Zora* 347). When she died in 1960, the hospital staff began disposing of Hurston's things—including manuscripts and letters—by burning them. The destruction of Hurston's belongings stopped only because the local sheriff believed they might include something of value to pay the debts she owed. When her obituary appeared in the *Fort Pierce News Tribune*, it described her as "penniless and almost forgotten" (Sharp n. pag.). Friends had begun a fund-raising drive to pay for her burial. In addition to soliciting Hurston's area friends, the funeral home also contacted Scribner's for a donation.[1]

Unknown to many and dismissed by others, Hurston's immediate literary legacy was controversy. Throughout her career, her life and her art had been subjects of debate. When she wrote about the black Florida folk she knew, some readers found her portraits suspect, at least in part because racist white readers could and did use her work to support negative black stereotypes. When she attempted to interest a publisher in a story of middle-class black life that she believed would counter popular stereotypes, it was rejected. When she tried to write her life story in *Dust Tracks on a Road* or share her experiences among the folk in *Mules and Men*, she was accused of ignoring the political and social realities of race in America. And finally, when she opted to write about white characters in *Seraph on the Suwanee*, she was ignored or silently condemned for having "abandoned" black ones. At every turn Hurston confronted those who would dictate—or suspend—her artistic work because she refused to conform to the contemporary politics of race. She understood that not every individual would appreciate the flavors of her "spice-box," but even those who had appreciated her work would have been unable to find it. By 1960 all of her books were out of print.

And yet, today Hurston is among the best-known, most-beloved, and most-studied of African American women writers. All of her books are back in print, with her folkloric work, short stories, and essays appearing in anthologies of African American, American, women's, and world literatures. Previously unknown works by Hurston are still turning up, including "Under the Bridge," "She Rock," "The Back Room," "The Country in the Woman," a number of plays available at the Library of Congress, and *Every Tongue Got to Confess: Negro Folk-Tales from the Gulf States*, which recently surfaced at the Smithsonian. As scholars continue to scrutinize previously neglected resources, as archivists sort papers on deposit in libraries around the nation, and as individuals empty attics and trunks, more pieces will surface and add to our understanding of Hurston as a writer. Each new discovery spurs new scholarship, further ensuring Hurston's canonicity.

Hurston has arrived. Her continuing place in the American literary canon seemingly was assured in 1995 by the release of two volumes of her work by the Library of America. She has become what Jonathan Arac terms a hypercanonical figure, one on a par with Mark Twain, William Faulkner, Edith Wharton, and former nemesis, Richard Wright, all of whom have also been published by Library of America. Such company clearly places her among the greatest figures in twentieth-century American literature. She has become a literary icon, so often considered a key figure that she has eclipsed other women of the period, who often published more traditional works.

The story of Hurston's rise from marginalized has-been to hypercanonical heights in twenty-five years is the subject of this chapter. Like her marginalization, Hurston's recovery is complexly rooted in the political and social moment, the upheaval of the sixties and seventies. Cultural critic Cornel West suggests that "cultural crisis" is the force "which prompts, guides and regulates" canonization (193). Just as racial and artistic ideologies marginalized Hurston in the first half of the century, the dynamic ideologies of black cultural nationalism and black feminism converged with changing university curricula, changing student and professor populations, and key publications to make her recovery and canonization possible. Hurston's contemporaries read her work through lenses created by the racial and artistic politics of the 1920s, 1930s, and 1940s, and through her existing public persona. More recent readers, however, have interpreted her works and her persona through new lenses—informed by changed politics and new scholarship—that have created new forms of bias, this time in Hurston's favor. Ironically, *Their Eyes Were Watching God* and *Mules and Men*, which proved pivotal in establishing Hurston as an exploiter of black folk traditions for white readers, are the two books upon which her recovery has hinged.

Early Efforts

On a superficial level, Hurston's recovery began almost immediately after her death. Reassessments of her life and art first appeared with obituaries attempting to define her place in American literature. The *New York Times*, for instance, describes Hurston as "among the foremost writers of Negro folklore" whose lack of "commercial success" was "the fault of the reading public" ("Zora Hurston" 27). The description of Hurston as "among the foremost writers of Negro folklore" was one even some of her harshest critics—Harold Preece, Alain Locke, and Sterling Brown—could not have disputed, and perceptively, the obituary turns attention to her readers, who over the years had read her work through mediating factors that too often cast her as an exploitative opportunist. The *Pittsburgh Courier* in its obituary mistakenly described her as a "prolific writer for motion picture studios" and, perhaps more accurately, as a "brilliant author and educator" (Reid 3).

Almost as if Hurston's death gave friends license and impetus to discuss her and her work, Fannie Hurst's personality sketch of Hurston appeared in the *Yale University Library Gazette*.[2] Although largely a memoir, Hurst's article makes an early and ironic claim for Hurston's place in the canon. The essay concludes with her assertion that Hurston's "short shelf of writings deserves to endure" ("Zora" 21). And they have. Ironically, Hurston's legacy has eclipsed that of Hurst, once Hurston's more powerful and more prosperous contemporary.

Equally important to Hurston's recovery is the editor's note appended to the end of Hurst's essay. The note identifies Hurston's manuscripts, books, and letters on deposit at Yale University. It also serves as the first posthumously published bibliography of her work, which identifies all seven of her books. The footnote made it possible for those interested in her writing to locate the rare and out-of-print books. For recovery of an author to take place, readers must have texts to read and study. This essay and its important footnote, then, were the first step toward canonization.

Turbulence and Its Creative Ferment

For Hurston's work to become widely available, however, she would first have to have a readership, and there would have to be a demand for her work. That readership and its demands grew out of the turbulent decades following her death. The 1960s saw America at war in Vietnam and the attempted overthrow of Cuba's Fidel Castro with the botched Bay of Pigs invasion. Domestic conflicts between civil rights activists and white racists mirrored the violence abroad. The civil rights movement gained momentum when nonviolent protesters began to press for equality with renewed energy. The integration of educational institutions—from elementary schools to universities—proceeded, even though black students often met violent opposition.

The year 1963, for instance, saw the March on Washington, with Martin

Luther King, Jr., sharing his vision of another America from the steps of the Lincoln Memorial, but it was also the same year Byron de la Beckwith assassinated Mississippi civil rights activist Medgar Evers. Following the televised assault by white police officers on nonviolent protesters in Birmingham, Alabama, Congress finally passed the Voting Rights Act of 1965. The law, however, failed to end public opposition, and the continued violence against black Americans exercising their constitutionally guaranteed rights spurred some to reject the concept of nonviolent protest. If whites wanted violence, they would be met with equal force. Integration was no longer necessarily the goal. As Hurston had pointed out in 1955, laws could do little to alter life if the minds of white Americans were opposed to the change. Black separatism, a separate black nation, emerged as an option. Black nationalism, particularly as manifested in the Black Power Movement, flourished.[3] In this social and cultural shift lies the first lens that altered interpretations of Hurston and her work. In this movement and its ideologies, readers found new forms of bias to make Hurston's work relevant and responsive to the "cultural crisis" of the moment.

The Black Power Movement resolved to empower African Americans politically and socially at any cost. That ideology gave birth to the Black Arts Movement, which was, in Larry Neal's words, "the aesthetic and spiritual sister of the Black Power concept" (184). Many date the beginning of the Black Arts Movement to LeRoi Jones's 1964 founding of the Black Arts Repertory/Theatre School in Harlem. At the heart of the movement was the struggle over images. Proponents argued for abandoning existing Western aesthetics so that "a separate symbolism, mythology, critique, and iconology" might be created. It aimed at addressing "the needs and aspirations of Black America" (Neal 184). It was a "cultural revolution in art and ideas" (185).

Proponents wanted art to be accessible to the common man and wanted art rooted in his experience. Jones, a frequent spokesman for the black aesthetic, condemned middle-class attempts to conform to white norms. He believed such attempts promoted "mediocrity" and diluted black traditions (166). In contrast, oral forms, those practiced by "the so-called lower class Negro" (168), represented the purest and the preferred forms of expression. Blues, jazz, and spirituals were reified. Interaction between artists and the people for whom they wrote was crucial. Artists' messages to the people took priority while form became transparent. Thus, the Black Arts Movement encouraged artists to rely on literary forms that did not require the mediation of a text. Poetry that could be recited on the street and drama that involved the audience ascended in priority.

As nationalists began crafting a new America, establishing a unified black community became central. To unify the community and overthrow white American mythology, the movement condemned individualism. The well-being of the individual became secondary to that of the community. On the artistic front the goals included the literary affirmation of "a cohesive, distinctly black cultural community" (Dubey 22). This community was to provide the "power and meaning" necessary to "counter the Western aesthetic privileging of the individual artist" (22).[4]

The unified community that proponents sought as liberation, however, also had the potential to stifle. The movement ignored gender issues in order to unify. Madhu Dubey argues that the community discourse "consolidated around the sign of race, discouraged any exploration of gender and other differences that might complicate a unitary conception of the black experience" (1). Black men, as Dubey and others have suggested, were the "true subject of black nationalist discourse" (Dubey 16–17). Ironically following the example set by white men, black men were, in the words of bell hooks, "obsessively concerned with asserting their masculinity" (177).

Black women found themselves marginalized and condemned in nationalist discourse. The Moynihan Report, a government study of the black family released in 1965, argued that black women were culpable for the emasculation of black men. Black matriarchal family patterns led to Moynihan's describing black families as "'a tangle of pathology,' inextricably knotted by a matriarchal head of the household" (Giddings 326).[5] Elliot Butler-Evans points out that "the symbolic destruction of a repressive matriarchy" was not only an acceptable goal, but a desirable one in nationalist discourse (34). The belief that men were to be leaders informed black nationalist organizations, which in Dubey's words, "clearly restricted roles for black women" who were to be secretaries, nurturers, and biological producers for future black male leaders (18). With the second wave of the Women's Movement gaining strength, black women were under attack for their autonomy.

For black women who felt restricted by misogyny within nationalist organizations, the Women's Movement offered nothing better. Just as black men were focused on asserting their masculinity, white women were focused on issues that ran counter to or ignored the needs of black women. All women do not necessarily want or need the same things. Dubey explains that white women looked to the workplace and to employment outside the home for liberation from patriarchal control. For black women, however, the workplace was yet another site of racial oppression. White women sought freedom outside marriage and the home; remaining single or divorcing husbands promised white women sexual and financial freedom. In contrast, most black women, Dubey argues, wanted to maintain their family units, which provided emotional and economic stability (16). In addition, nationalist discourse emphasized the importance of black families, which "superseded the desires and needs of Black women" (Butler-Evans 32). In fact, creating and protecting a family were among the few ways black women could actively advance and participate in nationalist ideology.

The needs of black and white women were also divided by the legacy of racially based sexual stereotypes. While white women sought liberation from the sexually repressive constructions of ladylike behavior, many black women continued to opt for sexual conservatism. With the lingering stereotype of black women as more overtly sexual or loose, Dubey argues, marriage provided black women with a kind of "social respectability," and it served as protection from "sexual exploitation" (16). The distinction between black and white females was embedded in everyday discourse: Whites were ladies, with the traditional connotations of soft, dependent femininity, while blacks were women, with the traditional connotations of strength and sexual independence.[6] As race and gender collided in the lives of black women, they responded with an alternative to the two dominant ideologies of nationalism and women's liberation: black feminism.

The term *black feminism*, like *black nationalism* and *feminism*, can be a challenge to define; even women who have identified themselves as black feminist thinkers have debated its meaning.[7] Generally in literary studies the term describes critics, most often black women, who interrogate the intersections of signs—most commonly race, class, gender, and sexual preference—in the lives of (often black) women and the power relations evident in those intersections. Being black and female generates a unique subject position from which women can treat artistic productions and lived experience. *Black Woman: An Anthology*, which was edited by Toni Cade, appeared in 1970 as an early manifestation of this self-conscious wave of black feminist thought as "a hardheaded attempt to get [women] basic with each other" in the midst of the struggle for "liberation" (Cade 7). Other anthologies followed.[8]

As black nationalist thought sought to remake American society and black feminist thought emerged as a discrete discourse, the university, which would ultimately canonize Hurston, was likewise undergoing radical changes.[9] By 1966 black nationalism manifested itself on college campuses in organizations of black students demanding new university structures, courses, faculty hiring, and student recruitment to better address the needs of increasing numbers of black students. The general goal, in the words of Roger A. Fischer, "was the 'de-honkification' of the universities" (291). While student demands and protests took various forms, Fischer suggests that "one demand was virtually universal and led nearly every list of priorities": the creation of black studies programs. Precisely what such a program should look like and hope to accomplish was a matter of debate, but central were (and are) courses in black history, art, literature, sociology, law, and economics. The late 1960s saw the formation of black studies (or Afro-American studies) programs at a number of universities, including San Francisco State, Yale, Harvard, and Cornell universities, as well as historically black colleges and universities including Howard, Morgan, Tuskegee, Atlanta, Fisk, and Lincoln (Brisbane 223–39). Imbued in this creation of black studies programs were efforts to recruit and offer financial support for black students and to recruit black faculty. In this educational context Hurston began surfacing at colleges and universities.

Making Hurston Accessible

In this era of social upheaval, the first reprints of Hurston's books began appearing. In 1965, only five years after her death, Fawcett Publications issued the first reprint, and significantly, it was of *Their Eyes Were Watching God*. Other publishers followed. Chatham reprinted *Moses, Man of the Mountain* in 1967, and in 1969 Arno Press reprinted *Dust Tracks on a Road*, while Negro Universities Press reprinted *Mules and Men*.

Rather than satiate the demand for Hurston's work, however, these reprints only increased interest. In "Zora Neale Hurston: A Cautionary Tale and a Partisan View," Alice Walker recalls her discovery of Hurston as a footnote in an African American literature class. Some time later, *Mules and Men* served as her "delighted" introduction to Hurston's folkloric work. She recalls that people in New York "sat around reading the book themselves, listening to me read the book, listening to each other read the book, and a kind of paradise was regained. For what Zora's book did was this: it gave them back all the stories they had forgotten or of which they had grown ashamed" (83–84). Ironically, the book that had first made Hurston and her artistic agenda suspect proved crucial to her recovery, in part for the reason Walker identifies.

A similar interest in Hurston's work was developing among academics. Mary Helen Washington recalls that about 1968 she discovered Hurston in a black book store. About the same time black writer Sherley Anne Williams first read *Their Eyes* in a course devoted to African American poetry and prose. Gayle Jones in 1971 introduced Ann duCille to *Their Eyes*, and she in turn shared it with her students (duCille, "The Occult" 23). By 1969, Washington explains, *Their Eyes Were Watching God* had a national readership ("Foreword" ix). "By 1971," Washington remembers, "*Their Eyes* was an underground phenomenon, surfacing here and there, wherever there was a growing interest in African American studies—and a black woman literature teacher" (x).

The emerging reprints of Hurston's work generated a smattering of reviews and notices. Although this new generation of reviewers did not find Hurston's works flawless, their evaluations of her books are markedly different from those of their predecessors. More recent reviews have an overwhelmingly positive tenor. The forms of bias had changed. Hurston's persona had faded, eliminating significant personal bias for readers of *Their Eyes* and *Mules and Men* who knew nothing of the author, and the political lenses created by black nationalist and feminist thought illuminated new aspects of Hurston's work, elements lost in the earlier horizon.

The reissue of *Mules and Men* generated high praise as reviewers hailed it as a "classic collection," even "invaluable" ("Book Notes" 455; Glassie 468). Even the *Journal of American Folklore*, which had not reviewed Hurston's work in her lifetime, reviewed the 1978 reprint positively. In his evaluation for the journal, John Roberts notes that concerns about the ways Hurston had collected, transcribed, and perhaps altered the tales and/or their contexts to create a narrative might present "problems" for the "professional folklorist," but he assures readers that *Mules and Men* remains a "worthwhile and extremely useful book" (464). In contrast to Hurston's contemporaries, whose criticisms focused on the political ramifications of the collection, Roberts focuses on her anthropological methodology. Roberts read *Mules and Men* from an entirely different horizon of expectations. The political context was different. Debates over whether lower-class folk characters perpetuated stereotypes had submerged in a broader celebration of folk life and aesthetics. Hence Walker could argue that in reading *Mules and Men* "a kind of paradise was regained" ("Zora" 84).

But no book underwent a more radical change in reception than *Their Eyes Were Watching God*. Hurston's use of the folk argot, which has become a hallmark of her work and which had elicited substantial praise from her contemporaries, actually generated complaints from reviewers in the 1960s and 1970s. *Publisher's Weekly* describes her language as "glutinous dialect" that might prevent readers from progressing (61), while Roger Sale, writing for *Hudson Review*, complains that "[i]ts chief problem is a language problem" (153).

Response to the novel's plot also saw a remarkable change, but for the better. While Hurston's contemporaries Richard Wright, Alain Locke, and Sterling Brown condemned the novel as lacking in social consciousness, critics from the 1960s and 1970s praise it for having important social implications. Carol Gregory in *Freedomways* argues that "Hurston explores the dynamics of color/class prejudice and male chauvinism in the lives of Afro-American women within the context of a love story" (307). Hurston's once-dismissed love story becomes "an often overlooked classic of Afro-American literature" (Roberts 465). Yet another critic suggests *Their Eyes* "belongs in the category—with that of William Faulkner, F. Scott Fitzgerald, and Ernest Hemingway—of enduring American literature" (Grumbach 49). The horizon had changed, illuminating new aspects of Hurston's writings and new reasons for praise.

The remarkable change in respect accorded Hurston and her work is rooted in the convergence of the Black Arts Movement and black feminist thought. What resonated personally for Walker and coincided with the tenets of black nationalist thought was Hurston's "sense of black people as complete, complex, undiminished human beings" (Walker, "Zora Neale Hurston" 85). In *Mules and Men* and *Their Eyes,* Hurston's black characters exist largely within separate black communities, and Hurston provides neither explanation nor apology for this black world. It just is. Hurston's fiction focuses on the folk characters who were the central focus of the Black Aesthetic, and she also treats her characters in the language of the folk. She describes her use of idiomatic narration as "stewing the subject in its own juice" ("Art and Such" 910). Her aesthetic choice, however, also carries political import, for it undermines traditional Western (white) norms, according to which "nonstandard" English was hardly the norm for narrative voices.

Hurston's use of vernacular narration and dialect, folktales, signifying, and sermons coincided with the new artistic agenda that made white readers and their needs peripheral to black readers and their needs. Thus, elements to which racist white readers of the 1920s, 1930s, and 1940s responded were read through different mediating factors. Critics were less concerned about whether Hurston was supporting stereotypes. The bias that emerged when Hurston's work was read against the background of the Black Aesthetic made the collection of folklore and the novel valuable evidence of cultural history and health. Even Janie's choice in *Their Eyes* to live on the muck with Tea Cake, rather than in her two-story white house, validates the class-conscious nationalist argument that middle-class blacks had traded their cultural wealth for an empty existence. Hurston's choices in subject matter, narration, and plot provided examples of the healthy all-black community advocated by black nationalist discourse.

Despite these ways in which *Mules and Men* and *Their Eyes Were Watching God* met the demands of the Black Arts Movement, Hurston also departed from them in important ways. Her departures, however, were less obvious during the 1960s and 1970s than they are today. First, cultural nationalists saw themselves as creating a separate nation within a nation. Hurston, however, fractures this whole by arguing that "*The Negro*" does not exist. She explains, "[o]ur lives are so varied, appearances and capabilities so different, that there is no possible classification so catholic that it will cover us all" (*Dust Tracks* 733). Hurston remained a staunch individualist, artistically and personally. Her autobiography, for instance, creates a "statue" of an individual woman who, through hard work, rises from poverty to become an anthropologist, essayist, and author. In addition, Hurston steadfastly considered herself an American. She was, in her later years, highly critical of the failings of American democracy, but she maintained her loyalties to America and remained distrustful of communists' attempts to recruit black Americans. Each of these aspects of Hurston and her values counters black nationalist thought, which prioritized community ties and subjugated women.

Importantly, however, the ways in which Hurston, her politics, and her aesthetics challenged black nationalist discourse were not necessarily obvious. They could be overlooked. Much of what we know today about her personal views, her politics, and her aesthetic values comes from Robert Hemenway's biography of her, which did not appear until 1977, and from her reprinted essays and letters, which were not available in the early years of her recovery.

Also working to Hurston's advantage was a more sympathetic attitude about the difficulties of publishing in the 1920s, 1930s, and 1940s. Reviews of reprints of *Dust Tracks on a Road* are remarkably different from those that appeared in Hurston's lifetime. Black reviewers in the 1970s approached the ambiguities and the circumstances under which she wrote her autobiography with greater sympathy than her contemporaries had shown. N. Owano's review for the *Village Voice* is perhaps one of the most thorough of the period. Owano describes Hurston as the "major female literary figure" of her time and notes the difference in political context by acknowledging that "in the early days of consciousness shaping, you do not make your own music" (22). Concerns about Hurston's personal values and her skepticism of racial solidarity make the autobiography problematic for Owano, but the power of mediating historical factors pervades the review. Owano acknowledges the problematic nature of the autobiography but, unlike so many predecessors, does so without condemning Hurston as an artist or as an individual.

Many readers, particularly black women, could relate to the difficulties under which Hurston labored as an artist. She transgressed the Black Aesthetic's privileging of the unified community by exploring issues of colorism, misogyny, and spousal abuse. This violation, however, worked to her advantage with female readers. In both *Their Eyes* and *Mules and Men*, men take center stage as storytellers, while women frequently find themselves marginalized and ridiculed. Hurston's female readers, black and white alike, found (and continue to find) themselves drawn to Janie's search for a loving relationship that will permit her to maintain her sense of self.

Black women writers emerging in the 1960s and 1970s were undertaking similar transgressions of the Black Aesthetic. As black women found themselves in the background of black nationalism and on the outer fringes of white feminism, they too questioned the notion of a unified, homogeneous community. While the black women writers who emerged during the period "respect the communal emphasis of Black Aesthetic theorists," they "question the specific model of community" (Dubey 23). The first novels of Toni Morrison and Alice Walker, *The Bluest Eye* and *The Third Life of Grange Copeland*, for instance, structurally reflect a communal voice by weaving together multiple narrators' voices. Yet these novels also "split the black community along gender lines, thus threatening the unified racial community projected in black aesthetic theory" (22). Dubey and Butler-Evans document the extent to which the writings of Morrison, Walker, Toni Cade, and Gayle Jones in the 1970s both drew from and yet fractured nationalist discourse by developing stories that reveal the unique subject position of black women and/or misogyny within a seemingly unified community.

As black women were searching for predecessors, they found that Hurston's experiences as a writer mirrored their own. Just as Hurston had struggled against a male-defined aesthetic promoted by Richard Wright, Sterling Brown, Alain Locke, and Ralph Ellison, her successors were doing the same. Dubey documents the censure contemporary black women writers faced from black male critics because their work fractured nationalist discourse and revealed a multidimensional black experience. Morrison's *The Bluest Eye*, for instance, won praise from Black Arts critics because it rejects white standards of beauty and advocates the need for black aesthetics. Yet *Sula*, which followed, generated harsh criticisms for what some saw as Morrison's emasculation of black male characters (Dubey 33–34, 51–52).

Walker has designated Hurston a literary foremother. Walker's search for predecessors has been a vital aspect of her work as a contemporary writer. The title of her essay "Saving the Life That Is Your Own: The Importance of Models in the Artist's Life" reveals the value Walker places on her literary links to other writers (4). Models, she suggests, offer an artistic and spiritual resource for endurance (4), and Walker needed that sustenance.

At one level, then, attempts by Walker, Washington, and Cade to recover

Hurston served to rescue a fellow female artist from male-imposed artistic oblivion. At another level, however, their efforts constituted an assertion of their own presence, their own power in contemporary literary culture. Their move to include Hurston in a male-dominated canon sought to change that status and confirmed the legitimacy of their own writings. If they could rescue Hurston and alter the course of literary history, they increased their own chances of literary survival and of writing themselves into that male-dominated literary history. To paraphrase Walker, the life they saved was their own (14).

As Walker, Washington, Williams, duCille, and others around the country were discovering Hurston in reprints, the first serious critical inquiries into her work were appearing. Catherine Juanita Starke, for example, in *Black Portraiture in American Fiction* (1971) discusses Janie in the chapter devoted to "Black Individuals." An essay by Robert Hemenway, who had not yet published his biography of Hurston, for *The Harlem Renaissance Remembered* (1972) describes her as "one of the most significant unread authors in America, the author of two minor classics and four other major books" (190).

The nominal emerging scholarship on Hurston's work, however, was not entirely positive. Darwin Turner's 1971 commentary on Hurston demonstrates the ways in which perceptions of her as an exploiter of black folk traditions continued to linger. In *In a Minor Chord* Turner concedes that Hurston "deserves more recognition than she ever earned," yet he prefaces his discussion of her novels with an examination of her politics, where he argues that she was "an imaginative, somewhat shallow, quick-tempered woman, desperate for recognition and reassurance to assuage her feelings of inferiority" (98). Her work, he asserts, must be interpreted in light of her obsequious behavior toward her "supposed superiors" (98). Hurston's character, her "shallow" nature (120), and her "obsequious behavior" (98) mediate for Turner. Despite these continuing concerns about her personal and public politics, interest in Hurston and her work continued to grow.

Keys to New Readings

By 1974 interest in Hurston had surfaced in the academy, and articles about her were showing up in popular periodicals, which would help develop interest in her outside academic circles. In 1975 when the Modern Language Association's Commission on Minority Groups and the Study of Language and Literature created "a list of out of print books most in demand at a national level," Hurston's *Their Eyes Were Watching God* "'unanimously'" topped "'the list'" (Washington, "Foreword" x). In 1974 June Jordan's essay on Richard Wright and Zora Neale Hurston had been published in *Black World*. Jordan's essay works to bridge the apparent ideological opposition between Hurston and her former nemesis, suggesting that "we almost lost Zora to the choose-between games played with Black Art" (5). Stressing that the differences in Hurston's and Wright's experiences in the South shaped their fiction, Jordan asserts the importance of accepting and supporting affirmative art: "*Their Eyes Were Watching God* is the prototypical Black novel of affirmation; it is the most successful, convincing, and exemplary novel of Blacklove that we have. Period" (6). Jordan wanted her readers to understand that Hurston and Wright were both critical to African American literary traditions. Readers did not have to choose. With the development of black nationalism, the emphasis on whole black communities helped to make Hurston's work relevant to the political and social crises facing black Americans.

In 1975, Alice Walker's "In Search of Zora Neale Hurston" appeared in *Ms. Magazine*. The essay recounts her search for Hurston's unmarked grave. Using the well-planned lie that she was the writer's niece, Walker located people who knew "Aunt Zora" and who shared their memories. What Walker's search revealed, however, is an appalling dearth of information—and a wealth of misinformation—about Hurston's life and death. Walker's personal tribute to Hurston, a long-overdue headstone to mark her grave, illuminates the tragedy of a lost literary giant. Walker's essay, too, offered readers a new lens through which to view Hurston's work—a greater appreciation for the time in which she lived and wrote, and a sense that someone of value had been tragically discarded.

These seminal essays were followed in 1977 by Hemenway's formative *Zora Neale Hurston: A Literary Biography*. The biography did more to stimulate Hurston's recovery than any other single text. Hemenway presented readers with new forms of bias by introducing new mediating factors, often to Hurston's advantage. Debunking the myths and explaining the contradictions in her personal life that had made her professional goals suspect, Hemenway's sedulous research made it possible to understand Hurston on her own terms. His attention to her politics showed that while her opinions were often controversial, and perhaps occasionally naive, they were never maliciously exploitative. Rather, she was the one often manipulated. Hemenway's biography, then, provided a positive form of bias, a mediating factor that offered a corrective look at the woman and her work.

The bibliography with which Hemenway concluded the volume also provided an important resource for early studies of Hurston's work, offering access to periodical publications and unpublished writings, which in turn spurred new scholarship. It hardly seems coincidental that the University of Illinois Press, which published Hemenway's study, the following year reprinted *Their Eyes*, for the first time making Hurston's best-known novel available on a regular basis.

With the foundation laid by Hemenway's biography and accessibility of *Their Eyes*, Walker, Washington, and Cade took additional steps to provide a framework that would allow serious, balanced Hurston scholarship to emerge. In 1979 Walker edited and Washington wrote the introduction for *I Love Myself When I Am Laughing*, which includes excerpts from all of Hurston's books, except *Seraph on the Suwanee*, as well as eight stories and essays. In the prefatory materials Walker and Washington both stress the need to read Hurston as an artist, not a politician.

Critical response to the collection was largely positive as reviewers acknowledged the need to reread and reevaluate Hurston's work in light of changing trends. The reviews reflect the sense that literary culture and Hurston's place within it are changing. Randall Kennedy, writing for *The New York Times Book Review*, bestows on Hurston an accolade she never had the pleasure of hearing by describing her as "the leading lady of black American letters between 1920 and 1950" (8). He believes the collection assembled by Walker "allows us to view, without the obfuscation of apology or special pleading, the work of a spirited woman whose talents were considerable" (17). For him the collection goes "beyond" an "attempt to redress an injustice of literary history" as it mirrors "the emergence of self-conscious feminism, increasing sophistication in the study of black literature, and a renewed emphasis on black nationalism" (8). Carol Gregory and Vivian Gornick also address "feminist" interpretations of Hurston's work. Gornick suggests, as I have, that Hurston's recovery hinges on *Their Eyes Were*

Watching God by describing it as "her masterpiece, the work on which all else depends for affectionate interest" (Gornick 34).

Clearly, then, the changing political climate was offering new forms of bias for readers of Hurston's work, shaping responses to *Their Eyes*, and binding her writing to the cultural ferment of the moment. And yet, old concerns about her politics lingered. Gregory, for instance, was unwilling to read her works without the filter of her politics, despite the encouragement offered by Walker and Washington. In her review for *Freedomways*, Gregory argues that in order to "honor" Hurston, readers "must address all of her complexities" (307), and she criticizes Walker's attempt to "sidestep Hurston's political conservatism" (306).

Walker and Washington were attempting to shift the perspective through which readers approached Hurston's fiction. While Walker reminded readers to see Hurston as an artist, she craftily included five of the writer's essays that offer a range of her ideas on race and politics. "How It Feels to Be Colored Me," "The 'Pet Negro' System," "My Most Humiliating Jim Crow Experience," "Crazy for This Democracy," and "What White Publishers Won't Print" traverse the span from Hurston's Harlem Renaissance celebration of her identity to her harshest criticisms of American democracy and publishing institutions. Walker must have known that to reestablish Hurston as a major literary figure she would have to offer readers a corrective, more complete look at the writer's politics. While the attempt to present her as an artist, not a politician, was not entirely successful, the collection offered a fuller picture of Hurston's work than had previously been available.

Two years later, in 1981, Toni Cade edited another volume of Hurston's writings, *The Sanctified Church*. The collection of her essays on folklore generated little critical response. Nevertheless, the slim volume made some of Hurston's finest folkloric essays accessible to readers. By that time, the Hurston critical renaissance was budding as articles and chapters of books began exploring her work.

Barbara Christian, for example, in 1980 situated Hurston within a tradition of black women novelists, and the same year a second biography of her by Lillie Howard appeared as part of Twayne's Author Series for undergraduate readers. In 1982 *Rainbow 'Round Her Shoulder*, the first book-length collection of essays devoted to Hurston's art, appeared (Sheffey). Essays exploring her work continued to emerge, but not until 1987 did Karla

F. C. Holloway's *The Character of the Word: The Texts of Zora Neale Hurston* offer the first book-length study. The same year, Adele S. Newson provided an important spur to Hurston scholarship by publishing the first book-length annotated bibliography of works by and about her.

Simultaneously the literary canon was undergoing important changes. The predominantly white male canon was under attack by scholars suggesting that assessments of literature are politically bound and that aesthetic standards of beauty are not monolithic, timeless, or universal. Women and minority writers began making their way in greater numbers into classroom anthologies as curricula expanded to create courses devoted to women's, African American, Native American, African, and Caribbean literatures. Likewise, black literary study became increasingly complex and theoretical in the 1980s and 1990s. Emerging scholarship often focused on the importance and use of oral forms, which we find in Hurston's works. Houston Baker's *Blues, Ideology, and Afro-American Literature: A Vernacular Theory* (1984) and Henry Louis Gates, Jr.'s *The Signifying Monkey: A Theory of African-American Literary Criticism* (1988) are but two examples of important literary studies that emerged in the decade that treated Hurston. Each of these shifts—attention to women writers, attention to minority writers, and new theoretical treatments of African American literature—helped pull Hurston to the center of the new canon.

Going Mainstream

Shortly thereafter, Hurston's works went mainstream as HarperCollins released new uniform editions of them with introductions written by prominent black scholars. The volumes released in 1990 and 1991 made her works widely available in bookstores across the nation. In addition, HarperCollins published *Mule Bone*, the play Hurston and Langston Hughes collaborated on in 1930. With an introduction, the text of the play, Hurston's short story "The Bone of Contention," and a collection of correspondence about the *Mule Bone* dispute, the volume brings together important resources for examining the play and a crucial controversy in Hurston's career. *The Complete Stories of Zora Neale Hurston* followed, making her known published and unpublished stories accessible. The ever-increasing availability has and undoubtedly will continue to foster new interest in and scholarship on Hurston's works.

Promise for the Future

The 1995 release of two volumes of Hurston's work from *Library of America* has also encouraged new scholarship. Edited by Cheryl Wall, the volumes contain all seven of Hurston's books, as well as selected short stories, essays, and folklore. These editions are the first to provide any discussion of textual issues, copy-texts, and emendations, which is typically the kind of attention devoted to classic authors and texts. The volumes have also offered readers a new version of *Dust Tracks on a Road*, the final version Hurston imagined. While Wall does not—and could not—recreate the text Hurston originally intended, she has restored nearly 10 percent of the final typescript the author submitted.

These volumes brought their own round of positive reviews. As critics across the nation noted the prestige of being included in the exclusive list of authors published by Library of America, their most frequent praise is for the restoration of Hurston's autobiography. They also note that Hurston is the first black woman included in the series, which is devoted to creating "definitive" editions of major American authors. Reviewers see the volumes as cinching her admission to the literary canon.

In addition, the reviews demonstrate another change in responses to Hurston. Many reviewers recount key biographical facts and mention her changed literary stature. Some mention her politics, including her opposition to court-ordered desegregation. Most reviewers, however, read the volumes with an awareness of the complexities of politics of race with which Hurston dealt. Richard Kaye in the *Voice Literary Supplement* suggests that "editorial meddling" generated the cool response to *Dust Tracks* when it appeared in 1942 (64). Likewise, Ellease Southerland in *Quarterly Black Review* admits that Hurston's politics can be disturbing, but asserts that "there is still much of value to consider" in her writings (n. pag.), which is a concession Hurston's contemporaries were unwilling to make.

Olin Chism's review for the *Dallas Morning News* is a rare example of a critic discussing at length Hurston's politics and their bearing on her reputation. He argues, "This [edition] can be seen as a sort of sealing of the reputation of one of the ambiguous American black writers." He continues by saying that "[f]or several decades she was little thought of as a writer"; this, he says, is because "people found it hard to pin her down" (n. pag.). A third of his review explores the ways Hurston's racial ideology differed from that of her contemporaries. Chism's review, however, is the exception.

An overwhelming number of reviews acclaim Hurston as an important author deserving of the prestige implicit in publication by the Library of America. Her personal values and behavior are substantially less important to this generation of reviewers. Generally only a paragraph notes that Hurston's work was not well-received by her contemporaries.

Respect permeates the reviews for the two volumes of Hurston's writings. Reviewers clearly consider Library of America an arbiter of fad and fashion; Hurston passed the test and has been admitted to a select group of predominantly white male authors including William Faulkner, Mark Twain, Eugene O'Neill, Richard Wright, and more recently James Baldwin. Still more impressive is that she is among only a dozen or so figures who are represented by more than a single volume in the Library of America collection. The highly selective nature of the series suggests that Hurston has finally been granted a place in American literary culture.

Conclusion

Well, that is the way things stand up to now.
I can look back and see sharp shadows,
high lights, and smudgy inbetweens.

—*Dust Tracks on a Road*

SINCE 1925 Zora Neale Hurston's critical reputation has undergone remarkable changes. From the 1920s through the 1950s her controversial persona combined with the politics of race and class to dictate much of the critical response to her work and to determine her position as an outsider. In the 1960s and 1970s, the confluence of black nationalism, new folk-centered, class-based politics and aesthetics, Hemenway's biography, and black feminist thought brought Hurston back to the center. Vernacular constructions of black literary traditions, new interpretations, the continued awareness of gender issues, and still-surfacing works have kept her there.

During Hurston's own lifetime her critics often viewed her work as exploitative. Although white critics praised her writing as it appeared, their recognition is often tainted by condescension and racial prejudice. Other contemporaries, black and white, recognized the negative impact her writings could have—when manipulated—on the struggle for social and political equality. It mattered little that her work is, from today's vantage, political in its repeated focus on whole black communities and women's issues, and its celebration of black oral traditions. It mattered little that Hurston did not intend to impede racial progress or that she did not intend to create stereotypes for white readers. Hurston found herself on the margins of American literary culture in large part because of concerns about her character and the ways in which racist white readers could manipulate her work to support their agendas.

Today scholars and popular readers alike acknowledge Hurston's place in the canons of African American and American literatures. Zora is everywhere. In every bookstore I have entered in the last decade, Hurston is on the shelf. Her life has been recorded for young readers in a children's biography, *Zora Neale Hurston and the Chinaberry Tree*. Mary Fleener's art work in 1988 transposed Hurston's *Mules and Men* into a graphically illustrated comic titled *Hoodoo* for new audiences. Audio tapes of her fiction now capture the rhythms of black idiomatic speech flowing from the mouths of characters and narrators alike. A PBS video titled *Zora Is My Name* recounts the story of her life in a manner she would have approved: with musical and theatrical performance. Popular anthologies contain her fiction as do anthologies published for classroom use. The trend continues in popular magazines. *Preservation* in 2000 ran a story on traveling to Eatonville titled "Hurston's Dusty Tracks" (Bose 65), while *Smithsonian* in 2001 ran a lengthy article titled "Zora Neale Hurston: Out of Obscurity" (Holmes 97).

The tide of academic scholarship likewise continues to rise. With each new anthology and each new edition or collection of her work, Hurston gains new readers, and the widespread distribution of her work by HarperCollins and Library of America promises, at least for the next decade or so, constant availability. Her stature has taken on such gigantic proportions that she has eclipsed her better-received black female contemporaries and has come to define, too narrowly, black female literary strategies. Ann duCille, in her study *The Coupling Convention: Sex, Text, and Tradition*, astutely points out that constructions of African American literary traditions, even those focused on a female tradition, which rely on oral or vernacular theories threaten to relegate other black women writers to the obscurity from which Hurston has returned. It is difficult today to pick up a study of American women writers and not find Hurston included, often as the subject of a chapter, virtually always mentioned—if only in passing. While such stature seems an unexpected and perhaps deserved boon for her, it also remains a threat. As duCille argues, "However attractive and culturally affirming, the valorization of the vernacular has yielded what I would argue is an inherently exclusionary literary practice that filters a wide range of complex and often contradictory impulses and energies into a single modality consisting of the blues and the folk" (69).

That threat of exclusion extends not only to writers like Nella Larsen and Jessie Fauset, the two female Harlem Renaissance figures with whom Hurston is often studied, but also to Hurston herself. While current vernacular constructions of African American literary traditions include Hurston, what happens when the historical moment has changed? When she no longer fits the current literary paradigm? Readers looking to Hurston for "real" or "authentic" portraits of black life must be aware that such constructions can limit, and they certainly limited Hurston in her own lifetime. No single text or author can define a people or a nation. Defining any tradition too narrowly promises to continue the pattern of exclusion. Hurston's story, if nothing else, invites us to look long and hard at the trends of American literary culture and the means by which we canonize or discard writers. Our constructions of the canon, like those in Hurston's lifetime, are bound up in the current horizons of expectations, not absolutes.

Hurston has, for instance, already come under attack. Hazel Carby, a well-respected black feminist literary critic and theorist, has emerged as openly critical of Hurston and the attention she has attracted. Carby's "The Politics of Fiction, Anthropology, and the Folk: Zora Neale Hurston" explores the ways in which Hurston is being "reread, now, to produce cultural meanings" (29). Carby suggests that Hurston's canonization reflects an attempt to return to the simpler, rural past and to avoid "the contemporary crisis of black urban America" (30). However, the numbers of contemporary black women writers—as diverse as Sapphire, Gloria Naylor, Terry McMillan, and Toni Morrison—who explore urban American landscapes and attract acclaim make me skeptical that Hurston's popularity stems from escapism.

Hurston has become a convenient figure for study. She is everywhere. Carby goes so far as to describe her as "an industry that is very profitable" (29), and I agree. I also believe that in classrooms today, she is too often lauded as *the* token representative of black women writers. As a result, other women writers of her era have been neglected. And, perhaps, some academics mistakenly find rural constructions of identity more "authentic" than urban identities. However, I believe more important to Hurston's current popularity is that her work continues to support—even invite—new investigations and new interpretations. The complexity of her fiction and folklore collections and her treatment of issues we continue to struggle with (marriage, domestic violence, gender stereotypes, class) account for her continued currency, among both scholars and popular readers.

Carby rightly challenges scholars to reflect on the roots of their interests in Hurston and to read beyond her work to that of other writers. Looking more widely at the writing of other African American women does not necessitate returning Hurston to obscurity, but Carby's attack demonstrates the potential for divergent voices and shifting aesthetic values once again to marginalize Hurston.

For the moment, however, it seems that Hurston has arrived. An ever-growing body of fiction, folkloric work, plays, articles and essays reminds us that her legacy is large. Her short fiction, unpublished dramatic works, a newly recovered folklore collection, and still surfacing stories offer fertile ground for new critical inquiry. Other promising avenues for new scholarship include her letters. A treasure trove of information, the letters provide access to Hurston's voice unmediated by publishers and editors. They reveal the ups and downs of her personal and literary relationships, her responses to criticisms of her work, and opinions not fully expressed in her published works.

Hurston's future seems secure. The part of me that is a fan wants that to be always true, and yet the critic in me must accept that stasis in literary studies is counterproductive. As readers' horizons change, critics and scholars must be willing to entertain new interpretations made possible by new forms of bias, new forms of social crisis. Readers must also forge deeper into Hurston's writings, beyond the self-discovery of *Their Eyes Were Watching God* and the laughter of *Mules and Men*. Critics and scholars—as well as the reading public—must turn anew to her work, even that which discomfits, challenges, or confuses.

New critical views, like those of John Lowe, Deborah Plant, Ann duCille, and Susan Meisenhelder, offer innovative readings of much-studied texts and insightful readings of neglected texts such as *Moses, Man of the Mountain*, *Seraph on the Suwanee*, and "The Conscience of the Court," which confound so many. Instability, change, and growth are necessary and inherent in the literary landscape, and in the work of such innovative scholars lies the promise of Hurston's continued place in the literary canon—for on the horizon is a new generation of readers who will interpret her writings through new forms of bias and the ever-changing politics of race, gender, and class.

Notes

Introduction

1. See, for example, Gates's treatment in the "Afterword" of *The Complete Stories of Zora Neale Hurston.*
2. While I disagree with Carby's implication that Hurston's canonization reflects Americans' attempts to avoid the ills of urban America, an issue I turn to in the conclusion, her *Reconstructing Womanhood* has proven crucial to my understanding of the works of black women writers.
3. For discussions of what constitutes black feminist thought, see McDowell's "New Directions for Black Feminist Criticism" (154), Collins's *Black Feminist Thought* (21), and Christian's "But What Do We Think We're Doing Anyway."

ONE. Negotiating Ideologies of the Harlem Renaissance: The Politics of Hurston's Art and Identity

1. "Harlem Renaissance" is a contested term some prefer to replace with New Negro Movement or New Negro Renaissance, since the artistic activity of the period was not limited to Harlem or even New York. Its participants, too, came from all over the country. Robert Stepto provides a summary of the debate ("Sterling Brown").
2. Scholars also debate the dates of the period. Baker's assessment in *Modernism and the Harlem Renaissance* reaches as far back as Booker T. Washington and as far forward as Richard Wright to define the modernist sensibility associated with the period. In addition, the canonizing influence of *The Norton Anthology of African American Literature* makes Henry Louis Gates, Jr., and Nellie Y. McKay's editorial decision to extend the Harlem Renaissance section of the anthology from 1919 to 1940 worth noting. My own dates for the period range from 1915, when the first cultural manifestations of the New Negro appeared, to 1935, when artistic and critical approaches focus increasingly on protest literature and social message. For other scholars' dates see Huggins (*The Harlem Renaissance* 3) and Kellner (xxiv).
3. The six poems include the four identified on page 16, "Home" and "Reveries." The prose paragraph is "Sun Set." The essays include "Mr. Schomburg's Library," "How It Feels to Be Colored Me," "The Hue and Cry about Howard University," "Characteristics of Negro Expression," "Conversions and Visions," "Shouting,"

"The Sermon," "Mother Catherine," "Uncle Monday," "Spirituals and Neo-Spirituals," "The Race Cannot Become Great Until It Recognizes Its Talent," "Cudjo's Own Story of the Last African Slaver," "Communication," "Dance Songs and Tales from the Bahamas," and "Hoodoo in America." The plays are *Color Struck* and *The First One*. The stories include "John Redding Goes to Sea," "Drenched in Light," "Spunk," "Magnolia Flower," "Muttsy," "Under the Bridge," "On Noses," "The Ten Commandments of Charm," "Possum or Pig," "Monkey Junk," "The Eatonville Anthology," "Sweat," "The Gilded Six-Bits," "The Back Room," "She Rock," "The Book of Harlem," and "The Country in the Woman."

4. Scholars have established that Hurston's autobiography, my source here, is less than reliable. Hurston, among other things, changed her birth date and omitted mention of other significant events. For a discussion of more recent biographical work see Bordelon's "New Tracks on *Dust Tracks*."
5. The clipping of "Sun Set" and dates on poetry manuscripts and typescripts on deposit at the Schomburg Center for Research in Black Culture suggest that Hurston was submitting (and perhaps publishing) as early as 1919. The three commonly identified poems are "Night," "Passion," and "Journey's End."
6. My definition of the folk derives from Hughes's essay.
7. I treat race, class, and gender as interlocking signs in Hurston's fiction, although sometimes one sign takes precedence over another. The signs do not signify independently but simultaneously, for one cannot be female without being also marked in terms of race and class. There are, as Deborah King so astutely points out, "multiplicative relationships" among signs "dependent upon the socio-historical context and the social phenomenon under consideration" (297–98).
8. See Hurston's "Art and Such" (910).
9. The context of Cunard's anthology may have prompted Hurston's feigned ignorance of the emotional and psychic functions of dialect and minstrelsy. She deliberately leaves white readers to indict themselves in an anthology driven by Cunard's communist ideologies and her belief that "'[a] number of the younger writers are race-conscious in the wrong way, they make of this a sort of forced *self*-conscious thing'" (qtd. in North 192).
10. Michael North sees Hurston's use of dialect similarly, as an attempt to "take back a language obscured by travesty and stereotype" (176).
11. Eric Lott makes a similar observation in *Love and Theft*: "The black mask offered a way to play with collective fears of a degraded and threatening—and male—Other while at the same time maintaining some symbolic control over them" (25).
12. Lott suggests other sources as well, including the African American trickster figure, and the clowns and harlequins of British drama (22).
13. There are at least two versions of this text. The version Wall includes in *Zora Neale Hurston: Novels and Stories* follows the same general outline of a man migrating North in search of a woman, but the specifics differ slightly from the version that appeared in the *Pittsburgh Courier* in 1927.

14. Hurston was, in these intervening years, more often in the South collecting folklore than in New York. Removed from an atmosphere where her stories were something of a tourist attraction, Hurston was able to focus on creating multidimensional fictional folk, rather than on the unusual *ways* of the folk.
15. Contract between Charlotte Osgood Mason and Zora Neale Hurston December 8, 1927 (MSHU).
16. This restriction accounts for the near six-year cessation in Hurston's creative publications between 1927 and 1933. Any temptation Hurston might have had to ignore Godmother's wishes were early put to rest. In May 1928 Hurston's "How It Feels to Be Colored Me" appeared, and her correspondence with Locke suggests that Hurston's transgression against Mason's publishing prohibition caused quite a rift. At the time she wrote Locke, she had already explained to Mason that the essay paid her debt for *Fire!!* Nevertheless, Hurston felt the need to remind Locke of his previous knowledge of how the essay came to be published, presumably so he might intercede with Mason. See ZNH to AL June 14, 1928 (MSHU).
17. Langston Hughes and Zora Neale Hurston's dispute over *Mule Bone* is legendary. The two had traveled together in the South, had conspired to circumvent Mason's restrictions, and between March and June 1930 had collaborated on a play based on a folk tale Hurston collected at home in Eatonville, Florida. They hoped to use "The Bone of Contention" to bring authentic black comedy to the theater (Bass 2). At some point, however, Hurston decided she no longer wanted to collaborate with Hughes and attempted to excise his contributions from the manuscript. The result was an extended controversy that ended their friendship.
18. It is worth noting that Rampersad's biography reveals that Hughes, too, often relied on various forms of white patronage, including that provided by Charlotte Osgood Mason, although at this point in the autobiography (his discussion of the "nigeratti"), Hughes neglects to mention it. The arrangement of his descriptions of Hurston suggests a rhetorical strategy: He introduces Hurston in unflattering terms long before he describes their dispute over *Mule Bone*, the effect of which is to destroy Hurston's credibility as a serious artist prior to recounting their dispute. It is also worth pointing out that although Hughes understood Hurston was not responsible for circulating her single-author version of the play in Cleveland (Van Vechten set that in motion), he implies that she bears more responsibility for the Cleveland debacle than she does.

TWO. Making a Way: Fighting "The Line of Least Resistance"

1. See ZNH to FB June 8, 1930 (Kaplan 190) and FB to ZNH June 13, 1930 (APSL).
2. April 1932 found Hurston in dire financial straits. On April 4 she wrote Mason, hoping the patron would pay for her to return south. Hurston was living beyond her means in New York, and Mason was dissatisfied with the progress she was making on the folklore manuscript. To make matters worse, intestinal disturbances

plagued Hurston. She hoped that returning South—where she might work more productively and live more economically—would provide a solution, and Mason agreed. By May 17 Hurston was settled in Eatonville, where her health improved and her work progressed. Hurston explains that she "edited the huge mass of material" she had been working on, "arranged it in some sequence and laid it aside" (*Dust Tracks* 714).

3. I argue the point more completely elsewhere. See my essay in *Women's Studies*.
4. The primary plot line of *Imitation of Life* follows the life of a white woman named Bea Pullman. Left a widow at nineteen with a paralyzed father and new baby to support, Bea enlists the assistance of Delilah, a young and very dark black woman, as a housekeeper and sitter. But Delilah soon becomes central to Bea's business prospects, as her face, her recipes, and her carefully cultivated mammy image promote a line of candy and a series of restaurants. The secondary plot line follows Delilah's light-skinned daughter, Peola, who refuses to be "a nigger" and decides to pass as white (Hurst 181).
5. Thomas F. Fletcher defended Hurst, while Martha Gruening and Emmett E. Dorsey sided with Brown.
6. Van Vechten wrote the introduction to Hughes's *The Weary Blues* (which also prompted protests from the black press) and assisted Countee Cullen's sale of verse to *Vanity Fair* (White 16).
7. Hereafter cited as *Books*. Advertisements are listed in the works cited under the title of the book being promoted.
8. Hereafter cited as *Book Review*.
9. Other characters make reference to his stature (17–18).
10. See ZNH to JWJ January 22, 1934 (Kaplan 287), JWJ to ZNH April 20, 1934 (Beinecke).
11. See ZNH to CVV December 4, 1934 (Beinecke), and ZNH to CVV February 28, 1934 (Kaplan 290).
12. Cheryl Wall mentions these elusive files in "Note on the Texts" in *Zora Neale Hurston: Folklore, Memoirs, and Other Writings* (982).
13. Only Hurston's last book, *Seraph*, sold more than 2,000 copies before going out of print, a fact that would have made it difficult for Hurston to make demands on her publishers.
14. See, for example, ads in the *New York Times Book Review* on March 10, 1940: 17; March 17, 1940: 21; and March 24, 1940: 15.
15. Julia Peterkin (1880–1961) was a white South Carolinian who wrote about Gullah life. *Black April* (1927) brought her national recognition; her novel *Scarlett Sister Mary* (1928) won the Pulitzer Prize.
16. Reviews signed only with initials, as this one is, appear in the Works Cited under the last initial.
17. By early 1931, Hurston had laid aside the mass of tales that would become *Mules and Men* and turned her attention to writing again about Cudjo Lewis, the last

surviving African brought to the United States as a slave. She had completed "Baracoon" by April 18 but was unable to find a publisher for it either. The manuscript, which dramatized Lewis's capture in Africa and transport to America, remains unpublished. For the date of the manuscript's completion see ZNH to COM April 18, 1931 (Kaplan 217).

18. The construction of "Injun-killers" as heroes is Lippincott's—not mine. This hero's role, of course, relies on stereotypical images of Native Americans as those who needed or deserved killing for the threat they posed to white settlers.
19. A number of critics have addressed the authenticity of the Uncle Remus tales and the frame Uncle Remus provides for the tales. Lowe suggests the tales are authentic, despite the racist depiction of Uncle Remus (18). For other discussions of Uncle Remus see Walton, Bretensky, and Howell.
20. What her critics failed to realize is that the title can signify positively on African American folklore and the concept of maintaining dual identities: the mule-like persona for a master or boss, and a human persona for others within the black community. Identification with mules was a mask.
21. For an account of Locke's pursuit of a romantic relationship with Hughes, see Rampersad's *The Life of Langston Hughes* (66–72, 91–94).

THREE. A Highway through the Wilderness

1. ERE to ZNH December 19, 1934 (Fisk).
2. ERE to ZNH January 21, 1935 (Fisk).
3. ERE to CSJ December 20, 1934 (Fisk).
4. FB to HAM November 29, 1933 (Guggenheim).
5. Ruth Benedict to HAM November 15, 1933 (Guggenheim).
6. FH to HAM c. November 1933 (Guggenheim).
7. CVV to HAM c. November/December 1933 (Guggenheim).
8. Eastman (1883–1969) was an intellectual, prolific author, editor of *The Masses*, and cofounder and co-owner of *The Liberator*.
9. Eastman had worked with McKay on *The Liberator* in the early twenties.
10. Max Eastman to HAM December 22, 1933 (Guggenheim).
11. See also ZNH's 1935 Guggenheim Fellowship application (Guggenheim).
12. FH to HAM December 11, 1935 (Guggenheim).
13. CVV to HAM c. December 1935 (Guggenheim).
14. Melville Herskovits to HAM c. December 1935 (Guggenheim).
15. Hurston also dedicated *Jonah's Gourd Vine* to him.
16. Henry Lydenberg to HAM c. January/February 1936 (Guggenheim).
17. Edwin Osgood Grover to HAM December 7, 1935 (Guggenheim).
18. See ZNH to COM April 18, 1931 (Kaplan 217–18).
19. Neither Hurston nor Hemenway reveals his name.
20. See Jennifer Jordan's "Feminist Fantasies" for an alternate reading.

21. For mention of Hurston's contract, see her 1935 application for the Guggenheim Fellowship.
22. I am deeply indebted to duCille's subversive reading of *Their Eyes* as Hurston's exploration of the ways in which for women "the dream is the truth" (117).
23. Hurston argues that race has less power to determine an individual's identity or fate than circumstance (*Dust Tracks* 713).
24. Despite the increasing emphasis on protest fiction, Hibben, for one, appreciated Hurston's departure from the norm. Hurston, she says, "writes with her head as well as with her heart, and at a time when there seems to be some principle of physics set dead against the appearance of novelists who give out a cheerful warmth and at the same time write with intelligence" (2).
25. Preece identifies himself in "The Negro Folk Cult" as a white man.
26. Du Bois did try to blend his focus on race with Marxism, but the younger Marxist thinkers were skeptical of his goals and his ability to use Marxist thought effectively (Young 126).
27. *Opportunity* refused to publish Hurston's vehement response. Locke must have known about Hurston's letter, however. The disagreement apparently ended their longtime friendship. While the two exchanged cordial correspondence in 1943, their friendship was never repaired. Changes in their relationship can be tracked through ZNH to AL October 29, 1934 (Kaplan 320), ZNH to AL January 10, 1943 (Kaplan 473), and ZNH to JWJ December 5, 1950 (Kaplan 634).

FOUR. Voodoo: Fact and Fiction

1. I capitalize all uses of *Voodoo* to connote Hurston's respect for the religion. Instances where it is not capitalized are direct quotes from Lippincott's marketing of the volume and from reviews. I have maintained the integrity of their usage in part because it suggests the lack of respect for Hurston's subject.
2. Hurston mentions practitioners of hoodoo in *Dust Tracks* (613).
3. Ethnobotanist Wade Davis argues that documented zombies are created by administering a poison that includes tetrodotoxin, a neurotoxin that in the correct dosage produces deathlike symptoms that cannot be distinguished from death by rural medical practitioners. Davis believes the puffer or blowfish to be the source for this poison (121–52).
4. Hurston distinguishes between Rada and Petro Loas. The Rada Loas and the Houngans or priests who serve them are not very powerful and can only do good. Their services require nothing more than small animal sacrifices. In contrast, the Petro Loas and Bocors who serve them have the power to do evil. In return for services from Petro Loa, the supplicant may sacrifice larger animals, those he loves, and eventually himself. The danger Hurston faced is that the Bocor and the Houngan are often the same man. See chapter 13 of *Tell My Horse*.

5. William Seabrook's book about Haiti, *The Magic Island*, appeared in 1929. In 1937 Melville Herskovits, the reputable anthropologist who had supported Hurston's bid for a Guggenheim Fellowship, published his own study of Voodoo, *Life in a Haitian Valley*.
6. As I discuss in the introduction, Hurston's work may be authentic, but the term implies that black characters (and by implication black people) who are not like her characters are inauthentic. Thus, Hurston's characters become "real" blacks, while middle- and upper-class blacks become fake or imagined.
7. Seabrook's narratives are sensationalized adventure/travel tales including *The Magic Island*, noted in the text above, and *Adventures in Arabia among the Bedouins, Druses, Whirling Dervishes & Yezidee Devil Worshipers*.
8. The same ad appears on November 13.
9. Carmer (1893–1976) was a popular writer in the 1930s, 1940s, and 1950s, publishing thirty-seven books in his lifetime. In addition to writing a number of books for young readers and the volume of folklore noted above, he published *The Stars Fell on Alabama* (1934), which is his best-known work and includes a fictionalized portrait of Alabama folklorist Ruby Pickens Tartt.
10. See Hurston's "Star-Wrassling Sons-of-the-Universe."
11. Woodson (1875–1950)—author, editor, publisher and historian—has become known as the Father of Black History. The son of slaves, Woodson founded *The Journal of Negro History* and created the first Negro History Week, the forerunner of Black History Month.
12. Untitled, anonymous reviews, like this one, appear in the works cited under the title of the work being reviewed.
13. Martin Luther King, Jr.'s last speech, "I've Been to the Mountaintop," also draws from this tradition.
14. Sigmund Freud also published two controversial essays in *Imago* that argue Moses was not Hebrew but in fact Egyptian. His essays, however, were not available until 1939, the same year *Moses* appeared (Lowe 250 n. 5).
15. Lester's experience with resistance to the twin laws of the folklore process demonstrates the challenges Hurston faced. Lester, in preparing his own version of Harris's Uncle Remus tales, faced an editor who wanted him to eliminate contemporary references from his versions ("The Storyteller's Voice").
16. See Bertram Lippincott's letter to Meyer in which he responds to her making the connection between Hitler and Pharaoh, October 3, 1939 (AJA).
17. See, for example, James Baldwin's "Everybody's Protest Novel."
18. His distinguishing the novel as a "Negro novel" raises questions about the standards Carmer used to evaluate authors. Were his standards for black authors different from his standards for white authors? Or did he mean to imply that the subject matter was "Negro," whatever that might mean?
19. Murphy's review provides a photo of her, which identifies her as a black woman, but the clipping does not indicate a publisher or date.

20. For positive reviews of *Uncle Tom's Children*, see "White Fog" and Sterling Brown's "Chronicle and Comment."

FIVE. "The Tragedies of Life"

1. For a closer look at the textual evidence of Hurston's revision process see Raynaud's "'Rubbing a Paragraph.'"
2. See, for example, Hurston's discussion of Fannie Hurst (734–38), her discussion of Charlotte Osgood Mason (688–89), and her discussion of Bertram Lippincott (716–17).
3. The autobiography contains occasional explanations that clarify Hurston's meaning for white readers. See, for instance, her explanation of using sugar to sweeten coffee: "That is a Negro way of saying his patience was short with me" (577).
4. It is worth noting here that Richard Wright made a substantial concession with his own autobiography, *Black Boy*. In order to appease readers of the Book of the Month Club, Wright eliminated the entire second section, which treats his encounters with racism in the North. See Rampersad's "Note on the Text" 487–89.
5. Hurston's treatment of sexual issues and other matters readers saw as coarse surfaces in several reviews. For an example, see Hurston's reference to the way young men can encourage a "big, thick mustache" (600–601).
6. Griggs's reference to "her people" here seems to indicate the Hurston family.
7. Hurston's autobiography mentions her having twelve visions of future events. The autobiography identifies several of them, but they disappear from view (*Dust Tracks* 596–97).

SIX. Talking Back: Taking a Stand on Race and Politics

1. Perkins was a well-known editor who worked with Marjorie Kinnan Rawlings and Ernest Hemingway, among others.
2. Recent treatments of whiteness abound. For example, see Awkward, Dyer, and Frankenberg.
3. This narrative is constructed from unpublished correspondence. See Mitchell to ZNH December 16, 1947, and January 21, 1948; Parker to Mitchell November 24, 1947 (Princeton).
4. I can only guess that this alludes to Jim's rape of Arvay, but I cannot imagine, from my own horizon, what readers might have found "hilarious" about it.
5. I do not treat all five here. For dates and locations see N. H. Snow to Mr. [Burroughs] Mitchell October 14, 1948 (Scribner's).
6. See "Zora Neale Hurston Pleads Not Guilty" from the *Iowa Register* and "Author Held on Unnatural Act Charge" from the *Ohio State News*.
7. See ZNH to FH February 10, 1949 (HRHC).

8. See Rawling's letter to CVV (qtd. in Meisenhelder 214 n.4).
9. See Butcher.
10. See Hurston's "Self-Association as Negro Policy."
11. See W. W. Taylor's letter to the editor (UF).
12. See undated postcard (UF).

SEVEN. The Making of an Icon

1. See the telegram from Percy Peak's Funeral Home to Scribner's dated February 4, 1960 (Scribner's).
2. See also the memoirs of Lomax and Pratt.
3. Scholars frequently distinguish between black cultural nationalism, which sought to create a new America, a nation within a nation, and revolutionary nationalism, which often sought the complete restructuring of American institutions. I use the first of the two terms to describe efforts to restructure American life, but it is an umbrella term for a large body of diversely motivated discourses.
4. See also Butler-Evans (32) and hooks (177).
5. Giddings devotes an entire chapter to the Moynihan Report (25–35).
6. The connotations of these two terms have changed. Most females, black and white, now prefer to be known as women, while the term *lady* often implies a class-based status or weakness.
7. For essays addressing these issues see McDowell's "New Directions for Black Feminist Criticism" (154), Collins *Black Feminist Thought* (21), Christian's "But What Do We Think We're Doing Anyway," and Carby's introduction to *Reconstructing Womanhood.*
8. I am thinking here of Noble's history *Beautiful, Also, Are the Souls of My Sisters: A History of Black Women in America*; Smith's *Home Girls: A Black Feminist Anthology*; Davis's study *Women, Race and Class*; Moraga and Anzaldua's anthology *This Bridge Called My Back*; Hull, Bell-Scott, and Smith's *All the Women Are White, All the Men Are Black, but Some of Us Are Brave*; and hooks's *Ain't I a Woman: Black Women and Feminism.*
9. I do not mean to suggest that black feminist thought is a late twentieth-century development; the tradition in the United States can be traced back to the eighteenth century.

Works Cited

Aaron, Daniel. *Writers on the Left: Episodes in American Literary Communism.* New York: Columbia University Press, 1992.

Alsterlund, B. "Zora Neale Hurston." Rev. of *Tell My Horse*, by Zora Neale Hurston. *Wilson Library Bulletin* 13.9 (May 1939): 586.

Athey, J. V. Letter. *American Legion Magazine* Jan. 1951: 8.

"Author Held on Unnatural Act Charge; Bail Is Set at $1500." *Ohio State News* 23 Oct. 1943. Clipping. Scribner's Author Files, Harvard University, Cambridge, Mass.

Awkward, Michael. "Negotiations of Power: White Critics, Black Texts, and the Self-Referential Impulse." *American Literary History* 2.4 (Winter 1990): 581–606.

Babcock, Barbara A. "'Not in the Absolute Singular': Re-Reading Ruth Benedict." *Frontiers* 12.3 (1992): 39–77.

Baker, Houston A. *Blues, Ideology, and Afro-American Literature: A Vernacular Theory.* Chicago: University of Chicago Press, 1984.

———. *Modernism and the Harlem Renaissance.* Chicago: University of Chicago Press, 1987.

Baldwin, James. "Everybody's Protest Novel." 1949. *Baldwin: Collected Essays.* Ed. Toni Morrison. New York: Library of America, 1998. 11–18.

Banana Bottom. Advertisement. *New York Herald Tribune* 2 Apr. 1933: 5.

Banana Bottom. Advertisement. *New York Times Book Review* 2 Apr. 1933: 13.

Bass, George Houston. "Another Bone of Contention: Reclaiming Our Gift of Laughter." Hughes and Hurston 1–4.

Beale, Frances M. "Double Jeopardy: To Be Black and Female." *Sisterhood Is Powerful: An Anthology of Writings from the Women's Movement.* Ed. Robin Morgan. New York: Random House, 1970. 382–96. Rpt. in Guy-Sheftall 145–56.

Beck, Clyde. "Books of the Day." Rev. of *Their Eyes Were Watching God*, by Zora Neale Hurston. *The Detroit News* 26 Sept. 1937: 18.

Bell, Bernard W. *The Afro-American Novel and Its Tradition.* Amherst: University of Massachusetts Press, 1987.

Bernard, Emily. "What He Did for the Race: Carl Van Vechten and the Harlem Renaissance." *Soundings* 80.4 (Winter 1997): 531–42.

Body, Boots and Britches. Advertisement. *New York Times Book Review* 26 Nov. 1939: 19.

Bone, Robert. *The Negro Novel in America.* New Haven: Yale University Press, 1958.

Bonner, Marita. "On Being Young, A Woman—and Colored." *Frye Street and Environs: The Collected Works of Marita Bonner*. Eds. Joyce Flynn and Joyce Occomy Stricklin. Boston: Beacon Press, 1987. 3–8.

Bontemps, Arna. "From Eatonville, Fla. to Harlem." Rev. of *Dust Tracks on a Road*, by Zora Neale Hurston. *New York Herald Tribune Books* 22 Nov. 1942: 3.

———, ed. *The Harlem Renaissance Remembered*. New York: Dodd, Mead, 1972.

"Book Notes." Rev. of *Mules and Men*, by Zora Neale Hurston. *American Anthropologist* 81 (June 1979): 455.

"Books." Rev. of *Jonah's Gourd Vine*, by Zora Neale Hurston. *Time* 19 May 1934: 36.

Bordelon, Pamela. "New Tracks on *Dust Tracks*." *African American Review* 31.1 (March 1997): 5–21.

Bose, Sudip. "Hurston's Dust Tracks." *Preservation* 52.3 (May/June 2000): 65–70.

Boskin, Joseph. "'Black'/Black Humor: The Renaissance of Laughter." *A Celebration of Laughter*. Ed. Werner M. Mendel. Los Angeles: Mara Books, 145–59.

———. *Sambo: The Rise and Demise of an American Jester*. New York: Oxford University Press, 1986.

Bowles, Eva. "Opportunities for the Educated Colored Woman." *Opportunity* Mar. 1923: 8–9.

"Boys, 10, Accuse Zora." *Baltimore Afro American* 23 Oct. 1948: 1–2.

Bradford, Roark. *"Let the Band Play Dixie" and Other Stories*. New York: Harper, 1934.

———. *Ol' Man Adam an' His Chillun: Being the Tales They Tell about the Time When the Lord Walked the Earth like a Natural Man*. New York: Harper and Brothers, 1928.

Brawley, Benjamin. *The Negro Genius: A New Appraisal of the Achievement of the American Negro in Literature and the Fine Arts*. New York: Dodd, Mead, 1937.

Braxton, Joanne M. *Black Women Writing Autobiography*. Philadelphia: Temple University Press, 1989.

Bretensky, Dennis F. "Uncle Remus: Mere Buffoon or Admirable Man of Stature." *Philological Papers* 2 (Dec. 1975) 51–62.

Brickell, Herschel. "Books on Our Table." Rev. of *Jonah's Gourd Vine*, by Zora Neale Hurston. *New York Post* 5 May 1934: 13.

———. "A Woman Saved." Rev. of *Seraph on the Suwanee*, by Zora Neale Hurston. *Saturday Review of Literature* 6 Nov. 1948: 19.

———. "Zora Neale Hurston's Second Novel Fine Story of Woman Who Loved and Enjoyed Life." Rev. of *Their Eyes Were Watching God*, by Zora Neale Hurston. *New York Post* 14 Sept. 1937: 11.

"Briefly Noted Fiction." Rev. of *Moses, Man of the Mountain*, by Zora Neale Hurston. *New Yorker* 11 Nov. 1939: 75.

Brisbane, Robert H. *Black Activism: Racial Revolution in the United States 1954–70*. Valley Forge, Penn.: Judson Press, 1974.

Brock, H. I. "Full True Flavor of Life in a Negro Community." Rev. of *Mules and Men*, by Zora Neale Hurston. *New York Times Book Review* 10 Nov. 1935: 4.

Brown, Sterling. "Chronicle and Comment." Rev. of *Uncle Tom's Children*, by Richard Wright. *Opportunity* Apr. 1938: 120–21.

———. "*Imitation of Life*: Once a Pancake." Rev. of *Imitation of Life*, by Fannie Hurst. *Opportunity* Mar. 1935: 87–88.

———. "Luck Is a Fortune." Rev. of *Their Eyes Were Watching God*, by Zora Neale Hurston. *The Nation* 16 Oct. 1937: 409–10.

———. "Miss Fannie Hurst." Letter to the editor. *Opportunity* Apr. 1935: 121.

———. "Negro Character as Seen by White Authors." *Journal of Negro Education* 2 (April 1933): 184.

———. *The Negro in American Fiction*. Washington, D.C.: The Associates in Negro Folk Education, 1937.

———. *Southern Road*. New York: Harcourt, Brace, and Company, 1932.

Burris, Andrew. Rev. of *Jonah's Gourd Vine*, by Zora Neale Hurston. *Crisis* 41 (June 1934): 166–67.

Butcher, Philip. "Our Raceless Writers." *Opportunity* Summer 1948: 113–15.

Butler-Evans, Elliot. *Race, Gender and Desire*. Philadelphia: Temple University Press, 1989.

Cade, Toni, ed. *The Black Woman*. New York: Mentor, 1970.

Callahan, John F., ed. *The Collected Essays of Ralph Ellison*. New York: The Modern Library, 1995.

Cameron, May. "A Black Moses Talks and Walks with God." Rev. of *Moses, Man of the Mountain*, by Zora Neale Hurston. *New York Post* 9 Nov. 1939: 16.

Carby, Hazel V. *Reconstructing Womanhood: The Emergence of the Afro-American Woman Novelist*. New York: Oxford University Press, 1989.

———. "The Politics of Fiction, Anthropology, and the Folk: Zora Neale Hurston." *History and Memory in African American Culture*. Ed. Genevieve Fabre and Robert O'Meally. New York: Oxford University Press, 1994. 28–44.

Carmer, Carl. "Biblical Story in Negro Rhythm." Rev. of *Moses, Man of the Mountain*, by Zora Neale Hurston. *New York Herald Tribune* 26 Nov. 1939: 5.

———. *The Hurricane's Children: Tales from Your Neck o' the Woods*. New York: Farrar and Rinehart, 1937.

———. "In Haiti and Jamaica." Rev. of *Tell My Horse*, by Zora Neale Hurston. *New York Herald Tribune* 23 Oct. 1938: 2.

———. *The Stars Fell on Alabama*. 1934. Tuscaloosa, Ala.: University of Alabama Press, 2000.

Carter-Sigglow, Janet. *Making Her Way with Thunder: A Reappraisal of Zora Neale Hurston's Narrative Art*. Frankfurt: Peter Lang, 1994.

Caston, Ruth Elaine. "Zora Hurston's Life." Rev. of *Dust Tracks on a Road*, by Zora Neale Hurston. *Pittsburgh Courier* 2 Jan. 1943: 7.

Chamberlain, John. "Books of the Times." Rev. of *Dust Tracks on a Road*, by Zora Neale Hurston. *New York Times* 7 Nov. 1942: 13.

———. "Books of the Times." Rev. of *Jonah's Gourd Vine*, by Zora Neale Hurston. *New York Times* 3 May 1934: 17.

Chase, Bill. "Noted Novelist Denies She 'Abused' 10-Year-Old Boy." *New York Age* 23 Oct. 1948: 1.

Cheney, Margaret. "Books for Christmas." Rev. of *Their Eyes Were Watching God*, by Zora Neale Hurston. *Scribner's* 102 (Dec. 1937): 57–58+.

Chesnutt, Charles W. *The Conjure Woman*. 1899. Ann Arbor: University of Michigan Press, 1969.

Chism, Olin. "Hurston Is an American Original." Rev. of *Zora Neale Hurston: Folklore, Memoirs and Other Writings* and *Zora Neale Hurston: Novels and Stories*, ed. by Cheryl A. Wall. *Dallas Morning News* 26 Feb. 1995. Unpaginated clipping. Library of America.

Christian, Barbara. *Black Women Novelists: The Development of a Tradition, 1892–1976*. Westport, Conn.: Greenwood Press, 1980.

———. "But What Do We Think We're Doing Anyway: The State of Black Feminist Criticism(s) or My Version of a Little Bit of History." Wall, *Changing Our Own Words: Essays on Criticism, Theory and Writing by Black Women* 58–74.

Chubb, Thomas Caldecot. Rev. of *Mules and Men*, by Zora Neale Hurston. *North American Review* 241.1 (Mar. 1936): 181–83.

Collins, Patricia Hill. *Black Feminist Thought: Knowledge, Consciousness, and the Politics of Empowerment*. Perspectives on Gender Series Vol. 2. New York: Routledge Press, 1990.

Connelly, Marc. *The Green Pastures*. New York: Farrar and Rinehart, 1930.

Cooper, Wayne F. *Claude McKay: Rebel Sojourner in the Harlem Renaissance*. Baton Rouge: Louisiana State University Press, 1996.

Courlander, Harold. Rev. of *Tell My Horse*, by Zora Neale Hurston. *Saturday Review of Literature* 15 Oct. 1938: 6–7.

Cromwell, Otelia, Lorenzo Dow Turner, and Eva B. Dykes, eds. *Readings from Negro Authors*. New York: Harcourt, Brace, and Company, 1931.

Cullen, Countee. "Heritage." Gates and McKay 1311–14.

Cunard, Nancy, ed. *Negro: An Anthology*. London: Wishart, 1934.

Curtis, Constance. "Zora Neale Hurston Reveals Key to Her Literary Success." *New York Amsterdam News* 18 Nov. 1944: N. pag.

Daniels, Jonathan. "Black Magic and Dark Laughter." Rev. of *Mules and Men*, by Zora Neale Hurston. *The Saturday Review* 19 Oct. 1935: 12.

Davis, Angela. *Women, Race and Class*. New York: Random House, 1981.

Davis, Wade. *The Serpent and the Rainbow*. New York: Warner Books, 1987.

Delbanco, Andrew. "The Mark of Zora." Rev. of *Zora Neale Hurston: Folklore, Memoirs and Other Writings* and *Zora Neale Hurston: Novels and Stories*, ed. by Cheryl A. Wall. *New Republic* 3 July 1995: 30–35.

Dixon, Thomas. *The Leopard's Spots: A Romance of the White Man's Burden, 1865–1900*. New York: Doubleday, Page and Company, 1902.

Dorsey, Emmett E. Letter. *Opportunity* May 1935: 154.

Dove, Rita. Foreword. *Jonah's Gourd Vine* by Zora Neale Hurston. New York: HarperCollins, 1990. vii–xv.

Dubey, Madhu. *Black Women Novelists and the Nationalist Aesthetic*. Bloomington: Indiana University Press, 1994.

Du Bois, W.E.B. "Books." Rev. of *Nigger Heaven*. *Crisis* 33.2 (Dec. 1926): 81–82.

———. "Criteria of Negro Art." 1926. Angelyn Mitchell 60–68.

———. *The Souls of Black Folk*. 1903. New York: First Vintage Books/Library of America, 1990.

duCille, Ann. *The Coupling Convention: Sex, Text, and Tradition in Black Women's Fiction*. New York: Oxford University Press, 1993.

———. "The Occult of True Black Womanhood: Critical Demeanor and Black Feminist Studies." *Female Subjects in Black and White: Race, Psychoanalysis, Feminism*. Eds. Elizabeth Abel, Barbara Christian, and Helene Moglen. Berkeley: University of California Press, 1997. 21–56.

Dunbar, Paul Laurence. "An Antebellum Sermon." *The Complete Poems of Paul Laurence Dunbar*. New York: Dodd, Mead, 1922. 13.

Dust Tracks on a Road. Advertisement. *New York Times Book Review* 6 Dec. 1942: 39.

Dust Tracks on a Road. Advertisement. *New York Herald Tribune* 22 Nov. 1942: 35.

Dust Tracks on a Road. Review. *The New Yorker* 14 Nov. 1942: 79.

Dyer, Richard. *The Matter of Images: Essays on Representation*. New York: Routledge Press, 1993.

———. "The Matter of Whiteness." *Theories of Race and Racism: A Reader*. Ed. Les Back and John Solomos. London: Routledge Press, 2000. 537–48.

Ellison, Ralph. "Change the Joke and Slip the Yoke." Callahan 100–112.

———. *Going to the Territory*. New York: Random House, 1986.

———. "Recent Negro Fiction." *New Masses* 40 (5 Aug. 1941): 22–26.

———. "Twentieth-Century Fiction and the Mask of Humanity." Callahan 81–99.

"Fall Book Index." *Publishers Weekly* 18 Sept. 1937: N. pag.

"Fall Book Index, 1939." *Publishers Weekly* 16 Sept. 1939: N. pag.

"Famous Author Working as Maid for White Folks Down in Dixie." *New York Amsterdam News* 1 Apr. 1950: 1+.

Farrison, W. Edward. Rev. of *Dust Tracks on a Road*, by Zora Neale Hurston. *Journal of Negro History* 28.3 (July 1943): 352–55.

Fauset, Arthur Huff. "American Negro Folk Literature." Locke, *The New Negro* 238–44.

Fauset, Jessie. "The Gift of Laughter." Locke, *The New Negro* 161–67.

Felton, Estelle. Rev. of *Jonah's Gourd Vine*, by Zora Neale Hurston. *Opportunity* August 1934: 252–53.

Ferguson, Otis. "You Can't Hear Their Voices." Rev. of *Their Eyes Were Watching God*, by Zora Neale Hurston. *New Republic* 13 Oct. 1937: 276.

Fischer, Roger A. "Ghetto and Gown: The Birth of Black Studies." *Current History* 57.339 (Nov. 1969): 290–94+.

Fleener, Mary. *Hoodoo*. Los Angeles: 3-D Zone, 1988.

Fletcher, Thomas Fortune. Letter to the Editor. *Opportunity* May 1935: 153.

"Florida Local Color." Rev. of *Dust Tracks on a Road*, by Zora Neale Hurston. Unidentified clipping. Zora Neale Hurston Collection, University of Florida.

Ford, Nick Aaron. *The Contemporary Negro Novel: A Study in Race Relations*. 1936. College Park, Md.: McGrath Publishing Company, 1968.

Forrest, Ethel A. Rev. of *Their Eyes Were Watching God*, by Zora Neale Hurston. *Journal of Negro History* 23.1 (Jan. 1938): 106–7.

Foster, Frances Smith. "African American Progress Report Autobiographies." *Redefining American Literary History*. Eds. A. LaVonne Brown Ruoff and Jerry Washington Ward. New York: MLA, 1990. 270–83.

Fox-Genovese, Elizabeth. "To Write My Self: The Autobiographies of Afro-American Women." *Feminist Issues in Literary Scholarship*. Ed. Shari Benstock. Bloomington: Indiana University Press, 1987. 161–80.

Frankenberg, Ruth. *White Women, Race Matters: The Social Construction of Racism*. Minneapolis: University of Minnesota Press, 1993.

Frazier, C. Leslie. "Zora N. Hurston's 'Men and Mules' Controversial." Rev. of *Mules and Men*, by Zora Neale Hurston. *Washington Tribune* 1935. Unpaginated clipping. Atlanta University.

Freud, Sigmund. *Moses and Monotheism*. Trans. Katherine Jones. London: Hogarth Press, 1951.

Fullinwider, S. P. *The Mind and Mood of Black America*. Homewood, Ill., Dorsey Press, 1969.

Gadamer, Hans-Georg. *Truth and Method*. New York: Seabury Press, 1975.

Gannett, Lewis. Rev of *Jonah's Gourd Vine*, by Zora Neale Hurston. *New York Herald Tribune* 3 May 1934: N. pag.

Gates, Henry Louis, Jr. Afterword. Gates and Lemke 285–94.

———. *Figures in Black: Words, Signs and the "Radical" Self*. New York: Oxford University Press, 1987.

———. *The Signifying Monkey: A Theory of African-American Literary Criticism*. New York: Oxford, 1988.

Gates, Henry Louis, Jr., and K. A. Appiah, eds. *Zora Neale Hurston: Critical Perspectives Past and Present*. New York: Amistad Press, 1993.

Gates, Henry Louis, Jr., and Sieglinde Lemke, eds. *The Complete Stories of Zora Neale Hurston*. New York: HarperCollins, 1995.

Gates, Henry Louis, Jr., and Nellie Y. McKay, et al., eds. *The Norton Anthology of African American Literature*. New York: W. W. Norton, 1997.

Giddings, Paula. *When and Where I Enter: The Impact of Black Women on Race and Sex in America*. 2nd ed. New York: Quill, 1996.

Gilbert, Douglas. "When Negro Succeeds, South Is Proud, Zora Hurston Says." Unidentified clipping. Chicago Historical Society, Chicago, Illinois.

Glassie, Henry. "From the Book Review Editor." Rev. of *Mules and Men*, by Zora Neale Hurston. *Journal of American Folklore* 84 (Oct. 1971): 468.

Gornick, Vivian. "Catching up with Hurston." Rev. of *I Love Myself When I Am Laughing*, by Zora Neale Hurston. *Voice* 31 Dec. 1979: 34–35.

Greenleaf, Richard. "'Let My People Go!'" Rev. of *Moses, Man of the Mountain*, by Zora Neale Hurston. *Orange County Chief* 14 Nov. 1939. Clipping, Zora Neale Hurston Collection, University of Florida.

Gregory, Carol E. "Hurston Revisited." Rev. of *I Love Myself When I Am Laughing*, by Zora Neale Hurston and ed. by Alice Walker. *Freedomways* 20.4 (1980): 305–7.

Griffith, D. W., dir. *The Birth of a Nation*. 1915. Los Angeles: Republic Pictures Home Video, 1991.

Griffiths, Gareth. "The Myth of Authenticity: Representation, Discourse and Social Practice." *De-Scribing the Empire*. Ed. Chris Tiffin and Alan Lawson. London: Routledge Press, 1994. 70–85.

Griggs, Hazel. "Moses Pictured as Voodoo Man in New Hurston Book." Rev. of *Moses, Man of the Mountain. Norfolk Journal and Guide* 13 Jan. 1940: 20.

———. "Zora N. Hurston's New Book an Autobiography." *Journal and Guide* 2 Jan. 1943. Unpaginated clipping, Atlanta University.

Gruening, Martha. "Darktown Strutter." Rev. of *Jonah's Gourd Vine*, by Zora Neale Hurston. *The New Republic* 11 July 1934: 244–45.

———. Letter to the Editor. *Opportunity* May 1935: 154.

Grumbach, Doris. "Fine Print." Rev. of *Their Eyes Were Watching God*, by Zora Neale Hurston. *Saturday Review of Literature* 16 Sept. 1978: 49.

Guy-Sheftall, Beverly, ed. *Words of Fire: An Anthology of African-American Feminist Thought*. New York: New Press, 1995.

H., W. Rev. of *Jonah's Gourd Vine*, by Zora Neale Hurston. Louisville *Courier-Journal* 8 July 1934: 7.

Hamilton, Edward W. Rev. of *Seraph on the Suwanee*, by Zora Neale Hurston. *America* 1 Jan. 1949: 354–55.

Harper, Frances E. Watkins. "Moses: A Story of the Nile." 1869. *The Complete Poems of Frances E.W. Harper*. Ed. Maryemma Graham. New York: Oxford University Press, 1988. 34–66.

Harris, Catherine. Letter to the author. 3 Oct. 2002.

Harris, Joel Chandler. *Nights with Uncle Remus: Myths and Legends of the Old Plantation*. Boston: Ticknor and Company, 1883.

Harris, Polly V. "Zora Hurston." Rev. of *Mules and Men*. *Chicago Defender* 2 Nov. 1935: 11. *Black Literature, 1827–1940* (1987–1996): fiche 1513.02.

Hedden, Worth Tuttle. "Turpentine and Moonshine." Rev. of *Seraph on the Suwanee*, by Zora Neale Hurston. *New York Herald Tribune Book Review* 10 Oct. 1948: 2.

Helbling, Mark. "Zora Neale Hurston." Kellner 180–81.

Hemenway, Robert E. *Zora Neale Hurston: A Literary Biography*. Urbana: University of Illinois Press, 1977.

———. "Zora Neale Hurston and the Eatonville Anthropology." Bontemps, *The Harlem Renaissance* 190–214.

Hernandez, Graciela. "Multiple Subjectivities and Strategic Positionality: Zora Neale

Hurston's Experimental Ethnographies." *Women Writing Culture*. Ed. Ruth Behar and Deborah A. Gordon. Berkeley: University of California Press, 1995. 148–65.

Herskovits, Melville. *Life in a Haitian Valley*. New York: Alfred A. Knopf, 1937.

Hex Marks the Spot. Advertisement. *New York Herald Tribune Books* 16 Oct. 1938: 21.

Heyward, DuBose. *Porgy*. New York: Grosset and Dunlap, 1925.

Hibben, Sheila. "Vibrant Book Full of Nature and Salt." Rev. of *Their Eyes Were Watching God*, by Zora Neale Hurston. *New York Herald Tribune* 26 Sept. 1937: 2.

Hill, Lynda Marion. *Social Rituals and the Verbal Art of Zora Neale Hurston*. Washington, D.C.: Howard University Press, 1996.

Holloway, Karla F. C. *The Character of the Word: The Texts of Zora Neale Hurston*. New York: Greenwood Press, 1987.

Holmes, Marian Smith. "Zora Neale Hurston: Out of Obscurity." *Smithsonian* 31.10 (Jan. 2001): 97–108.

hooks, bell. *Ain't I a Woman: Black Women and Feminism*. Boston: South End Press, 1981.

Howard, Lillie P. *Zora Neale Hurston*. Boston: Twayne Publishers, 1980.

Howell, Marcella. "Will the Authentic *Hare* Please Stand Up: An Analysis of Joel Chandler Harris' Uncle Remus Tales." *Afro-American Folklore: A Unique American Experience*. University of Wisconsin-LaCrosse, 1977: 23–31.

Huggins, Nathan Irvin. *The Harlem Renaissance*. New York: Oxford University Press, 1971.

———, ed. *Voices from the Harlem Renaissance*. New York: Oxford University Press, 1995.

Hughes, Carl Milton. *The Negro Novelist*. New York: Citadel Press, 1953.

Hughes, Langston. "Advertisement for the Waldorf-Astoria." *The Collected Poems of Langston Hughes*. Ed. Arnold Rampersad. New York: Knopf, 1994. 143–46.

———. *The Big Sea*. New York: Alfred A. Knopf, 1940.

———. "The Blues I'm Playing." *The Ways of White Folks*. New York: Vintage Classics, 1990. 99–123.

———. *Fine Clothes to the Jew*. New York: Alfred A. Knopf, 1927.

———. "I, Too." Gates and McKay 1258.

———. "The Negro Artist and the Racial Mountain." 1925. Angelyn Mitchell 55–59.

———. "The Negro Speaks of Rivers." Gates and McKay 1254.

———. *Not without Laughter*. 1930. New York: Scribner's Paperback Fiction, 1995.

———. *The Ways of White Folks*. 1934. New York: Vintage Classics, 1990.

———. *The Weary Blues*. Intro. Carl Van Vechten. New York: Alfred A. Knopf, 1945.

Hughes, Langston, and Zora Neale Hurston. *Mule Bone: A Comedy of Negro Life*. Ed. George Houston Bass and Henry Louis Gates, Jr. New York: HarperPerennial, 1991.

Huie, William Bradford. *Ruby McCollum: Woman in the Suwanee Jail*. New York: E. P. Dutton, 1956.

Hull, Gloria T., Patricia Bell-Scott, and Barbara Smith, eds. *All the Women Are White,*

All the Blacks Are Men, but Some of Us Are Brave: Black Women's Studies. New York: The Feminist Press, 1987.

Hunton, W. A. "The Adventures of the Brown Girl in Her Search for Life." Rev. of *Their Eyes Were Watching God*, by Zora Neale Hurston. *Current Literature on Negro Education* 7.1 (Jan. 1938): 71–72.

Hurst, Fannie. *Imitation of Life*. New York: Harper and Brothers, 1933.

———. "Mr. Sterling Brown." Letter. *Opportunity* Apr. 1935: 121.

———. "Zora Hurston: A Personality Sketch." *Yale University Library Gazette* 35 (July 1960): 17–22.

Hurston, Zora Neale. "Art and Such." Wall, *Zora Neale Hurston: Folklore, Memoirs and Other Writings* 905–11.

———. "The Back Room." *Pittsburgh Courier* 19 Feb. 1927, sec. 2: 1. *Black Literature, 1827–1940* (1987–1996): fiche 1627.05.

———. "A Bit of Our Harlem." *Negro World* 8 Apr. 1922: 6. *Black Literature, 1827–1940* (1987–1996): fiche 1217.10.

———. "Bits of Our Harlem." *Negro World* 15 Apr. 1922: 6. *Black Literature, 1827–1940* (1987–1996): fiche 1218.01.

———. "Black Death." Gates and Lemke 202–8.

———. "The Bone of Contention." Gates and Lemke 209–20.

———. "The Book of Harlem." *Pittsburgh Courier* 12 Feb. 1927, sec. 2: 1. *Black Literature, 1827–1940* (1987–1996): fiche 1626.11.

———. "Characteristics of Negro Expression." 1934. Wall, *Zora Neale Hurston: Folklore, Memoirs and Other Writings* 830–46.

———. "The Chick with One Hen." Unpublished Manuscript. James Weldon Johnson Memorial Collection, Yale Collection of American Literature, Beinecke Rare Book and Manuscript Library, Yale University.

———. *Color Struck: A Play. Fire!!* 1 (Nov. 1926): 7–15.

———. "Communication." *Journal of Negro History* 12 (Oct. 1927): 664–67.

———. "The Conscience of the Court." Gates and Lemke 162–77.

———. "Conversions and Visions." 1934. Wall, *Zora Neale Hurston: Folklore, Memoirs and Other Writings* 846–51.

———. "The Country in the Woman." *Pittsburgh Courier* 26 Mar. 1927, sec. 2: 1. *Black Literature, 1827–1940* (1987–1996): fiche 1628.05.

———. "Court Order Can't Make Races Mix." 1955. Wall, *Folklore, Memoirs and Other Writings*. 956–58.

———. "Crazy for This Democracy." 1945. Wall, *Zora Neale Hurston: Folklore, Memoirs and Other Writings* 945–49.

———. "Cudjo's Own Story of the Last African Slaver." *Journal of Negro History* 12 (Oct. 1927): 648–63.

———. "Dance Songs and Tales from the Bahamas." *Journal of American Folklore* 43 (July–Sept. 1930): 294–312.

———. "Drenched in Light." 1924. Gates and Lemke 17–25.

———. *Dust Tracks on a Road*. 1942. Wall, *Zora Neale Hurston: Folklore, Memoirs and Other Writings* 558–808.

———. "The Eatonville Anthology." 1926. Wall, *Zora Neale Hurston: Folklore, Memoirs and Other Writings* 813–25.

———. *Every Tongue Got to Confess: Negro Folk-Tales from the Gulf States*. Ed. Carla Kaplan. New York: Harper Collins, 2002.

———. "The Fire and the Cloud." 1934. Gates and Lemke 117–21.

———. *The First One: A Play*. *Ebony and Topaz: A Collectanea*. Ed. Charles S. Johnson. New York: National Urban League, 1927. 53–57.

———. "The Gilded Six-Bits." 1933. Gates and Lemke 86–98.

———. *Go Gator and Muddy the Water: Writings By Zora Neale Hurston from the Federal Writers' Project*. Ed. Pamela Bordelon. New York: W. W. Norton, 1999.

———. "High John de Conquer." 1943. Wall, *Zora Neale Hurston: Folklore, Memoirs and Other Writings* 922–31.

———. "Home." *Negro World* 8 Apr. 1922: 6.

———. "Hoodoo in America." *Journal of American Folklore* 44.174 (Oct.–Dec. 1931): 317–418.

———. "How It Feels to Be Colored Me." 1928. Wall, *Zora Neale Hurston: Folklore, Memoirs and Other Writings* 826–29.

———. "The Hue and Cry about Howard University." *Messenger* 7 (Sept. 1925): 315–19+.

———. *I Love Myself When I Am Laughing and Then Again When I Am Looking Mean and Impressive*. Ed. Alice Walker. New York: The Feminist Press, 1979.

———. "I Saw Negro Votes Peddled." *American Legion Magazine* Nov. 1950: 12–13+.

———. "John Redding Goes to Sea." 1921. Gates and Lemke 1–17.

———. *Jonah's Gourd Vine*. 1934. Wall, *Zora Neale Hurston: Novels and Stories* 1–171.

———. "Journey's End." *Negro World* 8 Apr. 1922: 4.

———. "Magnolia Flower." 1925. Gates and Lemke 33–40.

———. "Monkey Junk." *Pittsburgh Courier* 5 Mar. 1927: 1. *Black Literature 1827–1940* (1987–1996): fiche 1627.09.

———. *Moses, Man of the Mountain*. 1939. Wall, *Zora Neale Hurston: Novels and Stories* 335–595.

———. "Mother Catherine." 1934. Wall, *Zora Neale Hurston: Folklore, Memoirs and Other Writings* 854–60.

———. "Mr. Schomburg's Library." *Negro World* 22 Apr. 1922: 6.

———. *Mules and Men*. 1935. Wall, *Zora Neale Hurston: Folklore, Memoirs and Other Writings* 1–267.

———. "Muttsy." 1926. Gates and Lemke 41–56.

———. "My Most Humiliating Jim Crow Experience." 1944. Wall, *Zora Neale Hurston: Folklore, Memoirs and Other Writings* 935–36.

———. "Negroes without Self-Pity." 1943. Wall, *Zora Neale Hurston: Folklore, Memoirs and Other Writings* 932–34.

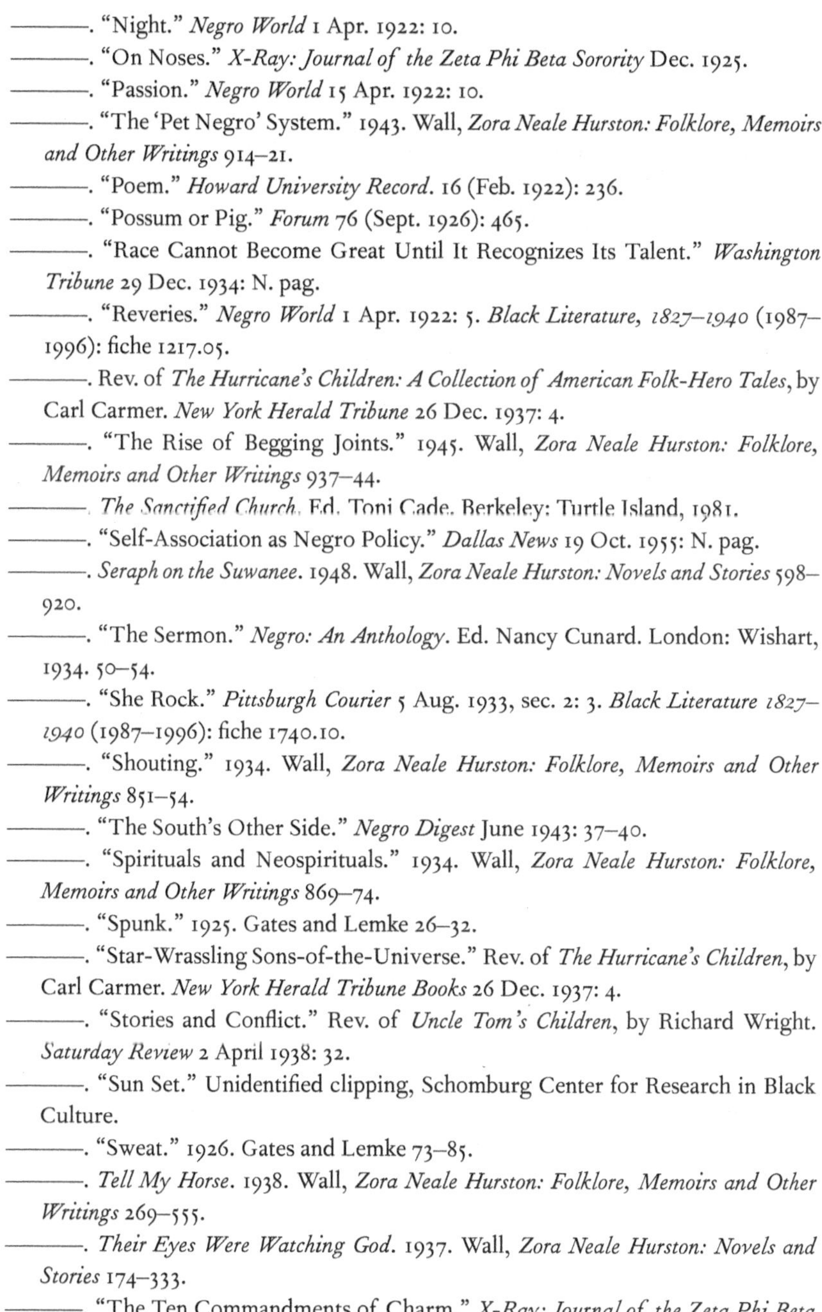

———. "Night." *Negro World* 1 Apr. 1922: 10.

———. "On Noses." *X-Ray: Journal of the Zeta Phi Beta Sorority* Dec. 1925.

———. "Passion." *Negro World* 15 Apr. 1922: 10.

———. "The 'Pet Negro' System." 1943. Wall, *Zora Neale Hurston: Folklore, Memoirs and Other Writings* 914–21.

———. "Poem." *Howard University Record.* 16 (Feb. 1922): 236.

———. "Possum or Pig." *Forum* 76 (Sept. 1926): 465.

———. "Race Cannot Become Great Until It Recognizes Its Talent." *Washington Tribune* 29 Dec. 1934: N. pag.

———. "Reveries." *Negro World* 1 Apr. 1922: 5. *Black Literature, 1827–1940* (1987–1996): fiche 1217.05.

———. Rev. of *The Hurricane's Children: A Collection of American Folk-Hero Tales*, by Carl Carmer. *New York Herald Tribune* 26 Dec. 1937: 4.

———. "The Rise of Begging Joints." 1945. Wall, *Zora Neale Hurston: Folklore, Memoirs and Other Writings* 937–44.

———. *The Sanctified Church.* Ed. Toni Cade. Berkeley: Turtle Island, 1981.

———. "Self-Association as Negro Policy." *Dallas News* 19 Oct. 1955: N. pag.

———. *Seraph on the Suwanee.* 1948. Wall, *Zora Neale Hurston: Novels and Stories* 598–920.

———. "The Sermon." *Negro: An Anthology.* Ed. Nancy Cunard. London: Wishart, 1934. 50–54.

———. "She Rock." *Pittsburgh Courier* 5 Aug. 1933, sec. 2: 3. *Black Literature 1827–1940* (1987–1996): fiche 1740.10.

———. "Shouting." 1934. Wall, *Zora Neale Hurston: Folklore, Memoirs and Other Writings* 851–54.

———. "The South's Other Side." *Negro Digest* June 1943: 37–40.

———. "Spirituals and Neospirituals." 1934. Wall, *Zora Neale Hurston: Folklore, Memoirs and Other Writings* 869–74.

———. "Spunk." 1925. Gates and Lemke 26–32.

———. "Star-Wrassling Sons-of-the-Universe." Rev. of *The Hurricane's Children*, by Carl Carmer. *New York Herald Tribune Books* 26 Dec. 1937: 4.

———. "Stories and Conflict." Rev. of *Uncle Tom's Children*, by Richard Wright. *Saturday Review* 2 April 1938: 32.

———. "Sun Set." Unidentified clipping, Schomburg Center for Research in Black Culture.

———. "Sweat." 1926. Gates and Lemke 73–85.

———. *Tell My Horse.* 1938. Wall, *Zora Neale Hurston: Folklore, Memoirs and Other Writings* 269–555.

———. *Their Eyes Were Watching God.* 1937. Wall, *Zora Neale Hurston: Novels and Stories* 174–333.

———. "The Ten Commandments of Charm." *X-Ray: Journal of the Zeta Phi Beta Sorority* Dec. 1925.

———. "'Twas the Night after Lobster—." Unpublished manuscript, Schomburg Center for Research and Black Culture.

———. "Uncle Monday." 1934. Wall, *Zora Neale Hurston: Folklore, Memoirs and Other Writings* 860–69.

———. "Under the Bridge." 1925. *American Visions* Dec./Jan. 1997: 14–19.

———. "What White Publishers Won't Print." 1950. Wall, *Zora Neale Hurston: Folklore Memoirs and Other Writings* 950–55.

———. "Why the Negro Won't Buy Communism." *American Legion Magazine* June 1951: 14–15+.

———. *Zora Neale Hurston: Stories*. Narr. Renee Joshua-Porter. Audiocassette. Audio Bookshelf, 1996.

Hutchinson, George. *The Harlem Renaissance in Black and White*. Cambridge, Mass.: Harvard University Press, 1995.

Hutchinson, Percy. Rev. of *Moses, Man of the Mountain*, by Zora Neale Hurston. *New York Times Book Review* 19 Nov. 1939: 21.

"In Brief Review." Rev. of *Moses, Man of the Mountain*, by Zora Neale Hurston. *College English* 1 (1940): 465.

Jacobs, George. "Negro Authors Must Eat." *The Nation* 128 (1929): 710–11.

Jauss, Hans Robert. "Literary History as a Challenge." *Toward an Aesthetic of Reception*. Minneapolis: University of Minnesota Press, 1982.

Johnson, James Weldon. *Along This Way: The Autobiography of James Weldon Johnson*. New York: Viking Press, 1933.

———. *Autobiography of an Ex-Colored Man*. 1912. New York: Penguin Books, 1990.

———. *Black Manhattan*. New York: Alfred A. Knopf, 1930.

———, ed. *The Book of American Negro Poetry*. 1922. New York: Harcourt, Brace and World, 1958.

———. *God's Trombones*. New York: Viking Press, 1927.

Jonah's Gourd Vine. Advertisement. *New York Herald Tribune Books* 6 May 1934: 18.

Jonah's Gourd Vine. Advertisement. *New York Times Book Review* 13 May 1934: 18.

Jonah's Gourd Vine. Advertisement. *New York Herald Tribune Books* 20 May 1934: 14.

Jonah's Gourd Vine. Advertisement. *New York Herald Tribune Books* 3 June 1934: 9.

Jonah's Gourd Vine. Advertisement. *New York Times Book Review* 10 June 1934: 14.

Jones, Dewey. "The Bookshelf." Rev. of *Jonah's Gourd Vine*, by Zora Neale Hurston. *Chicago Defender* 12 May 1934: 12.

Jones, Gavin. *Strange Talk: The Politics of Dialect Literature in Gilded Age America*. Berkeley: University of California Press, 1999.

Jones, Gayle. *Liberating Voices: Oral Tradition in African American Literature*. Cambridge, Mass.: Harvard University Press, 1991.

Jones, LeRoi. "The Myth of Negro Literature." 1966. Angelyn Mitchell 165–83.

Jordan, Jennifer. "Feminist Fantasies." *Tulsa Studies in Women's Literature* 1 (Spring 1988): 105–17.

Jordan, June. "On Richard Wright and Zora Neale Hurston: Notes Toward a Balancing of Love and Hatred." *Black World* 33.10 (August 1974): 4–8.

J., R. E. M. Rev. of *Jonah's Gourd Vine*, by Zora Neale Hurston. *Boston Chronicle* 5 May 1934: 4.

Kane, Harnett T. "Suwanee River. Carolina Swamp." Rev. of *Seraph on the Suwanee*, by Zora Neale Hurston. *Chicago Sun-Times* 17 Nov. 1948: 58.

Kaplan, Carla, ed. *Zora Neale Hurston: A Life in Letters*. New York: Doubleday, 2002.

Kaye, Richard. "Zora! Zora! Zora!" *Voice Literary Supplement* 26 Apr. 1994: 64.

Kellner, Bruce, ed. *The Harlem Renaissance: A Historical Dictionary*. Westport, Conn.: Greenwood Press, 1984.

Kelly, Robin D. G. *Race Rebels: Culture, Politics, and the Black Working Class*. New York: The Free Press, 1994.

Kemble, Frances A. *Journal of a Residence on a Georgian Plantation in 1838–1839*. Ed. John Anthony Scott. New York: Knopf, 1961.

Kennan, Hugh T. "Twisted Tales: Propaganda in the Tar-Baby Stories." *Southern Quarterly* 22.2 (Winter 1984): 54–69.

Kennedy, Randall. "Looking for Zora." Rev. of *I Love Myself When I Am Laughing*, by Zora Neale Hurston and ed. by Alice Walker. *New York Times Book Review* 30 Dec. 1979: 8+.

King, Deborah. "Multiple Jeopardy, Multiple Consciousness: The Context of a Black Feminist Ideology." *Signs* 14.1 (Autumn 1988): 42–72. Rpt. in Guy-Sheftall 294–312.

King, Martin Luther, Jr. "I've Been to the Mountaintop." Memphis, Tenn. 3 Apr. 1968. *A Call to Conscience: The Landmark Speeches of Dr. Martin Luther King, Jr.* Ed. Clayborne Carson and Kris Shepard. New York: Intellectual Properties Management, 2001. 207–23.

Kirschke, Amy Helene. *Aaron Douglas: Art, Race, and the Harlem Renaissance*. Jackson, Miss.: University of Mississippi Press, 1995.

Knickmeyer, W. L. Rev. of *Their Eyes Were Watching God*, by Zora Neale Hurston. *St. Louis Dispatch* 19 Sept. 1937: 4H.

Knopf, Alfred. "As I See It." Rev. of *The Ways of White Folks*, by Langston Hughes. *American Mercury* 33.127 (July 1934): xv.

Larsen, Nella. *Passing*. McDowell, *Quicksand and Passing* 143–242.

———. *Quicksand*. McDowell, *Quicksand and Passing* 1–135.

Lester, Julius. *Black Folktales*. New York: Grove Press, 1991.

———. "The Storyteller's Voice: Reflections on the Rewriting of Uncle Remus." *The Voice of the Narrator in Children's Literature*. Ed. Charlotte F. Otten and Gary D. Schmidt. New York: Greenwood. 69–73.

Letter. *American Legion Magazine* Jan. 1951: 8.

Leverty, Sally. "Beauty, Freshness, Poetry Make Novel Noteworthy." Rev. of *Their Eyes Were Watching God*, by Zora Neale Hurston. *Richmond Times Dispatch* 26 Sept. 1937: 16.

Levy, Eugene D. *James Weldon Johnson: Black Leader, Black Voice*. Chicago: University of Chicago Press, 1973.

Lewis, Theophilus. "Harlem Sketchbook." Rev. of *Jonah's Gourd Vine*, by Zora Neale Hurston. *New York Amsterdam News* 2 June 1934: 8.

Lindsay, Vachel. "*The Congo" and Other Poems*. New York: Macmillan, 1914.

Lippmann, Walter. *Public Opinion*. 1922. New York: The Free Press, 1965.

Locke, Alain. "Art or Propaganda." 1928. Huggins, *Voices from the Harlem Renaissance* 312–13.

———. "Deep River, Deeper Sea." Rev. of *Mules and Men*, by Zora Neale Hurston. *Opportunity* Jan. 1936: 6–10.

———. "Dry Fields and Green Pastures." Rev. of *Moses, Man of the Mountain*, by Zora Neale Hurston. *Opportunity* Jan. 1940: 4–8.

———. "The Eleventh Hour of Nordicism." Rev. of *Jonah's Gourd Vine*, by Zora Neale Hurston. *Opportunity* Jan. 1935: 8–12.

———. "Fire: A Negro Magazine." Rev. of *Fire!! The Survey* Aug.–Sept. 1927: 563.

———. "Jingo, Counter-Jingo and Us." Rev. of *Their Eyes Were Watching God*, by Zora Neale Hurston. *Opportunity* Jan. 1938: 7–11+.

———. "The Negro: 'New' or 'Newer.'" Rev. of *Tell My Horse*, by Zora Neale Hurston. *Opportunity* Feb. 1939: 38.

———. "The New Negro." Locke, *The New Negro* 3–16.

———, ed. *The New Negro*. 1925. New York: Atheneum, 1992.

Lockhart, Jack. "Zora Hurston Pens Novel of Own Race." Rev. of *Their Eyes Were Watching God*, by Zora Neale Hurston. *Memphis Commercial Appeal* 3 Oct. 1937, sec. 4: 9.

Lomax, Alan. "Zora Neale Hurston: A Life of Negro Folklore." *Sing Out* Oct.–Nov. 1960: 353.

"Lore of Haiti." Rev. of *Tell My Horse*, by Zora Neale Hurston. *New York Times Book Review* 23 Oct. 1938: 12.

Lott, Eric. *Love and Theft: Blackface Minstrelsy and the American Working Class*. New York: Oxford University Press, 1993.

Lowe, John. *Jump at the Sun: Zora Neale Hurston's Cosmic Comedy*. Urbana: University of Illinois Press, 1997.

Lyons, Mary. *Sorrow's Kitchen: The Life and Folklore of Zora Neale Hurston*. New York: Scribner's, 1990.

Martin, Gertrude. "Reviews: Read More—Learn More." Rev. of *Tell My Horse*, by Zora Neale Hurston. *Chicago Defender* 26 Aug. 1939: 19.

Maxwell, William J. *New Negro, Old Left: African American Writing and Communism between the Wars*. New York: Columbia University Press, 1999.

McCabe, Tracy. "The Multifaceted Politics of Primitivism in Harlem Renaissance Writing." *Soundings* 80.4 (Winter 1997): 475–97.

McDougald, Elsie Johnson. "The Task of Negro Womanhood." Locke, *The New Negro* 369–82.

McDowell, Deborah E. Introduction. *Quicksand and Passing*. By Nella Larsen. American Women Writers Series. New Bruswick, N.J.: Rutgers University Press, 1986. ix–xxxv.

———. "Lines of Descent/Dissenting Lines." Introduction. *Moses, Man of the Mountain*. By Zora Neale Hurston. New York: HarperCollins, 1991. vii–xxiv.

———. "New Directions for Black Feminist Criticism." *Black American Literature Forum* 14 (1980): 153–59.

McKay, Claude. *Banana Bottom*. New York: Harper and Brothers, 1933.

———. *Banjo*. New York: Harper and Brothers, 1929.

———. *Gingertown*. New York: Harper and Brothers, 1932.

———. *Home to Harlem*. New York: Harper and Brothers, 1928.

———. "If We Must Die." 1919. Huggins, *Voices from the Harlem Renaissance* 353–54.

———. "The White House." 1922. Huggins, *Voices from the Harlem Renaissance* 354.

McNeill, B. C. Rev. of *Mules and Men*, by Zora Neale Hurston. *Journal of Negro History* 21.2 (Apr. 1936): 223–25.

Meisenhelder, Susan. *Hitting a Straight Lick with a Crooked Stick: Race and Gender in the Work of Zora Neale Hurston*. Tuscaloosa: University of Alabama Press, 1999.

Miller, William. *Zora Hurston and the Chinaberry Tree*. New York: Lee and Low Books, 1994.

Minter, David. *A Cultural History of the American Novel: Henry James to William Faulkner*. New York: Cambridge University Press, 1994.

Minus, Marion. "Present Trends in Negro Literature." *New Challenge* April 1937: 9–11.

M[inus], M[arion]. Rev. of *Their Eyes Were Watching God*, by Zora Neale Hurston. *New Challenge* Fall 1937: 85–88.

Mitchell, Angelyn, ed. *Within the Circle: An Anthology of African American Literary Criticism from the Harlem Renaissance to the Present*. Durham, N.C.: Duke University Press, 1994.

Mitchell, Joseph. "Girl Stalks Negro Lore." Unidentified clipping, Zora Neale Hurston Collection, University of Florida.

Mitchell, Margaret. *Gone with the Wind*. 1936. Reprint. New York: MacMillan, 1964.

Moraga, Cherie, and Gloria Anzaldua, eds. *This Bridge Called My Back: Writings by Radical Women of Color*. Watertown, Mass.: Persephone Press, 1981.

"Morals Charge Hurled at Zora Neale Hurston." *New York Age* 16 Oct. 1948: 1.

Morgan, Robin, ed. *Sisterhood Is Powerful: An Anthology of Writings from the Women's Liberation Movement*. New York: Vintage Books, 1970.

Morris, Timothy. *Becoming Canonical in American Poetry*. Urbana: University of Illinois Press, 1995.

Morrison, Toni. *The Bluest Eye*. 1970. New York: Plume-Penguin Books, 1994.

———. *Sula*. 1973. New York: Plume-Penguin Books, 1982.

Moses, Man of the Mountain. Advertisement. *New York Times Book Review* 5 Nov. 1939: 23.

Moses, Man of the Mountain. Advertisement. *New York Times Book Review* 26 Nov. 1939: 19.

Moses, Man of the Mountain. Review. *Booklist* 15 Dec. 1939: 150.

Motley, Willard. *Knock on Any Door*. New York: D. Appleton-Century Company, 1947.

M., S. "Literary Caravan." Rev. of *Tell My Horse*, by Zora Neale Hurston. *Modern Quarterly* 11 (Winter 1939): 96.

Mules and Men. Advertisement. *New York Times Book Review* 13 Oct. 1935: 18.

Mules and Men. Advertisement. *New York Times Book Review* 20 Oct. 1935: 29.

Mules and Men. Advertisement. *New York Times Book Review* 8 Dec. 1935: 18.

Murphy, Beatrice M. "The Book Worm." Rev. of *Moses, Man of the Mountain*, by Zora Neale Hurston. Unidentified clipping. Atlanta University.

"National Best Sellers—October." *Publisher's Weekly* 13 Nov. 1937: 1951.

Native Son. Advertisement. *New York Herald Tribune* 17 Mar. 1940: 21.

Native Son. Advertisement. *New York Times Book Review* 17 Mar. 1940: 21.

Neal, Larry. "The Black Arts Movement." 1968. Angelyn Mitchell 184–98.

"Negroes Heatedly Deny Votes Bought in Miami." *Miami Herald* 26 Oct. 1950: N. pag.

"Negropings." Rev. of *Their Eyes Were Watching God*, by Zora Neale Hurston. *Time* 20 Sept. 1937: 71.

"A Negro Writer and Her People." Rev. of *Mules and Men*, by Zora Neale Hurston. *New York Post* 26 Oct. 1935: 7.

Newson, Adele S. *Zora Neale Hurston: A Reference Guide.* Boston: G. K. Hall, 1987.

Nichols, Charles H., ed. *Arna Bontemps-Langston Hughes Letters.* New York: Dodd, Mead, 1980.

Nicholson, David. "The Mark of Zora." Rev. of *Zora Neale Hurston: Folklore, Memoirs and Other Writings* and *Zora Neale Hurston: Novels and Stories*, ed. by Cheryl A. Wall. *Washington Post Book World* 5 Mar. 1995: 4–5.

"1943 Anisfield Awards." *Saturday Review of Literature* 20 Feb. 1943: 11.

Noble, Jeanne. *Beautiful, Also, Are the Souls of My Sisters: A History of Black Women in America.* Englewood Cliffs, N.J.: Prentice-Hall, 1978.

North, Michael. *The Dialect of Modernism: Race, Language, and Twentieth-Century Literature.* New York: Oxford University Press, 1994.

"Other New Books." Rev. of *Their Eyes Were Watching God*, by Zora Neale Hurston. *Newsweek* 27 Sept. 1937: 41.

Ottley, Roi. "Roi Ottley Says." *Chicago Defender* 10 Sept. 1955: N. pag.

Ovington, Mary White. "Book Chat." Rev. of *Jonah's Gourd Vine*, by Zora Neale Hurston. *New York Age* 5 May 1934: 4.

Owano, N. "What Was Your Slave Name?" Rev. of *Dust Tracks on a Road*, by Zora Neale Hurston. *The Village Voice* 17 Aug. 1972: 22+.

P., H. A. "Folk-Lore and Voodooism in the Deep South." Rev. of *Mules and Men*, by Zora Neale Hurston. *Boston Evening Transcript* 16 Oct. 1935: 2.

Page, Thomas Nelson. *In Ole Virginia.* 1887. Nashville: J. S. Sanders and Company, 1991.

Pells, Richard. *Radical Visions and American Dreams.* New York: Harper and Row, 1973.

Peterkin, Julia. *Black April.* Garden City, N.Y.: Triangle Books, 1940.

———. *Scarlet Sister Mary.* Garden City, N.Y.: Triangle Books, 1940.

Petry, Ann. *Country Place.* New York: Houghton Mifflin, 1947.

Pickney, Josephine. "A Pungent, Poetic Novel about Negroes." Rev. of *Jonah's Gourd Vine*, by Zora Neale Hurston. *New York Herald Tribune Books* 6 May 1934: 6.

Plant, Deborah. *Every Tub Must Sit on Its Own Bottom: The Philosophy and Politics of Zora Neale Hurston*. Urbana: University of Illinois Press, 1995.

Poe, Edgar Allan. "The Raven." *The Norton Anthology of American Literature*. 3rd ed. Vol. 1. Ed. Nina Baym, et al. New York: W. W. Norton, 1989. 1369–75.

Pratt, Theodore. "A Memoir—Zora Neale Hurston—Florida's First Distinguished Author." *Negro Digest* Feb. 1962: 52–56.

———. "Zora Neale Hurston." *Florida Historical Quarterly* 40 (July 1961): 39–40.

Preece, Harold. "The Negro Folk Cult." *Crisis* 43.12 (Dec. 1936): 364+.

———. Rev. of *Dust Tracks on a Road*, by Zora Neale Hurston. *Tomorrow* Feb. 1943: 58–59.

Rampersad, Arnold. Introduction. *Native Son*. By Richard Wright. New York: HarperPerennial, 1993. xi–xxviii.

———. *The Life of Langston Hughes*. Vol. 1. New York: Oxford University Press, 1986.

———. "Note on the Text." *Black Boy*. By Richard Wright. New York: HarperPerennial, 1991. 487–89.

"Raps Hurston Criticism of Haiti 'VOODOO.'" *New York Amsterdam News* 11 Dec. 1937: 4.

Rascoe, Burton. "Who Trun That Brick?" Rev. of *Tell My Horse*, by Zora Neale Hurston. *Newsweek* 21 Nov. 1938: 4.

Raynaud, Claudine. "Autobiography as a Lying Session." *Black Feminist Critical Theory*. Ed. Joe Weixlmann and Houston A. Baker. Studies in Black American Literature. Vol. III. Greenwood, Fla.: Penkevill Publishing Co., 1998. 111–38.

———. "'Rubbing a Paragraph with a Soft Cloth': Muted Voices and Editorial Constraints in *Dust Tracks on a Road*." *De/Colonizing the Subject: The Politics of Gender in Women's Autobiography*. Ed. Sidonie Smith and Julia Watson. Minneapolis: University of Minnesota Press, 1992. 35–64.

Redding, J. Saunders. "American Negro Literature." 1949. Angelyn Mitchell 107–16.

———. *On Being Negro in America*. Indianapolis: Bobbs-Merrill Company, 1951.

Reid, Jim. "Authoress Dies Impoverished." *Pittsburgh Courier* 13 Feb. 1960: 3. Clipping. Atlanta University.

Roberts, John. Rev. of *Dust Tracks on a Road* and *Their Eyes Were Watching God*, by Zora Neale Hurston. *Journal of American Folklore* 93 (Oct. 1980): 463–66.

Rose, Ernestine. Rev. of *Dust Tracks on a Road*, by Zora Neale Hurston. *Literary Journal* 67.19 (Nov. 1942): 950.

Sale, Roger. "Zora." Rev. of *Their Eyes Were Watching God*, by Zora Neale Hurston. *Hudson Review* 22 (Spring 1979): 153.

Salier, Steve. "The Secret of Zora Neale Hurston." Rev. of *Zora Neale Hurston: Folklore, Memoirs and Other Writings* and *Zora Neale Hurston: Novels and Stories*, ed. by Cheryl A. Wall. *National Review* 3 Apr. 1995: 58–60.

Schuyler, George. "Looks at Books." Rev. of *Moses, Man of the Mountain*, by Zora Neale Hurston. *Pittsburgh Courier* 2 Dec. 1939: 7.

———. "The Negro Art-Hokum." 1926. Angelyn Mitchell 51–54.

———. Rev of *Jonah's Gourd Vine*, by Zora Neale Hurston. *Pittsburgh Courier* 12 May 1934: 1.

———. "Views and Reviews." Rev. of *Nigger Heaven*, by Carl Van Vechten. *Pittsburgh Courier* 6 Nov. 1926. N. pag.

———. "Views and Reviews." Rev. of *Their Eyes Were Watching God*, by Zora Neale Hurston. *Pittsburgh Courier* 25 Dec. 1937: 12.

———. "What's Wrong with Negro Authors." *Negro Digest* May 1950: 3–7.

Seabrook, William. *Adventures in Arabia among the Bedouins, Druses, Whirling Dervishes, and Yezidee Devil Worshipers*. New York: Blue Ribbon Books, 1927.

———. *The Magic Island*. New York: The Literary Guild of America, 1929.

Seraph on the Suwanee. Advertisement. *New York Herald Tribune Book Review* 10 Oct. 1948: 11.

Seraph on the Suwanee. Advertisement. *New York Herald Tribune Book Review* 31 Oct. 1948: 14.

Seraph on the Suwanee. Advertisement. *New York Times Book Review* 24 Oct. 1948: 15.

Seraph on the Suwanee. Review. *Christian Science Monitor* 23 Dec. 1948: 11.

Seraph on the Suwanee. Review. *Kirkus Reviews* 15 Aug. 1948: 415.

Sharp, Howard. "Seek $ for Zora's Funeral." *Fort Pierce News Tribune* 4 Feb. 1960. Unpaginated clipping, University of Florida.

Sheffey, Ruth T., ed. *Rainbow 'Round Her Shoulder*. Baltimore: Morgan State University Press, 1982.

Sherman, Beatrice. "Zora Hurston's Own Story." Rev. of *Dust Tracks on a Road*, by Zora Neale Hurston. *New York Times Book Review* 29 Nov. 1942: 44.

"Shorter Notices." Rev. of *Jonah's Gourd Vine*, by Zora Neale Hurston. *The Nation* 13 June 1934: 683.

Singh, Amrijit, William Shiver, and S. Brodwin, eds. *The Harlem Renaissance: Revaluations*. New York: AMS Press, 1988.

Slaughter, Frank. "Freud in Turpentine." Rev. of *Seraph on the Suwanee*, by Zora Neale Hurston. *New York Times Book Review* 31 Oct. 1948: 24.

Slomovitz, Philip. "The Negro's Moses." Rev. of *Moses, Man of the Mountain*, by Zora Neale Hurston. *Christian Century* 6 Dec. 1939: 1504.

Smith, Barbara, ed. *Home Girls: A Black Feminist Anthology*. New York: Kitchen Table: Women of Color Press, 1983.

Smith, Henry Nash. "Voodoo as a Crude Piety and a Practical Magic." Rev. of *Tell My Horse*, by Zora Neale Hurston. *Boston Evening Transcript* 18 Nov. 1939: 2.

Snelling, Paula. "Signposts along the Way." Rev. of *Their Eyes Were Watching God*, by Zora Neale Hurston. *North Georgia Review* winter 1937–38: 8.

Southerland, Ellease. "Jump at the Sun." Rev. of *Zora Neale Hurston: Folklore, Memoirs and Other Writings* and *Zora Neale Hurston: Novels and Stories*, ed. by Cheryl A. Wall. *Quarterly Black Review* June 1995. Unpaginated clipping, Library of America.

Spingarn, Arthur. "Books by Negro Authors in 1937." Rev. of *Their Eyes Were Watching God*, by Zora Neale Hurston. *Crisis* 45.2 (Feb. 1938): 47–48.

———. "Books by Negro Authors in 1939." Rev. of *Moses, Man of the Mountain*, by Zora Neale Hurston. *Crisis 47.2* (Feb. 1940): 46+.

———. "Books by Negro Authors in 1942." Rev. of *Dust Tracks on a Road*, by Zora Neale Hurston. *Crisis* 50.2 (Feb. 1943): 45–46.

Starke, Catherine Juanita. *Black Portraiture in American Fiction: Stock Characters, Archetypes, and Individuals*. New York: Basic Books, 1971.

St. Clair, Janet. "The Courageous Undertow of Zora Neale Hurston's *Seraph on the Suwanee*." *Modern Language Quarterly* 5.1 (Mar. 1989): 38–57.

Steinbeck, John. *The Grapes of Wrath*. New York: Viking Press, 1939.

Stepto, Robert. "Sterling Brown: Outsider in the Harlem Renaissance." Singh, Shiver and Brodwin 73–81.

Stevens, George. "Negroes by Themselves." Rev. of *Their Eyes Were Watching God*, by Zora Neale Hurston. *Saturday Review of Literature* 18 Sept. 1937: 3.

Stoney, Samuel Gaillard. "Wit, Wisdom, and Folklore." Rev. of *Mules and Men*, by Zora Neale Hurston *New York Herald Tribune Books* 13 Oct. 1935: 7.

Stong, Phil. "Zora Hurston Sums Up." Rev. of *Dust Tracks on a Road*, by Zora Neale Hurston. *Saturday Review of Literature* 28 Nov. 1942: 6–7.

Story, Ralph. "Gender and Ambition: Zora Neale Hurston in the Harlem Renaissance." *The Black Scholar* Summer/Fall 1989: 25–31.

———. "Patronage and the Harlem Renaissance: You Get What You Pay For." *College Language Association Journal* 32.3 (Mar. 1989): 284–95.

Strom, Sharon Hartman. "Challenging 'Woman's Place': Feminism, the Left and Industrial Unionism in the 1930s." *Women and Minorities during the Great Depression*. Ed. Melvyn Dubofsky and Stephen Burwood. Vol. 6 of *The Great Depression and the New Deal*. New York: Garland, 1990. 262–89.

"Summer Book Index." *Publishers Weekly* 5 May 1934: N. pag.

Sundquist, Eric J. *To Wake the Nations: Race and Making of American Literature*. Cambridge, Mass.: Belknap Press, 1993.

Taylor, Robert. "Hurston Enters the Canon, at Last." Rev. of *Zora Neale Hurston: Folklore, Memoirs and Other Writings* and *Zora Neale Hurston: Novels and Stories*, ed. by Cheryl A. Wall. *Boston Globe* 22 Feb. 1995. Unpaginated clipping. Library of America.

Taylor, W. W. Letter. *Orlando Sentinel* 25 Aug. 1955. Unpaginated clipping, University of Florida.

Taylor-Guthrie, Danielle. "To Seek the Horizon." Rev. of *Zora Neale Hurston: Folklore, Memoirs and Other Writings* and *Zora Neale Hurston: Novels and Stories*, ed. by Cheryl A. Wall. *Chicago Tribune Books* 26 Feb. 1995, sec. 14: 1+.

Tell My Horse. Advertisement. *New York Herald Tribune Books* 16 Oct. 1938: 21.

Tell My Horse. Advertisement. *New York Times Book Review* 23 Oct. 1938: 23.

Tell My Horse. Advertisement. *New York Times Book Review* 6 Nov. 1938: 23.

Tell My Horse. Advertisement. *New York Herald Tribune Books* 13 Nov. 1938: 31.
Tell My Horse. Review. *New Republic* 7 Dec. 1938: 155.
Tell My Horse. Review. *The New Yorker* 15 Oct. 1938: 71.
Their Eyes Were Watching God. Advertisement. *New York Times Book Review* 26 Sept. 1937: 19.
Their Eyes Were Watching God. Advertisement. *New York Times Book Review* 3 Oct. 1937: 20.
Their Eyes Were Watching God. Advertisement. *New York Herald Tribune Books* 10 Oct. 1937: 20.
Their Eyes Were Watching God. Advertisement. *New York Times Book Review* 10 Oct. 1937: 26.
Their Eyes Were Watching God. Advertisement. *New York Times Book Review* 17 Oct. 1937: 22.
Their Eyes Were Watching God. Advertisement. *New York Herald Tribune Books* 12 Dec. 1937: 31.
Their Eyes Were Watching God. Review. *Publishers Weekly* 21 July 1969: 61.
Their Eyes Were Watching God, *Mules and Men*, *Jonah's Gourd Vine*. Advertisement. *New York Amsterdam News* 11 Dec. 1937: 2.
Thompson, Edgar. Rev. of *Tell My Horse*, by Zora Neale Hurston. *Rural Sociology* 4.2 (1939): 261–62.
Thompson, Ralph. "Books of the Times." Rev. of *Their Eyes Were Watching God*, by Zora Neale Hurston. *New York Times* 6 Oct. 1937: 23.
Three Harbors. Advertisement. *New York Times Book Review*: 35.
Thurman, Wallace. *Infants of the Spring*. 1932. Boston: Northeastern University Press, 1992.
Toelken, Barre. *The Dynamics of Folklore*. Boston: Houghton Mifflin, 1979.
Toll, Robert C. *Blacking Up: The Minstrel Show in Nineteenth Century America*. New York: Oxford University Press, 1974.
Tomaševskij, Boris. "Literature and Biography." 1923. Trans. Herbert Eagle. *Readings in Russian Poetics: Formalist and Structuralist Views*. Ed. Ladislav Matejka and Krystyna Pomorska. Cambridge, Mass.: MIT Press, 1971. 47–65.
Tompkins, Jane. *Sensational Designs: The Cultural Work of American Fiction, 1790–1860*. New York: Oxford University Press, 1985.
Tompkins, Lucy. "In the Florida Glades." Rev. of *Their Eyes Were Watching God*, by Zora Neale Hurston. *New York Times Book Review* 26 Sept. 1937: 29.
Toomer, Jean. *Cane*. 1923. New York: Liveright Publishing, 1975.
Torgovnick, Marianna. *Gone Primitive: Savage Intellects, Modern Lives*. Chicago: University of Chicago Press, 1991.
Turner, Darwin. *In a Minor Chord: Three Afro-American Writers and Their Search for Identity*. Carbondale: Southern Illinois University Press, 1971.
"Two Harlem Bodies Protest Lynchings." *New York Times* 20 Dec. 1926: 15.
Two Loves I Have. Advertisement. *New York Times Book Review* 10 June 1934: 14.

Uncle Tom's Children. Advertisement. *New York Herald Tribune Books* 15 May 1938: 17.

Untermeyer, Louis. *Moses*. New York: Harcourt Brace, 1928.

———. Rev. of *Moses, Man of the Mountain*, by Zora Neale Hurston. *Saturday Review of Literature* 11 Nov. 1939: 11.

Van Vechten, Carl. Introduction. *The Weary Blues*. By Langston Hughes. New York: Alfred A. Knopf, 1945. Originally published 1926.

———. *Nigger Heaven*. 1926. New York: Knopf, 1973.

Walker, Alice. Foreword. *Zora Neale Hurston: A Literary Biography*. By Robert Hemenway. Urbana: University of Illinois Press, 1977. xi–xviii.

———. *In Search of Our Mothers' Gardens: Womanist Prose*. New York: Harcourt Brace Jovanovich, 1983.

———. "In Search of Zora Neale Hurston" ["Looking for Zora"]. Walker, *In Search* 93–116.

———. "Saving the Life That Is Your Own." Walker, *In Search* 3–14.

———. *The Third Life of Grange Copeland*. New York: Harcourt, Brace, Jovanovich, 1970.

———. "Zora Neale Hurston: A Cautionary Tale and a Partisan View." Walker, *In Search* 83–92.

Wall, Cheryl A., ed. *Changing Our Own Words: Essays on Criticism, Theory, and Writing by Black Women*. New Brunswick, N.J.: Rutgers University Press, 1991.

———. "Note on the Texts." Wall, *Zora Neale Hurston: Folklore, Memoirs and Other Writings* 981–97.

———. *Women of the Harlem Renaissance*. Bloomington: Indiana University Press, 1995.

———, ed. *Zora Neale Hurston: Folklore, Memoirs and Other Writings*. New York: Library of America, 1995.

———, ed. *Zora Neale Hurston: Novels and Stories*. New York: Library of America, 1995.

Wallace, Margaret. "Real Negro People." Rev. of *Jonah's Gourd Vine*, by Zora Neale Hurston. *New York Times Book Review* 6 May 1934: 7.

Walters, Keith. "'He can read my writing but he sho' can't read my mind': Zora Neale Hurston's Revenge in *Mules and Men*." *Journal of American Folklore* 112 (Summer 1999): 343–71. WillsonSelect Plus. Ferris State University Library for Information, Technology, and Education, 2 Feb. 2003. <http://newfirstsearch.oclc.org>

Walton, David A. "Joel Chandler Harris as Folklorist: A Reassessment." *Keystone Folklore Quarterly* 11 (Spring 1966): 21–26.

Washington, Mary Helen. "The Black Woman's Search for Identity." *Black World* 21 (August 1972): 68–75.

———. Foreword. *Their Eyes Were Watching God*. By Zora Neale Hurston. New York: HarperCollins, 1990. vii–xiv.

"Weekly Record." *Publishers Weekly* 2 Oct. 1937: 1458.

"Weekly Record." *Publishers Weekly* 18 Nov. 1939: 1933.

West, Cornel. "Minority Discourse and the Pitfalls of Canon Formation." *Yale Journal of Criticism* 1.1 (1987): 193–201.

West, M. Genevieve. "Feminist Subversion in Hurston's *Jonah's Gourd Vine*." *Women's Studies* 31.4 (2002): 499–515.

White, Walter. "The Spotlight." *Pittsburgh Courier* 19 June 1926: 16.

"White Fog." Rev. of *Uncle Tom's Children*, by Richard Wright. *Time* 28 Mar. 1938: 63.

Wilentz, Gay. "White Patron and Black Artist: The Correspondence of Fannie Hurst and Zora Neale Hurston." *Library Chronicle of the University of Texas* 35 (1986): 20–43.

Wilkins, Roy. "The Watchtower." *New York World Telegram* 27 Feb. 1943: 7.

Williams, Joseph J. Rev. of *Mules and Men*, by Zora Neale Hurston. *Folklore* 47.4 (Sept. 1936): 233.

Wintz, Cary D. *Black Culture and the Harlem Renaissance*. Houston: Rice University Press, 1988.

Wood, Clement. *Deep River*. New York: William Godwin, 1934.

Woodson, Carter G. Rev. of *Tell My Horse*, by Zora Neale Hurston. *Journal of Negro History* 24.1 (Jan. 1939): 116–18.

Worth, Robert F. "*Nigger Heaven* and the Harlem Renaissance." *African American Review* 29.3 (Fall 1995): 461–73.

Wright, Richard. "Between Laughter and Tears." Rev. of *Their Eyes Were Watching God*, by Zora Neale Hurston. *New Masses* 5 Oct. 1937: 22, 25.

———. "Big Boy Leaves Home." Wright, *Uncle Tom's Children* 15–61.

———. *Black Boy*. New York: HarperPerennial, 1991.

———. "Blueprint for Negro Writing." *The New Challenge* 11 (1937): 53–65.

———. "Bright and Morning Star." Wright, *Uncle Tom's Children* 221–63.

———. "The Ethics of Living Jim Crow." Wright, *Uncle Tom's Children* 1–15.

———. *Native Son*. New York: HarperPerennial, 1993.

———. *Savage Holiday*. 1954. Jackson, Miss.: University Press of Mississippi, 1995.

———. "A Tale of Folk Courage." *Partisan Review and Anvil* 3 (April 1936): 31.

———. *Uncle Tom's Children*. 1938. New York: HarperPerennial, 1993.

Young, James O. *Black Writers of the Thirties*. Baton Rouge: Louisiana State University Press, 1973.

"Zora Hurston Denies Saying Race Better Off in South." *Atlanta Daily World* 2 Mar. 1943: 3.

"Zora Hurston, 57, Writer, Is Dead." *New York Times* 5 Feb. 1960: 27.

Zora Is My Name. Dir. Neema Barnette. PBS, 1989.

"Zora Neale Hurston Pleads Not Guilty." *Iowa Bystander* 21 Oct. 1943. Unpaginated clipping. Scribner's Author Files, Princeton University.

Index

M. Genevieve West is professor of English at Texas Woman's University in Denton, Texas.

www.ingramcontent.com/pod-product-compliance
Lightning Source LLC
LaVergne TN
LVHW091106080826
845145LV00008B/1823

9780813081083